EMOTIONAL CURRENTS
IN AMERICAN HISTORY

EMOTIONAL CURRENTS
IN AMERICAN HISTORY

BY
J. H. DENISON

AUTHOR OF "EMOTION AS THE BASIS OF CIVILIZATION" AND
"THE ENLARGEMENT OF PERSONALITY"

CHARLES SCRIBNER'S SONS
NEW YORK · LONDON
1932

973
D39

CONTENTS

v

CONTENTS

vii

INTRODUCTION

THE BATTLEGROUND OF GHOSTS AND VISIONS

Back of the events that are chronicled in the pages of history—back of the achievements and ambitions of the individuals that hold the front of the stage—there is in progress a stupendous drama, a battle of vast forces in whose hands the heroes of history seem but the painted figures of a marionette show, whose arms and legs are moved by invisible agencies that they but dimly discern. Correlative with the great process of evolution in the material world, in which the struggle for existence is continually eliminating the less fit while those better adapted fight desperately for supremacy, there is another battle in progress, no less stupendous because it is invisible. I refer to the Battle of Ideas. Here in the realm of thought the same struggle for existence is in progress, the same survival of the fittest. Ancient ideas that once dominated the world have been crushed out of existence like the prehistoric dinosaurs, and other forms now occupy the field.

We are prone to think that an idea is just a thought. It is that and something more—just as a copper wire may be something more than a piece of metal. An idea may carry an emotional charge that will drive a man to suicide or a nation to revolution. I should like to define an idea as an emotionalized thought. The power of an idea depends on the emotional charge which it has accumulated. A mere intellectual formula has little effect on men. But when, like the Nicene creed, such a formula has gathered an emotional fringe of reverence, enthusiasm, prejudice, and other such dynamic, it can set men by the ears, and turn the world upside down. The idea of the Divine Right of Kings or the Infallibility of the Pope or the Doctrine of the Atonement is more than mere thought. All these ideas now carry powerful emotional charges. Moreover, they grow. It is astonishing to see a tiny acorn grow into an oak, but the way in which an idea will take root and throw out branching ideas and logical corollaries until it becomes a vast thought system—a Theology, or Philosophy or Science—is equally amazing. A simple idea once set in motion, like a rolling snowball, will gather emotion at every turn, until its original content is lost to sight in a mass of prejudice or reverence or fear or enthusiasm.

A great Thought System like Communism or Catholicism may sway profoundly men who understand little of its intellectual content. Such a thought system we sometimes call a spirit, and speak of the Bolshevik Spirit, or the Democratic Spirit, the Spirit of Tyranny or Freedom. Some of those spirits originated in an idea brought to birth centuries ago, and have grown into vast systems of thought and feeling that have swayed men and dominated civilization. The Spirit of Feudalism, based on a few ancient beliefs, possessed Europe for centuries, and kept the masses in subjection more by the emotions it carried than by its thought content.

There are ancient superstitions still lingering here and there in dark corners, mere ghosts of powerful spirits that once ruled the world, now driven from the field by the fire of logic from modern ideas. Other ideas are just forming— visions of the future that are gathering emotional power every day and may soon dominate the nation. One scarcely realizes how one's acts are controlled by these vast spirits —ideas from the past that sway one by their emotional power. When one has once learned to see them it seems that all the heroes of history—statesmen, politicians or generals, are mere puppets in the great Battle of Ideas, which can end only in the survival of the fittest.

In old-world civilizations some ancient spirit, hoary with age, usually dominates and controls men beyond all thought of rebellion.

But America has been a field where the spirits of the past met with new spirits that belonged to the future. It has been in a peculiar sense the battleground of ghosts and visions.

Back of Burgoyne and Cornwallis and their armed red-coats, and back of Washington and his ragged Continentals, were forces far mightier than they. The old spirit of autocracy, armed with phrases like "the Divine right of Kings," and "the King can do no wrong," clad in garments of reverence and awe and with the shield of impermeable prejudice, was battling with the new spirit of liberty. Sprung from an ancient idea of the "rights of man," charged with enthusiasm, resentment and wrath, this new spirit was growing to a mighty force. Here, then, the spirit that had set up thrones and built empires and ruled the ancient world was fighting a battle to the death against the spirit that was to rule the world in the future, a ghost against a vision.

Every such spirit has at its roots an idea or a thought in which it originated, as we are told the spirit of the Reformation sprang from Luther's thought: "The just shall live by faith." But as the spirit grows the element of thought becomes of less and less importance—the phrase is lost in its emotional cover—it is the emotional charge upon the words rather than their meaning that sways men. It was not so much the abstract theory of democracy that stirred the average American citizen as the emotional charge in such phrases as "Give me Liberty or give me death!" It was not the divergent theories of the Northern Industrialists and the Southern Slaveholders that brought about the Civil War so much as the terrific emotional charge that had gathered upon the Slavery question and which made rational discussion impossible. I do not wish to minimize the importance of thought and ideas, but emotion is the driving force, and thought is a power chiefly because it is the throttle which turns on emotion. A new idea can set a continent in a turmoil, but this is because of the emotions it arouses. The effect of a thought on history is usually proportioned to the amount of emotion it can release. Everywhere in the world this battle between emotionalized ideas or spirits is going on and one object of this book is to follow their effect upon the development of the American nation.

Without impugning in any way the importance of other

agencies such as commerce and industry upon the progress of America, it is the object of this book to suggest that emotion has played a part even more fundamental. Every now and then the nation is swept by emotional storms that sometimes leave a trail like a cyclone. In certain areas emotion of a certain type reaches high pressure and, unless released, causes an explosion. Certain desires are permanent and can be reckoned upon; other emotions are ephemeral and explosive.

In every nation there are groups which are continually generating emotion of this explosive type,—prejudice, suspicion, antagonism, hatred, fear, which threaten to split the nation into fragments. We find Europe divided into racial and cultural groups which create antagonistic emotions and maintain an attitude of mutual suspicion so that a unified nation embracing them all would seem impossible. In America these same groups have been fused into one nation. They are held together by emotions that unite them, and that have proved strong enough to counteract the mutual suspicion and prejudice. It is most important that you, like every other American citizen, should understand what these emotions are and how they were generated. For, if we carelessly allow them to evaporate and cease to function, we shall soon see the nation disrupted by antagonisms.

It is not long since everyone was writing history from the standpoint of economics and we were shown how national development was due to material resources and climate and trade facilities. Now the world is beginning to appreciate the importance of the emotional factor. It seems self-evident that this is fundamental in all that affects human progress.

It should be unnecessary to explain that by emotion I mean any or all of the feelings and desires that stir the human soul, but I find there are many to whom the term signifies only the type of feeling to which a feminine hand has the key. While this latter motive power has launched its thousand ships and determined the fate of ancient Egypt and modern France at times, it is but a small part of that great store of energy that I denote by the term "Emotion," which by derivation from the Latin *Emoveo* should indicate any feeling that can move a man to action.

It is interesting to note that to-day business men and politicians are coming to recognize the supreme importance of this emotional element and the country is deluged with propaganda designed to awaken emotion. If our development is determined by economic causes and by the growth of wealth and industry and agriculture, we must remember that back of all values is emotion—a desire of some sort. Diamonds could have no value unless women wished to wear them. I have talked with men in New Guinea for whom silver and gold had no value. When I offered silver for a spear they returned it with a scornful laugh and demanded pig's tusks or dog's teeth. It is the desires of men that create values. For men without wants nothing has value. Salt alone has value in the forests of Central Africa, for the pygmies who inhabit them want nothing else. They threw aside with contempt the other gifts we brought them.

We are told that the Civil War was due to Economic causes—to King Cotton and the huge profits he brought the slaveholders, and to the rivalry of Northern Industrialism, but all these solid economic causes could be upset by a mere emotion. If women become "ashamed to be seen" in cotton stockings and will wear no garments but silk, they might easily wreck both the cotton planter of the South and the cotton manufacturers of the North, as indeed they are now in danger of doing. A mere feeling of shame can thus upset the economic world. Economic laws are based on the assumption that a certain emotion is as stable as the law of gravitation. We assume that it is inherent in human nature to desire wealth, to prefer profit to loss. History proves that this assumption is false. The desire for wealth is not an inalterable constituent of human nature but a mere emotion subject to the laws by which emotions are generated and neutralized.

The preaching of the ascetics in Egypt in the second

century persuaded some twenty thousand youths that to possess wealth was wicked and sent them to live in the desert. They regarded wealth with horror instead of with greed, and we are told by investigators like Hindus that the Bolsheviks in Russia have caused the people of that nation to feel ashamed to possess wealth. The roots of the economic system can thus be destroyed by cultivating an emotion. It is hard to imagine the economic laws that will control trade in a land where everyone aims at poverty instead of wealth, and really feels that it is more profitable to give than to receive.

Since a Savonarola or a modern revivalist might upset all the laws of supply and demand by a wave of emotion, there is evidently something back of economics which it pays to study, and modern business is beginning to appreciate the fact.

Every business man to-day knows that his success depends on this emotional element. He must create a desire for his wares. He must make people want what they don't want. If the garments he makes go out of style then women will be "ashamed to be seen in them," and he will be ruined by their feelings, unless he can produce something that they will feel proud to wear. Thus the back of every magazine to-day is devoted to emotional culture; for this is really what modern advertising is. Sit down some day and amuse yourself by seeing to how many different emotions the up-to-date business man appeals in order to induce the public to purchase. Pride, shame, sex, fear, ambition, parental love, greed, curiosity, vanity, appetite—every feeling to which flesh is heir is made use of to stimulate the reader to purchase, and deterrent emotions are avoided with almost diabolic ingenuity.

If emotion is important in industry and commerce and business, it is no less so in politics. The appeal to reason seems but insignificant in comparison with the appeal the politician makes to prejudice and suspicion and greed, and to racial and religious feeling. Party loyalty seems more important than wisdom and justice. In attacking an opponent an appeal to prejudice will counteract any amount of faithful service.

It is only recently that the terrible engine of propaganda has been set in motion and under skilled hands it seems as if the public could be roused to almost any emotion by its persistent use.

The object of this book is not to present new historic facts which are the result of independent research. My object is to induce you to read over the story of familiar events and note the emotional forces that brought them to pass and the emotional waves which they in turn have set in motion. The book is not based on original research; the facts are taken from the records of history as presented by recognized authorities. Nor shall I set forth a new and original view of history and prove that all the men you thought great were mean and petty, and those whom you thought wicked were noble and heroic.

I merely wish to persuade you to read over your history with an eye to the manner in which the emotions of the people have been manipulated, and to call attention to the great emotional storms that have swept the nation—with a vague hope that you may discover whether you yourself are anything more than a chip tossed about on these great psychic waves, or a pawn moved hither and yon in the great battle of ideas. And more especially I wish to call attention to the amazing changes in the emotional attitude of the nation and of individuals; and to the storms that are now brewing in the strange incoherent welter of feeling that has resulted from the disintegration of the ideas on which the social order was built. In spite of our claim to be creatures ruled by intelligence we shall always be swayed by emotions. I trust that those who read these pages will not allow themselves to be blindly swept away by emotional storms engineered by clever manipulators, but will choose intelligently the emotions to which they will yield and which they will cultivate in themselves, and in others. For those who read these pages must see that disaster threatens unless those emotions are cultivated which counteract the divisive effect of prejudice, greed, and group antagonism. History shows that certain emotions are essential to progress and prosperity, while others, which are being deliberately cultivated by certain groups, threaten the nation with disaster unless they are checked. It is foolish to regard emotion with contempt. It is a stupendous force. Left uncontrolled, like a cyclone, it may sweep the nation and leave death and destruction in its path. Intelligently directed it may bring unity, peace, prosperity, and happiness to all, or if those who direct are unscrupulous it may be used to breed hatred and suspicion and break down the whole social order.

Great as have been the changes in the emotional attitude of the average citizen since the Declaration of Independence was promulgated, still greater changes seem to impend. It is only by understanding the past that we can hope to direct the future, and I trust that those who read, even if they disagree with my interpretation, will be stimulated to think out some solution of the present situation. It would be silly to be swept unprepared into the midst of the dangers that threaten. The old emotions that held the social order together are disintegrating as the old ideas are crushed by new thoughts in the struggle for existence. In the general confusion you can at least decide what emotions you consider worth cultivating as the basis of unity and happiness, and if your eyes are open to the danger, you can help to thwart those ideas and agencies that are generating prejudice, antagonism, greed, and such other emotions as threaten the general welfare.

EMOTIONAL CURRENTS
IN AMERICAN HISTORY

CHAPTER I

THE MIRACLE OF AMERICAN UNITY

I

THE National Convention was in full blast. The leading candidate approached the rostrum and was about to speak. The whole vast assembly rose to their feet and cheered. A band struck up "Hail, Hail, the gang's all here," and ten thousand voices shouted vociferously in time. The excitement grew. Banners waved inscribed with the names of various states and clubs—handkerchiefs fluttered. Still the noise increased; cheer followed cheer, rising above the steady roar of applause. Men jumped up and down and threw their hats in the air. Well-dressed ladies climbed on the seats, waving their scarfs, and screamed their salutations in an abandon of enthusiasm.

In a gallery somewhat apart, an elderly Chinese* gentleman was seated. Educated in the old imperialism he had come to America to discover how a democracy was operated, and how China could fit herself for republican government. He looked on in mild astonishment.

"Why this cheering—this madness?" he asked his American interpreter. "This man has not saved them from ruin or conquered their enemies. Do they mock him, or perhaps does he pay them to shout?"

"Some of them may have hopes, but they are not paid," said his companion. "They cheer the leader of the party, but why so much or so loud?—You will have to ask a professor of psychology."

"It cannot be meaningless folly," said the Oriental. "What has he done for them?"

*The comments of the Chinese gentleman who attended one of our party conventions are more or less imaginary, for it was impossible, of course, to get any accurate report of what he said.

"Yonder group from his own state are his personal friends. Undoubtedly he has given them a chance to fill their pockets. The rest cheer him as they would cheer at a race for the horse on which they have put their money. They all want him to win."

"Such behavior one expects from a mob. But here, I think, are men of rank and ladies of fashion. How can the same feeling stir the gentleman and the coolie?"

"It does seem queer," responded the American. "But they all belong to the party and for the moment they all want the same thing."

"But how? The wants of a gentleman and coolie clash at every point. One would expect each to shun the other. And here they join in one madness!"

It really was puzzling. "Well," said the American, "I guess you are right. Their interests do clash, but they have managed to forget the fact. They want their candidate to win, for different reasons, but they all want him to win."

"I know nothing that would unite our people," said the foreigner. "Our provinces are distinct. They have different governments. They speak different languages and different dialects. Each section has its own interests and cares nothing for the rest. Possibly we could unite in one party if we spoke one language and had the same interests as your people do."

"But we don't," said the American. "We speak different languages and have divergent interests."

It is easy to see how incomprehensible this would be to the Chinese scholar. He grew up under an ancient imperialistic system that had endured four thousand years. He was trained in the Confucian ethic and in the conviction that the common man is incapable of education and of understanding the mysteries of government. As a philosopher he would hold that every man is driven by his desires and passions, and as the desires of every group conflict with those of the next, the only way to keep them at peace is by training them to obedience and punishing them with death or torture or confiscation for any rebellion. He would naturally think that democracy succeeded among Americans because they were homogeneous and had common desires which could all be satisfied by some one policy of the party. Supposing that the Democratic party originated as an effort to over-throw the power of the aristocrats, it was reasonable to ask if it was this purpose that still united them and aroused such enthusiasm.

As the American attempted to describe the various groups that were present he would find himself involved in hopeless incongruities. Here in front was the New York delegation with the Tammany Tiger to the fore, and a collection of names that seemed to combine old Ireland with the New Jerusalem. Here was the old organization created back in the time of Jefferson to gain control of the government from aristocrats like Hamilton for the common people and to enable them to enjoy its perquisites. They seem to be still running true to the Democratic ideal.

But next to them are the delegations from Virginia and South Carolina, the F. F. V.s and haughty Southern colo-nels and planters. No group represents the old American aristocracy and its pride more perfectly than they. To dis-cover any cause which would lead them to link arms with the Irishmen and Jews of Tammany and shout with them in mad enthusiasm would tax the imagination. They have no wish to secure the perquisites of government control for the proletariat. It is resentment against the party that freed their slaves and launched armies to burn their plantations that holds these groups together. In their view no decent man could be anything but a Democrat.

Here again is Mississippi with its vast population of negroes. These Mississippians cheer for the party because they trust it will keep the negroes in subjection and quash their demands for social equality. The life of the white man would be unendurable with the negroes in control, they say. These men, who stand for the subjection of the alien stock, might find it difficult to shout in harmony with the men of New York who are working to enable groups of alien de-scent to control the government.

Here is another group, sufficiently individual and picturesque to be celebrated in prose and poetry, the mountain folk of Tennessee and North Carolina. They are pure American stock, with a code of their own. A man's purse is sacred though they would shoot him down for an insult. They are primitive Protestants who abhor both Modernist and Catholic. It would tax one's ingenuity to find a common ground for enthusiasm between them and the Boston delegation, for example, who are seeking to put their government into the hands of Roman Catholics.

Here is the Massachusetts delegation, many of whom have left the Republican party because they hoped a change of administration would end the hard times caused by the closing of the textile mills. And next them are the men from North Carolina and Alabama, who have taken away the textile business from them by cheap labor and production, due in part to the fact that these states have not the laws which Massachusetts has passed to protect the workingman. One would imagine them at swords' points rather than cheering together.

One would scarcely expect Frenchmen to have a part in the government of an Anglo-Saxon nation. And yet here are enthusiastic representatives of sections in Louisiana where the traveller would think himself in France and hear no language but French and where the old French customs still hold sway.

Here again are Texas and New Mexico, with towns that are entirely Spanish or Mexican, where the swarthy inhabitants speak no English and keep to their old traditions. We are told that the most powerful political organization in New Mexico is that of the Penitentes, who maintain their processions at the Easter season where men are lashed with scourges of nails and cactus until the blood streams, while some stagger under huge crosses of heavy beams on which they hope to be crucified. The government has forbidden them to be nailed to the wood, so now they can only be tied to the cross. What have such men to do with twentieth-century America?

Here too are Arizona and Oklahoma with thousands of

Indians who have just been made citizens. Gathered in their own cities and reservations, with their old customs, their kivas and snake dances, it is hard to imagine them joining in the enthusiasms of the gentleman from Virginia.

And here is California with its own problems involving Chinese, Japanese, and the whole Pacific, which often put her into antagonism with the rest of the nation. Surely the Chinese Republic can have few incongruities greater than these, or interests more divergent. One might well ask, How were all these diverse elements brought into one group swayed by the same feeling of passionate enthusiasm? How was the feeling created and how did it get its grip upon men of such utterly different character and interests?

No American appreciates the miracle that has taken place. It takes a Chinaman to appreciate it. It is evident enough that it is possible to hold the innumerable communities of half a continent in obedience to one ruler if they know that rebellion means the destruction of their homes, the slaughter of their children, the torture of their bodies and the wreck of all their hopes, as Peter the Great proved in Russia. It can be done if they consider their ruler to be the representative of God and worship him as a divinity, as in Egypt or Japan. But to get a group of free and fearless men to remain obedient to one leader and to work under him in mutual co-operation is another matter. If they are all in quest of plunder or inflamed with the lust of battle it can be done until the plunder is divided. It is not natural or easy to remain obedient or united, as history has sufficiently proved. There must be some motive or strong feeling that holds each man and each group to the common cause, or they will break away as did the various states of Central Europe from Austria, or of South America from Spain, or as the horde of Attila disintegrated at his death. The mutineers of the *Bounty* settled on a beautiful island where they had all that was necessary for a serene and happy life, and ended by fighting until all but one were killed. One communistic experiment after another has failed and ended in division because the interests of men diverged, and no common desire or feeling was found strong enough to hold them to any joint endeavor or even to keep them from quarrelling.

It is not necessary that the same desire or motive should hold every man, but it is necessary that every man should be held by *some* desire or feeling which impels him to work with the others and holds him obedient to their leader or to the rules and regulations which the group has made and upon which its existence depends. Different members of the group may be held to it by quite different motives, and it is evident that the problem of arousing the emotion adapted to each individual, and then of fusing all these desires and feelings in a common enthusiasm, is by no means a simple one. It is this which has been accomplished in the American Republic and it is certainly of interest to inquire how it was done.

2. POLITICAL DYNAMICS

The force that drives all the wheels of the world's machinery, industrial, social, and political, is quite limited in quality. The mass of men are moved by one or two desires or emotions. The same desire may move them to good or evil, to unity or division. It has been said that the love of money is the root of all evil, but it is also the root of nearly everything else. This is because it is the key to the satisfaction of nearly every human desire. It gives a man power and position and control of all the world's resources and of the great forces of nature. The lamp of Aladdin did not confer as great and mysterious powers upon its holder as does the coin which a man holds in his hand to-day. With it he can summon the Djinn and tell him to fly forth and gather a report of all that has happened that day in the farthest corners of the world, and spread it upon his table. He can bid his Afrit to collect the fruits of the tropics, the fish of the distant sea, game from the mountains and spices from farthest Ind, and lay them all before him. He can bid his sprite to paint on the wall visions of distant lands or to portray in beautiful moving forms some thrilling tale of passion, or to collect sweet music and wise words from the air for his amusement. He can command the Djinn to carry him, flying over the ground by the power of an electric spark, or soaring through the air on mysterious wings. All that in previous ages would have been sheer magic, beyond the dream of mortal man, is in his power if he holds in his hand this disk of gold that represents the concentrated power of man over nature. To gain it man will toil and fight. For the sake of it he will attack his friend or unite with his enemy. The life of the individual and the social order to which he belongs depends on how this desire for wealth is directed. If men see that they can gain by working together they unite. The desire for plunder held the Norsemen together in irresistible solidarity on their varied campaigns. The hope of gain by commerce has repeatedly kept one community at peace with the next. Just so long as men see prospect of gain through their association, the desire for wealth will hold them together, unless some other emotion interferes.

A corollary of the same desire is found in the fear of losing wealth already acquired. This also binds men together to secure protection for their possessions.

An emotion which has proved equally potent to unite men as well as to divide them is that of resentment. Man has a great deal of dynamite in his composition. A slight touch, a flick in the face, or even a sharp word flung at him is enough to cause an explosion that may wreck a friendship or cause a social earthquake and an entirely new alignment and stratification of society. The root of all this emotion is what is called by some psychologists the ego-maximation instinct. It includes pride, vanity, the sense of self-importance. Its basis is a man's desire for recognition at the hands of his fellows, and it reacts violently when he receives insult instead of admiration and wrongs instead of favors. When several men or several groups think they have been wronged or robbed or insulted by some tyrant or class or nation, there is often developed a powerful feeling of resentment which fuses all the injured persons or groups into unified opposition toward their oppressor. It was this feeling that first united the American Colonies. Their feeling of resentment toward England made them forget their local quarrels. It was as much the supercilious treatment they received as the taxes imposed that aroused them.

The sense of justice and the desire for freedom seem closely associated with this ego-maximation instinct which impels every man to demand recognition of his rights and a free scope for development. These desires sufficed to hold together such groups as the Swiss cantons and the English Puritans through long periods of trial and opposition.

The feeling which would most naturally hold men together is that of sympathy, but that emotion is decidedly feeble in comparison with the others and needs violent stimulus to make it operant. It is difficult to make one man feel sufficiently the wrongs of some one at a distance to be willing to espouse his cause. It was an ancient custom when a man had been outraged and slain by some tyrant or dominant group to send around his dismembered limbs among his neighbors to awaken in them a keen sense of his sufferings and to unite them through sympathy in opposition to the perpetrators of the crime.

An earthquake or cyclone or flood or terrible disaster will often unite men who have been in antagonism. Hate can unite men as well as separate them. When a common enemy appears they will forget their differences and join forces to defeat him. And the most diverse persons are often held firmly together by a common prejudice.

No emotion is more potent to unite men as well as to divide them than that generated by religion. The crusades, by religious fervor, once united all the nations of Europe, and all the tribes of the east and south were thus brought together by Mohammed for the conquest of the world. Egypt and India to-day dread nothing more than the proclamation of a Jehad or holy war, which arouses the most violent emotions and unites warring tribes and separate communities of all types in a common effort to conquer all who hold a different religious belief.

Under autocratic government men were controlled by fear, horror, reverence and awe. That whole system seems to have passed away, and the forces that can be used to control the ordinary man are chiefly the emotions described above.

Men of superior quality can be united by a common devotion to truth or beauty or justice or the public welfare, but these feelings are rather beyond the scope of the man on the street.

We say that men combine under one government because they are governed by reason rather than passion. But this means merely that intelligence shows them that by thus combining they can satisfy their desires more surely and adequately than by seeking their immediate gratification. It is therefore the desire which is the real driving force and which causes them to hold together. It supplies the power and reason merely points the way.

It would seem unnecessary to state anything so self-evident, but men are continually speaking of reason as if it were in opposition to emotion, and as if some men were impelled by intellect rather than by feeling or desire.

Such are the emotions which a great leader must know how to harness if he is to combine men into a group of any size and strength. He must understand his constituency and promise to each man some object of his desire as the reward of his allegiance. Most men are governed by selfish desires, such as that for wealth. They prefer, however, to deceive themselves with the idea that they are working for noble and unselfish ends. The wise leader, therefore, while making it evident that his followers will gain increased prosperity, gives to them as an ostensible motive which they can proclaim to the world, some benefit which his party will confer upon mankind. Nearly every man and most groups have certain strong prejudices and enthusiasms. What will win one group will often antagonize the next. Here, of course, is the great difficulty. A man will throw off a life-long allegiance because he hears that his leader has infringed upon some prejudice. This is the great game of politics, to detach groups from their leaders by an appeal to their special prejudices, as the opponents of Roosevelt sought to detach the Prohibitionists by reports that he drank beer, and the Southerners by accusations that he ate with a colored man. It is more often petty prejudices than great principles that unite or divide men.

In England it is usual to enunciate some great principle and men gather to support or oppose it. In America the common method is to study the whims of the people and to present as bait such principles as will draw them together in a party. In England parties gather to support principles. In America principles are gathered to support parties. The party secures national solidarity by creating a united group from all sections under one leader. If the party is on sectional lines so that all its members are in a certain group of states and all its opponents in another section and feeling runs high, there is then danger of civil war, but ordinarily sections are so divided in their allegiance that the checks of government are sufficient to hold the parties in balance.

3. STORM AREAS AND TRADE WINDS

We are familiar with the maps prepared by the weather bureau, showing the areas of high pressure and the dominant wind currents. Some such map of the emotional status of the country would be of value to the politician who must trim his sails and shape his course by favoring winds. We have already spoken of the trade wind, the prevailing desire for wealth, which blows steadily all the time and changes its direction but little. Every man desires conditions that will favor success in his business and unless the politician trims his sails to this breeze he will gain but little support. There is the foreign-trade wind which blows from across the Atlantic and involves a desire for amicable relations with the nations of Europe. But there is also the domestic-trade wind which at times blows in direct opposition and sometimes is strong enough to create a protective barrier which interrupts the foreign trade. This is an emotional current of tremendous force which has wrecked many an organization in the past.

Then there are areas of high pressure, sections where a conflict of interests exists which is likely to burst forth in some violent emotional explosion. Such an area is that of the coal mines, where miners and operators are at high tension, each accusing the other of injustice, and each in danger of great losses at the hands of the other. Such areas exist in the South, where it is feared that the negro is putting in a claim for social equality, and the white man is determined to preserve his position of superiority. Other such areas are continually appearing all over the continent and may easily blow a party to pieces unless they are reckoned with.

There are also areas of low pressure which are equally dangerous. Some sections are exposed to suffering and loss, which create an atmosphere of discouragement and discontent. Such an area is now found among the textile cities of Massachusetts and also among the farmers of the Northwest. It is the part of the wise politician to satisfy the desires of such sections before they become violent enough to start a tornado.

We are told that cyclones are caused by overheating some spot so that the hot air, rising, creates a vacuum toward which the air rushes from all sides. So much heat was generated over the prolonged trial of two Italians that a veritable cyclone of feeling was started which is still eddying around the farthest corners of the world. Some such occurrence may at any minute start an emotional cyclone that will sweep across the whole country and tear to pieces organizations and alliances that have stood the test of years.

When tension has been gathering for many years an unexpected spark may set off an emotional explosion that will rock the nation. The raid of John Brown, the shot at Lexington, the sinking of the *Maine,* each of them released forces that wrought the most stupendous changes, before they were exhausted.

In addition to these areas of high and low pressure there

are certain eddies and currents in the emotional atmosphere that are more or less permanent and that have to be reckoned with. Some of these are racial antipathies against Jew, Italian or Japanese, or between English and Irish, or German and French. Many of these have their origin in the old country, but continue to reverberate through the United States. No less violent are the prejudices of religion and the currents of feeling between labor and capital, the working class, and their employees. When these feelings have accumulated because of the abuse of power and a growing sense of injustice, a revolution may very easily be precipitated. The clever politician can ride on these violent blasts of feeling to power and prestige, but the great statesman tries to modify them before they become dangerous. There are those who think that Roosevelt averted such a revolution, by legislation limiting the powers of the trusts and big business, just in time to prevent the popular discontent from breaking forth in a socialistic revolt. The leaders of the I. W. W. and of Socialism who sought to ride to power on the storm of public discontent, were dropped to earth as it changed to a gentle breeze.

4. EMOTIONAL FETISHES

The medicine man claims to possess certain objects which contain such demonic power that by means of them he can raise the wind and control and direct it. It is possible to charge certain objects with emotional force in such fashion that by means of them a storm can be raised or subdued. A piece of cloth can be so charged with power that it will draw men like a magnet and hold them to it even when to remain means wounds and death. Merely to raise a flag in the air will at times send waves of emotion through a great multitude that will stir them to intense activity. A flag is not the only object charged with emotion. Symbolism can work as great magic as fetishism, and when an object has become a symbol of some person or truth or fact it acquires the power to stir emotion and sometimes to arouse a veritable storm. This is true of objects consecrated by religion—a chalice or altar or ikon. Such an object may act as an emotional transformer and can change enmity to friendship, rage to reverence, and pride to humility, as history testifies. In the hands of Ambrose it reduced the pride of the Emperor Theodosius to humility. Held aloft by Saint Bernard it changed the rage of the fierce William of Aquitaine to terror. Garments may be charged with emotion by their wearers. The mantle of Cæsar, the glove of Conradin stirred men to change the course of history.

The priest and medicine man had other means of controlling the winds and storms than by fetishes and sacred objects. Certain words and phrases were thought to be so charged with demonic power that to pronounce them would cause the wind to arise or the clouds to fall back. All through the Orient the mystic syllable "Om" has power to control the forces of nature and the minds of men. In the world of emotion the same thing holds true. Certain phrases and syllables become charged with emotional power and produce the most violent effects. My first experience of this was as a small boy in Italy. My companion said he had learned an Italian word and wished to try it on some one to determine its meaning. He selected the first passer-by—a fierce-looking desperado with pointed moustaches, clad in a huge cape—and addressed the man with this word. The effect was phenomenal. It was only our agility and safe retreat at hand that saved our lives. We never knew the meaning of the word but we saw its emotional effect.

Use and association will give a certain phrase the power to stir multitudes to fury or calm them to silence. Any phrase which has become a subject of controversy acquires this astonishing emotional force. Gibbon tells of the riots in Alexandria over the Gloria, between those who said, "Glory be to the Father and to the Son, and to the Holy Ghost," and those who repeated, "Glory be to the Father in the Son and by the Holy Ghost." The repetition of either phrase was sufficient to rouse the crowds in the streets to fury. It was like waving a red flag in front of a bull, or the green flag and harp in front of an old-time Orangeman. Certain phrases are used as a standard around which a party rallies, and these acquire an emotional charge and affect men either positively or negatively.

Paul made use of this fact when he was attacked by the mob in the Temple at Jerusalem. As soon as he mentioned the word "resurrection" the crowd divided into warring factions and he was momentarily forgotten. Phrases used in religious controversy like the Vicarious Atonement, or the Inerrancy of the Scriptures, or the Miraculous Birth, or the Deity of Christ, have had this same power to arouse violent emotions. Feeling stirred by such a phrase would run so high that any rational discussion of the subject was impossible. The same holds true in politics, and phrases like Free Trade and Protection, or Women's Rights, or Prohibition, or Militarism, or The League of Nations, in certain groups never fail to awaken an emotional storm. Instead of arguing the merits of the case with scientific detachment a wave of violent feeling is discharged into the discussion and every decision is predetermined by emotion. The discussion of politics is forbidden in certain clubs for this reason.

The effect of such phrases apparently is due to prejudice implanted in childhood. The politician is aware of this fact and uses these emotional talismans with great cleverness to arouse the crowd. The word "King" among the Romans, or "tyrant" among the Greeks, could be counted upon to waken such a reaction against any man to whom it was applied. Subtle influences in childhood create an antipathy toward certain groups and enthusiasm for others. The name of the group then ceases to be a scientific term and becomes an emotional talisman. I can mention a mollusk or a crustacean, or perhaps even a Thibetan or Malay without stirring your emotions, but if you will analyze your state of mind when I apply to some one such a term as Bolshevik, Jew, Pacifist, Armenian, Republican, Fundamentalist, Catholic or negro, you will find that some of these words arouse a distinct antagonistic reaction and others perhaps a feeling of sympathy or enthusiasm. You may not know why you dislike Armenians or spring to defend Republicans. There may be no reason or sense in it. The reaction is instinctive and has nothing to do with reason or intelligence.

This emotional peculiarity makes possible the gentle art of calling names, which is one of the great resources of the politician. If he wishes to win over the adherents of an opponent he studies their emotional reactions and then calls his opponent a Socialist or an Atheist, or Pro-British, or whatever name will arouse this antagonistic reaction. It may have nothing to do with his fitness as a leader, it may not even be true. The man with a prejudice against the Socialist usually has no definite idea of what the word really means. He is so geared that he reacts emotionally at the mere word. It is not necessary to supply logical proof. Some chance phrase which the man has uttered is accepted as sufficient evidence of his socialism. The name sticks; the antagonistic reaction is produced, and his followers desert. Again and again we have seen this trick successfully turned in our politics. In each group there is a fund of antagonistic emotion in storage. Some such word is the key that will set it free and launch it upon the head of the victim.

The politician is the medicine man who by waving his fetishes, such as the flag or the Monroe Doctrine or naval supremacy or protection to American industries, can raise the wind, and who can shut off the breeze of popular favor from his opponents by launching against them some word electrically charged, such as "Pacifist" or "Pro-German." Of course, to succeed he must have a well-prepared map of the emotional storage centres of the country. In the vicinity of Milwaukee "Pro-German" would not produce the same reaction as in some other quarters.

5. WORDS WITH AN EMOTIONAL CHARGE

By means of historic experience or continued propaganda an idea or the word that expresses it gradually becomes charged with emotion and it is very interesting to watch this growth of emotional potential. During the reign of the Tudors the word "Liberty" had little emotional content. Under the house of Hanover in England it was carrying a decided positive charge, and "Slavery" had acquired an equally potent negative content. It had not yet attained any such potency in France, but in the American Colonies its potential was even higher. One has only to study the speeches in the Colonial assemblies to see the tremendous emotional storm it could produce.

Associated with this word was the phrase "No taxation without representation," which had been the nucleus of the controversy between Parliament and the Stuarts, and which became the watchword of the Liberal party in England. The application of the phrase was very vague even under the House of Hanover. Quite a large percentage of Englishmen who were taxed, and especially those in the industrial cities, had no real representative in Parliament. Nevertheless, the phrase stirred their souls. It was carried over to the Colonies with its full emotional potential and attention was also given to its meaning.

In the adjacent colonies of France and Spain such a phrase had no significance. They expected to be taxed to the limit that they could endure, and had no dream of being represented in the government that disposed of their wealth. The English colonies did not object to being taxed. They were quite willing to tax themselves and turn the money over to England, but to be taxed by an assembly in which they had no representation—this they defined as "Slavery" —an infringement upon their "liberty."

CHAPTER II

THE GREAT AMERICAN DRAMA. WAR WITH FOREIGN SPIRITS

1. CURRENTS OF FEELING

THE politician has not merely to deal with the various desires and passions of mankind as they are stimulated by chance and circumstance. There are in addition certain combinations of these emotions and emotionalized phrases which become associated by chance or intent and which are passed from man to man and generation to generation so that they form a more or less permanent emotional current. The universe seems to be so constituted that when masses of material are brought together currents of some kind are usually generated. In the vast masses of liquid that constitute the ocean we find the Gulf Stream and the Arctic Current. When metals are brought into contact electric currents are promptly generated. Human beings seem to have the same singular property. The meeting of even one man and one woman can start an emotional current that will last for years, and when men are brought together in large numbers it is usually not long before emotional currents are generated, some of which persist for decades and even centuries. We might start a science of emotional dynamics and state that these currents increase in force in proportion to the mass thus emotionalized. This is almost self-evident. If ten men are angry with you or ten women are shocked at you, you are conscious of a much greater force than when but one person is thus affected.

Resistance to an emotional current raises its voltage almost in proportion to the square of the resistance offered. If you resist a man with fist, boot and curses, you develop ten times more current than if you resisted with gentle words.

If I assert that you are swayed by emotional currents generated hundreds of years ago and still running strongly, you may protest. Nevertheless, when you turn in anger upon an officer who has unjustly arrested you and assert your rights, instead of cringing before him as certain Orientals would do, it is because of an old current of feeling that has been flowing for some hundreds of years in the veins of your ancestors and which had much to do with the creation of the American commonwealth. And when your neighbor is sadly disturbed because he has inadvertently eaten meat on Friday it is because of the impact of a current over a thousand years old, an emotional attitude handed down for generations.

Now an emotional current may serve to immobilize or to produce action. If you are "rooted to the spot" by some powerful emotion, we may call it static in its effect. If it stimulates you to leap, shout and throw your hat in the air, we may term it dynamic in its effect. These currents that come down through history are some of them dynamic and produce revolutions and upheavals, like the passion for liberty handed down in Switzerland or England. Others are static and hold men in passive obedience. Every successful tribe or nation has a religion which acts as a dynamo to generate a current of sufficient fear, awe and reverence to immobilize those whom passion impels to steal or kill or rape. These static currents are very complex and are composed of a dozen different emotions and emotionalized ideas. They usually create reverence for the national God and for the King as his son or chosen, and they can so fill the common folk with emotion that they feel honored if the ruling class walk on their necks. They so hedge the priest and the ruling class about with sanctity that the common man would be as horrified at the thought of disobeying their commands as if he saw the goblins and demons of the Pit waiting in rows to seize him.

For centuries the social order of Europe had been stabilized by the current of reverence generated by the Catholic Church. It was the eternal fires of Hell that supplied the power for that dynamo and kept the common folk in humble obedience to King and priest, who could put upon them the terrible curse. We might call this current the Roman Static, or stabilizing, current. When it came to action, under this system many works were accomplished by the drive of fear. In addition there is that world-wide current which needs no dynamo to generate it, since it seems to spring up spontaneously wherever men meet together. It is the power behind all business and commerce, the Trade Wind which blows steadily through all the world. This is of course the desire of wealth, or the Commercial current, described in an earlier section.

To understand the forces that are driving the wheels of progress in America to-day we must turn back to the Reformation Earthquake which short-circuited the old Roman current and turned it into a Dynamic of dangerously high voltage. In the Roman system the current of the Divine Will and the curse of God was conveyed in a carefully constructed power line running through Pope, priest and church, with switches that were controlled by proper officials, who could thus direct it to uphold or to blast whomever they would. The Reformation short-circuited this whole system and connected the Command of God directly with the mind of the individual through direct inspiration and guidance, and brought the curse of God to bear directly upon the individual conscience without the intervention of the priest. When, therefore, the individual felt himself inspired of God to oppose the commands of priest and King as unjust and sinful, the whole force of the current generated by the fires of Hell, instead of supporting the social order, drove him to overturn it, for his conscience told him that unless he obeyed the Divine voice he would be eternally punished.

The Reformation current, then, put all the dynamic of awe and terror generated by religion behind the conscience and intelligence of the individual and against any authority, whether of King or priest, that conflicted. Such an astonishing reversal of the emotional order would soon have disintegrated the social fabric had it not been recaptured and run back onto power lines of the old pattern. In England, Henry VIII succeeded in cleverly turning this Reformation current to his own uses so that he appeared as its vehicle and the representative of the Reformation God, thus replacing the Pope in the Roman system and creating an independent English static system. He and his daughter Elizabeth were, however, greatly annoyed by a group that kept clear of this power line, who were still swayed by the old Reformation dynamic and who, therefore, followed their own consciences and felt that they ought to obey God rather than man.

There was in England another emotional current troublesome to any autocratic system. The old Anglo-Saxon had been possessed of a very strong feeling of his rights as a free man which for him had an authority superior to the King's command. This feeling, handed down from generation to generation, had gathered up many emotionalized ideas, and, by violent resistance, had been raised to high voltage, to enable men like Pym and Hampden to stand against the sweeping current of awe radiating from the King's majesty, and demand the rights of the people. Combined with this current was that feeling which is especially annoying to one's opponents and which gives a drive stronger than almost any other force, namely, the feeling that they were right and those who opposed them were wrong. This feeling of right and wrong, or of conscience or of a duty to perform, has behind it a primitive urge that is well-nigh irresistible. When you have resisted it you have doubtless been conscious of the intolerable goading and pricking, resulting from the friction of the current, until you take action. When the Anglo-Saxon current had taken up this element it was raised to sufficient voltage to resist any current of fear and awe that autocracy could generate, for under its impulse men would endure torture and face death, and it naturally became extremely obnoxious to Kings, priests and autocrats. In the course of its conflict with the English throne many phrases and ideas received a high emotional charge and were taken up into the tide of the current. We have already noted the more important, such as "liberty," the "rights of man," and "no taxation without representation."

It is evident that groups charged with this sort of dynamic were as incompatible with the autocratic Tudor or Stuart régime that ruled England as fire is with water. One of the two had to go, and the King being the stronger, these devotees of liberty, whether inspired by the Anglo-Saxon or Reformation current, were suppressed and persecuted until they fled and sought a home across the sea. Such a current of feeling we often term a spirit. Great men and stirring events seem to have the magic power of evoking a spirit that lives after them. Clothing itself in institutions and ideas it goes forth to battle with other such spirits. Taking possession of human hearts it drives men sometimes to death and sometimes to glory. It is such a battle of spirits that we shall describe.

The History of America is a great drama not of the ephemeral struggles of individuals, but of the titanic conflicts of streams of feeling that endure for centuries, armed with prejudice and entrenched in logic, a drama in which the hero and protagonist is that stream of feeling that originated with the free men of old England, and their love of liberty and justice, their hatred of tyranny and privilege, with its ally the Spirit of the Reformation and its feeling that in the enlightened conscience of the individual is the supreme authority which none may disobey. It is that old Anglo-Saxon spirit handed down from man to man, gathering strength from conflict, that has been the great dynamic behind each forward step. There is a fascination in watching the drama of its conflict with the opposing systems that through past ages held it imprisoned by walls of fear and prejudice, by awe of King and priest, until it burst free in this new land and built for the first time a government which should express the spirit of liberty. We see it as the old systems creep upon it and hem it in once more with the walls of aristocracy or plutocracy, until it bursts forth again in some unexpected quarter and carries the nation forward once more. We see it caught up in other currents of feeling and swept aside for the moment by rage or fear or greed, but always returning to rouse men again against tyranny and injustice and corruption.

Again and again politicians build their systems to ensnare and bind it and twist it to their uses and again and again it breaks free and triumphs. It is this great drama that we shall follow.

2. THE FORMATION OF THE NEW ENGLAND DYNAMIC CURRENT

It was by various groups driven out from England that America was settled, and they were animated by feelings strong enough to make them face savages and endure hunger and privation, for in them all was this drive compounded of the Anglo-Saxon love of liberty, and the Reformation consciousness of a direct Divine guidance. It was the combination of these historic streams that formed the dominant emotional impulse in New England, and when it reappears we shall call it the New England Dynamic.

In the Quakers of Pennsylvania the religious or Reformation Dynamic was more preponderant than the Anglo-Saxon, but otherwise their emotional attitude was similar.

Virginia had begun with groups of men wafted by the Trade Wind or desire of gain, but it required a more powerful emotional drive to surmount the dangers and sufferings of the wilderness. The first settlements had failed and it was not until men of a type similar to the New Englanders began to arrive that they succeeded. Although these men had in them the Anglo-Saxon love of liberty they were not as sure as the New Englanders of direct Divine guidance and still clung to the Church of England. In America, then, we find that the current from the old autocratic systems was cut off and the drive that held men to their new home was the old liberty current and that product of the Reformation which caused them to feel that the supreme authority for any man was his own conscience. Incidentally, the old Trade Wind soon made its urge felt both in the North and South.

The American Colonies had been granted charters which left them fairly free to carry out their own ideas of religion and government, and the first difficulties which they met were the necessary consequences of the dominant currents that animated them. As we have shown, these were dynamic in character and were not designed to construct a stable social order. The Reformation impulse especially had a little too much dynamite in its composition. When a group of men try to live together, each one of whom feels that he has direct guidance from God and that he must obey his conscience or be eternally lost, it is almost certain to be split by men who feel conscientiously impelled to interfere with their neighbors' rights and privileges and to force others to act in accord with their eccentric views of right and wrong. Such was the Quaker lady who threw the inkwell at the minister in the pulpit of the Old South Church. Such was Roger Williams, who cut the cross from the flag, and refused to associate with his wife after she went to the Episcopal Church.

The colonists had to protect themselves against vagaries of this sort. They could not allow this Reformation current of absolute freedom of conscience to run wild. They accordingly set to work to codify their feelings as to what was right and wrong, and though it produced a code so strenuous that a man could not travel or even kiss his wife on the Sabbath Day, it did produce a stable social order which was not subject to the eccentricities of the individual conscience. They gathered these dynamic currents into a power line of their own through the organization of the Congregational Church, of which every citizen was a member, and thus developed sufficient reverence to form a stable emotional system in which the ministers took in some measure the position of Pope and King as the source of authority. They built up a deep reverence for the Bible, the Sabbath, the Church, the doctrines of Calvin, and for the ministers, which sufficed to maintain an orderly, peaceful community, extraordinarily free from vice and crime and from all elements tending to division.

In each community the minister was the father and adviser of his people—their intellectual stimulus as well as spiritual guide—for he was often the only man with a university education. He was looked up to as a superior socially as well as spiritually, and was regarded as chosen and called of God.

The New England Static current was then composed of reverence for the minister and the Bible on the one hand and on the other of a reverence for the law, which was a part of the old Anglo-Saxon current.

The Colonies had just reached a happy emotional balance, when interference came from across the seas. It had come before under James II and been quieted, and now George III was determined to re-establish the old royal prerogative and rule as Lord and Master of his Colonies. Everything was serene so long as he did not touch any of those questions which had a high emotional charge from the old Anglo-Saxon current, but the moment he attempted to place a tax no matter how slight upon them without their assent, or to interfere with their rights as free men, they were upon him like a nest of hornets disturbed.

In the feelings of the outraged Colonists we would find, then, a current which embraced all these phrases of high voltage and had behind it the force of the united Reformation Dynamic and the old Anglo-Saxon Dynamic, resting back not upon a Deity who upheld autocrats, but upon a God who gave men the right to be free, and condemned those who remained in cowardly submission. It found expression in the words of James Otis in 1764:

"The omniscient and omnipotent monarch of the universe has by the grand charter given to the human race, placed the end of government in the good of the whole. . . . There can be no prescription old enough to supersede the law of nature and the grant of God Almighty, who has given all men the right to be free. . . . A time may come when parliament shall declare every American charter void, but the natural, inherent, inseparable rights of the colonists, as men and citizens, can never be abolished."

3. The Colonial Spirit Arms for Battle

We come now to the period when the hero of our drama began to gird up his loins and gather up his armor and prepare for combat, and we must follow the process by which this Anglo-Saxon Spirit, latent in the psychological structure of the Colonies, was stimulated and roused to battle. Each spirit has its own magic formulæ by which it can be evoked. To change the simile, emotional currents may be running in the minds of men, quite unperceived and inactive until the stimulus of some highly charged idea sets them in motion. Each current has its key words which turn the switch and set it free. It is at this job that politicians are cleverer than men of science. When a man of intelligence and with a scientific mind hears a politician use phrases in a Fourth of July oration with no regard to their accurate meaning or application he is apt to regard the performance with contempt as mere claptrap. If so, he entirely misses its significance. The politician is not trying to influence the reason. He has no regard for the intellectual content of the word. He is using it for its emotional charge, or as a key to release some great store of dammed-up feeling in his constituency. It was thus that men like Samuel Adams set the current in motion, and it was these phrases rather than their wrongs that gave the impetus.

The men of the Colonies were naturally swayed by the desire for wealth. This tended to create antagonisms not only between certain individuals but between the Colonies themselves, each of which sought to gain advantage over the others. The men of the North wanted to secure a market for their fisheries and furs, those of the South for their rice and cotton. The English navigation act which restricted their market to England and prevented the profitable trade with France and Holland, would naturally have aroused resentment in them all. But it did not; for they considered that England had the right thus to hamper their trade.

Then England by the Stamp Act attempted to put a direct tax upon them to defray the expense of the army sent to defend them. Most men would have regarded this as a reasonable demand. But their leaders at once arose and waved the talisman "No taxation without representation."

In May, 1764, Samuel Adams of Boston said, "If taxes are laid upon us in any shape, without our having a legal representative where they are laid, are we not reduced from the character of free subjects to the miserable state of tributary slaves?" The colonies of France and Spain were being taxed regularly without representation, but no such emotional high-pressure area existed among men of these nations. They had never felt the pressure of the old Anglo-Saxon Dynamic Current and therefore no such phrase could have aroused them. But we have shown that in all the American Colonies these two currents, the Reformation and Anglo-Saxon Dynamic, were dominant, in different proportions but in such strength that they responded as one man, and joined in a universal protest, which was backed by such strong resentment that the men of New York said they would wear nothing but homespun, or even sheepskins with the wool on, rather than submit. (Bancroft, vol. III, ch. 7, p. 78.) "If we are not represented we are slaves" was the cry in the Boston Assembly. In the Anglo-Saxon current the term "slave" carried with it the utmost opprobrium, and the application of it to a man who paid a slight tax but was otherwise free to govern himself is an illustration of the way in which terms were used with reference to their emotional content, rather than their scientific meaning.

At about the same time New Orleans had been transferred to Spain and when the leading citizens protested and said they wished to remain loyal to the King of France or else to be independent, the King of Spain in 1769 sent a squadron of twenty-four vessels and 3,000 men. The leading citizens were invited to dinner by the Spanish officer, were treacherously arrested, their estates were confiscated and the five who were most prominent and most honored were brought out and shot in the presence of the people. The whole of Louisiana then received the Spaniards with "silent submission." No one thought of suggesting that they were "slaves." They were emotionally trained to react with reverence to the assertion of royal sovereignty and there was no storage of emotion to be released by such a phrase as "liberty or death."

Among the Colonists there was still some of the old reaction toward the term "King" and the word "Treason" awoke a reaction of horror which resulted from long centuries during which any one who attacked the King was promptly disembowelled and torn to pieces.

When Patrick Henry, voicing the resentment of Virginia to the Stamp Act, made his famous speech and said, "Tarquin and Cæsar each had his Brutus, Charles I had his Cromwell, and George III—" he was interrupted by cries of "Treason" and ended by saying, "may profit by their example." It was to take some years to generate sufficient feeling to overcome the emotional power of that word "Treason." Until then Dulany of Maryland recommended "a legal, orderly and prudent resentment." (Bancroft, vol. III, p. 146.) It was this feeling that united the Colonies in the Congress of 1765 which based its claims and found its grounds for union in "those natural rights which we all feel and know as men and as descendants of Englishmen," to quote Gadsden of South Carolina. "There ought to be no New England man, no New Yorker known on the continent," he said, "but all of us Americans." Their basis of union, then, was not in any charter or bill of rights, but was the result of that great dynamic Anglo-Saxon current in which they all shared.

There were still those in England who were swayed by the same emotional current. Nowhere was it more powerfully expressed than by Pitt on the floor of the House of Commons. "The Americans," he said, "are the sons, not the bastards of England. As subjects they are entitled to the common right of representation, and cannot be bound to pay taxes without their consent."

Against him stood Grenville, the representative of the old-world static current which felt that a tax was a subsidy paid to an overlord for immunity from attacks by his soldiers, and for protection from other such licensed bandits.

The Stamp Act was finally repealed as inadvisable, but the feeling of resentment persisted because Parliament passed a declaration of its right to tax whenever it chose so to do. From thenceforward it was really a conflict for supremacy between the two emotional systems—the old English current based on reverence for the King and his authority, and this new one which had come from the fusion of the Reformation and Anglo-Saxon dynamic currents and which, as it differed slightly from the New England current, we may call the Colonial Dynamic. The King and his party were determined to assert their authority and to withdraw every charter that denied it, and to send armies to enforce it, and the Colonists were equally firm in asserting that no one could dispose of their property without their consent. Choiseul, watching the situation from France, understood it better than any one in England. "The Colonists are enthusiastic for liberty," he said, and again, "Next to fanaticism for religion, fanaticism for liberty is the most daring in its measures and the most dangerous in its consequences."

He saw what a tremendous emotional charge had accumulated in the Colonies about this word liberty, and that this question of the right to be taxed was the trigger that would explode it, and he could not understand the folly of the British in not seeking to conciliate at a time when a mere word would have sufficed. It was a case of Sovereignty vs. Liberty; Lord North and the King were determined to "bring America prostrate to their feet," and the Colonists were equally determined to stand by their rights. One can see the wave of emotion spread from town to town in Massachusetts as the coercive measures began. Marlborough says, "Death is more eligible than slavery." Lenox responds, "Neither nature nor the God of Nature compels us to crouch between the burdens of poverty and slavery."

Leicester says, "We prize our liberties so highly that we think it our duty to risk our lives and fortunes in the defense thereof." Petersham invites the men of Boston, if they cannot withstand, to retire with them and "seek repose among the aboriginal inhabitants" rather than submit.

The event that finally pulled the trigger was a matter so trifling as to be absurd. The tax placed on tea was an insignificant matter and it was so arranged that the tea when purchased would be cheaper than it had been before. But it was a test case. Should the authority of the King prevail or the rights of the Colonists? The tea was dumped into the harbor and the explosion came. The port of Boston was closed and the colonial system of government by town meetings, the cornerstone of their liberty, was abolished, and an army was sent to seize Boston, to arrest their leaders and send them to England for trial. If Boston had been alone this would have been the end. Reduced to penury, deprived of her government, invested by an army of the enemy, her situation was hopeless. But the same emotional charge had been gathering in all the Colonies, and it took but the news from Boston to set it free. Connecticut, Rhode Island, New York, New Jersey and Pennsylvania in rapid succession sent to express their sympathy and their determination to stand by Boston to the end. On travelled the wave through Maryland and Virginia, until from South Carolina came the message, "The whole continent must be animated with one great soul, and all Americans must resolve to stand by one another even unto death." Bancroft says, "In three weeks after the receipt of the port act, the continent as one great commonwealth, made the cause of Boston its own." The various ambitions of the Colonies were all fused in one great Colonial Dynamic Current.

It is easy to see now that but for the repression of the British, which continually raised the emotional charge on this idea of liberty to higher potential in all the Colonies until they were all fused in a common resentment, the American Commonwealth would have been improbable if not impossible. The dominant emotion was not the old

Trade Wind—desire for gain—for they risked the loss of all. As has been explained, it was a great emotional current that had gathered force through the centuries and which had come to centre in the idea of liberty. Resistance had only served to dam it up to higher voltage, and friction with British autocracy was continually raising the charge on its emotionalized phrases.

Some emotions, like the desire for gain, resemble the permanent electric currents that are found in the material world. Others are chance frictional charges due to conflict, suffering or injustice. Others again, like the currents just described, are artificial products. Some, like the Roman Static Current, are like power generated from a dynamo constructed definitely for that purpose. No dynamo of institutions had been constructed to develop this Colonial Current, but it was nevertheless an artificial product, resulting from the turn of events upon ideas that had become highly magnetized, so that, like the dynamo, at every turn of the wheel, the friction of the brushes generated more power and poured its current into the hearts of the citizens.

4. THE FAULTS THAT ADMIT THE FOE

We have spoken of the heroic qualities of the protagonist in the American Drama, but like most who attempt such parts, the Anglo-Saxon Spirit had annoying traits which have caused it to be disliked if not abhorred by State builders. An unfortunate feature in these Spirits, or permanent currents of feeling, is that they gather up many violent feelings and prejudices appropriate to the past which may yet be harmful in the present, but which are entirely uninfluenced by an appeal to the intelligence.

There were certain grave defects in the old Anglo-Saxon Dynamic Current which at once began to manifest themselves when it became the dominant factor in American psychology and which nearly wrecked the American Commonwealth. Foremost of these was a veritable horror of tyranny or autocracy in any form, which went so far as to create suspicions of that legitimate authority without which concerted action is impossible. The "standing army" had been the chief agent in enforcing tyranny in the old-world system and the men of the Colonies regarded with suspicion any permanent military organization. They had the "Cincinnatus" idea,—that of a group of farmers who laid down the plough to beat off their assailants,—a militia coming and going as it wished, subject to no dictator, and receiving its orders from the various state governments.

At first Washington had no power to appoint or remove officers and no real authority to make them obey. It is pathetic to note how his efforts to secure the unified control that was essential to success were broken up time after time as some one hurled the word "tyranny" or "standing army" into the discussion. When at last by his wisdom and courage, and the confidence he inspired, Washington gained some real authority over his men, Adams did his best to overthrow this supremacy won by sheer force of character in spite of all that Congress could do to limit Washington's powers. He says, "I have been distressed to see some of our members disposed to idolize an image which their own hands have molten. I speak of the superstitious veneration which is paid to General Washington." To weaken this growing authority he sought to discredit Washington. When Howe marched into Philadelphia, and Washington was obliged to retire before him to Valley Forge, because Congress, by denying all his requests as to the organization of the army, had left him with a mere handful of half-starved, half-clothed militia, Adams, the head of the war board which had thwarted him, exclaimed: "Heaven grant us one great soul! One leading mind would extricate the best cause from the ruin that seems to await it."

It is easy to see how utterly disastrous was this horror of centralized control. It seemed to be entirely divorced from reason, for no reasonable man could expect armies to succeed which were subject to orders from ten different states and whose officers could disregard the commands of their General whenever they chose. It was only after they had repeatedly proved that they met with disaster when they disobeyed Washington, and succeeded when they yielded to his control, that adequate powers were granted him. Only terrible losses and suffering could counteract the ruinous effect of these emotional talismans. When bills were brought in to give Congress the power to levy permanent taxes and pay its debt to the army, which suffered untold hardships because neither men nor officers had received their pay, some one would interject the emotional talisman, "tyranny,"— "control over free states," and the bill would be blown to atoms. Thus they nearly brought about the dictatorship they dreaded, for the army, knowing that the civilians were always well paid while the men who fought and suffered received nothing, would have mutinied under this outrageously unjust treatment and established a dictatorship, had Washington been the man that Congress feared he was.

5. Transatlantic Storms Foreign Rivals That Supplant the American Spirit

There are those to-day who are still exasperated by annoying qualities in the Anglo-Saxon spirit, and it is not perhaps surprising to see it succumb to the attacks of two rivals from across the sea. Although it had supplied the dynamic that had carried the Colonies through the war, when the war was over it was more likely to split them to fragments than to unite them into a stable nation. Under the urge to freedom and independence, each colony seemed ready to go its own way. Reverence for Washington, which might have held them together, was the last emotion that could live in such an antagonistic tide.

While they thus backed and filled under the influence of this Spirit of Independence, and the Ship of State lay in the doldrums with flapping sails, they were caught in two currents from across the seas that threatened to sweep away all that was characteristically American in their psychology and to make of them a mere adjunct to one of the emotional systems that were dominating Europe. The first was the old familiar English current that stabilized the British monarchy. As the difficulty of forming any stable constitution from the various conflicting elements became increasingly manifest, a group of the leaders with Hamilton at their head began to advocate a return to the British system. They had kept out of the main current of enthusiasm for liberty and, if they rejected George III, they had the same reverence for the aristocracy, the same contempt for the common herd, the same respect for the ceremonials of church and state which characterized the English system, and which were anathema to all imbued with the Anglo-Saxon Dynamic. They wished to keep the government out of the hands of the people and if they could have introduced a King into the system would doubtless have been glad to do so. This group of men, known as the Federalists, recognized their emotional unity with England, and had there then been such a thing as Dominion Status would doubtless have been glad to apply for it.

In the direct opposition to them a new current was flowing across the country from a new quarter. We may call it the Gallic Dynamic Current. It had swept the old Roman current completely out of France, somewhat as the Puritan Revolution had swept away for a time the English system. But whereas in England the Revolution had been caused by emotional currents long in formation and with a definite content, in France it had been an explosion resulting from long-continued suffering and injustice.

In England the Reformation current had supplied faith in a God who stood behind the individual conscience in its struggle for freedom. The Anglo-Saxon current supplied belief in a law which transcended the authority of the King. The only God known to France was the one who upheld the old autocratic system, and the sudden cyclonic outburst had carried away God with all the institutions of the past. The Gallic Dynamic Current therefore differed fundamentally from the New England Dynamic because it was produced by entirely different forces.

In France there had gradually been accumulating areas to high emotional pressure, due to the suffering and discontent of the people. While Louis XV revelled in unrivalled magnificence, his people were housed like cattle and plundered by taxation, until nearly a third of them died of starvation. This tremendous pressure of suffering had been held in check by the old Roman current of reverence. This was so effective that the French people regarded their King and overlords with a sort of adoration as emissaries of God placed over them by Divine law. This barrier of reverence had been persistently undermined by Rousseau, Voltaire, and the Encyclopedists, and from their side the aristocracy recklessly aided in its destruction. Suddenly under the terrific pressure the barrier gave way, and a vast wave of mingled fury and enthusiasm swept before it the old Bastille and all the barriers of the old régime, hurling crowns, thrones, palaces, churches along in a raging welter of destruction.

Other kingdoms, in which the old barrier of reverence still held, gathered all their forces to stem the flood. The vortex of the cyclone was found in the word "liberty." This word had had but little emotional content in France during the years when it proved such a talisman in America, but it had been gradually acquiring enormous potential, and together with "Equality" and "Fraternity" it became a fetish that could conjure up a hurricane.

In England the emotional tension had been released in the course of recent revolutions, and the barriers of reverence for law and order had been reconstructed. Hence England became the chief bulwark against the advancing flood and her stabilizing emotional attitude had its effect on the Colonies across the seas.

In Hamilton and his party the words Liberty and Equality aroused antagonism rather than enthusiasm, and he was thrown continually into closer sympathy with England. With him were the bankers and merchants of New York and Boston whose trade was chiefly with England, and most of the men of wealth. Hamilton's policy of redemption of the currency at par, and assumption of state debts, had resulted in putting behind him nearly all the men of wealth. Aware of his intentions they had bought from the poor farmers all the government paper at its depreciated value, and therefore were sure to gain large fortunes when they were paid at par. They were naturally swept into the old English current. On the other hand the poor men who had received their pay as soldiers and disposed of it at a tithe of its value, as a result of this measure, were all to be taxed to enable the government to pay the par value to the wealthy men who had acquired their paper. The state governments were heavily in debt and they added so heavy a tax that the poor were unable to pay. Those in debt, instead of being allowed to work and pay off this obligation, were arrested and jailed. The prisons were full of poor ragged starving wretches whose only crime was that they had neglected their farms to fight for their country. The result was an area of terrific low pressure that threatened a cyclone.

Jefferson on his return from France was shocked by the unrepublican atmosphere that surrounded the President. He saw Washington conveyed in a gorgeous royal coach ornamented with cupids and with six prancing steeds. Around him was gathered a society that liked to term themselves "the court," which had its centre in the stately mansion of the fascinating Mrs. Bingham. Otis comments on the pride, haughtiness and ostentation of these social lights and says that nothing would make them happier than the institution of an order of nobility which would enable them to overawe the public with their titles. Travellers stated that in no court of Europe had they seen ladies of more exquisite charm. They were magnificently dressed in imitation of the portraits of Gainsborough and Reynolds in silks and gauzes and all the latest furbelows imported from London, and Liancourt complains of the manner in which the flamboyant rich displayed their costly furniture and rare English glass and old china to a guest one day, and dropped him the next with rude indifference. The English Static Current was apparently sweeping all before it. But there was resistance. Liancourt notes that this assertion of superiority was resented by the common people, who took quite seriously the idea of the equality of mankind. A question addressed to a working man usually met with an impudent answer, he says, and he notes that many people of this class were living beyond their means in their effort to copy the wealthy in a display of their goods.

All this created a situation of high tension and of such a type that the emotional explosion in France might well awaken sympathetic vibrations. For there were not only men of the upper classes trained to emotional response at the word "liberty" but also masses of the common folk who felt themselves abused because the equality for which they had fought was still as far as ever from their reach, and who were ready to respond to something more radical than the New England current. It is interesting to note the manner in which the new Gallic current swept across the sea and caught the people of America in its tide. It is a general law that when powerful frictional charges have accumulated, any dynamic or revolutionary current that touches them tends to discharge them and gather up into itself their accumulated force.

When the news of the French Revolution reached America it created great excitement. John Adams said there were more cannons fired in celebration of French victories than the French fired to win them. He notes 22 grand civic festivals in honor of the French Revolution, 51 inferior festivals and 193 public dinners. Even in Boston, the centre of the pro-English party, there was a grand procession in which twelve men robed in white and with cleavers, escorted the Ox of the Aristocracy to his death. Wagons of bread and punch followed in his wake to provide a feast for all. Frenzied crowds packed the streets and shouted madly while bells rang and cannon roared. Some banqueted in a chamber decorated with broken crowns and sceptres. In the theatres the play was stopped while actors came out and sang the Marseillaise and the audience joined in the chorus. A favorite ditty that spread all over the country stated that "Louis Capet has lost his caput."

When Genet, the Ambassador of the new republic, arrived in Charleston on April 9, 1793, he was received with a frenzy of excitement and overwhelmed with banquets and processions. His progress to Philadelphia was a triumphant processional. Every one donned the cockade and the liberty cap and shouted "Down with Royalty." A mob attacked the relief of George III in front of Christ Church and tore it down. Mobs of rough men swaggered through the streets shouting for liberty and equality and jostling the rich in their path. The English uniform was hissed, and all over the land, in all the drinking-houses and streets, was a mad outburst that rivalled and re-echoed the terror of Paris. The common man felt that at last his day had come. A dinner of one hundred covers was given Genet at Philadelphia with a liberty tree and cap as a centre piece and he gave the toast: "May all heads find themselves united under the same bonnet," and passed around his liberty cap for all to wear.

Under the old French treaty Genet claimed the right to fit out privateers, and to bring their prizes into American ports, and when Washington, knowing that such action would bring on war with England, denied him that right, Genet, feeling that he had the enthusiasm of the people behind him, threatened to appeal to them over Washington's head. In the storm which followed, Washington himself did not escape from vilification and vituperation. He was accused of falsehood, treachery and even of embezzlement, so violent and unreasoning was the storm of feeling.

One would suppose that French enthusiasm for Liberty would coalesce readily with the spirit of New England, and that it did not is demonstration of the fact that it had a fundamentally different emotional content. Both had produced a revolution; but for the Americans, with the Anglo-Saxon tradition behind them, liberty was something that came from God and was based on Divine laws and rights, while, for the French, God and the old laws were part of the system that liberty must overthrow. This new enthusiasm from France, then, carried contempt for religion, disbelief in God, and antagonism to all established institutions and ancient laws. Its adherents were regarded with horror by the Federalists as Atheists, Sansculottes, and criminals. In a later age they would have been termed Bolsheviks. The new current released all the accumulated discontent. Men rebelled against the established order and several miniature wars were started. Shays's rebellion in Massachusetts had been put down by General Lincoln, but now came the Whiskey Tax revolt in Pennsylvania, against which Hamilton conducted an army.

A period followed in which the country was nearly torn in twain as the two currents—the old modified English aristocratic and the Gallic Dynamic that had gathered up the whirlwind from the low-pressure centres—met and clashed. It really looked as if the French Revolution might spread to America, when Napoleon began his juggling with the map of Europe and incidentally upset its psychology. Between the Empire and the Pope the French revolutionary Dynamic hardly knew itself and became as stable as the old aristocracies. In the contest of France and England America had the happy position of a neutral who receives kicks from both sides. The partisans of England were enraged by the blows of France and the French adherents were infuriated by British insults, so that for a time the crossed wires of the two currents emitted more threatening fireworks than ever.

In this turmoil of violent emotion between the partisans of France and Equality and England and Privilege, it was for several years touch and go whether there would be war with England or France. First, when England was seizing American ships and goods (and she seized one hundred ships at one time and held them), the infuriated populace almost carried the country into war in spite of all the efforts of Hamilton and the Federalists. This was averted by the treaty negotiated by Jay, a treaty considered so humiliating that Jay was cursed and burnt in effigy by the enraged people. Then in 1798 the French, angered by this treaty, grossly insulted the American commissioners, and in their turn seized upon every American ship on which they could lay their hands. President Adams, with his sword by his side, stood forth and called the nation to arms in a ringing speech. An army was raised and drilled under constant alarms of a French invasion, and a wave of madness swept over the country, destroying all the liberty caps and memorials of France that had been erected. Adams finally ended the quarrel by sending other Commissioners to Paris, but the tide of feeling aroused by this embryonic war resulted in completely cutting off the Gallic current from its source. The current persisted, however; little by little the Gallic content fell away. More and more Colonial elements were gathered up, until finally it merged with the old spirit of the Colonies.

The fundamental current in the Colonies had always been the old Anglo-Saxon Dynamic and although it had been in part diverted by Hamilton it was still dominant among the middle class and gathered power as the aristocracy grew more oppressive. The Gallic current had been strongest among the lower classes, and as it lost its atheistic and anarchistic elements it fused naturally with the old Anglo-Saxon Spirit and between them the people were stirred to a point that threatened the stability of the government.

6. THE OLD SPIRIT EMERGES TRIUMPHANT

The Anglo-Saxon Spirit differs from the celebrated Djinn in that it is most unsafe for Authority, even with the seal of Solomon, to bottle it up. It was such an attempt that raised its feeble remnants to explosive power and brought it once more to dominance.

The Federalists saw the danger that the various storm centres that were starting up throughout the country would merge in an opposition current. Everywhere there were these points of high pressure where, because of some wrong or loss or injustice there were explosions of violent criticism of the administration, usually in one of the opposition journals. To Hamilton and his following it seemed both dangerous and outrageous that such waves of antagonistic feeling should be ricochetting around the country and finding ribald and insulting expression. In the old country such

emotional outbursts were promptly checked by the cry of
"Treason!" and, at the threat of being disembowelled and
torn asunder, a wave of fear eliminated all other feeling.
The Federalists apparently thought that the government of
this new country would be swept away unless something
were done to stop these explosions of discontent, not realizing that the outburst was often a safety valve through
which the high pressure found relief. They attempted to
bottle up and suppress all these centres of emotion by a
Sedition Act, which provided that any man who uttered a
criticism of the government or of those in authority, could
at once be thrown into prison. Such was the final expression
of the old autocratic spirit that flowed in from England.

To create a cover adequate to suppress an incipient tornado
requires the iron force of a Pretorian guard and the ruthlessness of a Russian Czar. Louis XVI had proved how incapable he was of carrying it out. In a country founded on
the idea of liberty, such an attempt was worse than futile.
The idea on which the country was based was that the feelings of the people should not be suppressed, but that they
should find full expression and be carried out in the policies
of the government. In this land alone, of all upon the earth,
the feelings of the people must not be compelled to conform
to the government, but the government must adjust itself
to the feelings of the people. It was an attempt to harness
half a dozen whirlwinds and make them saw wood, a
method totally alien to men imbued with the psychology of
the English Static current who naturally wished to organize America on the plan of England. But they had not the
power of the old autocracies. The feelings suppressed only
rose to higher pressure, and the masses became infuriated
as they saw their champions seized, beaten and thrown
into jail, and the opposition current gathered more and
more adherents from the old American stock who were
incensed by these attempts to curtail their liberty. The
man who attempts to sit on the lid of all the smouldering
emotions of a democracy might just as well try to drive a
plug into the throat of a volcano. This Sedition Act nearly

split the nation, for Virginia and Kentucky threatened to nullify it and secede from the union.

Here was the critical point in American development. It was to determine whether this country would go back to the usual method of government by suppressing the will of the people, or whether the feelings of the people should rule. It was again a conflict of the same two currents that had fought the Revolution, only now the English Static was established on American shores, and the old Anglo-Saxon Dynamic was fighting for liberty against Americans instead of British. Under the stimulus of the Gallic current clubs similar to the Jacobin clubs had sprung up all over the country, and there were other groups of men chiefly of the poorer classes, who were dissatisfied with the treatment they had received, and with the ruling class, which was supported by the government, and which, in its luxury and pompous disregard of the masses, differed but little from the old aristocracy of France and Britain. These clubs were the best means of voicing the discontent of the country with the Sedition Act.

It was Jefferson who took note of all these various Democratic organizations, of which the Tammany Club of New York was one, and who first thought of combining all these local centres of high pressure into a hurricane that would sweep the country. They were all dynamos in which the old Anglo-Saxon Dynamic was being generated and only needed to be connected up to create an irresistible current. This Jefferson accomplished and the strength of the resulting current carried him into the Presidency and destroyed the Sedition Act, and before it the old Federalist party gradually disintegrated. The new Republican party controlled the government for many decades. Its slogan was: "Equal Rights for all, and special privileges for none." Its creed is found in Jefferson's first inaugural. He based the party on the fact that men are constitutionally divided into two classes, those who distrust the people, and those "who consider them the most wise depository of the public interests." His followers were contemptuously termed

"Democrats" until they adopted the name themselves in the time of Jackson. In the force that animated them we can always recognize the old Anglo-Saxon Dynamic Current.

The emotions that centred in the old aristocratic ideal were swept away and all their representatives were put out of office, and the country was carried along on a steady breeze of democratic feeling. This lasted not only through the eight years of Jefferson's administration, but also during those of his followers, Madison and Monroe, and also of John Quincy Adams, who virtually came over to his party. For more than fifty years Jefferson dominated American politics. From his retirement in Monticello he still advised and directed. Even the Monroe Doctrine was promulgated by his advice. Perhaps no other man has ever had so long-enduring a control of any Democratic government.

7. THE DISINTEGRATION OF THE ANGLO-SAXON DYNAMIC

After all the years of conflict America seemed at last to be sailing in peaceful waters. Borne along on the current of the old Anglo-Saxon spirit with its love of liberty and respect for majority rule, the opposition of the Federalists was hardly enough to ruffle the surface. Washington had had his difficulties in riding that current and it was now to be seen if Jefferson could manage it by giving it its full head, and if a stable government could be organized while an emotional attitude was dominant which carried with it a horror of authority and of all agencies that compel obedience, including army and navy. Cromwell had found this spirit of liberty unmanageable without the control of his Ironsides. Jefferson wished to leave all to the will of the people and to destroy all the machinery that would control by force the feelings of the masses. He did what he could to weaken the central control of the government over the States. It was like driving a team of a dozen horses without any reins. He could only hope they would all want to go the same way. He allowed the army and navy, organized by Adams, to disintegrate to such a point that it became impossible for America to defend herself against aggression.

The old Anglo-Saxon love of liberty reached its acme, when through its antagonism to authority it rendered itself defenseless.

The result was a humiliating pacifism. Americans had long been irritated by the British practice of searching American ships and impressing seamen. The annoyance reached its climax in 1807 when the American frigate *Chesapeake* refused to submit to search, and the English ship *Leopard,* regardless of the fact that America was a neutral nation and that the *Chesapeake* was unprepared for war, fired shot into her, killed three men, wounded eighteen, and having forced her to strike her colors, seized and carried off four of her sailors. This called for some action, but, instead of fighting, Jefferson took the ground that if our ships could not sail without being insulted and outraged by the British, he would not allow them to sail at all, and placed an embargo on all our ports, forbidding all commerce and preventing any ship from leaving or entering American harbors.

This measure was like a rock appearing in the bed of a river which splits the current into diverse channels. Any man with a vestige of the Anglo-Saxon spirit is roused to wrath by a blow in the face, and now the provocation was greater than that which brought on the Revolution. There were many who resented Jefferson's peaceful equanimity, and still more resented the interference with trade.

The average man, when his attention is not diverted and his emotion absorbed by a fight of some kind, is usually occupied in acquiring wealth, and his soul begins to vibrate to the old Commercial current. Any measure that cuts off from him the good old Trade Wind is then sure to produce an emotional discharge of no small violence. The people of New England were now actively engaged in trade and commerce and Jefferson's measure cut off their trade completely. There were still enough Federalists there to keep alive a strong contempt for Democrats and a horror of Jefferson and all his works. A minister in Stockbridge in one of his sermons stated that he did not know that all Demo-

crats were horse thieves, but he was sure that all horse
thieves were Democrats. In retaliation the Democrats each
day drove an old rawboned horse through the streets hung
with placards expressive of their contempt for Federalist
pomposity. One Democrat had all his windows opening on
the lot of a Federalist neighbor closed up, as he refused to
receive air and light from Federalist sources. This new
measure added the force of the Trade Wind to the old aristocratic antipathy and roused all prosperous New England
against Jefferson with redoubled violence. Jefferson was an
atheist, an anarchist—no word was too strong. He found
that the measure was splitting his following in two and
before the united blast of the Trade Wind from North and
South he withdrew the measure.

During the Napoleonic wars, America from her neutral
position continued to suffer violent blows from both sides
until goaded beyond endurance she did not know which side
to hit first. Her efforts to acquire wealth were seriously
impeded as France and Britain, in their fight with one
another, attacked in turn the ships and commerce of America, that lay temptingly between them. The desire for wealth
can generate as much feeling as the love of liberty, and in
1812, under Madison, the people reached a state of wrath in
which they must hit somebody. The craft of Napoleon decided that England rather than France should draw their
fire and war was at last declared. But as the feeling behind
this war was desire for wealth, rather than any more patriotic emotion, it nearly split the country, for it immediately
cut off from New England a most profitable trade with the
British. The New England Federalists, already attached to
the British system and bitter against the National administration, and now stung by their losses and driven by the
Trade Wind, refused to enlist or send their militia, and
finally called a Congress to propose the secession of New
England. A few shells from the British served to reverse
this current in time to send the militia hurrying to Boston.

It was the most humiliating war ever undertaken by
America. Owing to the confused emotional status there was

no active resistance. The Anglo-Saxon love of liberty had wrecked the army. When the British marched into Washington without difficulty and burnt the Capitol, a change of feeling began, and by the time that Jackson had won the battle of New Orleans, and the Treaty of Ghent had ended the war, enough patriotic sentiment had accumulated to cause triumphant celebrations all over the country. The chief effect of the war was to cut the remaining links between America and the old world.

Thus closed the period when the chief emotional currents in America had their origin across the sea, and this continent was swayed by the same storms of feeling that swept across Europe. Washington had nearly been swept from his position in the hearts of his countrymen by these transatlantic hurricanes and well understood their danger, and his protest against "entangling alliances," which connected America with the emotional power houses of Europe, has become a classic. The phrase itself has become so emotionalized as actually to hinder necessary alliances. This policy was accentuated during the administration of Monroe under the guidance of the Secretary of State, John Quincy Adams, whose wise judgment and wide knowledge of European affairs did more for America than the work of any other man of the period. The Monroe Doctrine was formulated as the expression of a determination to keep America free from the turmoil of European politics and the violent rivalries of the transatlantic peoples, and above all from the domination of the old Static autocratic emotional systems. The Monroe Doctrine has acquired as great an emotional charge as that upon certain doctrines of the church, so that in the eyes of many it has an inviolable sanctity, and politicians have found it a valuable fetish to conjure with.

CHAPTER III

THE SPIRIT OUT OF THE WEST

1. The Enchantress That Ensnares and Blinds

In most dramas, after the battle is over the hero settles down to home life. It was at this time that the Anglo-Saxon spirit, resting from warfare, came under the domination of that ancient scheming adventuress, the Commercial spirit, and an alliance resulted in which, like Delilah, she robbed her companion of his noblest characteristics and made him quite unrecognizable.

We have shown that under the Federalists the North had been the seat of an aristocracy, while the South had supplied the leaders of the democracy. It seems as if it must have been that magic wind, blowing both hot and cold, that transformed the Southern democracy to an aristocracy and the Northern aristocracy to a democratic plutocracy. There are few things that the good old Trade Wind cannot accomplish. In the North the desire for wealth combining with the old Anglo-Saxon love of liberty produced that familiar Laissez Faire Commercial system in which every man felt that he had the right to pursue wealth and happiness in his own way, but without interference from his neighbor or the government. Driven by these feelings New England and New York developed a financial and industrial system and increased in prosperity. The commercial current can stabilize a community after a fashion, for it produces a respect for wealth and privilege almost as potent to hold men in subjection as reverence for a Lord.

The South was prospering under the same favoring Trade Wind and should have been borne along peacefully on the same current with the North, had not certain rocks appeared which split the current in twain, and which gave the Southern branch quite a different direction. The first was the question of slavery. The main charge of the old

Anglo-Saxon current had been on the idea of "liberty," and conversely "slavery" carried a violent negative charge through all the American Colonies. There was a general feeling in the world of that day that the negro was not really a human being and that the assertion that all men are free and equal applied to him no more than to the horse and dog, which were formed by the Creator to be the servants of men. The American Colonies, however, soon began to include even the black man in their ideas of freedom, and most of the Colonies protested against the introduction of slavery into this continent.

England, however, had profited by the slave trade to such an extent that she had compelled the Colonies to continue it. The protest, strange to say, was especially strong in Virginia and the Southern Colonies. As soon as independence was declared the slave trade was forbidden, and the leaders in Virginia nearly all registered the hope that slavery would soon cease to exist. The feeling against it gradually increased along with the charge on the idea of liberty, and by a natural and gradual process slavery was made illegal in one state after another. In some places in the North it was strongly intrenched and supported by the leaders of wealth and fashion. At Newport, R. I., the courageous Dr. Samuel Hopkins risked his position and almost his life in protesting against it. But his appeals awakened a response and soon over all New England there was strong feeling against holding any man in slavery.

In New England slavery was of value only to a small circle of the wealthy who enjoyed the pomp of black men in gorgeous livery. Industry and agriculture were carried on by white men and in their system intelligence was of more value than brute force. They preferred white labor, and the emancipation of the slaves was accomplished without any counter blast from the Trade Wind.

In the South the situation was different. It was difficult for white men to work on the Southern plantations and the prosperity of the planters depended more and more on slave labor. With the invention of the cotton-gin and the conse-

quent enormous growth in cotton production the demand
for slaves increased. It was here that the old Enchantress,
the Spirit of Commerce, ensnared the Spirit of Liberty and
began to blind its vision. My grandfather went from New
England to teach school on a Virginia plantation in 1820
and his letters gave a vivid picture of this conflict. The
planters felt that slavery was wrong but saw no way out.
They were outnumbered by the blacks and emancipation
would subject them to the domination of an ignorant race.
The Trade Wind always assists them to find arguments in
favor of a course necessary to their prosperity. They are
convinced by emotion rather than logic, or rather their
desires control their logic. In the mountains of Tennessee
and Kentucky where men for the most part did their own
work, the feeling against slavery increased, but when the
lands of Alabama, Mississippi and Louisiana were opened
to cotton, and slaves were imported, there soon developed
a strong feeling in favor of slavery. At first no one ventured to advocate it as right or desirable, but for the first
few decades it was defended as a necessary evil. In 1820
Ried of Georgia likened the South to an unfortunate "who
wears a cancer in his bosom."

Thus, although they were under the stimulus of the same
Commercial current, the North and South began to grow
apart. In the South the old Anglo-Saxon spirit was gradually shorn of its strength by the great Enchantress and
bound with the chains of the old aristocracy. The old planters of established family were dominant, and were regarded
by the blacks with the reverence due to a race of demigods,
while the poor whites felt toward them as the British com-
moner does to the House of Lords. Thus slavery served to
create a type of aristocracy of men who scorned to labor
with their hands, and who were supported by the labor of
the blacks.

In the North the old Anglo-Saxon Dynamic was not
entirely shorn of its strength. There was still scorn for the
aristocrat. Men of education worked in the fields or in
industry. It was felt that every man should work for his

living and be independent of his neighbors. In addition
there was a residuum of the old Reformation current which
caused a man to feel that he was directly guided by God
and that he must obey his conscience when it impelled him
to correct the conduct of his neighbor, no matter what the
consequences. Since the day of Roger Williams this current
had had its dangers, and now under its influence a group of
men were impelled to attack slavery as sinful and contrary
to the will of God. They had no appreciation of the problems of the South, they acted under the irresistible dynamic
of the animating current. Most Northerners, though they
did not want slavery for themselves, sympathized with the
difficulties of the South and the attacking group met with
ridicule and obloquy.

Thus gradually took form the two divergent emotional
systems of the North and South, supporting two different
economic systems, one based on industry and white labor,
the other on agriculture and black labor. The South which
had supplied the great leaders of democracy gradually became an aristocracy, while the North where the Federalists
had planned an aristocracy verged toward a plutocracy.

Another rock which divided the current was the Tariff
question. Men were used to taxes for revenue, but when it
came to placing a tax which should exclude or raise the
price on certain products so that the industries producing
them might profit, there was infinite opportunity for conflict. An infant can sometimes perpetrate an emotional explosion that will terrify a grown man and the infant industries
of America certainly did their share in the contest for
favors. Any tariff that could be arranged was bound to
bring profits to some and losses to others. Friction naturally
developed between states that profited and those that suffered. Gradually this also brought about a cleavage between
North and South. The tariff favored the industries of the
North, but was of little assistance to the raw produce of the
South. The Southerners saw with indignation the price of
the manufactured articles they needed being pushed arti-
ficially to heights beyond their reach. Their resentment

grew until South Carolina finally declared she would either break the Tariff wall or secede from the Union.

During the first period of American Development the South had been dominant in national affairs. Difference with the North did not annoy her so long as she could control legislation and have her own way. But as time went on the North gradually outstripped the states to the South in her energy and industrial development. The drive in black labor came from without and in white labor from within. The black worked for another, the white for himself and the Southern system could not keep up with the Northern. Even a horse does not like to be passed in a race, and here there were considerations that added fear to the natural charge of ambition and jealousy. The Southern planters began to fear that the North would gain control of the government and then knock the keystone from their system by abolishing slavery. The matter first came to an issue when in 1819 Missouri applied for statehood. In a closely balanced tug of war it makes a great difference on which side a new contestant lays hold. The South feared that if Missouri came in as a free state it would mean the preponderance of the North in the affairs of the nation. The majority in the North, with characteristic Anglo-Saxon Laissez Faire attitude, did not wish to interfere with slavery in the South, nor on the other hand did they wish the South to interfere in new territory and force slavery upon the people. The friction developed much heat and many sparks and when the matter had been finally settled by the famous Missouri Compromise, which allowed slavery in Missouri and forbade it in future states north of Latitude 36° 30′, there came about a change from the amicable development by two sister economic systems into a desperate rivalry between two hostile camps.

The North, licking its chops over large morsels of prosperity, was inclined as yet to be peaceful and somnolent, but the Southern lion was as rampant as if the North had intentionally trodden upon its tail. We find then that in the East the old Enchantress, the Spirit of Commerce, had ensnared the Spirit of liberty, and torn the South apart from the North, binding it with the gilded claims of pride and privilege into a settled aristocratic system, bitterly opposed to the North, where something of the Anglo-Saxon spirit remained, held by its alliance with the Spirit of Commerce to a stable plutocratic system. Within it were remnants of the old Reformation Spirit churning up explosive energy which was later to threaten both systems with ruin.

2. THE OLD SPIRIT RISES IN NEW GARMENTS

The old spirit that had fought the war of Independence seemed to have died out in the East or to be so disguised as to be unrecognizable. But just when it seemed to have disappeared from the stage it leaped once more from an unexpected entrance. While in the East it was robed in the garments of fashion and chained with links of gold, apparently a helpless prisoner, it suddenly emerged, rising like a mighty Djinn from the far Western forests and plains, manifesting the same devotion to liberty, the same staunch independence, and the same hatred of authority and pomp and privilege, that had always been its distinguishing characteristics. It had been borne westward by pioneers from the old Colonies who had not been bound by the gilded fetters of the plutocracy. It took on a new form and we may term it the Western Spirit or the Western Dynamic Current, while remembering that its main characteristics are derived from the old Anglo-Saxon Dynamic. Its appearance was cyclonic and seemed to be due to the unequal atmospheric pressure in the East and West.

As stated, the Plutocracy with its moneyed interests centred along the Atlantic Coast. Here were the wealthy manufacturers, the rich planters, the merchants and bankers, the men of culture and the institutions of learning. West of the Alleghanies dwelt a race of hardy pioneers who wrested their living from nature by hard toil, who fought the wild beast and the Indian, cut down the forests and dwelt in log cabins, moving ever farther West like an advancing battle line. They thought little of culture and book learning and many could hardly read and write. They were independent and self-sufficient. They could gain their own food, build their own houses, weave their own clothing, without help from any man. All they wanted was a free hand to carve their own way to fortune. They resented government interference and government control. They felt able to defend themselves and to make their own laws and enforce them. They were in the same circumstances with the early Colonists and it was natural that the same emotional currents should flow in them. They came naturally into conflict with the static systems of the East and resented the authority of aristocracy and wealth. They became increasingly suspicious of the men of wealth and culture and resentful of the fact that the government was run by them for their benefit.

But it was not until these antagonistic forces assumed in their eyes the form of a greedy and terrifying monster that they roused themselves to fight. The panic at the close of the War of 1812 and the demand for specie payments caused many failures and the foreclosure of mortgages and threw the control of a vast amount of property into the hands of the U. S. National Bank. Nearly all the real estate in Cincinnati was thus controlled in 1819. Many of the pioneers owed the government for their land and, being unable to pay, found themselves in the grip of the National Bank. It was this which they came to regard as a huge monster created by the moneyed interests to prey upon them and devour them. They did not understand the system and merely knew that the bank refused their paper money and yet hounded them for payment, and they cursed the cultured and wealthy East that sat chuckling in the seats of the mighty and watched while this giant vampire of theirs clutched the pioneers and drained their life's blood. Benton expressed this feeling when he said, "All the flourishing cities of the West are in the jaws of the monster."

Here then was a storm generating as the result of different atmospheric conditions in adjacent areas. Across the mountains they were men of entirely different type from these effete Easterners with their palatial mansions and feathers and furbelows, and conventions and forms. All that finely organized, delicately articulated social life, where each man contributed some one thing and was dependent on the work of others for everything else—all this mutual dependence was anathema to the West, where each man stood alone on his two feet against nature, man and devil. All his relations were personal—not social or industrial. He understood friendship. When he once chose a pal he would be loyal to him to the death. In that life of danger and adventure it was necessary to know one's enemies, to have friends that one could count upon to the bitter end. Men of this type despised the Easterners as effeminate and cowardly, as crafty money-grabbers, who had won supremacy by trickery, while the Eastern merchant despised the pioneer as rude, coarse and ignorant, impossible to meet socially, and incapable of a share in the government.

A gathering current of this sort is seldom dangerous until some low-pressure centre sets it in violent motion, and it was not until these men of the West began to suffer hunger and loss that the current became active.

Here, then, back of the smooth breeze of united feeling during the administrations of Monroe and of John Quincy Adams, there were three signs of storms to come, one due to a difference in the personal characteristics of the men in adjacent areas, one to a difference in the social-economic systems in vogue, and one to differences in the industrial conditions. The first threatened a clash between the East and West, the second between North and South, and the third had a shifting centre which seemed inclined to settle in the South and add to the increasing difference in potential between North and South.

Now the governments of the old world were not equipped to handle conflicting currents of this sort. They could only survive by suppressing them. It was now a question whether the American Government could handle them or whether they would split it in twain. Instead of suppressing them the American Government was designed to give them full expression and to enable them to issue in action. It was a gigantic commutator in which the various currents were received, combined and transformed into power. Each section had its representative in Congress where he could express the desires of his constituency. If he failed to do this they could elect another man. In Congress such a representative should be able to secure action in conformity with the desires of his section. If the administration refused to accede to his demands he could work with others to overthrow it and to elect men who would favor his purposes. Congress was therefore a most ingenious mechanism designed as a vent to the desires and passions of the nation. No administration could stand unless it did something to satisfy these desires that came raging in upon it from the Western plains, or the Southern plantations, or the farms of New England. Here, as in Africa, were the great rainmakers and weather conjurers, who had by means of some fetish to charm away the storm before it annihilated them and to transform it into a favoring breeze. Charms and fetishes, concessions and compromises all were in use by the medicine men of the nation, and many a tornado was diverted or changed to a prospering wind.

The dissatisfied West found its representative and spokesman in the national hero General Jackson, who at New Orleans had defeated the veterans of Wellington's army with the loss of less than a dozen men. He became the candidate of the West and drew votes all over the country from those dissatisfied with the aristocratic atmosphere and environment of John Quincy Adams. Maine, New Hampshire and Vermont, and Georgia also, had many men of the pioneer type and these sympathized with Jackson. The Republican party, which came to power with Jefferson, had been animated by the same old Anglo-Saxon Dynamic and represented a reaction against the aristocratic principles of the Federalists, and the old English Static system, but although its principles were democratic, its leaders were aristocrats by nature if not by belief, and represented the best culture and brains of the land. John Quincy Adams had gone over to their party and there was now scarcely a remnant left of the old Federalists.

The reaction under Jefferson was quite a different matter from that under Jackson. Though the current was the same the latter was much more radical in its action. The former was a protest against aristocratic government, the latter was against aristocrats. Jefferson brought about a government democratic in principle in which the masses had a share, and freed it from autocratic control, but the men who were at the head remained of the aristocratic type. It was a government run for the masses by aristocrats. In the time of Jackson the protest was not against the principle of the government, but against the type of men who were running it. John Quincy Adams, at his accession, had kept in office every man who had rendered good service—even his personal enemies. Jackson made a clean sweep of all the men of the old cultured type. Not one was kept. The White House was besieged by backwoodsmen, many of them in deerskin and coonskin caps—men with no learning and culture, but friends of Jackson and of the party. The fundamental feeling of the West was that a man should stand by his friends whether worthy or not, and this Jackson did. Regardless of their ability he filled the offices with men loyal to him. Then he proceeded to give expression to the feeling of the West. His first attack was upon the Bank. In spite of remonstrances and protests, and utterly regardless of disaster to the finances of the country, he vented the pent-up animosity of years, and autocratically proceeded to demolish the Bank. He vetoed the bill renewing its charter and in spite of the censure of Congress withdrew all the government funds.

The West had found the man they wanted, a typical Westerner, without culture and learning, but courageous, independent, loyal to his friends, bitter to his enemies, resenting any opposition as a personal insult. He carried out his purposes like an autocrat, he frightened South Carolina into submission by his violent threats. Now instead of a democratic government run by aristocrats, the people had an autocratic government run by democrats. The commutator had functioned successfully. The gathering discontent of the West was discharged—the storm was averted, for the new Western Current dominated the nation.

3. The Great American Stabilizer. The Political Machine

The law of entropy demands that power should always seek lower levels, and it seems to apply to the realm of emotion. These highly charged dynamic currents inevitably sink to static forms. Otherwise they would probably tear society to pieces. The Anglo-Saxon spirit had been raised to high levels in the current from the West but was destined to fall again. And this time its decline was assisted by a machine designed to reduce it to low levels—a machine whose deadly product was often to smother it in future days. We have shown how in the Old World the Static Currents that maintained the Social Order were generated by the institutions of religion. In the New World a mechanism was built up designed to stabilize, not by reverence and awe, but by means of an emotion more prevalent and unfortunately far more demoralizing.

Politicians were well aware that this powerful current of feeling from the West would soon break down, and they made use of it to construct a machine that would hold all their constituency together in a permanent organization by means of an appeal to emotions always latent in the mind of man—namely, greed and personal ambition. By rousing in each man the hope of personal gain they held their group together as by a magnetic current. This current of low-grade selfish emotions proved powerful enough to displace most of the unselfish enthusiasms, and ever since, by the law of entropy, the great American Reform Movements one by one seem to sink to its level and become absorbed. It is naturally of interest to note how this great political stabilizing machine was constructed.

Originally the number of voters had been small and they had been limited by property qualifications to a group of a certain intelligence and position, easily reached by political leaders. When these restrictions were removed and full white manhood suffrage was introduced, the general situation was changed. The unorganized enthusiasm of the people had swept Jackson into power. The astute leaders who surrounded him did not propose to allow this vast and useful force to go to waste. The wind of public favor had blown as it listed, and no one knew whence it came. They made it their business to know. In every state a party organization was built up and machinery was set in motion to influence and hold every possible vote. These men did not wish to depend for their support on the casual and ephemeral emotions of the common man. They proposed to link him up by feelings that were more permanent and more reliable. It was then that they determined to bring into action that desire for wealth and position which glows in so unflickering a fashion in the heart of nearly every man. It must be made to his advantage to stand by the party and vote its ticket.

Here began that disastrous "spoils system" which was to cause such difficulties and corruption in years to come. Party organization was built up, which included every precinct; every man was catalogued, and the great principle was introduced that "to the victor belong the spoils," and every faithful heeler must have his share. The Federal Offices were deliberately distributed as the perquisites of those who had done the party a service, with little regard to their fitness for the job, and pains were taken to make every man feel that he would receive some benefit for his adherence to the party. Thus the whole of modern party organization came rapidly into being, with this use of Federal patronage to build up the party machine. The party press appeared— the party platform, the National Convention, and all those devices which seem so indispensable to-day. A channel at such a low level was sure to drain into itself all the lower feelings—the emotional sewage of the nation and transform it to a current of power. Bowers says, "With the appearance of Democracy in action came evils that have persisted through the ensuing years—the penalties of the rule of the people. Demagogy then reared its head and licked its tongue. Class consciousness and hatred were awakened. And on the part of the great corporations intimidation, coercion and the corrupt use of money to control elections were contributed."

This was all due to the effort to stabilize the political party and make it permanent. Ideally a party should be a group of men gathered together to carry out some common purpose for the public welfare, or in support of some man in whom they trust as their leader. But such purposes are ephemeral, and such leaders give offence and lose their following, and the group naturally would tend to change and shift. It might be far better for the country that it should do so, and that men should be free to group themselves for and against every principle that is presented. That, however, does not suit the politician who wishes a permanent backing. And so, instead of attempting to hold the enthusiasm of the people by the offer of political principles, he makes his appeal to feelings that he knows to be more stable, and the party, instead of being a group united to carry out some policy for the public welfare, becomes a machine to provide its participants with money and position. This was believed to be the only way to hold the loyalty of the common man.

We have seen that sometimes a party or political movement started in some wave of popular feeling that swept the country, and that at times some great leader would rally the people about him to defend some cause. But this third method of holding men together, by their greed for personal gain, now replaced the other two. Greed is a dangerous emotion to rouse, and although it is constant enough in its operation, it is likely to turn men into a pack of wolves that are ready to rend, not only their enemies, but their own pack. It is strange that the same men who are ready to lay down their lives for their country when the war-time enthusiasm is upon them, can be turned into howling wolves and wallowing swine when the appeal to their greed is once made. Instead of a machine by which men could shape the destinies of the nation the party became a mechanism to enable a certain group to keep their noses in the trough, and to keep the trough always full. It was to take forty years before this system reached its full development, and we shall note the change in the Republican party later on. We may call the system of emotions, such as greed and loyalty and ambition, that held a man to his political party, the Political Current.

Jackson was the magnet that gathered the party together. But it was his henchmen and his kitchen cabinet who spun the web of party organization. Jackson himself was no politician or crafty demagogue. His appeal was an echo of the old call of Jefferson, and it has stood ever since as the creed of the Democratic party. It has in it a national ideal for which men might well be willing to sacrifice time and treasure—a standard to which they might rally, a plan in accordance with which they might toil through future years to rear the political structure of this new nation which was to grow so great.

In his first message in 1828 he gave true expression to all that was best in the great Western current that had put him in power. "Distinctions in society will always exist under every just government. Equality of talents, of education or of wealth cannot be produced by human institutions. In the full enjoyment of the gifts of heaven and the fruits of superior industry, economy and virtue, every man is equally entitled to the protection of the law. But when the laws attempt to add to those natural and just advantages, artificial distinctions—to grant titles, gratuities and exclusive privileges—to make the rich richer and the potent more powerful—the humbler members of society—the farmers, mechanics and laborers—who have neither the time nor the means for securing like favors for themselves, have a right to complain of the injustice of their government." To create a government on the earth where the poor will have an equal chance with the rich—where there will be none of those special privileges that create this ever increasing disparity between the classes, which has characterized every

government hitherto, this should be an aim sufficiently great
to stir enthusiasm and to bind men together to work for the
common cause, and it was sad to see these feelings sink to
the level of Greed.

Jackson had an amazing power to stir the people, and
many were moved by his appeal "to right the wrong of
1824." For he claimed with passionate bitterness that a
fraudulent league of his enemies had cheated him out of the
Presidency and put Adams in his place.

Jackson's strength was in his personal appeals, as man
to man, and friend to friend. Everything that he did was
done as a personal matter. He did not deal with abstrac-
tions or principles. His fight against the Bank became almost a personal battle with Biddle, its president, and his
fight against Nullification took in his mind the form of a
bitter personal contest with Calhoun, whom he regarded as
a traitor and an unscrupulous enemy. He put into these
fights a dash and vigor that is rare in political contention
and that had a charm for the people. Moreover, in spite of
the personal bitterness his final appeal to South Carolina
had in it a tenderness and beauty that might well have
softened his bitterest opponent. Had such a man been in the
Presidential Chair in 1860 when South Carolina again revolted, the great Civil War might have been prevented.

4. EMOTIONAL DYNAMOS

There are few batteries as powerful as the human personality and you have doubtless many times been conscious
of the impact of a current positive and alluring or negative
and repellent, radiating from such dynamic individuals.
Hitherto we have been following the great historic emotional currents as, raised to high potential by friction or suffering, they stirred men to action and created a new nation.
While ordinarily it is some institution such as the church, or
some pressure of events that is the battery which sets these
currents in motion, there are these personalities that seem
to act on their environment as emotional dynamos, and who

can thus initiate powerful currents of feeling. We have come now to a period when men of this type exercised a determining effect on the cost of events, and we must stop to consider the manner in which such personalities effect the public. Some were charged with the old Anglo-Saxon spirit and set its current in motion again. Others, filled with reactionary prejudice, served to block its path. But all bore a part in the great drama and left their mark on the spirit of the times.

The influence of some men is due to their ability to sense the feelings of those about them and then to express these feelings with clearness and to direct them to a definite goal. The usual politician is depicted with his ear to the ground listening for the footfall of the multitude and ready to swing into line and lead them. Van Buren was a man of this type. But there are also men of this other type who generate within themselves or by their actions such powerful emotions that they radiate in widening rings and carry along all who are near them. Violent emotion nearly always produces some effect, but in many men the effect is negative rather than positive and their emotion only arouses an antagonistic reaction. Such was John Randolph, who seemed to possess an amazing ability to stir men into a fury of opposition. Men who suppress violent emotion are likely to find that it emerges in spite of them and arouses strong antipathies. Such was the case with both the Adamses, who were men of violent feelings which they always sought to cover up. Emotion thus suppressed usually suppurates and becomes malice of the sourest kind, or it turns to a vitriolic venom which issues in unguarded moments and stings the bystander. Perhaps no man did more for his country than John Quincy Adams, but he seemed also to radiate antipathies, so that every measure he proposed was bitterly opposed merely because it was he who proposed it.

There are, however, fortunate men who have the power not only to generate powerful emotions but to carry others along with them. Some crowds are better conductors of emotion than others. In general it may be said that education and culture tend to insulate a man, so that he is little affected by the feelings of his neighbor. He is accustomed to weigh arguments pro and con, and he distrusts emotion. The uncultured men of the West were peculiarly susceptible to emotional dynamos of the personal type. Preachers with this power of generating intense feeling would conduct camp meetings in which they would transmit their feelings to a Western crowd in such fashion as to produce the most violent excitement.

Andrew Jackson was an emotional dynamo of this type. He was no politician and paid little if any attention to public opinion or the advice of his counsellors. He did what he felt like doing whether it was consistent or inconsistent, careless if thereby he caused the heavens to fall. When he first appeared in Congress Gallatin described him as a "tall uncouth personage, with long locks of hair hanging over his face, and a queue down his back tied with eelskin; his dress singular, his manners and deportment that of a backwoodsman." Such a person would pay little attention to the opinions and feelings of others. Jefferson says, "his passions are terrible. He could never speak (in Congress) on account of the rashness of his feelings. I have seen him attempt it repeatedly and as often choke with rage." I. J. Turner describes him as "a six-foot backwoodsman, angular, lantern-jawed and thin, with blue eyes that blazed on occasion. This choleric, impetuous, Scotch-Irish leader of men, this expert duellist and ready fighter, this embodiment of the contentious, vehement, personal West was in politics to stay."

Such violent feeling might easily have made him ridiculous or it might have merely aroused antagonism. Instead he aroused the most intense and wide-spread personal loyalty and enthusiasm yet accorded to any American save perhaps Washington himself. We have spoken of the power of an individual to awaken emotion by the use of fetishes or by the appeal to prejudice—by intentionally pulling the strings that release hatred or enthusiasm. Jackson did not do this consciously. He said what he thought and said it very loud and clear. He did what his feeling urged him to do even when it meant pursuing the Indians into foreign territory and seizing Pensacola where he had no shadow of right to be. Here on Spanish soil he executed two British subjects— one an ex-officer! But he voiced the feeling of the great inarticulate West, and went a little ahead even of where they would dare to go. Moreover, he had the prestige of a hero. If a man is to radiate emotion widely through the land he has to stand upon a pedestal high above the heads of his fellows. Otherwise his emotion, no matter how intense, will be smothered in penetrating his immediate entourage. But from a dominant height he can project feeling far and wide, and the intensity of it, instead of being decreased with the square of the distance, is increased with the square of the height at which he stands.

The case of Washington differed from that of Jackson. He did not seem to radiate emotion so much as to draw emotion toward him. It is possible for a man to create about himself an emotional vortex that draws men irresistibly to him. This may be done unconsciously by some heroic deed or word that stirs their souls, or it may be done intentionally by some political schemer who works upon the feelings of the people with telling and calculated phrases, such as Bryan's cross of gold.

Prestige merely brings a man into the public eye, and does not necessarily create any emotional reaction. Prestige may be due to wealth or achievement or merely to clever advertising. But a man who creates an emotional vortex acquires an amazing influence. In the first place he causes a wave of unifying emotion that sweeps together the most diverse elements and holds them in unison by a common loyalty. And secondly all who come within the sweep of this vortex seem to be so polarized that a word from him has incalculable emotional force, even when uttered with little feeling or with hesitancy. The emotional vortex created about Washington was so great that, in spite of the virulent attacks made upon him, it remained one of the dominant forces in politics, and Hamilton on several occasions exerted himself to induce Washington to speak even a word in favor of his policies, knowing that it would carry irresistible emotional power. For a long time any attempted action on the part of the democratic leaders was made impossible by the pretense that they were attacking Washington.

Washington made use of this vast power entirely for the good of the country and with no thought of himself, repelling with stern rebukes every attempt to put the supreme power in his hands, and advocating those measures which he saw to be essential to the unity and welfare of the people.

It was largely due to this emotional vortex that centred in him and gave every word of his such emotional power, that the country held together during those trying days until the Constitution was framed and put into practice. His name has always remained a fetish for politicians to conjure with.

The victory of Jackson at New Orleans gave him prestige and also created an emotional vortex of enthusiasm which drew the people toward him, and thus rendered them receptive to the violent feelings which he was continually radiating. Otherwise it seems hardly probable that they would have tolerated so long measures that were certain to bring disaster upon the country. Reaction was inevitable when the people began to suffer, and it was only the great enthusiasm centring about Jackson that staved it off during his two terms of office. He remained a democratic autocrat, acting on his own responsibility and paying little attention to his cabinet. There was a small group of personal friends, known as the Kitchen Cabinet, with whom he consulted, but he was not at all bound by their advice. He himself was the government, and the people were glad to have it so.

Jackson was by no means the only person who had power to stir the feelings of the people at this time. Clay and Webster were both emotional dynamos of high voltage and could sway the country from end to end by their words. Each of them had become a projecting station for the feelings and desires of a certain group, and was sure therefore to antagonize certain other groups.

Clay, though he began as representative of the South and West, had been swept backward by the violent storm of ultra-Southern feeling which voiced itself in Calhoun, and by the blast from the West which spoke through Jackson, until he became the spokesman of the prosperous middle states. A man of great charm, true representative of the sporting blood of Kentucky with the standards of the Southern gentleman, he was regarded with suspicion by conscientious New England Puritans of the type of John Quincy Adams, as a man who was wild and dissipated. In spite of such antipathies, however, Adams had made Clay his Secretary of State, and worked with him for the good of the Whig party.

Calhoun was of good Scotch-Irish fighting blood. Clay had power to charm, Calhoun carried men along by the fire that smouldered in his eyes and flamed in his words. He started in with a real devotion to the Union, but the intense feeling of his state, South Carolina, little by little took possession of him until he was charged with it, and became the voice of the dissatisfied South, irritated by the tariff, infuriated by the abolitionists, and ready for instant secession.

CHAPTER IV

NATIONAL AND SECTIONAL SPIRITS

1. WEBSTER AND THE NATIONAL SPIRIT

IF we may again personify the great currents of feeling or spirits that sway men's hearts, we shall now see two new actors enter upon the scene, each of which in turn made an appeal to the American people, and each of which, had they given whole-hearted response, might have preserved them from disunion and disaster. Both had a charm that should have made the people deaf to the disputes of others on the stage. Each ruled men's hearts for a time and then was driven from the field by the clamorous attacks of quarrelsome spirits. The first, the new-born Spirit of the Nation, was destined to a prolonged battle with the old Spirit of Liberty, which should have been her ally.

That heroic Spirit which had held the centre of the stage, dressed in more stately garments by Jefferson, and which, when faint and nearly dead, had risen again clad in the uncouth garb of the Western pioneer, we shall see ensnared in the South by the wiles of the aristocracy, while in the North, clad in the panoply of war, we shall see our hero transformed into a vindictive plunderer, ready to attack, and do to death, the fair young Spirit of the Nation.

The latter Spirit was evoked in all her beauty and glory by a great magician—one of those dynamic personalities whose power has been described. No name is better known in America than that of Daniel Webster.

In him intellect seemed more prominent than emotion. He had the gift to state in clear, irresistible logic the points he wished to make. He had a power to convince men that few possessed. The British had claimed the right to search American ships and had bolstered it by innumerable arguments. Webster as Secretary of State wrote a protest. Lord

Aberdeen read it with growing astonishment. He read it over a second time and then remarked: "That statement is unanswerable." He did not answer it, and the British never again attempted to assert the right. In addition to clarity there was behind his words a tremendous force; there was a majestic power in his address; he seemed to radiate an Olympian authority. He became the spokesman of New England and its nobler, saner ideals, as distinguished from the rabid denunciations of the abolitionists.

We have noted the various centres in the country where storms were gathering—the black clouds that were rolling up as the barometer steadily fell—the sense of inevitable disaster to come. When such a storm is brewing it seems that certain clouds act as a condenser. They seem to gather up the force of the storm and hurl it forth in blazing thunderbolts that rend the sky asunder. Just so there are certain personalities that seem to have the power to gather up within themselves the force of the storm, to take that which had been blind dissatisfaction or incoherent rage, and transform it by their genius until they can hurl it forth in a lightning flash that makes clear the whole issue and concentrates it upon some one point. Such were the men who have just been named, and with them might also be mentioned Benton, who represented the West, and its ideas of expansion, as Calhoun spoke for the South.

There is always sublimity in watching the beginnings of a great storm, and it should stir the soul of any man to look back and see rolling up the great storm clouds that were to tear the nation apart, and to watch as these titanic figures wrestled with them and gathered up the dark masses of incoherent rage and blind passion and dumb suffering to hurl them forth in the dazzling flashes of their oratory. At times the pressure was thus relieved, and at times it would only seem to be rendered more intense. Clay was voicing the discontent and suffering of the great central section of manufacturers and producers and their desire for relief from the policies of Jackson. Calhoun was concentrating the passion of the South, Benton was expressing the demands of the growing West—its resentment of government control and its desire for expansion. The abolitionists, on behalf of a section of New England, were denouncing the slaveholders, another group, that was to become the Know Nothing men, was finding its spokesman to attack the increasing power of the immigrants with the cry "America for Americans!"

In the midst of all this clashing turmoil Webster stood for something more than the mere voice of a discontented group. To understand his position we must turn back to 1830 to his famous speech against Hayne. It was an amazing achievement. The anger and distrust of South Carolina had reached its climax and was being poured out in the vivid speeches of Calhoun and Hayne, who were threatening Secession unless their wishes were heeded, while the abolitionists were almost ready to stir New England to secede, unless the South was compelled to relinquish her slaves. Webster stood forth in the midst of the turmoil with the storm rushing in upon him from all sides, and there began to weave with magic words an image men had never seen before though often in their dreams they had caught a pale reflection of its likeness—the image of a nation greater than any the world has known, clad in the forms of that Constitution shaped by the heroic men of the past, majestic in its dignity, enthralling in its beauty, based on ideas never before thought compatible, but here at last finding their true expression—Liberty and Union, now and forever, one and inseparable.

Out of the black mists of opposing thunderclouds this magic wove its compelling image, until it rose serene above them all, gathering to itself the light of loyal devotion, while the muttering thunder of the storm died away, as there rose throughout the land the roar of an applause more vast and unanimous than had yet greeted the words of any American. He had put back the storm for twenty years by the power of the image he had evoked.

It was the finest expression of the American spirit yet attained—enthusiasm not for liberty merely, but for a nation based on liberty, not for any one man or for the cause of any group, but for a new ideal of the Nation and its Constitution—a Nation united, indivisible and yet free. The current thus originated was to sweep through the country and carry men from their homes and the selfish pursuit of gain to give their lives and all they had on its behalf. We may well call it the National American Current, for in it for the first time the old currents were merged and the Nation became a unity.

2. THE VORTEX OF DISTRESS

It was to take many years before this new idea of loyalty to the Union grew to a tide that could sway the Nation, and we come now to a point in the drama where the heroic spirit that fought for progress seemed to be swept entirely from the field by whirlwind and disaster. For Jackson continued his furious tilt at the pillars that supported the National finance till he brought them crashing to earth. Like a modern Saint George he had slain the Monster with the plaudits of the West, and seemed thereby encouraged to feel that he could ride rough-shod over the whole financial system and lead his Western following to prosperity. But finance has laws as inevitable as gravitation. A man may defy gravitation and, spurning the solid earth, he may leap forth into space and fare well for a time. But the further he leaps the greater is the crash at the end.

The country was prosperous enough to run for a time without a stable financial basis. It was Jackson who knocked out the last feeble support and sent it hurtling into the abyss. He saw that, owing to mismanagement, the paper of the State Banks, which he had favored, was becoming depreciated. He was violently opposed to an inflated currency and, with his usual precipitation and contrary to the advice of all financiers, in July, 1836, at the end of his second term, he issued a sudden demand that all payments for the government lands should be made in specie. Lands to the value of twenty-five millions had been taken up. In payment for these the paper of the State Banks was refused, which forced the banks to redeem it at once. This they were unable to do, and there followed a general collapse that has never been equalled in the history of the United States. Prices rose to incredible heights—then there was a crash and all credit went dead. There were bread riots in New York and universal distress throughout the country. It was due entirely to tampering with the financial system, for the country had never been more prosperous; production was increasing by leaps and bounds, the newly constructed railroads were supplying the needed transportation, and there was every indication of progress.

Jackson, protected by the vortex of enthusiasm about him, escaped, but the Western Current was shattered to fragments in the disaster. Van Buren, Jackson's henchman, whom he put into office in 1836, on the wave of emotion he still had power to radiate, had to bear the force of the storm. He did what he could to better the situation, but nothing could avail to stay the indignation of the nation. Nevertheless in 1840 he sought a second term.

The general distress had been like one of those appalling low-pressure centres that set in motion the cyclones that sweep across the country and leave devastation in their track. The one dominant feeling in the country was resentment against the cause of their suffering, and the chief desire of the people was to sweep the party of Jackson from the face of the earth. But to do this unity and organization were necessary, and in the turbulent state of their feelings they were more ready for riots than for calm political procedure. Never had the country been in such a welter of conflicting purposes. In this time of distress all the old currents we have described seemed to be running with redoubled violence.

In the Northwest the old Plutocracy whose emotional attitude we have termed the Northern Static current, under the leadership of Adams, were vociferously demanding the restoration of sound money. The old party of Jefferson, once animated by the love of liberty, and now transformed into an organ of the Southern Aristocracy and of the Plutocracy of the Central States, had split on the rock of the Tariff. The Protectionists had gathered about Clay, and the Free Traders bitterly opposed him. The Nullifiers of South Carolina who had been adherents of Jackson, under his violent attack upon them, had revolted under the leadership of Tyler. The old Reformation Current was still animating the Abolitionists, who were now termed "Free Soilers." There was still a Western group with something of the old Anglo-Saxon spirit, suspicious of wealth and culture, and now strongly anti-Jackson, and there were minor parties such as the Anti-Masons, driven by prejudice to oppose Clay.

How to build a political platform in such cross currents was a problem. Any plank that was launched would divide them into warring tides. The more purposes they announced the greater the number of fragments into which their constituency would split. It was like trying to harness in one team assorted animals from the cages of a zoo. Never had any group had greater leaders than were at hand in Webster, Adams, Clay, and Benton, but each, as the leader of a certain party, had radiated a wave of feeling that, by its impact on the other groups, had awakened prejudices so violent that to propose him for President would send the rest flying to the opposition.

But somehow the whirlwind of resentment swept them all together into the New Whig Party. The feeling against Jackson was the only link that held them together and was strong enough to overcome their feeling against one another. The chief problem was to select a leader who would not split them to fragments, and who would awaken enthusiasm in all and prejudice in none. They hoped that they had found in Harrison one who would rival Jackson in emotional appeal. A typical Westerner like Jackson, and the victor of Tippecanoe, the party managers felt that there was in him material which could be used to stir the people.

Jackson's powerful personality had needed no assistance in generating enthusiasm. It was otherwise with Harrison, and his managers set to work to build a machine that would create the necessary current. The log cabin and the cider barrel became his emblems, designed to stir the souls of those who once held to Jackson, and whom they hoped to win from the New Yorker who stood in his shoes. Tippecanoe was exploited as one of the great battles of the age and Harrison as the national hero who had saved his country from the brutal atrocities of the red man. The Southern Nullifiers, whom they could not hope to hold by this means, were conciliated by nominating Tyler as Vice-President and with shouts of "Tippecanoe and Tyler too" the great vortex was started in motion. The Democrats called it the Campaign of Noise, Nonsense and Numbers. It worked sufficiently to put Van Buren out of office and to give Harrison the Presidency in 1840.

This was the beginning of a new type of leadership in politics, a period when the politicians shunned every man of dynamic personality. So long as there had been a simple division of the people between those who were swept by a breeze from the East and those who were carried along on the Western gale, it had been easy to choose for each side the leader who would best express their feelings and carry out their desires. And when there was no emotional storm, it was natural to choose some man whose deeds or words had created about him an emotional vortex of enthusiasm which fitted him for leadership, since it gave his words the necessary emotional power.

But when the country was torn by cross winds blowing in all directions, and a dozen questions were before the public which aroused the most violent antagonisms, it was necessary to choose a leader for what he was. It was then the job of the politician to pick a man without dynamic, who had never taken any stand, or stirred the feelings of any one, and create around him an artificial current of enthusiasm.

3. The Rise of the Imperialistic Dynamic Current

We now come to the entrance of the second of the new actors in the drama, a tide of feeling which the spirit of the fathers had faced with antagonism, but which, like the National Spirit, had the power to charm and unite the warring factions, namely the Imperialistic Spirit.

By successful use of the methods described above, Harrison was carried into the Presidency by the support of a complex of antagonistic currents—a dangerous situation for any man. By the appointment of Webster as Secretary of State, and with Clay as Speaker of the House, he had just succeeded in drawing together the main groups into a majority sufficient to pass the measures necessary to the return of prosperity, when Fate suddenly threw the whole government machine into the control of the smallest and most violent of all the groups to whose support the election was due. Harrison suddenly died and Tyler became President in his place.

Tyler was the head of that small group of Nullifiers and states-rights men, who were bitterly opposed to every measure advocated by the Whigs, and who had joined them only because of their hatred for Jackson. Their support had been bought by the nomination of Tyler as Vice-President, and the Whigs now realized that they had paid too high a price. The folly of attempting a coalition of irreconcilables was soon demonstrated. Every measure of Congress which Clay brought forward to re-establish credit and restore the old national Bank was promptly vetoed by Tyler. The commutator of the government was out of gear. The powerful Static currents of North and South that were working together to re-establish sound money were completely shut off, and the ponderous wheels of government revolved only under the feeble trickle of an adverse current.

It is a dangerous matter to shut off the will of the great majority and dam up the strongest currents of feeling in the nation. Tyler was equally at variance with Whigs and Democrats, and yet by a quirk of destiny the power was in his hands and he could block the purposes of both. To suppress the will of the majority is a dangerous pastime for any one without a Pretorian guard at his call. An explosion was imminent when a diversion occurred which turned all the old currents into new channels and generated this new current of feeling which was destined to have a vast effect on the future of America. Texas, then an independent republic, asked for annexation. Instantly the whole force of the Southern Static current poured in to support the plea. Slavery had been introduced into Texas when it broke away from Mexico, and the South would win the support of a powerful new state. In the North the old Reformation current threw its vitriolic tide against an increase of slavery. Those animated by the Anglo-Saxon spirit, with its keen sense of justice, opposed annexation because they thought it unjust to Mexico and certain to end in war. But everywhere in the country, and chiefly in the West, were men who were stirred by the prospect of increasing the power and territory of America. This enthusiasm for increased power and domination created a powerful current of feeling new in America, where sentiment had been against expansion, and it is this which we term the Imperialistic current.

Tyler, as a Southerner, advocated annexation and pushed it with all his strength. The question was under discussion when the campaign of 1844 came on. The Whigs determined this time to have a real leader as their candidate and chose Henry Clay. Clay had been swayed by that Static current which was dominant in the Central States and which animated a society prone to Plutocracy. He had strong convictions on the Tariff and on sound money, but was doubtful about annexation. The Anglo-Saxon spirit in him finally prevailed and he came out against it.

Van Buren, who was the supposed Democratic candidate, with the feeling of the Northern Democrats behind him, opposed it firmly, in spite of Jackson's rebuke. It was the finest and most heroic act of his life, and reveals in him far nobler qualities than those indicated by the sobriquet "Red Fox," given him because of his clever political manœuvres. For conscience' sake he lost the favor of Jackson, his hold on the party and the nomination. When it became evident that he could not gain the requisite two-thirds vote the name of James K. Polk was presented, with nothing to recommend it save that he favored annexation, and on this he was triumphantly nominated.

It would seem that a man of genius like Clay, who had about him such a vortex of enthusiasm, and who stood for the financial measures desired by the solid mass of his countrymen, with the support of the North and central states, and with the confidence of the South since he was a Southerner himself, and who thus had behind him the dominant static currents of feeling, would have won an easy victory over a comparatively unknown Tennesseean. But this New Imperialistic enthusiasm was gaining head every moment and, supported by the Southern aristocracy, it swept aside all the old party groups. The South and West voted solidly for Polk and annexation; the Central States, save Pennsylvania, voted for Clay as did New England, excepting Maine and New Hampshire, where the pioneer element was dominant and the Imperialistic Current had taken hold. He lost New York and Michigan because the Abolitionists, who had organized a separate party, divided the vote against annexation, and Polk won by an electoral vote of 170 to 105. The new Imperialistic current, with its enthusiasm for power and expansion, had overcome the Anglo-Saxon Dynamic with its hatred of slavery and injustice. Polk carried out the annexation and war with Mexico followed.

Nothing so arouses enthusiasm as a successful war, and it had often paid a leader whose popular support was uncertain, to start a war, and ride to glory and popularity on the waves of united patriotic enthusiasm. The war raised the Imperialistic Current to higher potential and temporarily swept the slavery question out of sight. The Northern and New England sections, who were always under the drive of the Anglo-Saxon Dynamic, became even more opposed to the war as unjust aggression, because General Taylor, who was not to fight until attacked, had to advance into Mexican territory before the Mexicans would assault him. Moreover, the Abolitionists and Antislavery party continued to attack the war as sinful since it would add to the extent of slavery. But these were small eddies in the dominant current. Lincoln lost his seat in Congress by attacking the war as unjust. The patriotic wave in his home section swept him aside as a "traitor."

All would have gone well had not the old Political Current come into action. The administration was unfortunate in that all the generals belonged to the opposite party. It looked as if the victorious generals would ride to fame and power with their party over the heads of the Democrats. Those who were bound to the party by greed or loyalty or ambition found this Political Current stronger than the Imperialistic dynamic. Their problem seemed to be to win the war and discredit the generals. They did their utmost to steer the waves of popular enthusiasm. After Taylor had won the victories of Palo Alto and Resaca de la Palma, and generated a dangerous vortex of enthusiasm that caused him to be suggested for the Presidency, the administration, swayed by this Political Current, took away all his men but 5,000, and put General Scott in command of an expedition which was to attack Mexico City from Vera Cruz, promising him all the men and supplies he deemed necessary for success. When he arrived at Vera Cruz, however, only a part of the necessary force was sent, and he was compelled to move on Mexico with inadequate equipment. Every means was used to prevent the generals from capturing the tide of the Imperialistic Current and riding to office on it.

In the meantime Santa Anna moved against Taylor with 20,000 men, and Taylor's annihilation was expected. To the astonishment of every one Taylor with his 5,000 men won the stunning victory of Buena Vista, and rolled up an overwhelming vortex of enthusiasm. Scott also, with his inadequate force, captured Mexico, and administered it admirably and developed an emotional wave of his own. He was promptly removed by the administration and summoned home to answer grave charges. Such were the characteristically unscrupulous methods of the political machine to quash the gathering emotional waves which favored the opposing party. A third man of the opposition, Frémont, had aroused enthusiasm by his picturesque career in the

California campaign, so that the administration now had three National heroes who were being borne along on the tide of the Imperialistic Current in opposition to their interests.

But as the war excitement died down the old storm centres gathered once more. Everything else sank into insignificance, as the struggle for and against slavery began again with more bitterness than ever.

4. The Northern and Southern Dynamic Currents

The Imperialistic tide of feeling, in spite of the opposition of the spirit of justice, had gathered up something of the American National Dynamic generated by Webster's famous speech. But Imperialism needs some war or national crisis to maintain its hold on the public. And both the new spirits of union gradually faded out or were crushed by the fierce attacks of the sectional spirits of North and South. There was a persistent force in the old Reformation Dynamic that had once carried it to victory through persecution, torture, and death at the stake, and which was scarcely less potent in America. The little group of Abolitionists who felt themselves Divinely directed to right the wrongs of the slaves, and whose conscience impelled them to constant attacks on the Southern planters, had been ridiculed, stoned, and persecuted, but had persisted until the tide began to turn in their favor. The North, still strongly swayed by the Anglo-Saxon Dynamic, felt it unjust that slavery should be forced by the South upon the New Western states, and though they had no wish to free the slaves in the South, they resented being obliged to return the wretched runaway slaves to their masters. Thus little by little they were swept along with the Abolitionists in a tide of opposition to the Southern demands.

The current in the South, which had been at first fairly peaceful and static, was raised by the attacks of the Abolitionists to a violent dynamic quality. The old Southern Aristocracy had been roused by fear and resentment to such a degree that its dominant feeling became an unrea-

soning wrath against the North, so that the country was
now divided into two main currents of feeling which we
may term the Northern and Southern Dynamic, and which
were in danger of submerging the old Spirit of the fathers
in a storm of blind passion.

Every question now seemed to involve slavery and accentuated the sectional cleavage between North and South.
Now it became a question of dividing the new lands acquired
from Mexico between the slave states and free states, and
of carrying the cleavage between North and South clean
across the New West. All the little local storm centres seemed
to withdraw one by one into the shadow of the two black
clouds that stretched across the continent, and in each of
which the mutter and roar of the thunder seemed to grow
each day more ominous. The South was infuriated by the
fact that the North, instead of returning their fugitive
slaves, aided them to escape into Canada. Certain Southern
slaveholders still asserted that the North was determined
to gain possession of the government, and overturn their
whole social system, and that their only protection from this
was to preserve an even balance of slave states so that they
could not be out-voted. They had the advantage that, though
the slaves did not vote, they counted for three-fifths of a
man in the apportionment of representatives. The North
declared it unfair that the South should maintain that the
negro was mere property and then count him as three-
fifths of a voter.

The whole country was torn with excitement over the
fate of California, New Mexico, and Oregon, when the
election of 1848 approached. The storm centre was the Wilmot proviso, a product of the Northern Dynamic designed
to exclude slavery from the new territory. The two political
parties were terrified by these two violent opposing currents. The Whigs dared not stand against the tornado of
feeling in the South. The Democrats feared to oppose the
violent rush of the Northern Current. Each tried to trim
their sails to both currents, a difficult feat. The Whigs still
had Clay and Webster, but Clay had been three times de-

feated, and every one knew where he stood. Webster aroused enthusiasm for an idea but very little for himself. He seemed to stand apart from the people in cold majesty. Their only hope was to resuscitate the Imperialistic Current that had borne General Zachary Taylor to such heights and which might still have sufficient power to carry him into the President's chair. He was a Southern slaveholder and no one seemed sure whether he was a Whig or not. He finally decided that he was, and was nominated with enthusiasm, with Millard Fillmore as his running mate, for the campaign of 1848.

The Whigs said nothing about the Wilmot proviso, and with a slaveholder as candidate, were out to catch the Southern votes. On the other hand the Southerners, though they came out strongly against the proviso, nominated Cass from the Northwest, to catch some of the Northern votes. This ruse failed, for the Democrats who had been caught in the Northern Dynamic would not support a man opposed to the proviso. They would not join the Whigs, however, and nominated Van Buren, on the platform of "Free soil, free speech, free labor," and thus were the only party that fully expressed the Northern Dynamic. They took just enough votes from Cass in New York and Pennsylvania to enable Taylor to win. It is strange that Van Buren, a former Democratic President, should have become the leader of that party which became the nucleus of the future Republican. The rock of slavery had split the Political Current that maintained the Democratic party into two sections. Strangely enough in the election the division was on East and West lines. All the Western states though they did not oppose the proviso, voted for Cass, and all the Eastern but four, for Taylor, the South in the hope that Taylor as a slaveholder would prevent the passage of the proviso.

It was a strange repetition of 1840. Webster and Clay were again the directing power while once more a National hero as figurehead held the Presidency. The situation was so ominous that the President, standing between two tigers ready to pounce, dared not move, even to settle the chaos in the California gold-fields, and the Californians were left to form their own government. Everything was at a deadlock, but with feeling mounting steadily to a higher and higher pitch some action was inevitable. The attempt by Meade of Virginia, in January, 1849, to pass a fugitive slave law started an explosion. The President, anxious to keep the Ship of State on an even keel, tried to avert the storm and requested Congress to avoid "introducing those exciting topics of a sectional character which have hitherto produced painful apprehensions in the public mind." But so violent a current could not be suppressed. The Southern Dynamic was reaching a point where its adherents preferred to secede rather than submit to the North. In December, 1849, finding that the candidate for Speaker had made terms with the Free Soilers in the midst of a fierce contest, Toombs of Georgia said: "I do not hesitate to avow before this house and the country, and in the presence of the living God, that if by your legislation you seek to drive us from the territories of New Mexico and California purchased by the common blood and treasure of the whole people, and to abolish slavery in this district, thereby attempting to fix a national degradation upon half the states of this Confederacy, I am for disunion." And here just as the country threatened to be rent asunder in this clash of opposing currents, came an appeal to that great tide beneath them all, nearly forgotten in the conflict, but still running deep in the hearts of men, the great American Dynamic of Webster.

Baker of Illinois replied, "in the name of the men of the North so rudely attacked, and speaking what I know to be their sentiments, I say a dissolution of this Union is, must be, shall be, impossible, so long as an American heart beats in an American bosom, or the Almighty sends His wisdom and goodness to guide us and bless us."

Could it prevail? Here were two opposing currents that seemed to be sweeping every man and every thought into their roaring vortex. Only about a fifth of the white men of the South were really slaveholders, but the Southern Dynamic had so grown in strength that it was beginning to stir the whole South. And the Northern Dynamic had swept the indifferent and careless into its bitter opposition to any encroachment of Slavery upon the new states. Could men still be stirred by that love of America, that devotion to the Union that had once so moved them to enthusiasm, and forget their passion and adjust their differences? Webster and Clay determined to make the attempt.

The new territory could not remain in chaos. Some government must be provided. These two great leaders of the party came together and launched a compromise measure which they knew would not satisfy either party, but which they hoped to carry by the power of the Great American Dynamic. It was like trying to sail a boat through a tide rip when two gigantic tides meet. Both Northern and Southern Currents fell upon them with equal violence. In the midst of the raging turmoil these two giants of the former days stood forth with all the power that prestige and old loyalties could give them, and sought to quell the storm. Each of them had built up around him a high potential of confidence and loyalty if not of enthusiasm, and they were risking their all in this attempt to stay the onward rush of the cyclone.

It was a magnificent sight, these two old heroes of the battles of the past, who loved their country and the Union more than any party or measure, risking the loss of all the prestige and devotion they had built up through long years of service, and standing firm in the midst of the waves of passion that assailed them on every side and threatened to wreck the country that they loved. Clay began by showing the danger of the emotional chaos. "Congress and the state legislatures are twenty odd furnaces in full blast, generating heat, and passion, and intemperance and diffusing them throughout the length and breadth of this broad land," he said. He showed the unreasonableness of the partisan demands, the fairness of the Compromise. He tried to lift them above the raging tumult of the conflict and ended by saying that in the Union he meant to stand and die. Calhoun, with the shadow of death already upon him, replied.

He had lived in the midst of the Southern whirlwind and he knew its temper and he stated the only means by which its fury could be quelled. The old Reformation current which, by its continental assertion that slavery was sinful, contributed the violent element to the Northern current, must be entirely shut off, and by some provision in the Constitution the political power of the South must be restored to an equality with the North.

Webster knew that the North, stirred by the propaganda of the Abolitionists, with the Reformation drive of Divine authority behind it, was aroused to intense feeling and about to demand, through its mouthpieces Seward and Chase, complete freedom in all the new territory and a denial that Slavery was permitted by the Constitution. He knew that if they carried their way it meant secession— the ruin of the Union to which he had given his life. It is hard to face a storm of violent feelings from one's enemies. Hardest of all is it to stand against the passionate convictions of one's friends. It was then that Webster stood forth facing the storm and the whirlwind, knowing that in a few moments all the confidence and loyalty he had built up through years of patient, faithful work, might be stripped from him as the hurricane tears the trees from a mountain side, and made that great speech, perhaps the greatest of his life, his final effort to preserve the Union whose image he had made so glorious twenty years before.

"I wish to speak to-day," he said, "not as a Massachusetts man nor as a Northern man, but as an American. The imprisoned winds are let loose. The East, the West, the North and the stormy South, all combine to throw the whole ocean into commotion, to toss its billows to the skies, and to disclose its profoundest depths. I have a duty to perform, and I mean to perform it with fidelity—not without a sense of surrounding dangers, but not without hope. . . . I speak to-day for the preservation of the Union."

He stood against the Wilmot proviso, on the ground that Slavery would die of itself in the new territory. In fairness to the South he demanded a better fugitive slave law, he stood for the Compromise which admitted the new states and territories without restriction as to slavery, because he knew that only thus could the Union be preserved. Thus he sought once more and for the last time to set in motion that great American National Current, that spirit of devotion to the Union which had sprung from his glowing words years ago. But now circumstances had changed. His following in New England were swept along in the vortex of the Northern Current, which fell upon him and broke over him. Because he had granted these Concessions to the South he was called a traitor to his party and his cause. And the vindictive Southern Current with Calhoun at its head fell upon him with equal force, since he had not granted what they considered the essentials. But wherever men were not blinded and deafened by the tumult of the conflict his words made their way, and in the hearts of men the tide of devotion to the Union rose once more, higher and higher, until it turned the wheels of destiny and carried the Compromise. Webster had lost his friends but he had saved the Union. The death of President Taylor and the hearty co-operation of the new President, Fillmore, with Clay aided to pass the various resolutions that made up the Compromise. It was carried by the central states, with the opposition of both North and South.

5. THE CONSOLIDATION OF THE NORTHERN DYNAMIC CURRENT

The passage of the Compromise created a momentary lull, during which the Southern current gradually broadened and deepened, sweeping the whole Democratic party into its stream. It sought to engulf what was left of the old Imperialistic Current in the North by nominating in 1852 Franklin Pierce of New Hampshire, a handsome and popular general of the Mexican War, and hoped that thus a number of Northerners would be carried into its stream. The Northern Current had no organ for its expression, for the Whig party was still seeking to gather up the blasts from a dozen different directions. So long as they had the

bitter animosity against Jackson to animate them there was
some unifying driving force, but that was gone. They were
an artificial conglomeration of such antagonistic forces that
the announcement of an opinion on any vital question would
split them into fragments. It was increasingly impossible
to deal with slavery in a fashion that would please both
slaveholders and Abolitionists. When the wind is blowing
from opposite directions the sail cannot be trimmed to both.
The sails of the Whigs were flapping idly. There was no
longer any emotional drive or moral purpose behind them.
They were doomed to sink out of sight in the great swamp
of innocuous futility. They made a desperate effort to
blanket the Imperialistic breeze from the Democrats by
nominating in 1852 the Mexican War Hero, General Scott
—a futile effort to gather potential. The great personal
dynamos were passing away. Clay and Calhoun were already gone. Webster heard with disgust the nomination of
Scott, predicted the end of the Whig party, and died, and
Pierce was duly elected.

We come now to a point in the drama when the old Anglo-
Saxon Spirit, dismembered and helpless, seemed lost forever. And then the very strength of the opposition seemed
suddenly to resuscitate it in a new line of power.

The Southern Current now turned the wheels of the National government. The opposition was so split into antagonistic currents that the Democrats had nothing to fear, and
the wheels began to spin rapidly according to their will.
Douglas as Speaker of the House turned on the power and,
so sure was he of success, that he actually put through the
repeal of the Missouri Compromise, which left the new
Northern states free to choose whether they should exclude
slavery or not. Douglas and his following were animated
primarily by the Anglo-Saxon current, and stood for liberty
and the right of each group to determine its own course,
and only secondarily did he follow the Southern Current.
But he had gone a little too far, and this repeal measure
tended to consolidate all the various branches of the Northern Current into one party and throw them into the channel

of the Free Soil party, which had once been led by Van
Buren. Those moved by the old Reformation Dynamic,
those whom the Anglo-Saxon spirit stirred to protest
against slavery in every form—every man whose conscience
and sense of justice had been roused, united in this new
party.

A New Emotional current had begun to make itself felt
in American affairs. Vast numbers of foreigners had been
pouring into America, most of them belonging to the Roman church and therefore imbued with old Roman Static
emotional attitude. The old Reformation current, flowing
from men who in time past had suffered greatly from the
Roman system, was still strong in the country and certain
of those in whom it flowed strongly, and whom it had not
carried into the Abolition movement, were swept by it into
violent opposition to all foreigners. A Society of United
Americans was formed, so secret in its dealings that when
any member was questioned about it, he replied that he knew
nothing. The group was thus christened the "Know Nothings," and their platform was to keep the government of
America in American hands. They gained so rapidly in
power that by 1854 they had won nearly one hundred seats
in Congress, and in 1855 they carried six Northern states
and nearly won as many more in the South.

There were two causes that threw these diverse currents
into one channel. The first was the enforcement of the
Fugitive Slave Law. The Abolitionists had been hooted and
ridiculed in the North and their meetings had been broken
up. But when the wretched, hunted, fugitive slaves appeared, starving and wounded, it appealed to the sympathy
of the public. They were indignant at being compelled to act
as police to catch slaves for the South, and they were infuriated that they were declared criminals if in common
humanity they aided the suffering wretches. Then secondly,
when the Missouri Compromise was repealed, they resented
it as an attempt of the South to overreach them unfairly,
and the results of the repeal stirred them even more deeply.
Douglas's bills granting popular sovereignty to the terri-

tories, threw Kansas open to the possibility of slavery, and
the South was determined to win that territory. The North
was sufficiently stirred to resent this encroachment. Money
was raised and thousands of men were sent in to vote
against slavery and drive out the Southerners. Fanatics
like John Brown came in, determined to kill and burn and
destroy, in order to keep the soil free. Here in "bleeding
Kansas" the full force of the Southern and Northern Currents met, in a terrifying tide rip, unchecked by the barrier
of law; and the storm burst in battle, murder, and sudden
death. Such fury and outrage cannot exist without sending
out waves in widening rings, and the whole country was
soon vibrating to it, and each current was raised to higher
voltage as men recounted the outrages of the other side.

These two causes, then, threw all the stray currents into
the channel of one party which took the name "Republican."
At last there was a party in the field which had behind it a
real emotional drive and a moral purpose. With them combined those of the Know Nothings who were against
slavery, and those of the Whigs who were "anti-Nebraska
men." Their war cry was "Free Soil, free speech, free labor
and Frémont," and they chose as their candidate the hero
of the Californian Campaign whose name fitted their platform so well. That old current of feeling that came from the
free men of old England and the reformers of Germany,
and that had been the most potent force in the formation of
America, had again found a channel through which its
power could be expressed. No one could remain indifferent
when a conflict to the death was going on in the new territories to determine whether they should be free or slave
states, and the new party put into their platform the following plank:

"Resolved: That while the Constitution of the United
States was ordained and established by the people in order
to form a more perfect union, establish justice, ensure
domestic tranquillity, provide for the common defense, and
ensure the blessings of liberty, and contains ample provision for the protection of the life, liberty and property of

every citizen, the dearest constitutional rights of the people of Kansas have been fraudulently and violently taken from them; their territory has been invaded by an armed force, spurious and pretended legislation, judicial and executive officers have been set over them, by whose usurped authority, sustained by the military power of the government, tyrannical and unconstitutional laws have been enacted and enforced, the rights of the people to keep and bear arms have been infringed . . . they have been deprived of life, liberty and property without due process of law, . . . murders, robberies and arsons have been instigated and encouraged, and the offenders have been allowed to go unpunished—that all these things have been done with the knowledge, sanction and procurement of the present administration; and that for this high crime against the Constitution, against the union and humanity, we arraign the President, his advisers, agents, and accessories . . . before the country and before the world, and it is our fixed purpose to bring the perpetrators of these atrocious outrages to a sure and condign punishment hereafter."

The party was too late in its organization to win. It had split the Whigs and Know Nothings, but they still had candidates in the field, and the new party had not had time to gather its full strength.

The Democrats, still strongly united under the impetus of the Southern Current, were clever enough to choose a Northern man who favored slavery, Buchanan of Pennsylvania, knowing that he would sweep a number of Northerners, in the vortex of his following, into the Southern ranks.

He was elected in 1856 and once more the wheels of the government began to revolve by the full tide of the Southern Current and regardless of the feelings of the North. A good way to raise a current of high voltage is that the party in power should press through measures violently offensive to the minority and to which it is opposing its full strength.

The North was carrying about all the charge it could safely contain, when the Democrats, realizing that now was their chance to subject the whole nation to slavery, carried through their final measure. The Dred Scott decision, by the Supreme Court, made it law that slavery could be introduced into the territories even if the people voted against it. This was the supreme goal of the ultra Southern Dynamic. But they forgot that the current which animated the Democratic party was a composite, and had in it a large residuum of the old Anglo-Saxon Dynamic which carried strong feeling against any attempt to force conditions upon the people contrary to their will. Douglas and the Northern Democrats would support slavery in districts where the people wanted it, but would not see it forced on those opposed to it. Those animated by the Northern Current were roused to intense indignation by this decision which delivered the whole Nation into the hands of slavery, and the Abolitionists burst forth with a new tide of invective.

The old Southern aristocratic emotional attitude, which underlay the Dynamic Current, was not one which could be insulted with impunity. The South was like a spirited horse, pricked incessantly by the spur, until it reached a state bordering on fury. They did not consider that the Abolitionists were only a small minority of fanatics. They held the whole North responsible for their utterances, and embraced all New England and its allies in the circle of their hate. The new Republican party, animated chiefly by the Anglo-Saxon spirit with its strong sense of justice, while indignant at the recent measures which it regarded as unjust, still wished justice done to the Southerners and supported slavery in the South and endorsed the Fugitive Slave Law. But the Southerners took no account of this. Roused to an unreasoning emotional state, they proclaimed the Republican party to be a conspiracy to rob them of their rights. Fear was added to fury. Just at this time the celebrated John Brown in whom the old Reformation current had risen to mad proportions and who felt that he was sent of God to free the slaves, subsidized by a group of Abolitionists and supported by a body of young men who felt themselves impelled by conscience to rouse the slaves to rebellion, seized

the Arsenal at Harpers Ferry and called on the slaves to
rise against their masters and join him. He was quickly suppressed by Colonel Robert E. Lee and executed. John
Brown's act was more than an outrage. It was a tragic
drama executed with high courage under the drive of that
old current which had driven thousands to lay down their
lives for conscience' sake, and it was certain to arouse
thrilling emotion throughout the land. Every one vibrated
to it in one way or another and "John Brown's body" became an emotional fetish. The South regarded the expedition as proof of a conspiracy in the North to start an insurrection among their slaves, in which the slaveholders might
all be murdered. They were thus free to retaliate and call
all Northerners criminals and potential murderers.

The Southern Dynamic had now reached a higher voltage than the old power lines would hold. They knew that
Douglas, and those animated by the Anglo-Saxon spirit,
were being split from the Southern Current by the Dred
Scott decision, but they only pressed it the more firmly.
They were determined to dominate or secede. Douglas was
the logical Democratic candidate but they would have none
of him. Against him they chose Breckenridge as their own
candidate, who would press their demands to the full. They
were tired of half measures and knew that, with Buchanan
or Douglas as President, they would be granted so much
that they would have no excuse to secede, and they preferred either to elect their own candidate who would demand all, or that a Republican candidate should be elected
against whom they could rouse the South in revolt.

As stated, the mass of the Republican party, still swayed
by the old Anglo-Saxon Dynamic, had no wish to interfere
with the rights of the South, but their leaders, Seward and
Chase, had taken such radical anti-slavery ground that the
choice of either would mean the loss of the votes of the
moderate group. Lincoln's debates with Douglas had been
reported all over the North and had brought him before the
public as a leader calm and sane, whose first aim was to preserve the Union and deal justly with the South, while pre-

venting unfair encroachments upon the rights of the North.

In some way he had kept free from the violent emotional charges of the day and had gathered up into himself the force of the great American National current, now nearly forgotten in the clash of North and South, with its sense of a common heritage and a noble tradition under the heroes of the past, and its consciousness of the thrilling shoulder touch of millions of free men marching triumphantly to a glorious future. Like Jackson he was of the common people and commanded their sympathy and enthusiasm. Seward and Chase were therefore passed by and Lincoln was nominated. He had kept clear of the madness of the Abolitionists, who were as virulent against the Union as the Slaveholders. Garrison had publicly torn up the constitution and threatened that Massachusetts would secede from the Union.

Here then were two violent currents threatening to split from the Union if they could not have their way, the Southern Dynamic, and the portion of the Reformation current concentrated on Abolition. Those who wished to preserve the Union were split into three channels, the Democratic under Douglas, impelled by that part of the Southern Dynamic which was mingled with the Anglo-Saxon current and which favored slavery, the Republican, composed of all the elements that opposed slavery under the impulse of the Northern Dynamic, now all collected in one channel, and a small party, the Constitutional Unionists, animated by the American National current, but ignoring slavery. If it had been possible to ignore so vital a question, Lincoln would doubtless have been with them. As it was their efforts were futile. They polled but few votes, and with the Democrats divided in half Lincoln was elected. For such troublous times the election was dangerously close. He polled little more than a third of the total vote.

6. The Undiluted Southern Dynamic

The drama has now reached a point when the characters have shifted parts in strange fashion. Under Jackson the old Anglo-Saxon spirit had found its chief expression in the Democratic party, but the election of 1860 served to split off that wing of the party in which it was dominant from the rest of the Southern Current, and to raise the residual current to its maximum voltage in opposition. In the meantime that ancient current of devotion to liberty and justice had found a new vehicle in the new Republican party. Although the extreme Southern Current still flowed through the channel of the Democratic party, it was as unlike anything hitherto known as Democracy as might well be, retaining the old spirit only in its extreme assertion of the states' rights. To understand the events that followed we must stop for a moment to analyze the emotional charge which it carried, and to review the various elements which had combined to create it. Its controlling force was found in the old Southern Static system which we have shown to be an aristocracy in which the same emotional currents were dominant as in the aristocratic system of England, from which it was derived.

The men of the South who held large numbers of slaves, and to whom slavery was a vital question, were but a minority of the population. It was these who formed the dominant aristocracy, and in some states like South Carolina they were an oligarchy, entirely controlling the government, and regarding the poor whites with almost as much contempt as the negro. They had been temporarily submerged by the tide of democratic feeling under Jackson, but now that that current had been sidetracked they were once more dominant. Slavery had given them an attitude somewhat different from the British aristocrat.

It would seem that the control of slaves is likely to create in the master a peculiar psychology. The habit of giving orders which cannot be questioned, of regarding a group of men as chattels, who can be punished if they fail to carry out every whim of the owner, and who can be treated without any regard to their feelings or desires, seems to produce in the master a character which is arrogant, wilful, and determined to have its way regardless of others. It accentuates the temper of the old-time aristocrat, who feels that his desires and comfort are of more importance than the sufferings of thousands. With all this they seem to acquire a certain charm of manner that has always given them great influence in the world. It was this aristocratic attitude that supplied the explosive element to the current. The denunciations of the Abolitionists, made without any real understanding of the negro problem and its difficulties, and implying that all Southern slaveholders were brutes if not criminals, in its effect on the group described above, was about as helpful toward a happy solution of the slavery problem as the discharge of a pistol into a barrel of dynamite.

Aristocrats such as these with the old-time code of honor were accustomed to wipe out in blood insults such as these, and Southerners only waited their opportunity.

Gentlemen as they were, this group was not insulated from the old Commercial current, and it had been the desire of wealth and fear of losses that had driven them from condemnation of slavery to an ardent support of its extension throughout the continent. If slavery were allowed in the new territories it increased the demand for slaves and therefore added greatly to their value.

From the old Reformation element in their psychology there was enough suppressed feeling that slavery was wrong, to cause the words of the Abolitionists to sting their consciences. This would have weakened their resistance had they not succeeded in constructing a transformer for this current of feeling. By searching the scriptures their clergy discovered that the children of Ham were ordained of God to be slaves, that slavery had been commanded by God and those who opposed it were resisting the Divine will and purpose, which had created the blacks, like the animals, to serve man. Thus the powerful drive of conscience instead of pushing against slavery was transformed to a re-enforcing current.

In addition this accumulating tide of feeling was raised to high power by resentment against the attacks of the

North upon slavery, and by fear of the political power of the Northern states, who, according to their ideas, were planning to control the government and free their slaves and overturn the whole social order. It was fear and resentment that changed the old static emotional status of the Southerners to a dynamic current of such terrific voltage that argument had no more effect than a bag of oats on a runaway horse. The only means now to quiet their fear was to give them again the control of the government which they had lost. To quiet their resentment, more was now needed than an apology. The North must retract and adopt their point of view, that the negro, like cattle and sheep, was personal property and to be dealt with as such, and that slavery was the will of God. On no other condition would they remain in the Union.

In a sense they were right. The currents of feeling in the North and South had now acquired such a charge of mutual antagonism that they could hardly coexist in the same nation. The Abolitionists regarded slaveholders with a sort of horror and contempt, and spirited gentlemen refused to remain in a group that thus regarded them. Such currents as these cannot be turned by the protests of intelligence, of prudence, or of conscience. They twist about all the guideposts of the mind and the moral nature until they point the other way. Some Southerners actually believed that unless slavery were reintroduced in the North its social and economic system would fail! Sandburg tells us that Lincoln was stirred by the reports of the lecture delivered by Fitzhugh, Virginia economist, at Yale, in which he said that free society was a failure. Fitzhugh had written to an Abolitionist: "I am quite as intent on abolishing Free Society as you are on abolishing slavery," and again "I believe slavery natural, necessary, indispensable." He published a book in which he practically said that the Anglo-Saxon and Reformation currents must end in wrecking society. "Men once committed to negro slavery agitation—once committed to the sweeping principle that man, being a moral agent, accountable to God for his actions, should not have these actions controlled and directed by the will of another, are, in effect, committed to Socialism and Communism—to no private property, no church, no law, no government—to free love, free lands, free women and free churches." In other words slavery was essential to a stable society and without it democracy was doomed to issue in anarchy.

The Richmond *Enquirer* said: "Northern free society is burdened with a servile class of mechanics and laborers unfit for all self-government and yet clothed with the attributes and powers of citizens. Master and slave is a relation in society as natural and necessary as parent and child, and the Northern states will yet have to introduce it." Lincoln also had preserved a clipping from the Muskogee (Ala.) *Herald* which gives full expression to the extreme Southern Dynamic. "Free Society! We sicken of the name. What is it but a conglomeration of greasy mechanics, filthy operatives, small-fisted farmers and moonstruck theorists? All the Northern and especially the New England states are devoid of society fitted for well bred gentlemen. The prevailing class one meets with is that of mechanics struggling to be genteel, and small farmers who do their own drudgery and yet who are hardly fit for association with a Southern gentleman's body servant. This is your Free Society which your Northern hordes are endeavoring to extend into Kansas."

The extreme Northern Dynamic was even more insulting in its attacks on the Southern Social order. In this conflict, then, there was something more than a mere local issue. Here were two great emotional currents confronting one another for yet another death grapple, two attitudes toward life with all their attendant emotions and philosophies—on the one side that complex of feelings that had stabilized the old world with all the pride and conscious power that dwelt once in the kings and potentates of long ago, the hauteur of the aristocrat, with his contempt of manual labor and for the man of common clay or of inferior race, his consciousness of a right inherent in birth and breeding to be honored and obeyed by the common herd—

and over against it the new system that had grown up under the impulse of the Anglo-Saxon Dynamic, with its growing sense of the worth of the individual and his right to freedom and equal opportunity, with its feeling of the dignity of labor, and its sympathy for the downtrodden. It was the aristocrat against the democrat, the past against the future.

In every fundamental feeling the two differed absolutely. Men brought up in all the feelings of an aristocracy and conscious of a right to override the wishes and welfare of the masses, cannot live in harmony with those brought up with democratic ideas. They are immersed in two separate emotional currents that train them to feel differently in every respect and produce an inevitable antipathy. The Southerners saw, and a few like Lincoln in the North saw, that the two systems could not coexist. One or the other must go, as he said in his famous "House divided" speech. Two emotional systems so radically opposed cannot rule the same country.

CHAPTER V

THE SOUTHERN CYCLONE

1. The Currents That Split a Nation in Half

AFTER a conflagration it is interesting to see how the fire started. That old Anglo-Saxon spirit that had set the torch to many earlier explosions was only incidentally responsible. It was handicapped by a rebellious offshoot that was supplying power to the other side. In the time of Jefferson the main force of that old current of love for liberty was devoted to maintaining states' rights and had generated a horror for the authority of any central government.

In the North the Anglo-Saxon spirit had advanced to an enthusiasm for the rights and freedom of the individual, but in the South the old Jeffersonian current was still flowing strongly. The Republican party who opposed the extension of slavery and the Dred Scott decision, and, to a lesser degree, the Douglas Democrats, were channels for the Northern branch of this current.

In the South were many Douglas Democrats and men who had been stirred by the current of loyalty to the Union. None of these wished for separation—still less for war. In the North the danger spot was the small group of Abolitionists who kept pouring their detonating mixture into the South. Driven by that stern Daughter of the voice of God they would be content with nothing but the freeing of all the slaves, and kept the finger of condemnation pointed at every slaveholder. Garrison was insisting that either the slaves should be freed or the North should separate herself from the iniquity of slavery.

In the South, as explained, it was the group of slaveholders who formed the danger zone. They had now reached the point where they were determined that either the North should approve slavery and accept it throughout the Union, or they would secede.

The Abolitionists sought in vain to raise the North to their level of moral indignation. The slaveholders were determined to rouse the whole South to a point where they would split from the North. Now it would seem impossible for a comparatively small group of men to stir the millions of the South to such a pitch of excitement that they would trample on their National Flag and attack the very government to establish which their fathers had given their lives. It is an interesting study in emotional dynamics to discover how they accomplished it and threw the mass of neutral people into the vitriolic tide of the Southern current.

Their first plea was that the election of a Republican candidate was an insult to the South. Although Lincoln and the Republicans had strongly opposed Garrison and his party, they were identified with him, as "Black Republicans," "Abolitionists" or "advocates of the nigger."

In South Carolina the slaveholding group formed an oligarchy which controlled the government and they were sure of that state.

A month before the election of Lincoln, Governor Gist of South Carolina wrote confidentially to all the governors of the cotton states, stating that if Lincoln were elected South Carolina would probably secede if the other states would join her, and asking what each of the other states would do. The governors of Mississippi, Alabama and Florida said they would join with South Carolina, but the governors of North Carolina, Louisiana and Georgia did not think a Republican election sufficient cause for secession and said that they would wait for some more overt act. This made it evident that Gist must devise some further stimulus to win all the states.

It was not difficult to carry South Carolina. It had been on the point of secession before in 1832, and was so controlled by the oligarchy that the people were not even allowed to vote for the President. On the day before Lincoln was elected, the Governor called an extraordinary session of the Legislature and recommended the immediate arming "with the most efficient weapons of modern warfare" of every white man in the state between eighteen and forty-five, and the acceptance of ten thousand volunteers. James Chesnut, a United States Senator, told them he had little doubt of Lincoln's election. "The Black Republicans," he said, "claim the doctrines of the Declaration of Independence as part of the Constitution and that it is their right so to administer the government as to give full effect to them. The people now must choose whether they will be governed by their enemies or whether they will govern themselves. For myself, I would unfurl the Palmetto flag, fling it to the breeze, and with the spirit of a brave man, determine to live and die as becomes our glorious ancestry and ring the clarion notes of defiance in the ears of an insolent foe."

Waving a flag is an emotional talisman that always seems to act. When the election of Lincoln was announced the Palmetto flag was flung to the breeze with wild enthusiasm and, after more speeches that told of oppression and wrongs, on November 12 the Legislature of South Carolina carried the vote to secede and the Union was formally dissolved on December 20.

A state controlled by a small group in the Legislature was not hard to move, but Governor Gist had found that to stir the other states some further cause was necessary than a Republican election. To move Georgia they told the people they were being unjustly coerced. When the Legislature assembled on November 7, the speakers announced that the Republicans were planning to nullify the fugitive slave act, to exclude slavery from the territories, and to force upon the Church a God opposed to slavery. In Alabama they secured the aid of the Church, and in January, 1861, the Conference of the Methodist Church resolved that "African slavery, as it existed in the Southern states, was a wise, humane and righteous institution, approved of God; . . . that the election of a sectional President was evidence of hostility to the South, which in fact, if not in form, dissolves the compact of union between the states."

They used as inflammatory epithets as did the Abolitionists; for example a legislator in Charleston said: "The Union is a dead carcass, stinking in the nostrils of the South."

But neither side wanted to fight. These agitators thought that they could force the North to let them go their own way. With this in mind, Floyd, the Secretary of War, in whom the Southern Current flowed at highest voltage, actually moved 135,000 muskets from the arsenals in Massachusetts and New York to North Carolina, Alabama and Louisiana, and arranged to turn them over to the states. He was barely prevented from sending the cannon at Pittsburgh down to Mississippi.

Everywhere they were disseminating the idea that they had a perfect right to secede. It was here that the current of feeling generated by the old Jeffersonian Democracy bore a part by supplying the conviction that any state had the right to go its own way and could not be coerced by the central government. This peculiar branch of the Anglo-Saxon Dynamic had almost died out in the North but unfortunately it controlled the administration of Buchanan.

Black, the Attorney General, gave it as his opinion that the government had no constitutional right to put down the rebellion of a state by armed force, and President Buchanan, fortified by this opinion, expressed his sympathy with the South in his message of December 3 in which he said, "Northern agitation has at length produced its malign influence upon the slaves, and inspired them with vague notions of freedom. Many a matron on retiring at night dreaded what might befall herself and her children before morning." Southern states would be "justified in revolutionary resistance to the government of Union" unless the Northern states repealed the laws they had made to protect their free colored citizens from being kidnapped under the Fugitive Slave Law. Such a message from the head of the government naturally led the people of the South to believe that they had the right to secede if they were treated unjustly. The job of the agitators then was to demand something which the North could not grant, and then to rouse the people with the cry of tyrannous coercion. This was by no means easy to do. Although the Northern Current in the Republican party was flowing strongly against the attempts of the South to force slavery upon new areas, they desired peace and were willing to go any length to preserve it. Every sort of compromise was offered by Congress. They even proposed to open the new territory to slavery; they agreed to enforce the Fugitive Slave Law. In short they granted every request of the South short of adopting slavery themselves. This then was the point upon which the agitators could concentrate knowing well that it could not be granted. Jefferson Davis, on December 24, 1860, offered a resolution to Congress which demanded: "That it shall be declared, by amendment to the Constitution, that property in slaves, recognized as such by the local law of any of the states of the Union, shall stand on the same footing in all constitutional and Federal relations, as any other species of property so recognized." That is, the Constitution was to be made to recognize property in man and slavery as a national institution. Senator Wigfall said: "If you wish to settle this matter declare that slaves are property. Declare this and the matter is settled."

To grant this the new current of feeling that had found its channel in the Republican party, would have to revise itself, and it had in it too much of that old Reformation Dynamic—that irresistible drive of the conscience—to make this possible. They would allow the South to keep their own views and to retain their slaves, and to have an equal chance to introduce slavery into new territory, but to declare themselves that human beings were property and put it into the Constitution, would be a violation of their most fundamental principles and of their conscience, and contrary to the ideal of freedom on which their whole government rested. The old Anglo-Saxon spirit once more took the field, ready to fight to the end rather than prove false to the fundamentals of liberty. The Southerners insisted upon this point. To assert that the whole anti-slavery agitation was wrong and contrary to the will of God, was the only way to extinguish the flames of passion and resentment that threatened the Union. On the basis of the refusal of the North the agitators generated enough feeling to carry the bitterest states into secession. They based this secession on the ground of the fundamental necessity and righteousness of slavery. Stephens of Georgia made the declaration on March 21, 1861, in terms the North regarded as blasphemous: "The corner-stone of our new government rests upon the great truth that the negro is not equal to the white man—that slavery is his natural and normal condition. This is the stone which was rejected by the first builders (*i. e.,* Washington and Jefferson) but is become the first stone of the corner in the new edifice." Here they took their firm ground on the rights of a superior and stronger race to enslave the weaker and more ignorant, and to live by the proceeds of its labor, and in his speech at Montgomery Jefferson Davis said: "All who oppose us shall smell Southern powder and feel Southern steel."

2. THE THREAT TO DEMOCRACY

While then the two groups of the slaveholders and abolitionists were driven by currents of dangerously high voltage, the majority of the people were being gradually carried into opposition by two divisions of the old Anglo-Saxon Dynamic, the Jeffersonian current of feeling that the states should be free, and the Northern Current which emphasized the freedom of the individual. Many in the North were sufficiently influenced by the Jeffersonian current to feel that the Southern states should be free to go their own way. To oppose this feeling, then, was only the National American current of feeling, which had been kept alive by the dynamic power of Webster and which had given to a portion of the people a real sense of Nationality, so that secession meant to them tearing asunder a living, sentient organism. If a man thus broke his oath of allegiance they felt it to be a traitorous act, which awakened the feelings once roused by High Treason. Lincoln was of this number. It seemed as if those who were swayed by democratic feeling, with that old horror of central authority that was the bane of the Anglo-Saxon spirit, would support the right of the Southern states to secede. We are told that it was Lincoln who provided a switch for reversing this current by demonstrating that such action would be the death blow to all real democracy. His point was that democratic government rested absolutely on an agreement to abide by a majority decision. By a long process of evolution representative machinery had been devised which enabled each section to present its case. After each section had declared its will, and the fairest possible compromise had been reached by a thorough discussion of the needs of all, all were bound to abide by the decision of the majority. If the majority disregarded the needs of the minority, or attempted to coerce them, or to exercise tyranny over them, their rebellion might be justified, but if their needs had been fairly considered and every adjustment offered compatible with the well-being of the whole, to rebel meant not only treason to the nation but to Democracy itself, and made the whole method of government futile and void. In this case the North had listened to the South, had been willing to compromise, and, rather than break, had yielded to the various demands of the South and even to those which seemed to them as unrighteous as did the Fugitive Slave Law, until it was demanded that they should accept slavery as a fundamental principle applicable to the whole nation. Because this was not granted the South proposed to secede. Their attitude was "give us everything we ask or we won't play." Now this is the familiar spirit of the autocracies of the old world, generated by the aristocratic society which in the South had gradually replaced the old communities of free men. It is the deadly foe of the Anglo-Saxon spirit. They cannot coexist and one of the two must perish. The age-long conflict was on again. The old spirit had risen again to overthrow the institutions built by the spirit of Freedom. Lincoln saw clearly that Democracy cannot exist among men each of whom is determined to have his own way without any compromise. Such an attitude means inevitable disintegration. The minute any section of a group is displeased it will withdraw, and, in the various sections again, smaller groups split off as they are dissatisfied, until nothing remains. Therefore to allow these states to secede meant their own ultimate ruin as well as that of the nation. If government of the people, by the people and for the people is not to perish from the earth these states must be compelled to stand by their agreement and remain in the Union.

It was a difficult situation, for the Southern states came in the disguise of the Spirit of Liberty, asking freedom to go their own way, and the masses did not see that beneath the disguise was their great enemy the autocratic spirit, insisting upon domination. It was to take some time to rouse them to the danger. In the meantime Lincoln set himself to evoke the National American spirit, for it was upon this that he must rely to stir men until they were ready to die for the Union.

The masses of the people, then, were in a balance between the Jeffersonian current and the National American spirit, and no one could tell whether the seceded states would return to the fold, or whether the remaining Southern states would be roused to join them.

3. Exploding the Mine

The Southern agitators were growing anxious lest their efforts might fail and the majority of the Southern states remain with the Union. They were in the main convinced that they had the right to secede. Some emotional explosion must be arranged that would detach them. They understood enough of emotions to fear that if they attacked the North they would lose the doubtful states. In some way the North must be driven to attack the South. The means was found in the situation in Charleston harbor. Forts Moultrie and Sumter were held by the government, and after her secession, South Carolina demanded their surrender. Major

Anderson, in command there, seeing that Moultrie could not be defended, moved his forces to Sumter and asked Washington for supplies and reinforcements.

After great friction in the Cabinet, in which Floyd, the pro-Southern Secretary of War, was forced by Stanton to resign, President Buchanan finally refused to surrender the fort and sent supplies in the steamer *Star of the West,* unarmed, to give no offense to the Secessionists. She came into Charleston harbor flying the Stars and Stripes on January 9, 1861.

The motive of keeping supplies out of a fort which they claimed as their own, gave the Southerners the excuse to offer the most deadly insult that can be offered a nation, an insult that they doubtless felt would stir the North to attack.

To fire on the flag of any nation is emotionally equivalent to a slap on the face. The Secessionists fired on the flag and compelled the steamer to retire. As if this were not enough to stir the North they proceeded to rub in the insult in every possible way. The Legislature issued resolutions commending the act, and their newspaper commented as follows: "Yesterday, the 9th of January, will be remembered in history. Powder has been burned by decree of the state, timber has been crashed, perhaps blood spilled. We are proud that the state of South Carolina so long, so bitterly, so contemptuously reviled and scoffed at, should thus proudly have thrown back the scoff of her enemies. Intrenched upon her soil she has spoken from the mouth of her cannon, . . . she has not hesitated to strike the first blow, full in the face of her insulter. Let the United States bear, or return at good will, the blow still tingling about its ears. We would not exchange or recall that blow for millions. . . . And if the red seal of blood be still lacking to the parchment of our liberties, and blood they want—blood they shall have—and blood enough to stamp it all in red. For by the God of our fathers, the soil of South Carolina *shall be free!"*

They must have felt that at last they had fired the train.

There are few governments that would not have been stirred to wrath by such a pronunciamento, or even by a shot at their flag without the added comment. But the national government was for peace at any price, and hoped to soothe the irascible state and smooth over the offense. The result was that the conspirators decided that more drastic action was necessary to touch off the desired explosion. They were soon informed of the only means by which Virginia could be made to join them.

In the meantime Lincoln was inaugurated and, like his predecessor, sought to pacify the seceding states although he kept his hold on Fort Sumter. On April 10, 1861, Roger Pryor of Virginia spoke to the populace in Charleston: "Gentlemen," he said, "I thank you that you have at last annihilated this cursed Union, reeking with corruption and insolent with excess of tyranny. Thank God it is at last blasted and riven by the lightning wrath of an outraged and indignant people. . . . Proclaim to the world that upon no condition and in no circumstances will South Carolina ever enter into political association with the abolitionists of New England. Do not distrust Virginia. . . . I will tell you gentlemen what will put her in the Southern Confederacy in less than an hour by the Shrewsbury clock. Strike a blow! The very moment blood is shed, old Virginia will make common cause with her sisters of the South."

Gilchrist of Alabama said: "Unless you sprinkle blood in the face of the people of Alabama, they will be back in the old Union in less than ten days." This was probably true. The prevailing sentiment was still for the Union. In North Carolina the Raleigh *Banner* said: "The big heart of the people is still with the Union. Less than a hundred thousand politicians are endeavoring to destroy the liberties and usurp the rights of thirty millions of people." And the politicians proved their ability to shape the people according to their will. Convinced that the seal of blood was essential they gave orders to Beauregard the next day, April 11, to open fire on Fort Sumter. The bombardment continued for thirty-six hours until the fort was set on fire and its ammunition exhausted. Major Anderson then surrendered and the flag was hauled down and replaced by the Palmetto flag of South Carolina.

Strange to say, in that appalling bombardment when three thousand shot and shell were hurled into the fort, no one was killed. It was enough, however, to serve the purpose. At last the agitators had roused the North to action. Those who wished for peace could no longer hold back the tide of the Northern Current that had been rising constantly and that now broke forth in an outburst of resentment. It is a pretty sluggish and untemperamental soul that can see the flag of his country fired upon and insulted, and a fortress of his government seized while a hostile flag is flaunted in his face, and feel no emotion. Before, only the anti-slavery current had carried high voltage. Now the great National American current, far more wide-spread than men had dreamed, became a raging torrent. Men who cared nothing for the slavery issue were stirred to the quick. With the wide-spreading wave of indignation and wrath behind it, Lincoln issued his call to arms and met an eager response. Thousands who had been ready to allow the South to withdraw from the Union without a protest sprang to arms under the lash of this insult.

But it did more than rouse the North. That was a side issue. The real intent had been to force the South to quick decision. In many states the dominant minority, intoxicated by the fumes of battle, terrorized the peaceful majority. Now that the North was really to attack, the extremists were strong enough to use fear and force. In Virginia on April 25, Mason threatened banishment to all who did not submit. A vigorous propaganda was set in motion. False reports of the wildest nature were circulated. In North Carolina the people were told their liberties were to be taken away and they were to be made subject to a military despotism in Washington. Texas, loyal at first, had been forced into secession by threats of the rope and the firebrand for every one who resisted, and Governor Houston, rather than see his people torn by civil war, finally gave his assent. In Alabama there had been strong resistance to secession, but the threats of the secessionists so terrorized the Unionists that at length they gave way. In Arkansas there was a majority of Unionists in the Convention. They were notified to change their votes under threat of assault and death. All yielded to the terror save one, Murphy, who was compelled to fly for his life. Unionists were exiled, imprisoned and murdered. Where men could not be roused to rage they were driven by fear, and thus state after state was carried. Western Virginia resisted threats and coercion and succeeded in forming a separate government and was able thus to remain in the Union.

In the border states all depended on the energy and decision of a few men. Whichever side gained the control terrified the rest to acquiescence. Missouri was saved by the prompt action and determination of Colonel Lyon, who held the arsenal, raised troops and drove out the Governor and his secessionists when they attempted to seize the government property. In East Tennessee loyalists were hunted, arrested, taken to camps and prisons and insulted and abused by mobs. Cavalry scoured the country, burning and plundering the property of Unionists. The jails were filled with loyalists and secession triumphed.

Maryland was at first in the hands of secessionists, who controlled the police of Baltimore, and stirred up a mob to attack the Massachusetts troops on their way to defend the capital. The prompt action of General Butler in seizing the city gave courage to the Unionists, who soon showed their strength and brought the state into the Union column. For a time Washington had been entirely cut off from the North and in imminent danger of capture by the Secessionists. Their threat to seize the Capitol and imprison the President served to arouse the North yet more. At last the nation was ready to fight. Some one said that when Uncle Sam was hit in the face he had blinked a little and said, "Hit me again, will you?" At the second blow, he said, "Just hit me once more." Not until the third blow was he mad enough to fight, and then he proceeded to clean things up. The emotions of the Yankee required violent and repeated stimulus to set them free, but once aroused they were just as difficult to suppress.

It is not an easy matter to split a great nation asunder, and we have tried to give somewhat in detail the means by which emotions were aroused which threw into violent antagonism those very groups that had fought side by side through three wars and labored together for the country they loved, and rejoiced together in its prosperity. Originally animated by the same spirit of love and liberty, the old commercial spirit, reacting to different environments, had developed antagonistic attitudes. Two different types of emotional culture, one aristocratic, one democratic, had created groups whose emotional reactions were antipathetic. Both groups, impelled by strong emotions, had developed their theories and morals and religion to conform to their feelings. One group with an over-sensitive sense of honor, the other with an over-sensitive conscience, had reacted on one another in constant emotional crescendo, until they had swept the whole nation into the vortex of their conflicting passions. The strangest feature was the manner in which the old Anglo-Saxon current had divided itself.

The men who framed the government had embodied in their Declaration of Independence the statement that all men are born free and equal—an ideal which they must have known impracticable at the time, even as regards equality in rights and opportunities, but to whose gradual realization they must have looked forward. Half of their descendants felt bound to an attempt to realize this ideal, and the other half repudiated it as impossible, unjust and harmful. Thus the old current was split, those in the South still clinging to the Jeffersonian interpretation and stirring men's souls with the demand that their own group should be free, while they were equally insistent that individuals in it should not be freed. To claim the right to be free to enslave, certainly seems an anomaly to the disinterested bystander, but it is an illustration of the strange way in which ancient currents of feeling are twisted by events.

Slavery was doomed; the sentiment of the world was against it; the South must have relinquished it of themselves in a few years. It was the violence of the old Reformation drive in the conscience of the abolitionists that had reacted on the Southerners until they were driven to assert that slavery was a Divine institution essential to society and to fight for it until their whole country was in ruins.

Every one knows that the success of a war depends on the heat generated in the feelings of the people. And nothing produces such high temperature as stories of atrocities. Both sides did their best. In June, 1861, before the National troops had entered Virginia, save to fortify Arlington, and when their only care was to defend Washington, Beauregard issued a proclamation which said: "A reckless and unprincipled tyrant has invaded your soil. Abraham Lincoln has thrown his abolition hosts among you, who are murdering and imprisoning your citizens and committing other acts of violence and outrage too shocking and revolting to humanity to be enumerated. All rules of civilized war are abandoned and they proclaim by their acts if not by their banners, that their war cry is 'Beauty and Booty.'" The only murders committed up to that time had been the assassination of the Massachusetts soldiers by the Baltimore mob. Such a proclamation, without a word of truth, isued by the commanding general, shows that 1861 was not much behind 1914 in the art of arousing emotion.

4. THE MASTER OF THE WHIRLWIND

War is not only the result of emotional charges. When once set in motion it is also the most powerful known generator of emotional currents of violent and abnormal potential, that sweep through a nation until even the most sedate are thrown from their balance and react like wild men to every stimulus. War in a Democracy is a most dangerous and terrible agent, for there is no authority to control these tides of wrath, panic, prejudice and enthusiasm that sweep men beyond the control of reason. The only hope then is that some dynamic figure will arise who can ride the storm and direct its currents, and, holding the enthusiastic support of the people, can guide them wisely when their wisdom is lost in passion. At the great emotional crisis that overtook the American nation there seemed to be no such person at hand. The man who stood at the head of the nation was singularly lacking in emotional dynamic. To-day the name of Lincoln is such a word to conjure with that it is hard to realize that at that time it was entirely devoid of emotional content. To Southerners, indeed, false report had made it the synonym for all that they detested most. They knew little of the real man or of his speeches, but his name stood to them for the brutal enmity of the North, and its determination to put them into the power of their slaves.

In the North he was merely a compromise candidate shoved forward to catch the Western vote. He was known as an exponent of the Northern Current of feeling against the extension of slavery, but the current that ran strongest in his heart was that of devotion to the Union. He had caught the vote and now it was expected that Seward and Chase would direct and control the affairs of the nation. Lincoln was known as an uncouth backwoodsman and rail-splitter, whose clever stump oratory had exposed the sub-terfuges of the Little Giant and occasioned his political downfall. He had a dry pungent humor and an uncanny power to get at the pith of a political situation and to por-tray it in telling humorous phrases. It was a power some-what akin to that of Will Rogers, and American audiences would rather listen to a political speech by Lincoln than at-tend a circus. They were sure of good entertainment, and some realized that beneath the humor there was a deadly seriousness and a vital grasp of the situation that no other politician possessed. At the same time, upon the average cultured New Englander the election of Lincoln had much the same effect as that of Will Rogers would have in 1930.

Superficially he appeared much the same type of man as Jackson—uncouth, vigorous, the champion of the plain peo-ple, and opposed to all aristocrats. Really he was as different a type as could be conceived. Jackson was passionate, violent-tempered, self-assertive, opinionated; he resented all opposition as a personal insult and played a lone hand in his own way, and as a national hero he was a tremendous emotional dynamo. Lincoln, though capable of absolute firmness on vital questions, disliked to assert himself and was willing to put up with the most outrageous treatment from overbearing men like McClellan or Stanton, for the good of the cause. He felt keenly the contempt of men of culture, but, instead of regarding them as bitter enemies, he rose above all personal feeling, and after Stanton had grossly insulted him and called him a gorilla, he actually appointed his detractor Secretary of War.

He was possessed of amazing patience and tact, and his management of his cabinet, with their bitter animosities and petty ambitions and contempt for himself, showed little less than genius. He deferred at first to the judgment of others until he found that it failed, and then he was able to disregard their clamorous commands and to stand calm and clear-headed in the vortex of violent emotion that surrounded him, and, uninfluenced by panic or prejudice, to direct the course of the Ship of State with a far-seeing sagacity and a deep understanding even of his enemies and detractors, and with sympathy even for those against whom he was fighting to the death. Since he was working for harmony, all sides regarded him as cowardly and vacillating, and even at the time of his death there was no general appreciation of his great qualities, and the negroes were the only ones among whom his name had high emotional potential. Leaders like Sumner had even talked of impeaching him as a menace to the state on account of his cowardice.

With no one at hand, then, whose personality could sway the public feeling or who would be accepted as a dominating influence, it behooved the leaders to move with great caution. It was necessary to study the great tides of feeling as they rose and swelled, to judge which of them could be used to bear the Ship of State upon its way and to determine how to pull out of the way of such hurricanes as threatened to dash the ship upon the rocks, and how to lie by cautiously until the wild wind of passion had blown itself out and it was safe to proceed. At all this Lincoln proved himself a past master. He seemed able to estimate just how long it was necessary to wait before launching on a new course, and just what tides he could trust to bear him on his course.

Better than any one in the North, Lincoln understood the temper of the South. Ardent Union man though he was, he realized that the South had never been brought to feel that sense of solidarity that made secession seem to him like a dismemberment in which vital limbs were torn away from a living body.

In 1789 the various states of the South had joined a federation for their mutual advantage. They had always insisted on the independent rights of the states and they had always felt at liberty to withdraw when the association proved disadvantageous. The South had been little touched by the great speeches of Webster that thrilled with the sense of national pride and throbbed with the consciousness of the bond that held together a mighty nation, united in their struggle against foes without, united against the great forces of nature as they conquered the vast wilderness, and built cities from the desolate forests, and harnessed the raging torrents to their will,—united more and more as they bound East to West with a girdle of steel and city to city with threads of power. These words, to which the North and West had thrilled with the consciousness of their united greatness, had left the South unmoved, and impermeable to the great current of national feeling that began to pulse through the land. The Southerners still felt themselves to be separate states, associated as long as their federation proved advantageous. They had threatened to withdraw, thinking to compel the North to grant their demands. It is probable that their leaders expected to rejoin the Union after they had made their own terms. They had no appreciation of the consciousness of union which made their withdrawal seem to the North like high treason, or the breaking of a marriage vow. But Lincoln knew that he had with him this great tide of National feeling, raised now to triple strength, and it was upon this that he hoped to ride to victory.

The Southern leaders, intent on forcing Secession, probably had no conception of the emotional effect of their attack on the flag upon the North, or how it would arouse the whole nation to avenge the insult. They still expected to give a little demonstration of their strength and determination and thus to be taken back on their own terms. They had little idea of the irrevocable nature of their act or of the emotional forces they had let loose.

We must picture then in the North a rapidly rising storm of mingled wrath and enthusiasm that swallowed up all the factions. All the various currents were fused in one great tide of war enthusiasm. The old-time Democrat who felt it sacrilege to vote the Republican ticket, the old Republican guard who abominated the abolitionist and was ready to mob him, and this party of Free Soilers and Anti-Slavery men were all swept together by the tide and united in a common wrath against the South and a common loyalty to the flag.

In the South propaganda and oratory were rapidly raising a wave of antagonism to the North and the war spirit was submerging what little opposition or loyalty to the Union remained. In Alabama, however, there was one county where the Unionists outnumbered the Secessionists four to one, and in Mississippi one county seceded from the Secessionists.

5. PERSONAL FEELING AND POPULAR CLAMOR

The first year of Lincoln's administration affords an admirable illustration of the difficulties of conducting a war in a democracy where violent waves of enthusiasm and prejudice make wise and intelligent direction well-nigh impossible. A leader cannot ignore popular clamor and do what he knows is best, because this blind emotion has its vote and will throw him out of office and turn over the control to those who will wreck his plans and bring disaster on the cause he loves. This was Lincoln's difficulty. He was undoubtedly ambitious, but his own success counted as nothing compared with the principles he sought to defend and whose overthrow was involved in his defeat. Almost unknown, the victim of violent prejudices, his wisdom doubted on every hand, he had to feel his way cautiously and use such instruments as time and fate supplied, and popular feeling endorsed. He could not afford to make enemies or resent insults and he had to hold all the raging, tumultuous, selfish forces around him in some sort of unity, and to avoid any act that threatened to split his following asunder. More difficult to manage than these tides of popular feeling, were the personal prejudices and antagonisms of those whom he chose to help him. No man ever understood better than Lincoln how to control and blanket and transform the violent feelings in the men about him. Where any other would have added fuel to the flame he always picked the word that would disarm prejudice and turn hate aside and quiet panic. No personal feeling interfered with his calm, humorous touch on their emotion. He rose above all petty animosity to appreciate the value of Chase and Blair to the country, and to ignore their treachery when he knew them to be plotting against him in his own cabinet. Perhaps no other would have refused to vindicate himself from the absurd charges of Horace Greeley because he knew that his vindication would cause the North to lose confidence in *The Tribune* and thus work disaster.

Perhaps his greatest triumph in manipulating both personal feeling and popular enthusiasm was in the case of McClellan. That youthful warrior by a fortunate chance and the skill of his subordinates had won a few trifling successes in West Virginia, which aroused one of those absurd waves of popular enthusiasm that are the bane of democracy. He was "the young Napoleon," "the great American Conqueror," "our little Mac." How Lincoln's military advisers could have been so carried away by this tide of feeling seems a mystery. Lincoln had not yet learned to distrust them and, doubting his own military knowledge, he followed their advice and made the popular hero General of all the Northern armies. His head completely turned by all this adulation, McClellan promised speedily to annihilate the armies of the Confederacy and capture Richmond.

He treated all his superiors with cool contempt. When Lincoln called on him, he kept the President of the United States waiting half an hour and then sent word that he had gone to bed and could not be disturbed. In spite of urgent requests and even commands from his superiors to dislodge the Confederates from their threatening position before Washington, he did nothing until the enemy retired of themselves, when he promptly claimed a great victory. Month after month he excused his inaction by abusing the administration and claiming that he was being thwarted at every turn. So clever was he that the people believed him and he remained their idol.

The story of his futile delays is a familiar one. When after idling eight months he was forced to fight on the Chickahominy, and by bad generalship or treachery so divided his army that he was defeated by an inferior force, the people still stood by this little Napoleon and threw the blame on Lincoln. When Lee marched on Washington, hoping to seize the Capital and proclaim a new government of the United States, McClellan, instead of hindering him, caused the defeat of Pope by refusing to send reinforcements when ordered, and in addition wrote his public letter to the President making it evident that he did not intend or wish to conquer the South; then when Stanton wished to remove him as a traitor, Lincoln forgot the insults to himself and considered only the danger to Washington and the harm that McClellan might do the cause if removed. Instead he put him where he was forced to fight and he won the Battle of Antietam. Then when it became known that McClellan had had Lee's plans in his hands and might have annihilated the Southern army, public opinion veered. McClellan had had his chance and failed. The National government was out of danger. Lincoln could act safely, and McClellan was removed. He left the army to

begin the campaign in politics by which he hoped to wreck
Lincoln and his administration. If Lincoln had ousted him
while the wave of popularity was running high, with that
enthusiasm behind him, he might easily have put Lincoln
out of the Presidency and overturned his efforts to preserve
the Union. With such genius had Lincoln handled the tide
of public feeling that instead of overwhelming him it swept
him on his way.

6. The Cyclone of Opposition

If enthusiasm can raise the currents of war to triple
power, discouragement can exercise upon them a counter
effect which is even more telling. It may be difficult to guide
a wave of unreasoning enthusiasm, but to face a giant wave
of discouragement and turn it aside requires courage and a
knowledge of emotional dynamics which few possess. The
way in which Lincoln met this great crisis, and abandoning
the support of the current of feeling upon which he had relied, turned on the only power line which had the strength to
resist and conquer the vast wave of discouragement that
had rolled up, is the most interesting feature in the history
of the war.

As in the case of the Great Panic, repeated defeats and
prolonged suffering had created one of these areas of low
pressure that generate a cyclone, and cyclones of this type
almost invariably sweep the controlling administration from
the face of the earth. This was the crisis that Lincoln had to
face, and we must review the history of the period to understand what he accomplished.

At first Lincoln had listened with reverence to the pro-
nouncements of army men, who told him he knew nothing
of war. He had humbly called on McClellan and been re-
buffed. He had promoted Halleck and listened patiently to
his authoritative statements. When nothing was done, he
began to see that he must take the reins into his own hands.
The men he had were accomplishing nothing. He could at
least try a change. His efforts seemed to bring forth nothing but disaster. The best generals he could pick from

their successes in other fields went down like a row of nine-pins when confronted by the consummate genius of Lee and Jackson. McDowell had failed, Pope had failed, Halleck proved inept. He picked Burnside, and the latter, declaring his incapability almost with tears, proved it conclusively at the stone wall of Fredericksburg. Lincoln put Hooker in his place and he, declaring boldly his ability to crush Lee at one stroke, barely escaped annihilation at Chancellors-ville when Jackson pounced unexpectedly upon his flank and rear, while he rested secure in the thought that Lee was retreating on Richmond.

Two years of such disaster served to change the emotional temper of the North. Enthusiasm and the triumphant assurance of victory gave way to despondency. The Southern sympathizers in the North, at first overwhelmed by the war enthusiasm, lifted up their heads. A party of Defeatists began to gather and grow. McClellan, embittered by his removal, made common cause with them. A wave of disgust with the war and of weariness at the prolonged struggle spread over the country. "Make peace and let the South go," was the cry. Distrust of the administration spread rapidly. Lincoln was incapable, a bungler, a menace to the country.

Disaffection and disorganization had crept into the army. At the time that Hooker took over the command, over 88,-000 enlisted men were A. W. O. L. and, worst of all, more than 2,000 commissioned officers—an army in itself. Orators such as ex-President Pierce were declaiming in turgid rhetoric against the tyranny of the administration while they declared the war an utter failure and urged the citizens to rise and free themselves from their bondage. Moreover, organizations such as the Knights of the Golden Circle were honeycombing the country with subterranean activities in which, under direction of Southern sympathizers, they plotted the overthrow of the government. If Lincoln could have answered them with a great victory all would have been well, but his every effort seemed to result in disaster. The state elections of 1862 came on and the pacifists and plotters carried all before them. Their candidates were elected in New York, New Jersey, Pennsylvania, Ohio, Indiana, Illinois, and Wisconsin, and the Unionists were left with a scanty majority of sixteen in Congress. The current of devotion to the Union was giving way before the old Jeffersonian current of states' rights. Had the Presidential election fallen that year it might have made an end of Lincoln. Discouraged and disheartened, the people distrusted their leaders and were swayed by plotters and malcontents.

Nothing can be more dangerous to a nation than such a wave of distrust and discouragement. It was accentuated by the attitude of foreign nations. England sympathized strongly with the South, partly because her cotton trade was broken up by the blockade, and partly because the Southern aristocrat appealed to her more than the Northern farmer and mechanic. The *Trent* affair, when the Southern commissioners, Mason and Slidell, had been forcibly taken from the British ship *Trent* by an American warship, nearly resulted in war, and would probably have done so but for the quick action of Lincoln. These were sad days for the Union and its leader. The contempt of England for the lanky clodhopper and rail-splitter, and the withdrawing tide of favor and support among his own people, left him standing almost alone, a tragic solitary figure, whose every effort to save the Union that he loved had failed, and who had won the distrust of his own party. Why sacrifice all this wealth and pour out all this blood to force a group of people to remain in a Union which they hated? This was the question that was everywhere asked and the wave of public feeling against the war was rapidly growing and seemed doomed to sweep Lincoln and his few loyal adherents to destruction at the next election.

CHAPTER VI

THE SPIRITS OF UNION AND VENGEANCE

1. The Shift to Ancient Power Lines

To Lincoln it was evident that the current of devotion to the Union that had been his main support was played out. He must find some new and more powerful emotional tide to carry the war forward or it was lost. So long as it was a question of holding the doubtful border states he had avoided any mention of slavery, and had relied simply on the spirit of Nationality and devotion to the Union. He had repeatedly asserted that he did not care what the South did about their slaves if only the Union were preserved. He still expressed this attitude in his famous letter to Greeley in August, 1862. But now that the question of Secession was decided the appeal to men to fight in order to maintain the Union had lost a large measure of its emotional force. There were more and more who resented it and refused to give their lives for a Union that was already broken.

There was, however, the great spirit that had carried America to victory in all the struggles of the past, and that still had a deeper hold upon the people than any other feeling, the old Anglo-Saxon devotion to freedom. To every man in the North, and to those in England also, the word freedom still had its emotional appeal. At great cost England had freed her slaves, and the majority of Northerners as they had witnessed the sufferings of the fugitive negroes, and as they had absorbed the teachings of "Uncle Tom's Cabin," had come to feel that slavery was wrong. Little by little the group of fanatics with that tremendous drive of the conscience behind them, had influenced the public mind until now it seemed as if the Reformation spirit was about to add its force to the old Anglo-Saxon current and direct its whole stream toward freeing the slaves.

If he could shift the cause of the war so that it would not be a war to compel men to submit to a government they did not want, but would become a fight to free a race from slavery and injustice, he would then have behind him a vast emotional drive—the conscience of all who thought slavery wrong—and with it that great heritage of emotional force that had been built up in America about the word "Freedom"—that blended current coming down from past ages that had the power to carry men forward in spite of suffering and death to ultimate victory. Moreover, he would win the approval of the European nations. If, by his authority as President and head of the American armies, he should declare the slaves free, then every man who fought in the Northern armies would be fighting to carry out this decree and to free the slaves from their bondage. It was a risk, for there were many in the North who still felt that the Southerners had a right to their slaves, and there was a section of the old current that would be against him. His advisers sought to dissuade him, but Lincoln had his hand on the pulse of the country and he felt that the time had come to set free this great wave of emotion which might carry the war through to success. There would be opposition and resentment, but by this time all in the North who favored slavery were already working secretly against him. He would really lose very few votes and would merely drive the opposition into the open. The old spirit that resented slavery, blocked by political considerations, had been rising higher and higher in the minds of men and reenforced by the drive of conscience it formed a reservoir of tremendous power that he could set free.

As already indicated, the abolitionists had stirred up enough emotion to blow up a nation, but most of it had been directed against themselves. It is strange how a group that feels strongly will ultimately communicate its feeling to the indifferent and even overcome a fairly vigorous opposition. These men had reached a white heat of passionate devotion to the cause of the negro and spared nothing that stood in the way. Garrison had been violently proclaiming that the Constitution was "an agreement with death and a covenant with Hell" because in 1789 the men who disapproved of slavery and thought it incompatible with the principles of liberty which they endorsed, nevertheless made an agreement with the Southern planter to permit it. At the time of Lincoln's inauguration, the feeling against abolition was strong and there was such fear that the abolitionists would attempt to alter the Constitution that an amendment was carried by a two-thirds vote in the House, forbidding any future amendment to alter the status of the slaves. So long as it was doubtful which side the border states would take, every concession was made to slavery. The territories of Colorado, Nevada and Dakota were organized with no restriction against slavery. The result was that the abolitionists and Radical Republicans regarded Lincoln as a shifty compromiser, an enemy rather than a friend, while the Republicans were most anxious to repudiate the epithets of "abolitionists," "slave drivers," "dough faces" and "blacks," that were hurled at them. The most capable Union generals, such as Grant, Sheridan and Sherman, at the beginning of the war would never have fought if the main objective had been to free the slaves.

But slowly a change had come over the minds of men. The status of the border states was determined. McClellan's Peninsular campaign had caused a shift of sentiment. In April, 1862, Congress forbade slavery in the District of Columbia. In June, it was forbidden in all the territories and in July permission was granted to enlist negro troops. The signs were favorable and Lincoln decided that the time had come to turn loose in his behalf that great mass of emotion that had been storing up in the reservoirs of the North, trusting that it would sweep before it the remnants of the old anti-abolition prejudice. And so in January, 1863, he issued the celebrated Emancipation Proclamation. It was not a law either of the states or of Congress. It was simply a war measure issued by the head of the armies, and it meant merely that the Union officers had the right to set free any slaves who came within their jurisdiction. It had surprisingly little effect on the mass of negroes in the South, who continued to work on in patient loyalty to the masters who, being absent in the army, could no longer compel their obedience.

In the North it seemed to hit those opposed to it first, and in the 1863 elections Lincoln lost many votes and it looked as if he had made a mistake. But little by little the Proclamation took hold of the mass of the people and a wave of enthusiasm spread throughout the country which carried the war forward with a new spirit.

2. The Crisis and the Conflict of the Tides

The change in the situation was due in part to the appearance of a new leader. While disaster followed disaster in the East, in the West a new star had risen. No star ever appeared in a fashion more unpredictable or confusing to all astrologers. After Lincoln's disastrous luck with the Generals he had chosen, it is perhaps surprising that he should have faced public criticism by committing himself to this new man, and supporting him so steadfastly. An officer who had served in the Mexican War and had left the army under a cloud; who had made a failure of one business after another, who was accounted a shiftless ne'er-do-well, and who was suspected of being often incapable because of over-indulgence in alcohol—surely, in the opinion of his fellows, no man appeared less likely to lead the armies of America to success. His biographer tells us that he had one peculiar quality. When once he chose a path, he never turned back. He seems to have had an almost superstitious horror of retracing his steps, and even when he found he had taken the wrong fork, he would still push on and reach his destination by roundabout ways and through great difficulties rather than turn back. It may be that this peculiarity accounts for much in an army whose generals seemed to do little but retrace their steps.

Slighted and overlooked at first by his superiors in Missouri, when he was once given a command, he achieved success after success and this, in a time of many failures, soon brought him into notice. In February, 1862, by the capture of Forts Henry and Donelson, he gained control of the upper Mississippi and started the movement to cut in two the Southern Confederacy. His achievement, as it was almost the only notable success for the North, awakened the wildest enthusiasm.

His peculiar psychology revealed itself at Shiloh, when he was caught asleep, without pickets or defenses, by General Johnstone and his army was nearly annihilated. His generals could not believe their ears when, instead of retreating, he ordered an advance. Fortunately for him, General Johnstone had been killed by a stray bullet and he won a great victory. Lincoln assumed responsibility for him; when he was accused of drunkenness and negligence and superseded by Halleck, Lincoln restored him to command with the celebrated suggestion that his other generals should drink a little of Grant's liquor.

Lincoln stood by him through the terrible Vicksburg campaign, when, to win the control of the Mississippi, Grant attempted the impossible, and threw his army against impregnable defenses by water and land, for month after month, with appalling losses. He became known as Butcher Grant. A violent wave of distrust swept over the country. The public clamored for his removal. Probably under the clamor any other leader would have removed him, but not Lincoln. Any other man would have given up and turned back, but not Grant.

Lee was advancing into the heart of Pennsylvania; Grant was helpless before the walls of Vicksburg, losing his thousands in continual carnage. Then was the hour of the Defeatists. The war was lost. Lincoln was an incapable bungler who insisted on directing affairs of which he knew nothing. Grant was a heartless drunken butcher. The only thing to do was to make peace and let the South go her way and keep her slaves.

All through those anxious days Lincoln held steadfastly by Grant, refusing to recall or hinder him in his obstinate course, though he knew it might mean the overthrow of his government. It was then that his great move in proclaiming emancipation was tested. Once more the heroic old Anglo-Saxon spirit was to face the supreme trial. The great wave of discouragement and despair that was sweeping the country had now to face this new enthusiasm that had risen under the impulse of the old current, a crusader's passion for freeing a downtrodden race. Conscience and moral determination stiffened it. If it could only once gain headway here was something for which men would give their lives, to which women would consecrate their children and husbands. The two waves were rolling up, discouragement, defeatism, pro-secessionism, distrust of the administration and hatred and contempt for Lincoln on the one side, and against it the passionate enthusiasm of the abolitionist, devotion to the Union, loyalty to Lincoln and faith in the cause. Even with the new current of feeling it was a doubtful balance and with only the support of the failing National spirit, Lincoln must have gone under.

The Pacifists and Southern sympathizers redoubled their efforts. In the great danger the President had ordered the suspension of the writ of Habeas Corpus and the arrest of those who were making seditious speeches. It was a dangerous move, for it was certain to split off and turn against him a section of that Anglo-Saxon current on which he relied, and which once before had risen against a similar exercise of authority. In Ohio an energetic politician named Vallandigham, who was apparently a high official of the Knights of the Golden Circle, went about stirring up sedition and urging the people to resist the President's order. He was finally arrested and a storm of bitter criticism burst upon the President from all the Democrats. To express their sympathy they even nominated Vallandigham as Governor of Ohio. The South were well aware of all this discontent, and knew that the President by his shift to the Anti-Slavery current now had against him in the North not only the Jeffersonian current and McClellan, but all their sympathizers with the South and all who were tired of the war. They were told that the Knights of the Golden Circle controlled Ohio and Indiana and that they had only to send a Confederate force over the border to have the people come over to their side in a mass. Accordingly Morgan started through Ohio in his famous raid, and carried all before him. He swept across the state and into Indiana, burning, plundering and slaughtering all who resisted.

With assurances of sympathy in New York and Pennsylvania, Lee had determined to invade the North and to count upon a rising of the people to support him. Hooker was still in command of the Union forces and Lee slipped past him and was soon on Northern soil. Irritated by an order from Halleck, Hooker resigned. It seemed a perilous matter to break with a popular general at such a critical moment. At such a crisis before, Lincoln had refused to remove McClellan. But Lincoln was stronger now and he relied on the strength of the new current behind him. Even so he knew the risk was great when he accepted the resignation and appointed Meade in Hooker's place.

Terror reigned in Philadelphia. Men began to move away and to hide their treasures. Lincoln made an urgent plea for volunteers and re-enforcements, but the response was feeble. In desperation at the small number of volunteers he had decided to compel the reluctant to enlist, and a general draft had been ordered. Once again he was tampering with the old Anglo-Saxon spirit of Freedom, and this measure brought all the opposition to a head and threatened to reverse the main current on which he relied and bring about hatred to the cause of the slaves. In New York feeling was intense, and finally broke loose in a riot on July 13, 1863, in which the mob dominated the city for four days. Negroes were attacked and slaughtered with no regard to age or sex. The colored orphan asylum was sacked and all abolitionists were threatened with death. Property to the value of millions was destroyed and four hundred were killed. This but shows how imminent was the peril. All through the North were thousands ready to rise at a word and join with the Southern armies in destroying the Union.

It was the crisis. The great wave of hatred toward the

abolitionists and toward the administration, which now appeared as their supporters, had reached its climax. It had gathered up all the malcontents, such as McClellan and his henchmen, all who were weary of the war, and all those who, animated by that cantankerous element in the spirit of freedom, resented all exercise of authority and the dictatorship of the President in particular, and it was sweeping on to overwhelm him. Against it the new wave of enthusiasm, so long checked and halted by the disfavor of the administration out of respect for the feelings of the South, and now at last set free, was stirring the North with this new passion of unselfish devotion. It had been checked by cross currents and disasters, but Lincoln had faith that one success could give it sufficient impetus to sweep the country and carry him to triumph at the next election. On the other hand if Lee should defeat Meade it looked as if the Union cause would be lost forever. In this balance of the tides one wave of enthusiasm or despair would mean victory or ruin.

And then just at the critical moment, in the first days of July, 1863, Vicksburg fell, and Lee, after a desperate three days' battle, was hurled back at Gettysburg. We can hardly realize to-day the effect of those two victories. A burst of wild enthusiasm swept the country from end to end and carried all before it. All the feeling pent up through two long years of discouragement and disaster burst loose and carried even the doubters and pessimists along with it. Lincoln had chosen rightly and now had behind him an increasing wave of enthusiastic devotion which was fanned to a constant blaze by the abolitionists. The counter wave of opposition had gone so far that it burst forth in the New York riots as already noted, but when these were suppressed and the injustices of the draft corrected, it simmered down, and in a few months colored troops marching through the streets where negroes had been hounded and butchered, were cheered to the echo.

What the Knights of the Golden Circle might have done in the way of rousing Ohio and Indiana to co-operate with Morgan we do not know, but with Gettysburg behind them

the Unionists of those states, no longer fearing and doubting, rose and drove the marauder from their borders. There
were setbacks indeed, but from that time the cause of the
Union moved steadily forward.

3. EMOTIONAL REPERCUSSION

It is a well-known law of emotional dynamics that when
two antagonistic currents of feeling are once started, each
act of violence on one side raises the voltage of the other
and stimulates to acts of yet greater violence, so that by
continual retaliation an emotional charge of such power is
rolled up that neither reason nor justice can control it. Each
side becomes blind to the merits and just claims of the other,
and, in place of a group of fellow men, sees only a horde
of treacherous brutes and devouring monsters.

We come now to that period of the war when, by constant
retaliation, that terrible charge of bitterness gathered which
was to work ruin for many years. It began with the Emancipation Proclamation. Though helpful in consolidating the
North, it intensified the bitter feeling in the South tenfold.
Southerners claimed that it was an attempt to arouse their
slaves to insurrection and, in April, 1863, ninety-six Southern clergymen sent forth an appeal to the Christian world
in which they stated that Lincoln's act would make it absolutely necessary for the South to slaughter all their slaves.
The worst effect of the Emancipation Proclamation and the
enlisting of colored troops was that the South announced
that negroes and their white officers, if captured, would not
be treated as prisoners of war. They threatened to enslave
the negroes and to put their officers to death. To protect them
the Union government retaliated by refusing to exchange
Confederate prisoners, and by threatening to give them the
same treatment accorded to Union prisoners. This occasioned the most terrible suffering to thousands of Union
prisoners who might otherwise have been exchanged.

Violent feeling was aroused in the North by the treatment of Union prisoners at Andersonville, at Libby prison,
and on the island prison near Richmond. They died like

flies from ill treatment and lack of food. Some prison camps were placed in unsanitary spots and in the North it was generally supposed to be the deliberate policy of the authorities to kill off as many Union prisoners as possible.

We cannot attempt to describe the series of retaliations that followed. The ill treatment of prisoners was revenged by Sherman's sack and destruction of the beautiful city of Jackson in July, 1863, and that in turn by the burning of Lawrence a month later and the slaughter of one hundred and forty unarmed men by Southern guerillas.

To punish colored troops for serving against the South General Forrest massacred three hundred of them at Fort Pillow and shot their commanding officer, Major Bradford.

Feeling reached such a point that the Confederate President and Cabinet voted to execute ninety prisoners of Dalgren's command, taken in a daring raid near Richmond, and would have done so but for General Lee's interference. When the heads of a government contemplate butchering prisoners of war in cold blood, it shows how their normal judgment has been warped under emotional stress.

The war went on and the North seemed to meet defeat everywhere save when Grant was in command. He snatched victory from defeat at Chattanooga when he replaced Rosecrans. Among all the generals who had refused to advance when ordered, or when they did advance went to defeat, or when they won the battle had refused to go forward and pluck its fruits, they had found one general who pushed steadily forward and never turned back, who had never lost a battle, and had twice turned defeat into victory, and they decided to use him to the full and put the whole war into his hands. General Grant was summoned to Washington and given command of all the armies of the United States. He kept Meade in command of the army of the Potomac, but assumed charge of that army himself, as it was here that the war must be decided.

The history of that tragic advance on Richmond is familiar to all. The Confederacy was at its last gasp. Its numbers were diminishing and those of the Union increasing. At the close of 1863 the Confederate Congress had passed an act which declared every white man in the Confederacy between the ages of eighteen and fifty-five to be in military service and that upon failure to report for duty within a certain time, he was liable to the penalty of death as a deserter. This appalling act, which in tyranny surpassed anything in the modern civilized world, and was worthy of Sennacherib or Timur, was the last desperate effort of the Southern aristocracy to force every man into the war. Cut off as they were by the blockade, the Confederate armies were short of food, many were ragged, and clad in homespun; their shoes were worn out and many were barefoot. And yet for more than a year the genius and courage of Lee kept their morale strong and checked the advance of Grant at every turn. It was only over the bodies of thousands of his best men, in the Wilderness, at Cold Harbor, and before Petersburg, that Grant could push his dogged way through, on that line that he had chosen and that with characteristic psychology no disaster or delay could cause him to abandon. He would "fight it through on that line if it took all summer." Lincoln had a bulldog at last who would not turn back or relax his grip on the enemy until the bitter end.

4. The Spirit of Liberty and Loyalty

In the midst of the war with the South, Lincoln faced a battle in the North which was hardly of less importance. The time of election approached and it was to be seen whether the people would approve Lincoln's administration or cast him out. Here was the final test of his policies. In the turmoil of conflicting currents of feeling most men would have been dazed and bewildered and carried to destruction. Lincoln had shown amazing intuition in riding out the storm. He had thrown himself fearlessly into the current that seemed to him the strongest and trusted his fate and that of the country to its power. He had chosen which tides to fight, and he had known when not to fight and patiently to wait the turning of the tide. At first all had been confusion. A dozen conflicting streams of feeling sought to push him hither and yon. He had given his allegiance first to the old spirit of Liberty and Justice, then to the fair young spirit of the United Nation, then, when that was rent asunder he had turned back to the old Reformation spirit in alliance with Devotion to Liberty, and now he sought to unite with that old warrior spirit the frail wounded spirit of love for the Union, the two from whose marriage had sprung the American commonwealth. Against him were all those who believed in Slavery, who thought the South should go free and who were against the war, the spirit of the old Aristocracy, of discouragement and disunion.

Although by the Proclamation he had come out strongly against slavery at last, there was a rabid wing of the Abolitionists and Radicals who continued to attack him as a backboneless blunderer and compromiser. Nothing seems so to blind the intelligence as that extreme branch of the Reformation current which leads men to feel that they are divinely guided and therefore infallible; and perfectly obedient to conscience, and therefore flawless in virtue. Charles Sumner was one so shaped by this eccentric current of feeling, and so warped in intelligence that he and his following actually proposed to nominate in Lincoln's place Ben Butler, the "Beast" and "Hero of the Silver Spoon" as he had been named from his grafting and robbery while governor of New Orleans, and whom the Abolitionists regarded as a true patriot and real statesman.

To divert this movement Lincoln offered Butler the Vice-Presidency, which was contemptuously refused. When Butler made a fiasco of his attack on Richmond and put himself out of the running, the Radicals tried Chase, and a western group of Abolitionists actually nominated Frémont at a convention of their own. But they soon found that the great mass of the people, as they put it, "were taken in by Lincoln's apparent simplicity and good-naturedness and his vulgar jokes," and that they were determined to have him and no other. The scheming politicians and the fanatics had to fall into line, for at last the great current was beginning to sweep the country. Lincoln wished to do away with the idea that he was a sectional candidate representing merely the Republican party, or the North. Many Douglas Democrats supported him who were bitterly opposed to the Republicans. He wished to gather the full tide of feeling for the Union and for freedom, and he managed indirectly to bring about the nomination of a Democrat and a Southerner, Andrew Johnson of Tennessee, as Vice-President. Thus by the time of election he had behind him all who were for the Union and the extermination of slavery. It was then a question whether this united current of feeling would carry Lincoln to triumph and the war to a finish, or whether the old tide of discouragement and defeatism would overwhelm it. The terrible loss of the Wilderness Campaign had started a new wave of discouragement, and Southern sympathizers were doing their best to push it along. To-day it seems so impossible that Lincoln should have failed that we must turn to contemporary writers to catch the spirit of that time, and to understand how great was the danger that that great wave of discouragement and war weariness should be used by Southern plotters to sweep Lincoln from power and establish the Southern Confederacy. These agents in disguise were working to gain control of the Democratic party through Vallandigham, and in Canada, by pretending that they were authorized to conclude a Peace; they caught Horace Greeley in their snare and turned the New York *Tribune* against the President for a time. The immeasurable tact and patience of the President saved him from disaster.

When the Democrats met at Chicago in August, 1864, Lossing states that there were among them large numbers of a secret organization then plotting against the government. It was a military body with a membership of half a million, west of the Alleghanies, bound to a blind obedience and pledged to a general rising in Missouri, Ohio, Indiana and Kentucky in co-operation with a Southern army under

General Price, which was to invade their territory. Eight thousand Confederate prisoners, confined at Fort Douglas near Chicago, were to be liberated and armed during the sitting of the Convention. The Confederate prisoners at Indianapolis were to be released and together with the Knights of the Golden Circle, forming an army of a hundred thousand, were to fall upon Grant's rear. Vallandigham, who had ventured across the line from Canada, was there to direct them with a host of Confederate refugees and sympathizers, and incendiary speeches were the order of the day. Their plan was to force a peace which would recognize the independence of the Confederacy.

They overwhelmed the Conservative element at the Democratic Convention and drew up a platform stating that the war was a failure, and should be ended at once; that the government was guilty of revolutionary action and usurpation, and should be resisted. McClellan was nominated as President and Pendleton of Ohio, a bitter opponent of the war, as Vice-President.

With the terrible war still in progress, and news of the devastating losses at Cold Harbor and Petersburg coming in, all this was enough to shake the nerve of the strongest leader. And in the midst of all this the man in supreme authority at Washington received all these reports with unbroken good humor, and calmly went his way doing his best with his job, unflustered, refusing to be excited or to lose his faith in the people. He had done his best in putting his administration in line with the finest ideals of the age, and with the strongest convictions of his people. He trusted that great tide of devotion to liberty that had carried the country safely through so many crises. If the people turned from him and supported his enemies, there was nothing he could do about it.

It was a perilous time for the Lincoln administration and there were moments when he himself thought all was lost. Now was the time when he proved his wisdom in refusing to remove McClellan until that popular hero by his own acts had disgusted the public, and his foresight in committing himself to a cause that would waken the enthusiasm of all the devotees of freedom and humanity. The Republican bolters came in to him first, and Frémont withdrew from the Presidential race. The Commandant of Fort Douglas, Colonel Sweet, discovered the plot of the conspirators to release his prisoners, and took such measures to thwart them that the plotters decided to postpone their action.

General Price did, indeed, carry out his invasion, but General Rosecrans, then commanding in Missouri, through his spies, got wind of the plot to co-operate with him, and took such effectual measures to block it that after a raid through central Missouri, Price retreated with heavy losses.

Then came the election, and it was here that Lincoln's wisdom was thoroughly vindicated. The Democratic platform proved a political error. The people were discouraged, but to declare the war a failure annoyed them and was especially irritating to the army. This, and Sherman's success in Georgia, started a backwash against the Defeatists. Then their platform so favored the establishment of the Confederacy that it created the suspicion that the party was co-operating with traitors. The result was a great triumph for Lincoln. Only three states, New Jersey, Delaware and Kentucky, gave their votes to McClellan and the army voted against him three to one. One has only to look back to the election of 1863 when nearly all the leading states were against him, to realize the triumph of Lincoln's policy.

The election was a knockout blow for the Confederacy. But in spite of the knowledge that all was lost the war still went on. There was a large section as yet untouched by war in Carolina and Georgia whose spirit was still as defiant as in the days of Sumter. Here was the seat of the old aristocracy that had brought on the war and forced the unwilling people into it. So long as that spirit, so fundamentally antagonistic to democracy, remained, the war would go on. Sherman had been detached with his army to march through Carolina and Georgia, where the spirit of defiance was strongest, and to destroy the resources which they were sending to keep their armies in the field. Until Sherman marched to the Sea the people of Carolina and Georgia, who had been urging on the war, had little understanding of what it had meant to the people of Virginia, who had borne the brunt and seen their beautiful estates ravaged and destroyed in battle after battle. Sherman's march broke down that old aristocracy of the South and ended the war, but it also added a final touch to that repercussion of retaliation and roused a bitterness that it would take decades to overcome, as men saw their houses burned, their produce destroyed, their livestock seized. Sherman claimed that all unnecessary plunder was checked, and that the conflagrations were started by the Southerners themselves, but in such a march there must be many wrongs and unforgivable atrocities. After the Union army had seen the prison pens in Georgia in which Union prisoners had been confined, it was difficult to check them had Sherman wished to do so.

Lee surrendered to Grant in April, 1865, and Johnston to Sherman soon after, and the terrible war was over. It had set in motion waves of passionate feeling that it would take many years to quiet, after they had taken a full toll of human suffering and misery.

5. War Currents in Time of Peace

During every war the dynamo of propaganda is busy churning out prejudice, hatred, revenge, ferocity and that whole stream of violent emotions that we might term the war current. When the war is over this current still continues to rage, and causes that period of unrest and disaster that follows every prolonged conflict. When cannon cease firing and shells no longer tear men's bodies to pieces, their tongues continue to launch projectiles which tear reputations to shreds, and the poison gas of hatred and malice does more harm than chlorine. It was only by raising the war current to the maximum that Lincoln had overcome the wave of defeatism. Now, however, that his one desire was to restore the Union, the current that had carried him to victory became his most dangerous opponent. It was not to be turned off by any twist of the wrist.

As we have shown, he had turned in behind the war current that old-time Colonial Current with its devotion to Liberty, and its sense of Divine Direction, by supplying as a motive the deliverance of a downtrodden race. It is a characteristic of the Anglo-Saxon, whether he fights for liberty or for love of the battle, that when the fight is over, he likes to shake hands with his enemy and sit down and talk it all over. This was true of the great mass of the men who, under the drive of the old current, had fought to free the slaves. The war was won and the question was settled, for, in January, 1865, the Thirteenth Amendment, emancipating the slaves, was carried through Congress by a tremendous outburst of emotion in which men broke down and wept.

The soldiers and fighting men had had enough of war, and, for the most part, wanted to treat the Southerners as returned brothers. General Grant, though he had been termed "Unconditional Surrender Grant" had made most liberal terms of surrender. He treated Lee and his officers as comrades and permitted them to retain their side arms. When he learned that the cavalry horses belonged to the men and not to the Government, Grant permitted them to be kept to be used in the spring ploughing. He had done all he could to feed and care for Lee's starving army.

Sherman had made such liberal terms with Johnston that he was severely reprimanded by Stanton. The mass of people in the North, in whom the old Colonial spirit of justice and liberty was strong, were ready to take the South back. Also in the South there were large numbers who had been forced into the war, who were glad it was over, and who were eager to return to the Union.

There was, however, the remnant of the old aristocracy whom the continual retaliation of atrocities had raised to even greater antagonism to the North, and who were returning to the Union with bitterness in their hearts, because there was nothing else to be done. Even they, however, would probably have quieted down but for a matter which roused a new current which was destined to leave violent and disastrous effects on American life.

When two races of markedly different characteristics and

traditions come in contact, human nature is so constituted that a feeling of antagonism is aroused. While a few individuals of such a race may merely awake curiosity and interest, the contact of masses almost inevitably creates an antipathy, based not merely on differences in manners and morals, but upon the innate fear that any group has of strange elements, and the dread that its own traditions will be modified or overcome.

So long as the negro was regarded as a slave, and a sort of superior animal, the Southerners were fond of him as of a pet dog or horse, and this emotional reaction did not take place. But as a free man and possible fellow citizen he awakened the bitterest antagonism, for thus he formed an alien group which was obnoxious socially and threatening from a political standpoint. Thus the war generated a powerful stream of racial antagonism between the Southerners and the negro. If the Southerners themselves had freed the negro the feeling would not have been so strong, but the fact that the North had forced the negro upon them as an equal, increased both the antagonism to the negro and their hatred of the North. Thus in the South, the spirit of the old aristocracy was strong against democracy, and, re-enforced by racial antagonism and war bitterness, created a strong head wind against any progress toward Union.

Even this, however, might have been overcome by tactful handling, but for two currents in the North which served to maintain and accentuate the virulence of the war spirit. There was still in the North that group of men with Sumner at their head who had behind them the dangerous dynamic of the Reformation, which gave them the sense that they were inspired of God and driven by conscience, and who had brought on the war by their bitter attacks on the slaveholders. They had always opposed Lincoln as weakly sympathetic with the South and tolerant of its wickedness. Not being in contact with the negro there was no antipathetic reaction. They sided with the negro in the race conflict, were agitated by his wrongs, and in revenge for his former sufferings they wished to give him the suffrage and social rights which would enable him to dominate his former masters. They had worked themselves up to a point where they felt themselves directed of the Lord to take vengeance on the South for its wickedness, and demanded that all the leaders should be executed as traitors. They claimed that by secession the Southern states had committed suicide and no longer existed as states.

In addition that old current of the lower emotions and desires that we called the Political current, sprang to life again, this time in the Republican party, and a large group of politicians and office-holders, swept by this tide of greed and ambition and party loyalty, were determined to keep their party in power and either to prevent the South from voting, or to allow them suffrage only on conditions that would give them into the control of Republicans, which meant the negroes. They insisted that the Southern states, as conquered provinces, should be put under military rule until a republican government should be set up.

It was these two currents which incarnated the old War Spirit and raised it to new extremes of hate and bitterness. Thaddeus Stevens, whose hand controlled the Political current, has been termed the Apostle of Hate. Handicapped by his club foot, he had fought his way up from poverty and ignorance, lashing and excoriating all who stood in his way by vitriolic invective and stinging wit. He could drive wavering Congressmen by the lash of his tongue to vote as he commanded. Although he had a colored mistress, at heart he cared little for the negro race, but he became their most ardent advocate as a means of securing political control of the South. He was frankly unscrupulous in the means he used, and sneered at the protests of law and justice.

It was a strange league that brought together Charles Sumner, the fanatical idealist, who considered himself the instrument of God to punish the South and to give the downtrodden negro his rights over his former masters, and Thaddeus Stevens, the unscrupulous politician, who stood for the rights of the negro and the flagellation of the South, not from any ideal motive, but to gain power for himself and his party.

Lincoln and the mass of the people then stood between this Scylla and Charybdis, two monsters spouting venom, the old aristocracy in the South, and in the North this duplex current of Divinely sanctioned ferocity and political unscrupulousness. Perhaps he alone among men had power to charm them—to take from them their sting, and to fuse this warring tumult in one great current of patriotism. His hope was to waken again that tide of devotion to the American Commonwealth, of pride in the great nation of self-governing free men, of determination to work side by side forgetting all personal grievances for the realization of a glorious future. In his eyes the war had been fought to prove that the Union could not be broken and that no state could secede, and he now was planning to treat the states as if they had never seceded. Already in 1863 he had issued a proclamation of amnesty and restoration of property and citizenship to all who would take the oath to support the Constitution and to accept the emancipation of the slaves, excepting only a few more heinous offenders.

Tennessee had already been recognized as restored to statehood, in accordance with his plan of reorganization, which allowed those negroes who could read and write, to vote, as well as all those who took the oath to support the Constitution with its last Amendment.

He planned that all the other Southern states should be received in the same manner. Here he ran foul of the opposition current. Sumner and Stevens were determined that no Southern state should be admitted until all "traitors" were punished and all negroes enfranchised. Lincoln knew the temper of the South and that such action would raise the current of bitter feeling there to such a pitch that any real union would be impossible. So virulent was the current of fanaticism in the North that Sumner denounced the Thirteenth Amendment because it did not include Suffrage for the negro, and so great was his assurance that he alone understood God's will that although Lincoln was his personal friend he proposed to impeach him because he would not accept Sumner's plan. And Stevens asserted that no Southern state should be recognized until the Constitution had been so amended "as to secure perpetual ascendency to the party of the Union."

To master such currents as these, one driven by greed and ambition, the other by the hallucination of a Divine Mission, requires infinite tact and patience. Direct opposition only increases the tension. It can only be done by one who has the power to exorcise and transform the antagonism of his opponents. We are familiar with the stories of Lincoln's cabinet meetings, when, aware of such high emotional tension that no sane decision could be reached, he would insist on reading some humorous tale until the tension was released and the antagonism dissipated. His dealings with Sumner at this period illustrate his marvellous tact.

Lincoln has so inspired the nation with the spirit that he sought at this time to evoke, that every schoolboy can repeat his words and every generation is thrilled anew by their spirit. Never has that great tide of feeling that we may call the American spirit, drawn in part from the ancient devotees of liberty and in part from the spirit of patriotism and of loyalty to the Union, found more perfect expression than in those golden words of the Gettysburg address and of the second inaugural, which are now inscribed on the walls of the marble shrine from which his form still looks toward the great dome beneath which he saw so fierce a battle rage to make his words come true. They were not then written in the hearts of the people as they are to-day, and his opponents could sneer at the Gettysburg address as a failure, but little by little he was succeeding in making his ideals felt a little more widely.

It seemed as if he must carry the nation with him on that great tide, when, suddenly, in the very midst of the jubilation over the surrender of the Confederate armies, the assassin's bullet struck him down.

The forces of hate sought to profit by his death to start

a wave of fury against the South, and accused the Southern leaders of responsibility for his assassination. For the moment they swept the North with unreasoning passion. It was then that all depended upon the man who stepped into his place.

The judgment of history, now that the excitement has calmed down, is that Andrew Johnson was a truly great and heroic man who stood inexorably for the right as he saw it. He made Jackson his hero, and was borne on that great current of devotion to freedom and democracy as modified by Jefferson and Jackson. Starting in poverty and ignorance as a tailor's apprentice, unable to write until taught by his wife, he had fought his way up by sheer pluck and native ability against tremendous odds and the scorn of the Southern aristocracy. He thus became a veritable dynamo for that current of feeling that opposed the advancing tide of hatred for the Union generated by the aristocracy. In Tennessee, fearless and often alone, he had faced infuriated crowds to defend the government and it was largely due to his efforts that Tennessee finally reentered the Union. He was a man of the Jackson type, pugnacious, irascible, self-assertive, and immovable in his loyalty to duty as he understood it. The situation then demanded just such a man, and his heroism as Governor of Tennessee won the enthusiastic plaudits of all Northerners. He was bitter against the Southern aristocracy, and apparently felt that they should receive the severest punishment for starting the war. On becoming President he said, "The American people must be taught to know that treason is a crime. It must not be excused as unsuccessful rebellion, to be overlooked or forgiven." Sumner and Stevens, therefore, rejoiced that they had a leader who would assist them to sweep away Lincoln's policies in the current of hate.

But he was truly devoted to Lincoln and evidently came to feel that his first duty was to the great departed leader, for on May 29 he endorsed Lincoln's policy by issuing a proclamation of amnesty similar to Lincoln's save that the old democratic current showed itself in his exclusion of all those whose taxable property exceeded $20,000, as a punishment to the aristocracy. His plan for admitting the states was the same save that he excluded all negroes from the preliminary vote. During the recess of Congress he carried out his scheme and by autumn all the former Confederate states had set up a new government and elected delegates to Congress and eleven of them had accepted the Thirteenth Amendment. It looked as if the Union were re-established as Lincoln had hoped.

But it had all been done in the grand Jacksonian manner, ignoring Congress and the protests of opponents. A man must be an emotional dynamo of the first order to act the dictator in a democracy, and it is doubtful if even Jackson himself could have succeeded at this period. The situation required the infinite tact of a Lincoln, not the dogmatic authority of a Jackson, and the very qualities that had won Johnson success in Tennessee now proved his undoing. The Political current was running strong in Congress, and in New England the abolition tide with its dynamic of conscience was dangerously potent. Neither greed nor conscience can be disposed of by ignoring or by suppressing them. It required humor rather than authority, humility rather than pride, and above all that wonderful power of transmuting emotion of which Lincoln alone seemed to have the key. With the convening of Congress the flood gates were opened and both currents came down upon the President with sound and fury. At first there was some pretense of standing by him, but as his stand became more uncompromising the attacks increased in virulence. At his inauguration as Vice-President, Johnson had made an unfortunate speech under the influence of liquor given him to enable him to resist an attack of illness and go through with the ceremony. This was just what would raise the old religious current to highest voltage against him, and Sumner undertook to turn that current to his assistance by stimulating prejudice and calling him a disgraceful drunkard. Stevens in the House quoted a passage from *The World* describing him as "an insolent drunken brute in comparison with whom even Caligula's horse was respectable." One cannot read without shame and disgust the epithets and insults that were hurled at the chief magistrate of a great nation in this tide of fury. Brownlow of Tennessee sent his salutations "to the dead dog in the White House."

It was not surprising that Johnson, in spite of his hatred of the aristocrats, should have been thrown into further sympathy with the South, as he tried to shield them from the vengeance of the same vindictive spirit that was attacking himself.

6. THE TRIUMPH OF HATE

In the meantime the helpless negroes, over whom this deadly battle was in progress, were in tragic condition. Thousands of them, freed from restraint, and thinking that the Day of Jubilee had come, started for the Promised Land, expecting that their hard toil was over and that they were to receive homes and lands and food and to live at ease in peace and plenty. Many thousands gathered at Old Point Comfort, and soon were in such a desperate state of starvation and want that something had to be done, and done quickly. At first, the army under the direction of General Butler attempted to handle the situation. Then the famous Freedmen's Bureau was created, with powers extraordinary and almost unlimited, to handle the situation and to do whatever they thought best for the negro. Hundreds of Northerners volunteered and at first handled the difficult situation with sympathy and understanding.

The newly organized Southern States found themselves overwhelmed with negro vagrants, who refused to work, and, in idleness and want, got into mischief of all kinds. Theft and assault became common and the whole social life was threatened. They were mere children and without a firm hand to direct them naturally fell into trouble of all kinds. The Southern states promptly took measures to remedy the trouble. They passed vigorous vagrant laws which compelled the idle to go to work under prescribed contracts. Minors were put under masters by laws of apprenticeship and all negroes were forbidden to be in the streets after the ringing of the curfew at nine P.M.

These vagrant laws did not differ materially from those of many Northern states, but while the North had merely a few scattered tramps to deal with, the South had a whole race of some millions on their hands, and the application of the law naturally caused great excitement.

The Northern enthusiasts, who were too deeply stirred by emotion to give the matter careful investigation, insisted that these laws were merely a dodge by which the South was re-enslaving the negro, and a new wave of indignation burst forth. The Freedmen's Bureau with its paternalistic powers interfered with the operation of these laws and matters were soon in a chaotic state again, and violent feelings were generated on both sides.

Here was a race of some millions, accustomed for centuries to arbitrary control, ignorant and utterly untrained in democratic government, suddenly turned loose on the public, and on one side of them a group of fanatical idealists, insisting that as the "Ebon image of God," the negro must be given social privileges and political rights that would make him the master of his former masters; and, on the other hand was the old aristocracy, aware of the utter futility of giving the vote to the negro and horrified at the danger to themselves and their institutions, protesting furiously against such attempts and seeking to re-establish some control over the vagrants. And between them was the President, receiving curses from both sides, that he did not with one word give the vote to them all, and on the other hand that he had attempted to fit them for equality with the white man. The Mississippians turned on him in wrath because he suggested that they should admit the negroes who could read and write to suffrage, and the turbulent currents in Congress hurled their fury upon him because he supported the laws by which the South sought to protect herself from the tyrannical interference of the Freedmen's Bureau. Finally, in April, 1866, the Abolitionists and the Politicians persuaded Congress that the South was trying to re-establish slavery and passed the Fourteenth Amendment over the President's veto, assuring equal civil rights to the negroes and declaring that no state should be readmitted without assent to this Amendment. Here the South made her great mistake. The Amendment still left it to the states to decide whether they would have negro suffrage or not, and most important matters were still in their hands. The current of hate was not yet strong enough to blind the intelligence of Congress, and if the Southern states had accepted the Fourteenth Amendment all might have gone well, but they counted on the President's support and under stimulus of the Southern aristocratic current they rejected it. Nothing could have helped more the effort of Sumner and Stevens to sweep the North into this current of hate. This was demonstration that the South intended to re-enslave the negro, they claimed, and thus they gathered up much of the old liberty-loving current that hitherto had kept apart.

The President had been carried into power by the old war current, but it was now running in direct opposition to all that he undertook. It was evident that he must get some other emotional drive behind him or fail. He decided to try to evoke once more that fair spirit of love for the Union that had gained beauty and form from the words of Webster and Lincoln.

A National Union party was formed and a convention called. But no sooner had the spirit begun to appear than the old Anti-war Democrats, with Vallandigham at their head, sought to hide beneath her robes, and former traitors clothed themselves in her garments.

This gave the Radical politicians the opportunity to accuse the President of leaguing himself with the enemies of liberty and traitorously conspiring against the North, and the great Northern current was gradually deflected into the current of hate. Just then the terrible insurrection in New Orleans, resulting in the slaughter of many negroes, added fuel to the flame, and although it was due to the plots of his enemies, the President was held responsible. He then determined to appeal to the people and made a tour through the chief cities. But his enemies were ahead of him and everywhere crowds of roughs were provided to interrupt and insult him. He was like some old lion baited by yapping terriors. At last stung beyond endurance by their shouts of "Traitor," "Judas" and "Drunkard," he burst forth in a personal attack on his enemies in Congress.

Perhaps no one but Lincoln would have stood such an assault better than Johnson, but his answer was a fatal move. It was misinterpreted and misreported by his enemies and served to set the whole country aflame. Once more a small group, stirred by violent emotion, had swept the masses of the people into their current.

The elections in 1866 went strongly against Johnson's party, and the House was so filled with Radicals that his veto could be easily overridden. Worst of all his enemies had even secured his cabinet, and Stanton, still Secretary of War, was working treacherously against him.

The current of hate then carried everything before it. A military Reconstruction Bill was passed over the President's veto, which put the whole South under bayonet rule. When the President, at last aware of Stanton's treachery, attempted to remove him, Congress passed a bill forbidding him to remove any officer without the consent of the Senate. But Johnson was essentially a fighter, and what he might have done earlier with a little tact, he now attempted when it was certain to bring disaster; although the election in 1867 proved that there was a reaction in his favor. He removed Stanton and laid himself open to the attacks of his enemies. He was promptly impeached for treason to the laws and Constitution.

During the trial the current of hate reached its maximum of fury. The most disgraceful insults were hurled at him, the most shameful accusations were made, and it was only by one vote in the Senate that he was acquitted.

The powers of hate had triumphed. The old war current of vengeance, pushed along by the politicians and kept at high voltage by the fanatical conscience of the Abolitionists, swept the whole North, and by their orders the South was crushed under the 'heel of the negro and the carpet-bagger. The old aristocracy were shut out from the vote, and the Constitutions of the Southern states were drawn up by negroes and those Northern adventurers who lived by exploiting the negro. When strong feeling is suppressed beyond a certain point it is bound to break loose in some fashion, and the old Southern spirit was being goaded beyond endurance. Their former slaves were encouraged to treat their masters with insolence, they saw their whole social order being wrecked by ruthless scalawags. They could do nothing through the channels of government, for they were shut off.

In the election of 1868 the old war current, revived and sweeping the North, was re-enforced by the vote of the negroes in the South, and the war hero, General Grant, who had gone over to the Radical side, was carried into the Presidency by 214 electoral votes against 80.

But there were indications of a backwash in the current. Grant failed to carry New York and New Jersey, and many Northern states showed a reaction against the negro.

7. The Southern Spirit Arms Again

Before Grant could be inaugurated, in February, 1869, Congress rushed through a Fifteenth Amendment to sanction beyond the possibility of interference the right of the negro to vote. Enthusiasm for control by the negro did not reign through all the North, for New Jersey, Delaware, California and Oregon rejected it, as well as Kentucky and Maryland. Virginia, Georgia, Mississippi and Texas had not yet been reconstituted, and their acceptance of this amendment was made a condition of their readmission as states. It was a cruel bargain that forced them to submit to the permanent domination of the negro before they could re-enter the Union.

It is tragic to contemplate the haughty states that had flaunted their defiance in the face of the Union a few short years before, now decimated by war, their beautiful estates laid waste, many of their cities burned and destroyed, their aristocracy robbed of its wealth and resources, their government in the hands of Northern adventurers and ignorant negroes, their men and women of education and refinement subject to insult from their former slaves and under the domination of unscrupulous politicians. The flame of vengeance still burned in the North, fanned by politicians who were determined to keep the vote of the Southern states, and this prevented any fair discussion or clear understanding of the situation and of the disaster that Military Reconstruction had worked. Robbed and plundered as they were and sunk in poverty, with their country wrecked about them, the old spirit of the men of the South was yet unbroken. Since there were no legal means of righting their wrongs and protecting their women from insult, as strong men of their type have always done, in the lack of just laws, they made and enforced their own laws. Taking advantage of the prank of some youths in Tennessee who had formed a secret society known as the Kuklos, and who delighted to throw the negroes into panic by their hideous disguise, the strong men of the South organized themselves as the Ku Klux Klan and created the "Invisible Empire of the South." Its object was "to protect their people from indignities and wrongs, to succor the suffering, to enforce the real laws, to defend the Constitution of the United States and to protect the people from unlawful seizures."

Here at last was an instrument through which the bitter resentment of the South could find expression. By terror they could control the growing insolence of the negro. The corrupt politicians and carpet-baggers could be checked in their plundering and extortion, by floggings and house burnings. If they proved obdurate they could be shot, and no one could trace the masked riders who disappeared in the darkness of the night. If this were all, our sympathy might be with these night riders. But unfortunately there were many fine men and unselfish women who had left their homes in the North to teach the ignorant negroes and attempt to fit them for the new privileges and responsibilities that developed upon them. The feeling of the South toward all those who tried to lift the negro to a higher position was bitter beyond words, and their vengeance fell upon these Northerners also.

The current of hate had aroused its inevitable reaction at last. Instead of treating the Southerners as lost brothers returned, as Lincoln proposed, they had been crushed as conquered enemies. The current of bitterness toward the North had been strong enough before, and instead of disarming it the North had raised it to higher potential, until it broke through the barrier of the law. The resentment of the South against the injustice of the Federal laws resulted in breaking up the respect for the law, that emotion which lies at the basis of all civilization, and there was a return to the primitive methods of personal vengeance. All this, of course, increased the violent antagonism of the North instead of creating sympathy.

Once more the Northern and Southern currents met in a clash more bitter than in time of war. Reports of house burnings and of men tarred and feathered and of the general lawless condition reached the North. Congress soon grasped the idea that the Ku Klux intended so to terrorize the negroes in the coming election that not one of them would dare go near the polls. This would mean a loss of Republican control in the House, and that they were determined to prevent. Instead of setting on foot a fair investigation of the grievances of the South and of its sufferings, they passed most stringent measures to break up the Ku Klux and put the whole matter into the hands of President Grant with extraordinary powers, even to suspending the writ of Habeas Corpus, to enforce it. After a warning to which no attention was paid, general arrests were made of leading citizens who were suspected of belonging to the Ku Klux, and machinery was provided to secure immediate conviction, so that in a short time the whole Invisible Empire was broken up.

The Spirit of the North at first so largely drawn from

the old current of devotion to liberty and justice, had been warped and twisted from its course, until it became an instrument of tyranny and injustice. The old Anglo-Saxon tide was reversed.

It would be interesting to know what would have happened if the whole situation could have been treated psychologically instead of politically. Here were two vast opposing tides of feeling, generated gradually through the events of a century, that had met at last in a clash of conflict, rousing such waves of fury and prejudice that clear thought was swept away in the passionate desire of each side to punish the other. In that welter of feeling each side distrusted the other, and considered every move of the opposition an attempt to injure or destroy them. The physical conflict had ceased, but the storm of feeling that drove the two tides into furious conflict still raged. Anything done by either side only served to increase the mutual suspicion and rage. What was needed was some Æolus to capture the winds by his kindly fatherhood and bottle them up safely in bags, before any ships were launched on that angry sea. And the country had such an Æolus whose soothing hand could have captured these wildly raging winds and made use of them to drive on the Ship of State. But alas, he was set aside, and his foolish followers proceeded to untie and unloose upon the troubled sea such winds as he had succeeded in confining. Instead of quieting the storm every act seemed designed to increase it.

By ceaseless agitation Sumner forced through a bill which compelled the Southerner to permit the negro to sit beside him in hotels, cars, restaurants, schools and juries. This was passed in 1875 after Sumner's death. Nothing, of course, could have been better calculated to prevent what Sumner wished to achieve. There are times when even wisdom and justice are futile and what is needed is some appeal that disarms emotion. This is the principle of turning the other cheek, which is both unwise and unjust, but has the merit of disarming violent feeling, and of discharging high emotional voltage with the least possible damage. It

allows the bottled-up feeling to express itself to its full
satisfaction and thus dissipate itself. When we once recognize the importance of the emotional situation in any problem, our laws and political methods may be entirely reconstructed. If men can be brought into the right emotional
attitude, they will solve most difficulties of themselves, but
we persist in forcing wise plans upon them in a fashion that
rouses antagonism, instead of devising some means to
awaken the emotions that are needed and to disarm those
that impede. It is surprising to find that of all of our statesmen Lincoln seems to be the only one who mastered this
art. He was continually being called weak, cowardly, and
undignified, but in almost every case it will be found that
the unusual act or word which occasioned criticism was a
device to disarm or awaken emotion. Whether he could
have succeeded with the tremendous emotions unleashed by
the war may be open to doubt, but the words he has left us
make us feel that if any man could have succeeded, he was
the man.

It was his place, as we have shown, to evoke again the
Spirit of Devotion to the Union to charm away the War
Spirit, but we have shown how the two groups of irreconcilables in the North, in a combined current of greed and
fanatical conscientiousness, crushed the National Spirit and
swept the whole North back in the tide of hate, thus driving the whole of the White South into the bitter current of
the Southern Extremists and into racial war with the negro.
They all resented this government of negroes and carpet-
baggers who plundered and blundered with equal success,
and when they found they could not secure justice by legal
means nor yet by force, they turned to craft. They devised
means of avoiding the laws by deceptions of all kinds and at
length gained sufficient control to administer the government in such fashion that prosperity began to return.

When Grant was re-elected in 1872, it was only by the
armed support of Federal troops that Florida, South Carolina and Louisiana were kept in the Republican column.
Rival claims were put in by the Democrats and suppressed

by force. The dissatisfaction resulted in a violent riot in Louisiana in 1874 which was suppressed by the Federal army.

But little by little the bitterness of the North was dying out. It is an interesting law of emotional dynamics that when feeling has expressed itself in violent action against an opponent there is usually a reaction to friendly feeling. Thus it happened that, although the feeling of the South was constantly raised in potential by repression, the feeling of the North, as they learned of the disaster wrought by the plan of "Thorough" became more friendly. Once more the old National feeling began to awake a sympathy with the South as suffering brothers, and disgust with the legislation which had wrought such havoc.

CHAPTER VII

THE RULE OF THE ENCHANTRESS

1. The Dominance of the Political Current

WE now come to a new act in the American Drama when the old actors, whose contests had held the front of the stage, seemed to sleep, while others slipped into their places and even stole their garments. The Political Spirit which had been an insignificant follower in the train of the Great Spirit of Liberty of the North, managed to slip into his garments and rule in his place, and made way for the return of the Great Enchantress, the Spirit of Commerce who always reappears when the High Gods drowse.

We have shown that the Political Current, through its strange junction with that stream of fanatical Idealism sponsored by Sumner, had carried the country into opposition to the President's policies and filled Congress with its adherents, both from the North and from the reorganized South, so that it completely dominated the Nation. The new tide of National feeling threatened their rule, and they began to arm themselves against it. In the beginning they had been but a small group in the Republican party, which party had been the body in which the old Spirit of Liberty and Justice had clothed itself. The party had been animated by strong feelings and stabilized by firm Convictions, and in the war had come to be the expression of the Spirit of the North. But this small group had succeeded in gaining possession of the party and twisting it to suit their will, until it became the instrument of injustice and cruelty. In like manner the Democratic party had become the vehicle through which the feelings of the South found expression. We have noted how in times of emotional stress certain objects or words or groups acquire a high emotional charge and even the mention of them stirs violent feeling. Something of this sort happened with the two parties. To those in the South the mere word "Republican" was anathema. It stood for all they detested most, and never failed to rouse violent feeling. In the North, on the other hand, in certain circles, instead of merely signifying a group who voted a certain ticket, it became a sacred symbol, commanding the same loyalty and devotion that was rendered a king or a god. A man who forsook the Republican party was a renegade and a traitor. A "dyed in the wool" Republican felt that his party contained all the virtue and intelligence in the country and was bound to it by feelings so intense that no argument or logical proof could have turned him from it.

This emotional charge survived when the great issues of the war were past, and the great "Cause" which had aroused so much feeling had ceased to be an issue. It was by this surviving emotional charge that the politicians found the means to hold their grasp on the people. The soul of the party had died, the old feelings and convictions were defunct, but astute politicians kept the body on its old throne, waving its arms and legs and going through the old motions, in order to retain the reverence and loyalty of the people who were not yet aware that they were lavishing their devotion upon a corpse, whose decay would only too soon become evident to their nostrils. The party once animated by the old Heroic Spirit was now a mere shell, still decked in the old panoply, but operated craftily by the Political Current to secure power and privilege and wealth for a certain group. The body through which the patriotic soul of the people had expressed itself in action was transformed into a framework where the political spiders spun their web to ensnare the whole nation. Greed and not glory was their appeal. When the creative emotions die the body can still be kept in motion by the appeal to greed. We must consider this strange Frankenstein monster that for so long dominated the people.

The Political Current had been strong enough in Jackson's time, but now it was far greater, for the party in power now had in its hands the appointment of some half million officials. Many of these, in turn, had authority to engage workmen to carry out various public works, so that in this way it was possible to reward a much larger proportion of the men who had voted the party ticket than in Jackson's day. The President became a vast plum distributor. As soon as he was elected he was beset by swarms of office seekers whose determined onset to secure some prize or booty knew neither courtesy nor reason, and was more akin to the squabbling of a pack of wolves over an unfortunate traveller. Each President, after being nearly torn in pieces by them, left his record of disgust at human nature in general, and the system in particular, but still it went on.

Moreover, although the President appointed, each senator had come to demand the right to control the lucrative patronage in his section. By means of the wealth they controlled, and the number of workmen and clerks they could appoint, such powerful officials as the Customs Collector in New York could almost control the vote in his section. Both parties now had their fully organized "machines" or party organizations in each state and large city, whose "boss" determined how the patronage should be distributed, who rewarded every man for his obedient vote, and disciplined every disobedient adherent by putting him on the black list where he could get no office or position. The mass of the people, though they were well catalogued, were ignorant how they were being manipulated, so that their votes merely served to provide jobs for greedy office seekers. The body politic was a helpless host on which battened this army of officials. The people were still stirred by the passionate eloquence of the boss, who appealed to their loyalty to the old flag and the "great cause" and kept alive their devotion to the Grand Old Party, while laughing in his sleeve at the gullibility of the public.

It is one of the extraordinary facts of emotional mechanics that a word or a cause that once had power to stir men to the highest pitch of feeling because of its tremendous significance and the vast issues that hung upon it, still retains its emotional power when its meaning is gone and the issues that originally awakened emotion have long been settled. It was this fact that the politicians understood and of which they made use with an amazing skill.

Thus began the great period in American history when the emotions and attitudes of the public were calculated and manipulated by a small group of men under the drive of the Political Current, and a few financiers and industrial magnates who understood the situation could deflect the current to secure wealth and power for themselves, leaving the public happy in the conviction that they were supporting their old ideals and loyal to their great leaders, and utterly unaware that they were becoming mere puppets in the hands of big business.

2. THE ENCHANTRESS CASTS HER SPELL

Twice before, when the old Heroic Spirit of Liberty had brought a war to its finish and laid his armor aside, the old Enchantress, the Spirit of Gain, had sought to bind him in her toils. And now again, as he lapsed into somnolence, she laid her spells upon him. From a shy and crafty adventuress who feared to show her face openly, she soon became a blustering termagant, who dominated the nation by her threats. She conquered and mastered those men of the stalwart fighting type, who, hitherto in the world's history, inspired by the warlike spirit, had been the great conquerors and tyrants, and who now, incarnating this commercial spirit, became a force hitherto unknown in the world. The conquest of the Nation by this new force is a drama so remarkable in itself that we must stop to call attention to it.

The war had prepared the way. As is usual, it was a great stimulus to industry. Not only iron and steel and munitions, but the textiles too, were working full blast to supply the army. The daughters of farmers and even of professional men went into the mills to work, and the famous Lowell lectures were inaugurated to supply the intellectual needs of New England factory hands. As the factories multiplied thousands were drawn from across the sea to supply labor. The great danger from immigration is that it threatens to destroy the emotional solidarity of a nation. But these came at first from the Northern countries of Europe—England, Scotland, Scandinavia, Germany and Holland, and amalgamated readily with the American people. Educated in American schools and trained to reverence American heroes and traditions, the second generation was hardly distinguishable from the old stock, and responded to the same emotional stimuli.

Farming was never over-profitable in New England, and industrialization progressed rapidly, spreading through the Middle West to the Mississippi, until the whole Northeast was as predominantly industrial as was England or Germany. Starting from private mills and enterprises, there began that amazing process of consolidation in which American genius has been so peculiarly made manifest. It was here that the commercial current gained its hold on the strong men of the nation, and the captain of industry appeared on the scene—a man of great organizing ability and vision, of inexhaustible energy and ruthless determination, who combined the small local enterprises into vast trusts with thousands of employees and millions of capital. It was through him that the Commercial Spirit set its stamp upon the national life and completely transformed it from the old independent individualistic life, to the co-operative standardized life of to-day, whose emotional characteristics are quite different as we shall show later on. With him as its instrument the Commercial Spirit, that in the old time Jew had been shy and crafty and sly, became as bold and ruthless as the Spirit of War. The small and weak were bought out or crushed mercilessly until each industry was controlled by one huge organization.

To-day every one is familiar with the story of the amazing growth of Standard Oil under John D. Rockefeller, when the "smaller buds were lopped off to secure one rose of supreme beauty on the stem." U. S. Steel under Andrew Carnegie had a growth as phenomenal as did the automobile industry under Henry Ford or the General Motors, and the

packers under Armour and Swift. Under such men the old
Spirit wrought miracles astounding to the old world. Carnegie put it among the wonders of the world that "two
pounds of iron stone mined on Lake Superior, transported
nine hundred miles to Pittsburgh; one pound and a half of
coal, mined and manufactured into coke, and transported
to Pittsburgh; one-half pound of lime mined and transported to Pittsburgh; a small amount of manganese, mined
in Virginia and transported to Pittsburgh—that these four
pounds of materials could be manufactured into one pound
of steel for which the consumer pays one cent!" No vaunted
miracle of ancient days was greater. Englishmen came to
America to see two things—the falls of Niagara and the
packing houses at Chicago, and to study how the latter made
use of every possible element except the odors, so that the
profits actually came from that which had been counted
refuse.

No Timur or Genghis Khan ever marched to greater
victories than did the army of the great Enchantress, now
robed in armor, and leading to battle these modern giants,
who were as determined, as heroic, as resourceful and as
ruthless as the great Mongol. Starting in poverty with some
petty clerkship, the story of the battle of each of these with
Want and Fate and Circumstance, is an epic. Gaining
wealth at first by hard-earned pennies, and power by desperate struggle, they fought their way to supremacy, bringing man after man to obedience, adding new cohorts to their
army day by day, until they became invincible. The magic
touch of the Great Enchantress transformed the world.
Industry grew as a mango tree under the hand of an
Indian juggler. In 1860 about one billion dollars was invested in manufacturing, and a million and a half were
earning their wages in industry. In less than fifty years
the capital invested had increased to twelve billions and the
workers to five and a half million. During this time the
value of manufactured products increased more than fifteen
fold. National power is measured by some in terms of iron
and steel. The American output increased in twenty years

from an insignificant amount to a third of the world's supply, surpassing France and England. As Carnegie said:
"The iron crown had been placed on the brow of Pennsylvania." Within twenty-five years from the close of the war,
America had become the leading manufacturing nation of
the world. The little sawmills by the rivers were replaced by
gigantic power plants; by a process of consolidation the
local plants were gathered up into huge organizations and
each staple was in the hands of some great trust that controlled its production, one of them, at least, reaching a
capitalization of a billion dollars.

3. The Armies of Capitalism

The Captain of Industry commanded but one cohort of
the army of the great Enchantress. Another division paved
for her a path of steel, harnessed the flaming fire to her
chariots and drove them in conquering phalanx across the
Continent, and united the nation under her dominion.
Transportation is important to prosperity. It is almost
equally important to the emotional solidarity of a nation. In
1850 California was as remote from New York in its emotional attitude as Australia. The steel roads reared by these
men of iron made possible the solidarity of the nation. It
had taken an heroic mind and indomitable leadership and
resourcefulness, combined with no little ruthlessness, to enable Drake to drive a furrow through the uncharted seas to
face the Spaniard in his lair and open a path for English
trade throughout the world. The same qualities appeared in
the men who made the paths of iron across the trackless
wastes on the Continent. Vanderbilt, Gould, Harriman,
Hill, their names are familiar to all. Like the leaders of
industry, they pushed their way up from small beginnings.
Like Drake they drove forward to their purpose with indomitable will, like him they crushed those who stood in
their way and gathered such loot as the gods put in their
path.

No character appeals more than that of the early pioneer who pushed his way with his Lares and Penates stowed

in the covered wagon hauled by stout oxen, over the vast plains where skulking bands of Indians waited the chance to strike, on till the snowy Rockies loomed before them, on still, driven by the consuming passion to see beyond the next range, into the land of mystery beyond, always with some new range ahead, tempting them onward. On still into the blazing desert with its horror of desolation, its waterless Valley of Death, on often without food, sometimes half mad with thirst, on till the pleasant valley is found at last where they can found a home beside the rippling streams.

Thus were the first homes of America founded. But as the roads of steel stretched out across the prairie, towns sprang up wherever these modern magicians drove in a stake, settlers gathered—the court-house, church and school soon were built, and new communities arose springing from the soil, armed not with the spear like Jason's men, but with the plough and ax and spade, and all this new un-known realm was connected up with the activities and emo-tions of the Eastern Coast. Such roads were of incalculable value to the nation and at first the government offered great prizes to induce men to undertake them. From 1850 to 1875 the government granted to such men an amount of public land equal to the whole area of New England and New York with quite a large slice to spare. The Union Pacific received, in addition to vast blocks of land, a free right of way and an enormous loan. Beard says that a chart of the railway land grants of this period looks like a map of the Roman Empire at its palmiest moment.

One would have supposed that such generosity would have contented the Barons of the Iron way. But driven by the great Enchantress it only served to whet their appetite. It was then that she began to ensnare and stifle the Spirit of Liberty and Justice, for these men proceeded to sell stock in the roads they had built far in excess of any real values. By this process of watering the stock the capitalization of the Erie increased in four years from seventeen to seventy-eight millions, without any corresponding increase in real values, and this process went on everywhere. No robber barons of the Middle Ages ever looted with a freer hand or with greater ingenuity than did the railway magnates of New York and Chicago during this period. Gould and Fisk, indeed, did not hesitate to attack the leaders of a rival road with hired gangs of Bowery toughs, but the methods of others were more subtle.

The two cohorts of the army combined and gained a stranglehold on the country. Certain firms were given a rebate on all products transported, which effectually crushed competitors. And in certain cases the favored firm was even given a rebate also on all products transported for their rivals. In the snares of the Enchantress the old spirit of Liberty was changed to a blustering assertion of independence, a selfish individualism, in which each claimed the right to run his business in his own way without interference, regardless of the sufferings of others. To such a brutal blusterer had the heroic spirit of the Fathers been transformed by the wiles of the great Enchantress.

There remained yet another division of the great army inspired by the Commercial Spirit. This was the money power, commonly known as Wall Street. A few leaders in banking and finance, such as J. P. Morgan, working with the Barons of Industry and the railroad magnates, gained a dominant control of the finances of the country, and thus at last the old Enchantress set upon her head the triple crown of Capitalism. Through the small group of her captains she could control the nation. There seemed nothing that this small oligarchy could not do. The whole country was in their hands, so completely that they could grind down their laborers to the lowest living wage, and if told that the people protested against their management, could contemptuously respond: "The public be damned!" And all the time that she was establishing her control the mass of the people were unaware of the spell that was cast upon them.

The history of these times and the methods of the great trusts are familiar reading to us to-day, but at the time of their growth and greatest power the general public was absolutely ignorant of what was going on. Every one took pride in the growth of the national resources, but no one understood the methods by which these great trusts were built up and gigantic fortunes made. The old Spirit of Liberty and Justice was not dead but only asleep. When the knowledge first leaked out of the methods employed by the Standard Oil, a storm of public indignation burst forth in which Rockefeller was assailed as an arch malefactor. Although subsequent investigation seems to indicate that the proceedings of the Standard Oil were no worse than those of other industries, and were in fact more defensible than the methods of many of the trusts, the evil deeds of the others were as yet unknown and Standard Oil had to bear the full weight of public condemnation, which was so severe that philanthropic agencies were pilloried for·receiving money which the hands of Rockefeller had touched. It is therefore absurd to hold the American public responsible for the craft and guile of that money-grubbing age, and to condemn as hypocritical the idealism which found such frequent expression and which critics would have us believe to be a mantle beneath which the average American pursued his sordid aims. The people were indeed the victims of a vast conspiracy. The great Enchantress was binding the old heroic spirit while it slept.

4. The Old Spirit Ensnared

There was a section of the country to which the old Spirit of Liberty had fled to escape the rule of the Enchantress. It was necessary for the capitalist to keep these folk content and for the politician to keep them subject to the Republican party by the old fetishes. Although the Northeastern and Central states were being swept by the Trade Wind of industrialism, in the West there were districts where the old-time pioneer farmer held his ground, with the same emotional reactions that characterized the farmer of Revolutionary days, and it was inevitable that there should be conflict between these two tides and their divergent desires and attitudes. The Democratic reaction under Jackson found its backing chiefly among the farmers, both those with small holdings in the South, and the pioneers who had acquired lands in the West and who were antagonistic to the industries and the money power, and a high tariff. They had been increasing in power and in numbers at a rate nearly equal to that of the industrial sections. In 1860 there were two million farms in the United States; in fifty years they increased to six million. In this so-called age of industrial development, the additional farm land brought under cultivation in the United States exceeded the total cultivated land of Germany combined with that of France. The wheat crop increased from 173 million to 700 million bushels. At the time the Republican party was organized the influence of the farmer was dominant in the United States and in the party, but industry had no sooner hitched on to the farmer's party than the tail began to wag the dog. To please the farmer, the Homestead law was passed in 1862 with the slogan, "Vote yourself a farm." It provided that the government should present 160 acres of the public domain to any adult citizen who applied.

The industrial wing was not to go without its plum. During the same period the tariff was raised from an average of seventeen per cent in 1857 to nearly fifty per cent in 1864. The accusation has been made that there was a definite agreement of these two great interests to control the country and share the loot. It may have been true that such an agreement was framed by a group of leaders on both sides under the influence of the Political Current. To the great mass of the farming population, however, any such deal was unknown. They were honest simple folk, whether God-fearing or hard-drinking, or both. They were busy tilling the soil and fighting wild beasts and Indians and they asked little of the government but to be given the land and let alone. It was only in time of distress that they began to inquire what enemy was sowing tares in their field. After the war they stood by the Republican party not because it had made a successful deal between agriculture and industry, but because they had been brought up to think of it as a sacred institution, hallowed by the blood of martyrs, and because they were convinced that if that party went out of power the country would go immediately and inevitably to the dogs.

It was this group whom the politicians deceived most successfully by their disguise, and they little dreamed that in voting for the Republican party they were really supporting the Political Spirit masked in its robes. The chief appeal of the politicians to them was not the hope of gain. They were more easily swayed by the old emotional fetishes. The party did confer benefits upon them and they were grateful. They did not ask how it was done. But even if it had brought them losses, the feeling of loyalty was strong enough to hold them, for a time at least. If its leaders behaved flagrantly, it was enough to tell the voters that they could not understand the dealings essential to politics, and their faith always survived. As already stated, the average citizen was bound to the party by a sense of loyalty almost akin to religious feeling. To-day it is hard to realize that most of the achievements of the past were accomplished by thus building up around some institution or "cause" this atmosphere of reverence. Men created an Ark of the Covenant to decry which was little less than sacrilege.

The Enchantress was busy in casting a similar charm upon the Tariff. Men who knew little or nothing of economic causes were brought up to feel that there was something sacred about the Tariff. Free Trade was anathema. A man who advocated it risked social ostracism in certain sections. In this emotional atmosphere the clever manipulator could work out his schemes unimpeded and meet every protest with a cry of "Sacrilege!" The government, which was intended to be the means for carrying out the will of the people, became a vast organization to secure wealth and privilege for a certain group. In a monarchy of the old type there is no cure for this state of things, for the reverence of the people for the king holds them subject in spite of his tyrannies. In a democracy the cure is found in the wrath of the people, which is roused when they begin to suffer and discover how they have been fooled. We must then trace the causes that led up to the outburst of feeling which caused the overthrow of the system.

5. THE WEB OF THE ENCHANTRESS

The Political Spirit now had its power lines built so that the whole nation was involved in its hidden network. Party organization was developed in each state and in every large city as a means to secure patronage and privileges so that the thousands of workmen employed in the public works, as well as the leading officials, were all dependent upon a strong political group, that kept its adherents under firm discipline, saw that they voted as directed, and rewarded them in proportion to their services. This vast organization was perfected merely to secure patronage and the loot that could be derived from such offices as the customs, and the presents which office seekers were willing to make in return for their appointment. In return for his office each Congressman was to secure the appointment of good organization men as postmasters, etc., in his district, and to advocate bills that would bring army posts or harbor facilities or other opportunities for lucrative employment into the section. Each senator must secure for the organization all the offices that controlled graft.

Here then was a web spun by the Spirit of Politics, but made for the service of the great Enchantress. In framing the Constitution it had been designed to create in the Senate a conservative body, representing the moneyed interests of the nation, and while the representatives were elected by popular vote, the senators were chosen by the state legislatures, on the theory that the conservative interests would here be dominant. The results exceeded all expectation. The Senate became the throne of the Enchantress. The senators in most states became the representatives of the leading industries of the state and became the chief mechanism through which measures favoring those industries were engineered. The most important issue for the industries was the tariff, and we have shown how, with the overthrow of the Southern oligarchy in the war, it became possible, even before the war was over, to put through a tariff which enabled the manufacturer to get for his product twice what he could otherwise have received.

We have also shown how the railways secured legislation handing over to them vast tracts of land and special privileges. The most notable instance was in connection with the building of the Union Pacific where not only was land granted, but also an issue of bonds. The financing was engineered by a group of men organized under the name of Crédit Mobilier, who bought up the bonds at a minimum and by various financial tricks were able to make enormous profits at the public expense and declare a dividend of $3,500 on every $1,000 invested. In order to secure the assistance of Congress in this graft various prominent members were either presented with shares or allowed to buy them at nominal price. The profits were too great to keep quiet and the news leaked out, awakening a storm of public wrath. Oakes Ames, a leader in the organization, was put on the stand and his testimony involved a number of prominent Republican Congressmen.

Every great war seems to break down the usual moral standards. When the inhibition that checks a man from killing his fellow is destroyed, other moral restraints seem to go with it. Even though the backbone of the country is still stiffened by the currents of religion and justice, there are large numbers who are swept from their moorings. It was these that the Political Current caught in its tide and used in the exploitation of the Southern states. Many of the worst grafters, such as Ben Butler, the plunderer of New Orleans, found a place in Congress, and proceeded to work for their own enrichment. They voted an increase to their own salaries and made it retroactive, so that it covered past years. Men of integrity, such as Garfield, who was chairman of the Appropriations Committee, were obliged to dicker with them in order to pass the bills essential to the government. No one doubted the honesty of General Grant, but politically he seems to have been a mere babe who floated, like Moses in his ark of bulrushes, helpless on the Political

Current. During his Presidency, he trustingly appointed unscrupulous politicians to high positions, believing that as
his friends they could do no evil. When it was proved that
his Secretary of War had been collecting large sums for his
private purse from office seekers, Grant allowed him to resign and accepted his resignation with regret. When his
secretary was implicated in the frauds of the Whiskey ring,
Grant interfered to defend him. Every one was seeking to
pull out a plum. The secretary of the Republican National
Committee in Garfield's time was found to have been drawing large sums to run postal routes which apparently existed only in imagination.

All honest men seemed to be caught in the web of the
Enchantress. Her hidden power lines ran through the whole
nation and controlled the whole mechanism of the government. Her captains had only to grasp the levers and the
machine would pour wealth into their pockets—land grants,
oil grants, mining grants, water power grants, bond issues,
concessions, franchises—there was no limit to what it could
churn out. On the other hand if any one interfered with
their projects, lo, at a touch out came injunctions, legal
decisions, with an army to enforce them if need be.

6. The Spirit of Liberty Awakes

Secure behind their interlocking power lines the henchmen of the Great Enchantress grew reckless in piling up
their fortunes. They could rob and fool the public and get
around the laws, but there were certain laws they could not
safely break any more than Jackson could in his day. In
their greed they built up a vast system of credit on watered
stock and empty promises and the great edifice founded on
water and air collapsed with a crash in 1873. The crash
roused the old Spirit of Liberty and Justice that had lain so
long asleep and helpless. He stirred in his slumber and
sought to break free from the snares of the old Enchantress.
Thus began a struggle for freedom which was to last many
years and which had many different phases.

Each of the cohorts of the Enchantress had made its

domination felt in a peculiar way upon a certain group, and in each of these three groups the old spirit took a new form as it woke and prepared to fight. Thus the attacking forces were separated and hardly recognized one another as allies, though they all sought to break the tyrannical rule of Capitalism, leagued with politics. The first attack was in the realm of politics and aimed to break the connections through which the corrupt Political Current turned the wheels of government.

In the second place there was an attack upon that cohort of the Enchantress which was entrenched in Wall Street. As in the time of Jackson the old spirit had risen in the West to battle with the monster, so again out of the West once more came the resurrected Spirit of the Fathers to battle once more against the chains with which it was being bound by the henchmen of the great Enchantress—the leaders of Capitalism.

A third division of the revolt was in the realm of Industry where the tyranny of Capitalism was reducing laborers to a condition worse in many instances than that of slaves in the South had been. The old Spirit of Liberty and Justice roused them at length to rebellion.

We must follow these three movements in series as the old dominant spirit woke to life and in the course of the battle was thrown into strange new channels where it was hardly recognizable. The conflict at first was indecisive, for the Reform Spirit woke slowly, and after winning a slight advantage would let the prize slip from its hands, and the old forces would re-entrench themselves. It was to take more than twenty years to rouse the nation to the point of revolution, and in this chapter we shall deal only with the preparatory skirmishes.

The battle began in the sphere of politics. It is a most fascinating struggle to watch. The Political Spirit dominated in so absolute a fashion by this time that even honest men had to yield to it. Although a politician who did not graft was a curiosity, yet the public trusted its leaders until a series of revelations pulled the wool from their eyes.

The panic, and the wide-spread losses resulting, started at last a wave of wrath strong enough to burst through the barrier of ancient fetishes and jujus built by the politicians around the Republican party, and was not even checked by the old dyke of hero worship for General Grant. It is emotional waves of this sort, started by the suffering and dissatisfaction of the people, that sweep the governing party from power in a Democracy. Here was the opportunity of the Democratic party to become once more the channel of the old Colonial Spirit and they did not let it pass. In their platform in 1876 they inserted the following plank: "Reform is necessary even more in the higher grades of the public service. President, vice-president, judges, senators, representatives, cabinet officers—these and all others in authority are the people's servants. Their offices are not a private perquisite but a public trust. When the annals of the republic show the disgrace and censure of a vice-president, a late speaker of the House marketing his rulings as a presiding officer; three senators profiting secretly by their votes as law-makers; five chairmen of leading committees of the House exposed in jobbery; a late secretary of the treasury forcing balances in the public accounts; a late attorney-general misappropriating public funds; a secretary of the navy enriched or enriching friends by percentages levied off the profits of contractors with his department; an ambassador to England censured in a dishonorable speculation; the President's private secretary barely escaping conviction upon trial for guilty frauds upon the revenue; a secretary of war impeached for high crimes and misdemeanors,—the demonstration is complete that the first step in reform must be the people's choice of honest men from another party. . . . All these abuses, wrongs and crimes, the product of sixteen years' ascendency of the Republican party, create a necessity for reform confessed by the Republicans themselves, but the party's mass of honest voters is powerless to resist the eighty thousand office holders, its leaders and guides."

If the people had been prosperous and content, as they

were during the Harding Administration, such an arraign-
ment might have passed unheeded, but suffering as they
were, it served to start a wave of indignation that swept the
country from end to end. Those who were kept from the
Democratic party by the old fetishes felt that a radical
change must be made. The public would still cheer for
Grant as a hero, but it was felt that he had become the tool
of unscrupulous politicians. The better men in the party
demanded another leader and the party leaders, although
they would have been glad to see him continue in office,
yielded to the popular feeling, and Rutherford B. Hayes, a
governor of Ohio, was nominated in his place in 1876. It
was then that the changed temper of the country was revealed. The Democrats had nominated Samuel J. Tilden,
the Reform governor of New York, who had been instru-
mental in overthrowing the Tweed ring, and who, as a man
of integrity and cultivation, had the confidence of the public.
Democratic majorities piled up in New York, New Jersey,
Delaware, Maryland, Indiana and Missouri. In addition,
ten Southern states had been mastered by the Southerners
by various devices such as placing the polls where the
negroes could not reach them, or by shifting them without
notifying the colored population, as well as by the old methods of frightening the negro voters.

This gave 184 electoral votes to Tilden of the necessary
185, and the election was conceded to the Democrats even
by Hayes himself. But there were nineteen votes in dispute,
and the old Spirit of Politics was determined not to allow
the Democrats to gain a hold upon the government. A politician named Chandler made up his mind to swing the election to Hayes. It was a most amazing and incredible performance. One doubtful vote was in Oregon where one of
the Republican electors had been replaced by a Democrat
through the authority of the Democratic governor. The
others were the votes of Florida, South Carolina, and
Louisiana, where the Republican regime had not yet been
overthrown, in spite of violent efforts. Each side presented
its own count and claimed the election. There was probably

fraud and coercion on both sides, and the whole country was torn by the violence of this dispute. For the South here was the hope of at last winning a Democratic government and President who would right their wrongs. To the North it was the threat of losing the control by which they had kept the South in subjection and of seeing all their plans overturned. The most interesting feature was that it provided a test of the old Anglo-Saxon Spirit that created democratic government. Could such a question be settled without fighting?

7. A Triumph for the Spirit of Democracy

Here was a test of the fundamental Spirit of Democracy so remarkable that we must stop in the history of the battle to consider it. It was difficult enough to develop the spirit of good sportsmanship, that adjunct of the Anglo-Saxon Spirit, so far that men would stand by the rules they had made, and the constitution they had shaped, when they thought it to their disadvantage to do so. It was to maintain this essential principle of democracy that Lincoln had thought it worth while to fight through the Civil War to an issue, and to settle this question for all time. It is hard for us to appreciate how great an achievement it was.

In a recent interview Ibn Saud, the ruler of Arabia, expressed his admiration for Wilson, and asked why the United States had not carried out his plans. He was informed that an adverse party had prevented it. He then inquired why Wilson did not fight it out. He was told that the reason was that in America men had agreed to stand by the decision of the majority without fighting. He contemplated this idea with amazement a moment, and then remarked that it was a wonderful idea and that it would solve all his own difficulties with his rebellious Arab tribes. But, he said, it would never work in Arabia.

It was a great achievement to get men to settle their disputes by majority rule, but the supreme test was as to whether a dispute could be settled in a democracy when there was no rule to guide men. With feeling at such an intense pitch as in the election of 1876, and with such important issues at stake, it did not seem possible. And yet it was done. The House was Democratic, the Senate Republican. A committee was chosen of five men from each, with five from the Supreme Court, to hear both sides and decide the election in the three doubtful states. Two of the judges from the Supreme Court were Republicans, two were Democrats, and these four were to choose a fifth. They chose an unbiassed man, but when he was taken ill, their choice fell on one who though honest, was an ardent Republican. As all the others voted on party lines, the decision rested on the vote of this one man. In the case of each of the four states presented for decision, he voted with the Republicans, and Hayes was declared elected. It was a rather tragic demonstration of partisanship that in every single case each man voted with his party. The people had made their own rules to settle the controversy, and the old spirit of Fair Play kept them loyal to the decision. Bitter though their feelings were, they never thought of disputing the decision. It was a supreme triumph of government by the people, and of good sportsmanship. There was undoubtedly fraud on both sides. It was generally said that the Democrats had stolen the election and the Republicans stole it back.

Hayes was duly inaugurated and struck his first blow to break the power of the Political Current. Realizing that, although he had won by the support of the Republican organization in the three doubtful states, that government was really against the will of the true people of the South and instituted by the politicians for their own gain, he withdrew the Federal support from the Republican administration in these states, and enabled them to establish a democratic government. From that time on the Southerners retained control of their own states. The carpet-baggers and negroes were turned out of office, and the South was able to express itself once more in the channels of government and present a united front against their arch enemy, the Republican party. That party as the channel of the Political Current was in bad way. The North had become disgusted with its policy and distrusted its administration, and had elected enough Democrats to give a Democratic majority in the House, which was to remain for many years, so that no party measures could be carried. As the Senate and President were Republican no Democratic measures could be put through, and the South had to remain subject to the old laws for another decade, and were compelled to resort to humiliating subterfuges to retain their control. In addition to the plan of appointing the polls at places unknown to the negroes and Republicans, they tried gerrymandering, creating districts they could carry by putting all the negro vote in one section, as in the famous Shoestring district of Mississippi, which ran all over the state. It was not until 1882 that the Supreme Court declared all the force acts by which Grant had maintained military control of the South, to be unconstitutional, and freed these states at length from their irksome bondage.

The old spirit was roused but the issue was confused. Insofar as the spirit animated the Democratic party it was against the whole North not distinguishing its real enemy in the Political Spirit. In the Republican party it was inspiring the people to wrath against their old leaders. But the crafty leaders had slipped behind the fence while the wave of wrath went by. Having put forward a President in whose honesty the people trusted, they thought they could still pull the wires from behind the screen, while they waited for the public indignation to cool. But Hayes was not the man to be manipulated. He refused to appoint their nominees and vetoed their bills. With simulated horror they branded him as a traitor to the party, hoping to appeal to that old party loyalty. The anger of the people had swept away the group around the former President, but had not been quite wrathful enough to make a sweep clean enough to give the new President a free hand; for the party leaders from behind their smoke screen could still block all his recommendations.

8. THE BATTLEFIELD OF POLITICS

For four years the old heroic spirit, roused at last, and incarnate in the President, sought to break the old Political Current, while the politicians fought desperately to break the President. The political leaders had been very far from the mass of the people in their ideals and attitudes. Hayes was tuned in as a perfect instrument to express the feelings and convictions of the solid, reliable, church-going element of the people in whom the old current ran strongly and who as yet were utterly ignorant of the machinations of big business and who had been taught that corruption in politics existed only in the Democratic party, and in the person of Ben Butler, whose grafting had become famous. In those pre-Prohibition days, President Hayes would have no wine in the White House, even at diplomatic dinners. The politicians were always at hand to ridicule him and discredit him. His honest efforts to keep out corruption were condemned as disloyalty to the party. When he became indignant and made a false move they made the most of it. By the end of his term they had prejudiced the whole party against him. The old machine, with Conkling at its head, was determined to reelect Grant, who would give them a free hand. Opposed to them were Blaine and his henchmen, who, although he was suspected of corruption, promised a cleaner administration than the Conkling machine, who regarded him as their bitterest enemy. The public indignation had died down, and they were once more in that somnolent state which gives the politician his opportunity.

We find in Conkling, Thad Stevens's successor, the true exponent of the Political Spirit and the cleverest of the old-time politicians, who regarded patriotism and moral convictions and the higher emotions merely as convenient levers by which the mass of the people could be controlled and swayed. He did not think it possible that any man should be in politics for any other purpose than self-enrichment. He was the kind of dynamo that generates the Political Current and keeps it going, and is worth study. He regarded high ideals as the twaddle which it was necessary to feed out to the public in order to keep them well fooled, while any politician who pretended really to believe these things he considered a double-dyed hypocrite. He was the typical leader of the old order, tall, domineering, arrogant, a past master of violent invective, an implacable enemy to any one who stood in his way or questioned his authority. He was the state boss of New York, and he was yet to learn that patriotism and moral standards could not always be manipulated and that the public, when once aroused to what was going on in politics and thoroughly indignant, was a dangerous animal to tamper with.

The revelations in New York City politics had aided in opening the public eye. Tweed had turned the Political Current into the city as Conkling had done in the state. Starting as County Supervisor where he had power to levy taxes and expend money for improvements, by 1869 Tweed and his Tammany friends had in their hands the mayor, the common council, the district attorney, the municipal judges, and for a time the legislature of the state and the governor himself. He had looted the public funds without mercy and was only caught through a quarrel over the plunder. He was convicted of stealing six millions and the power of Tammany was broken for the moment. Conkling succeeded in manipulating the public indignation in such fashion as to secure control of the state for his machine. Then he reached the acme of his power. He could deliver the whole machine into the hands of whatever capitalist would pay the price.

The old Spirit of Liberty and Justice had turned somnolent and abandoned Hayes to the mercy of the politicians. He had lost the first round. At the Convention in 1880 Conkling hoped that the Political Current would carry all before it and nominate Grant for a third time. He was opposed by Blaine, and in the contest a number of Conkling's New York delegates went over and voted for Blaine, thus making Grant's nomination impossible. Conkling branded them as traitors and pursued them with undying hatred. The convention, reaching a deadlock between Grant and Blaine, finally turned to Garfield and nominated him with great enthusiasm. The Political Current was so strong that he had to promise, if elected, not to follow Hayes in disregarding the suggestions of Senators as to patronage, but he would give no definite pledges as Conkling wished him to do. He was still carried by the Political Current and felt bound by the patronage system. But though ready to reward those who had worked for him, he proposed to follow his own judgment and not the dictation of the machine.

He felt that the independent section of Conkling's men who had determined the nomination by their disobedience to their leader, should be rewarded, and although he appointed a majority of machine men, he reserved one or two of the most lucrative positions for these men. The fury of Conkling knew no bounds. When volumes of fiercest invective had no effect, he finally resigned his senatorship, thinking that the old feeling of loyalty to the party leader was strong enough to return him with a triumphant vindication. But the public was waking up and was no longer swayed by the old blind loyalties. He never was returned, but lost his hold on politics forever. Hayes's protest had served to call some attention to the evils of the patronage system, and a small group of reformers, such as Godkin, George William Curtis, and Carl Schurz, had attacked the Spoils System in general, and advocated some form of civil service examinations. There were too many who derived benefit from the old system for their protest to have much effect. The general public had been stirred by political corruption, but they did not yet understand the evils of the Spoils System.

Conkling, who could not conceive that any one would enter politics without gainful motives, was perplexed and evidently thought the reformers expected to be bought off. "Some of them are man-milliners," he said, in a burst of his characteristic invective. "The dillettanti and carpet knights of politics, men whose efforts have been expended in denouncing and accusing honest men,"—presumably such as himself. "They are wolves in sheep's clothing. Their real object is office and plunder. When Dr. Johnson defined patriotism as the last refuge of a scoundrel, he was unconscious of the then undeveloped capabilities of the word 'reform.'" No passage could show better the manner in which the "Stalwarts" repelled with indignation any suggestion that their conduct of affairs was not the noble disinterested devotion to the public welfare that their Republican constituency had once considered it to be.

The odds so far were with the Political Current which was once more dominating the nation. It was not until it carried down to death a hero of the people that the old spirit was roused again to decisive action. The chief magistrate of the nation, who was also a hero of the war and the political idol of many thousands, was done to death as a sacrifice to the corrupt system that like some foul bird of ill omen had got its claws into the heart of American politics and overshadowed White House and Capitol with its dark wings. President Garfield was shot by a disappointed office seeker, because he had refused to yield to the system. In all the months that the President lay in suffering, awaiting the approach of death, the people were pondering with increasing indignation upon the evils of a system that made such things possible. The whole Spoils System came in for a frank discussion, and although Arthur was a machine man, put in to placate the Conkling forces, he was nevertheless a man of finer type, and during his administration a Civil Service bill was passed at last, which was an entering wedge to break the power of the invincible machine, upon which capitalism was riding to power and wealth.

The mass of the people are sluggish and easy-going in their action and ideas. The old Spirit of Liberty with its hatred of injustice is there, but hidden and asleep. When they are convinced that their government is noble and patriotic it takes a period of depression and heavy personal losses to rouse enough emotion to overturn it. Their dissatisfaction and wrath had been increasing little by little, but it needed some great appeal to the public sympathy such

as Garfield's assassination to raise it to such heat that the
politicians had to give way before it, and to vote the tempting morsels out of their own mouths.

9. THE BATTLEFIELD OF AGRICULTURE

We have shown how the hero of our Drama, the old
Spirit of Liberty and Justice, woke and began the struggle
to break the hidden magic web by which the great Enchantress held the Nation. Having described these thrilling and
indecisive skirmishes in the field of politics, we must turn
to another battleground.

We have told how the politicians had kept the pioneers
and farmers of the West loyal to the Republican party by
that process known to their opponents as "waving the bloody
shirt," which signified reawakening the emotions of the
war by violent ebullitions of oratory. They, who had opposed Lincoln, had now developed a Lincoln cult, and made
it plain that any one opposing the Republican party could
not be a true patriot. These Western farmers were becoming an increasingly important factor. In twenty years the
population of Kansas grew from 100,000 to 1,000,000, and
in twenty-five years from the passing of the Homestead
Act all the available farm land as far as the Rockies was
occupied, save that held by the Indians.

The politicians kept them so well in hand by their emotional fetishes that they turned elsewhere to look for their
enemy when trouble came, and, as in the time of Jackson,
they fell upon the money power in Wall Street. The old
spirit that fights for freedom is not always clearsighted
and sometimes attacks a friend instead of a foe. In this
case the forces of the great Enchantress were well disguised, and the spirit of the West, by mistake, struck at
the very pillars on which the credit of the Nation rests.

Conditions were so similar to those in the day of Jackson
when the West rose to fight the "monster" that it seems like
a repetition. As before, in the West was this vast class who
were dependent on the fortunes of farming, and who were
most of them either in debt or living on such small margins

that any disaster or period of hard times threw them into the keenest distress. When conditions were favorable, they were contented enough and built up their self-governing communities into prosperous towns where law and order reigned. During the war the farmers prospered. They gained high prices for their crops. Specie payments were suspended and government notes were made legal tender. These fell gradually in value, but the farmers were able to pay off their mortgages with them as if they were really worth the full amount, so that they profited enormously by the process. Thus was laid the groundwork of future discontent by giving them something for little more than nothing.

It was evident that if the business of the country was to be restored to a normal basis and trade with other nations was to be made possible, there must be a return to sound currency. While Garfield was in the House he made it his chief effort to restore the gold standard and to resume specie payments. A law was finally passed in 1875 that after 1879 the greenbacks outstanding should be redeemed in specie. This restoration of the purchasing power of the dollar meant that the farmer must expend nearly twice as much of his purchasing power in the payment of each coupon on his mortgage as he had to pay before, and it naturally awakened a storm of discontent. A party of Greenbackers was organized, and when they failed other methods of acquiring easy money were devised. Acting under the violent stimulus of their constituency the representatives of the farming sections sought to pass a law that debts could be paid in the old underweight silver dollar. This was attacked by Garfield as sheer robbery, and defeated. But after silver had fallen in value, repeated attempts were made to substitute the silver dollar as legal tender in place of gold, in the hope that they could thus escape paying the full value of their debts. Whenever hard times made an inroad, the great Northwest, stirred to intense feeling by the pinch of necessity, would send forth a blast like a western cyclone that threatened to overturn the

currency system of the nation and which never failed to
throw Wall Street and Capitalism into a panic. They finally
forced through a compromise law compelling the government to accept a certain proportion of silver each year. For
twenty years the East looked with dread at the Western
Plains as the breeding place of cyclones that might sweep
away their whole financial system at any moment. Thus
the Western Spirit, instead of striking direct at Capitalism,
attacked the foundation on which the prosperity of the
whole nation was built.

10. The Battlefield of Industry. Liberty versus Independence

It was in the third division of the Great War and on the
battlefield of Industry that the fighting was most bitter and
most confused. Here the Spirit of Liberty, springing to life
among men enslaved by ignorance and poverty, was compelled to fight with a bogus blusterer who wore his own
form and was decked in his armor. To make any headway
against the entrenched forces of Capitalism it was necessary
to summon as ally a new Spirit, one extremely difficult to
coax into life, but, when once really alive, the fairest and
strongest of earthly spirits, namely, the Spirit of Brotherhood. Many have presented themselves in her image only
to be unmasked and shown to be the spirit of greed or
tyranny in disguise. But when she truly rules in men's
hearts there are few feats she cannot accomplish.

The old Spirit of Liberty can never fight alone successfully, as has repeatedly been shown. The urge to independence drives his followers apart. He must have as ally
some spirit to preserve union. The evocation of the Spirit
of Brotherhood among the workers of America was one of
the most surprising achievements of modern times, and
without it the battle for liberty would have been impossible.
Strangely enough the battle for liberty put an end to the
dominance of that old Anglo-Saxon Spirit of Independence
which had been the leading component in all the great cur-

rents of American life, and the nation became subject to new spirits which enforced a unity and conformity almost as great as that produced by the systems of the old world.

The farmer tended to preserve the old American Spirit of Independence. But Industry was growing at an even more rapid rate and to meet its needs thousands of laborers were imported from abroad. As already stated, they came at first from Northern and more amalgamable nations, but ended by advancing in thousands from Slavic Austria and Poland, from Southern Italy and Russia. Most of them were ignorant and illiterate, and brought with them a standard of living wholly foreign to the ideas of America. The condition of labor was none too good before the arrival of the foreign hordes. During and after the Civil War prices moved rapidly upward and wages did not keep pace with them. In the old days the factory was usually a village affair where all the hands were known to the employer and in personal relations with him. Now personal relations were replaced by a relentless machine organized to grind the last dollar of profit and the last ounce of work from each sweating employee. Ten, twelve, even fourteen hours were at times exacted, and the pay was often hardly enough to keep soul and body together.

The society and government of America were adapted to old-time conditions when each man had his own house and field and asked only to be let alone to make his own way. But here was another world than any one had ever imagined. A vast organization had sprung up by control of which a small group of men had gained a throttle grip upon their fellows. With law and government, wealth and power, behind them, they could deal as they chose with their helpless underlings and with the general public. No law had been formed to check them, and the whole genius and spirit of the Anglo-Saxon race was with them in their demand to conduct their own business in their own way with no dictation from outsiders. The Anglo-Saxon Spirit fought for them, then, dressed up as a selfish and brutal bully, the Spirit of Independence, opposed to Liberty.

We can all remember the furious indignation of such lords of enterprise when their men combined to resist some dictum, or when reformers sought to pass a law that limited their authority. "This is a free country. No man has a right to dictate to me," was their refrain. The barons of the Industrial System were proving as autocratic and merciless to the man beneath as were the men of the old aristocracy, and even more so, for the aristocrat knew nothing of the sufferings of the poor, while the Industrial Baron knew the starvation conditions of his laborers and used the knowledge to drive harder bargains with them, often forcing them to take their pay through the company store where they got only half value.

To meet these conditions the old individualism was helpless. Co-operation was necessary, but extremely difficult to attain. How in the face of such organized power the workmen ever managed to form their Unions and to gain enough strength to secure their rights, seems a mystery. To those of us to-day who have suffered from the injustice and unreasonableness of the Unions it seems as if there could be in them nothing good. But if any of us have tried to get men to stand together when it means suffering and loss, we must realize that to produce in these ignorant, illiterate men of all races and nations a sense of brotherhood so that they would suffer and starve to help one another, was an amazing achievement. Before electric welding was known a friend of mine showed me a rod composed of sections of copper, iron, nickel and several other metals and explained how by turning an electric current through these separate metals they had been united into one solid rod. To me it seemed a miracle, and it seems one equally surprising that these men should have been able to evoke a current of brotherhood that would fuse German, Irish, Polak and Italian and black and white into one solid coherent implement. Such men did not have the Anglo-Saxon heritage and it took violent stimulus to start the current of liberty running in their veins.

We have noted that wherever there were conditions causing suffering, the emotional temperature was raised. The heat would set the air in motion and before long an emotional cyclone would be sweeping over the whole country. This proved true in the case of the laboring man, though at first their troubles were localized. Such a sore spot in the Pennsylvania mining district occasioned the organization of the famous Molly Maguires, who did to death some scores of men, among them superintendents and managers of the mines, before a plucky detective penetrated into their organization at the risk of his life, and broke it up.

The same cause that started the rebellion in the realm of politics and on the Western plains, served to set in motion the armies of industry. This was the panic of 1873, following the war inflation. The railroads started to reduce wages and continued the process until a final cut in 1877 brought them below what the men considered a living wage. When the men of the Unions remonstrated, their committees were discharged wholesale by managers who said they would have no workmen telling them what to do. Some men on the Baltimore & Ohio finally struck and refused to work. The strike spread over the whole country from New York to the Pacific coast, and radiated from each outburst the most violent waves of public feeling. Pictures were circulated of the starving children of the workmen, and of their employers rolling about in private cars, with comments on the enormous fortunes they had made by watering their stock, while they were still too poor to pay a fair wage. Between the grievance of the men and the rage of their employers, and the annoyance of the travelling public, the whole country was in a turmoil of excitement. There were riots in Baltimore, Pittsburgh, Chicago, and Saint Louis, in which many were killed and much property was destroyed. For two weeks the fight went on, and then the militia, with the aid of federal troops, restored order, and the men were forced to yield.

Attempts had been made by the Unions to effect a general organization. The National Labor Union existed for a while, but difficulties beset its path. The attempt to create any sense of unity between the diverse groups of labor seemed futile. Here was a mass of negro workers to deal with, unacceptable to the whites. Then numbers of women began to enter industry, and to lower wages by their competition. The interests of these groups conflicted and they proved unamalgamable. Then had come the hordes of foreigners, who could not understand the purposes of the Union and who swamped all efforts by sheer numbers. To train these men to stand by one another, to suffer for the sake of the group, to feel any sense of solidarity or brotherhood with elements so diverse seemed hopeless and the Union broke up into various crafts.

The Knights of Labor followed who sought to bring all laborers, white, black, native and foreign, men and women, into one mass organization. They grew rapidly in power, and by 1880 were able to secure higher wages and shorter hours for many of their members, and to score several victories over the railroads, ending in a triumph over the Gould roads which made the name of Powderly, the labor leader, a terror to Capital everywhere. From an emotional standpoint it was an amazing achievement to bring these diverse groups to a sense of unity.

If they had continued simply in the current of Liberty and Brotherhood, all might have gone well, but there was a spirit from abroad that was beginning to penetrate American life which caught them in its current. It is familiar to us under the name of Socialism and its fundamental feeling was a hatred of Capitalism, root and branch. Instead of seeking, like the American Spirit of Liberty, to correct the injustice and tyranny of Capitalism, it aimed to overthrow the whole system and to replace it by government control and ownership. Though it made its appeal to the Spirit of Liberty, it was really the spirit of autocracy in disguise. This spirit repelled a large proportion of the membership of the Knights of Labor. They succeeded in influencing various legislatures to pass the eight-hour day, to exclude importations of contract labor and to pass various other measures in favor of labor. But because of their socialistic and revolutionary ideas they lost the conservative element in their constituency and raised up many bitter enemies.

Noting their failures, Gompers, when he organized the Federation of Labor, determined to keep its objective such that it would appeal to all workmen and at the same time would not arouse unnecessary antagonism. He would not work against the capitalistic system but would simply endeavor to secure for the workman a larger share of its products.

11. The Second Round on the Political Field

The war against the great Enchantress continued in the three battlefields of Politics, Agriculture and Industry with varying success. So long as the government was controlled by the Political Current but little progress could be made. There was a growing discontent among the people and an increasing distrust of the Republican administration. The politicians were by this time such masters of the art of juggling with emotional fetishes and turning in cross currents of prejudice that the people seldom saw a square issue.

This was especially true when Blaine was nominated in 1884. Although he was never actually caught in any flagrant misdemeanor, Blaine's name was associated with many dubious transactions. The country at large felt there was something sinister about him and his relation to the money power. His main hope lay in carrying the Irish vote of New York by turning in a blast of religious prejudice. His mother was a Catholic, while he depicted Cleveland, the Democratic nominee, as a narrow Presbyterian anti-Catholic. The balance was so close that this appeal to religious prejudice might have turned the trick, when it was all blown sky high and reversed by the congratulatory speech of the Reverend Dr. Burchard with its famous alliteration of Rum, Romanism and Rebellion. The noted clergyman was evidently proud of his eloquence, but never before or since did his vocal pyrotechnics produce so cataclysmic an effect. Blaine for some reason did not detect the dynamite in the phrase in time to repudiate it, but his enemies saw its possibilities and detonated it with such effect that its echoes still reverberate. Blaine's chance with the Irish vote was slim when they got through.

The Democrats nominated Cleveland, who had not been in national politics and was therefore untainted and who had given a strikingly honest administration of the local government of New York State. The campaign was characterized by the most unscrupulous efforts to arouse prejudice against the candidates. Instead of considering their fitness for the job, or the great issues of the battle, various acts in the private life of the candidates that would arouse the antagonism and prejudice of certain groups, were hunted out and broadcasted, and the most violent personal antipathies were created, so that the election went forward in an emotional vortex, most of which was as much aside from the vital points at issue as was the speech of Dr. Burchard. It was all a wonderful display of the politicians' methods of manipulating emotions. One factor in the result was the feeling of Conkling toward Blaine, whom he had characterized as "a grandiloquent swell with a turkey gobbler strut."

It was an election apparently determined by the most absurd trifles, but there were deeper feelings underneath. The Commercial Current was once more running wild. In the mad effort to gain riches, the henchmen of the great Enchantress had been speculating wildly in the stocks of competitive railroads, and the crash came in 1884. General Grant went down to ruin, and discovered that his name had been used by unscrupulous speculators to back their wild and dishonest schemes. In Ohio there were terrible floods causing great suffering and discontent which expressed itself in violence. A mob raged for six days in Cincinnati. With all these local centres of suffering and with the general causes of dissatisfaction already described, the barometer was falling all over the country and a storm was rolling up which vented itself first in an attack on the party in power. The old Spirit of Liberty and Justice was aroused and on the war path again. Reformers such as Carl Schurz and George William Curtis joined in the assault and carried with them a large party of Republicans who were stigmatized by the old guard as traitors and "mugwumps." The result was that for the first time since the war the bloody shirt waved in vain, and the Democrats came into power once more after a Republican rule of twenty-four years. It was a narrow squeak, for Cleveland only carried New York by 1,000 majority. It was an indication that the old spirit was awake again and fighting mad, though it had not yet discovered the real enemy.

It was strange that the Democratic party, which had so long been the vehicle through which the feelings of the Southern Aristocrat found expression, should now be the channel for the old Spirit of Liberty and Justice. It was the man rather than the party, for Cleveland was a dynamic personality in whom the old spirit was raised to high voltage and intelligently directed. He saw the issue and was out to fight the Political Current. Unfortunately the people were fickle and variable; they were dissatisfied, but they could still be influenced by the old party leaders. Cleveland made his position plain and stood by it. He had the courage to stick to the course he believed best for the country when threatened with loss of votes, and even when it looked as if he would have to stand alone. He attacked the Republican Political Current by turning practically all Republicans out of office, but he also attacked the Political Current in the Democratic party by ignoring their candidates and appointing only men who proved themselves fit in the Civil Service examinations. Cleveland felt that he had a commission from the people to smash the old Republican machine that had generated the current that had wrought so much corruption. Constructive legislation was impossible, for the Senate was still Republican, but by use of the veto he killed more than two hundred pension bills by which public funds were being doled out to thousands of Republican adherents. He destroyed a river-and-harbor bill which would have provided untold graft to the contractors, and he managed to force various corporations and individuals to disgorge some eighty millions of acres of the public lands which they had illegally obtained from the corrupt Republican land offices.

Some of the secret charms of the old Enchantress leaked out. He learned of the system of rebates by which the railroads were able to favor certain concerns and crush others, and the Interstate Commerce Commission was appointed to regulate railroad rates. The old battle of labor and capital was going on steadily. The success of such a movement depends on whether it is borne along on the same great current that sways the mass of the people. If they are sympathetic the movement progresses. So long as it kept to the old Liberty current all was well. Unfortunately for Labor the sympathy of the public was lost by the injection of a current from across the seas which aroused such distrust that the labor movement has hardly yet recovered from it. Among the imported laborers were those who were swayed by the tide of Anarchism, a thousand times more bitter and dangerous than that of Socialism, and they sought to enlist the American working man in the cause of anarchy. The efforts of the Chicago workmen to secure an eight-hour day precipitated a row with the McCormick Harvester Company, resulting in a lockout and a battle with the police in which several were killed. At a protest meeting at Haymarket Square, feeling ran high but no violent action was taken until a body of police advanced. Then a bomb was suddenly exploded which killed one policeman and wounded several. The old Liberty current reacted against this and a violent wave of antagonistic feeling swept the whole country and left a strong prejudice against all the activities of labor. Four of the anarchists were hanged, several more imprisoned, and a horror of all anarchists spread far and wide through the nation. For a time the Unions were associated with them in the public mind and sentiment turned violently against them and even their reasonable attempts to better conditions were regarded with suspicion. Thus, by a disastrous alliance the public were thrown into opposition to a current which was moving in a direction they approved.

Cleveland apparently felt that his mandate was against

all Republican abuses, and having done his best with those at hand he finally turned to the tariff. This, however, proved to be a different matter. Hitherto, his chief enemy had been concealed. Now he met the full force of the Commercial Current in the open field and attacked ideas that were emotionally intrenched. The tariff was protected by a wall of reverential prejudice, and public feeling had not yet been aroused against it. Moreover, there were many Pennsylvania Democrats directly benefited by the high tariff, and violent protests arose. Every attempt at legislation was crushed in the Republican Senate, and when the four years were over and a new election was in order, the Enchantress assembled her forces and Cleveland went down to defeat. He faced the issue squarely and knew that his stand would probably lose him the election, but he said: "What is the use of being elected or re-elected unless you stand for something?" The Enchantress still had her hold upon the public and the old Spirit of Liberty and Justice was still blind to her snares, but Cleveland had faith that if he stood firm the people would come back to him when the evils of the tariff system had really stirred them.

The chief reason that the war with the great Enchantress continued so long in doubt was that the issue was so confused that few understood it. Conditions had been so altered by the material progress of the nation that liberty meant something almost the opposite to that which it had signified. In the old days all that the Spirit of Liberty demanded was freedom from all interference. Now the freedom of the individual was impossible without interference. If the men who controlled the vast and delicately articulated system of industry were left free to do exactly as they chose, it meant practical slavery for the mass of the people. This produced the anomalous situation that the old Spirit of Liberty had to fight against independence, and it took many years to make this clear.

In the beginning America was a nation of householders, each making his living in his own way and dependent on his own resources. Each man wished freedom to carry on his own plans without the interference and repression that characterized the old world. But in 1888 there had grown up an elaborate industrial and social mechanism in which each man had his part and upon which he was dependent for life and happiness. Even the farmer had his part in it. With the advent of farm machinery and of the grain elevator and the modern system of marketing, the individual could do nothing alone. He was only a cog in the vast machine, and if he lost his place, he might not find another into which he could fit. He could not, like the pioneer, produce all that he needed himself. He could only revolve with the machine and take his share of the product which it poured forth. The same laws could not apply as when each man led his independent life, and yet the men who had worked their way to a controlling position in the machine claimed that the industry they controlled was *their* business, and no one could interfere with them. Theirs was a spirit as arrogant as that of the old Southern Aristocracy, but it was based on wealth rather than birth. We may term the feeling that animated them the Plutocratic Current. Their attitude toward their employees differed little from that of the aristocrat to the serf and it was bitterly resented. It was evident that there must either be a radical change in the laws of the land or a revolution. Where thousands are dependent for life and happiness on the whims of one man, and he denies that they have any rights, or claims upon him, and asserts that he can deal with them precisely as he chooses, it is evident that there is likely to be trouble ahead. As long as men have enough to eat and are contented with their work, they are likely to acquiesce in almost any government that is not flagrantly unjust, and the nation will hold together. But as soon as they begin to suffer or become discontented, explosive forces gather that are likely to blow up the government and the whole machinery of society unless something is done in time.

The trouble now was not that the new mechanism of society did not work and produce enough to keep all men happy and content. It did. Its product exceeded anything hitherto imagined. Every day new inventions added to the efficiency and rendered less manual labor necessary. The trouble was with the division of the product. There were no laws to regulate this. It was possible for a few men to get control of the product of the social mechanism and so to manipulate it as to acquire enormous fortunes, while the workers were left to starve. Even in the normal distribution their share was so small that it left a very small margin between them and starvation. The story of the next few years is the story of how a revolution was avoided, that might easily have been the most terrible the earth has yet seen, and which did in fact transform both the government and the characteristics of the American people. Strange to say, few people in America realized how imminent was the danger of a violent catastrophe or how extraordinary it was that such vast changes were produced by peaceful means.

CHAPTER VIII

THE REVOLUTION IN SPIRIT

THE CONVERSION OF THE ENCHANTRESS

1. The Threatening Storm

WHEN one looks over the wide Western plain, through the clear atmosphere that seems to bring the distant purple mountains almost within reach, it is impossible to believe that in that clear air is latent a force that can uproot trees and destroy cities and carry ruin and destruction far and wide. A little extra heat here or there can set that air in motion. It carries moisture which a little extra cold can precipitate in the form of clouds and these have in them that mysterious force electricity, which gathers into a charge that can be hurled down to blast and destroy whatever stands in the way. So as one looks over the face of the country and sees men at their peaceful pursuits, there seems here no force that can harm or destroy. Yet there are latent feelings that some event may rouse to fury; there are ingredients—prejudices implanted in childhood, superstitions, strange fears, that a word may kindle into a destructive explosion, or stimulate into violent action.

It is from their knowledge of this situation that politicians gain their power. When they see among the constituency of a man they wish to defeat, a large number of people with some latent prejudice, it is their cue to turn it loose. If they are respectable folk with a horror of any man who is lax in his relations with the other sex, they rake up the story of some early peccadillo and by concentrating the attention of the public on this, they arouse a wave of violent antagonism, causing them to forget that the candidate is an honest man who would purge the government of graft. It was such appeals that were attempted against Cleveland and which served to distract and break up the gathering wave of discontent among the people. Politicians stopped at nothing to awaken prejudice and distract attention from the valiant service he had done. It made no difference how trivial the accusation or how brazen the lie. He sat in the White House in his shirt-sleeves! He went on hunting expeditions to indulge in an orgy of intoxication. They even ventured to say that he beat his wife. Each statement was designed to rouse the prejudice of a certain group. When a story was thus started, it was almost impossible to arrest it, and it inflicted a permanent and irreparable injury, for a large number of people always believed it and never read the other side. A similar story about Garfield, made up out of whole cloth, without a shadow of truth behind it, gained such general circulation that it was believed even by those friendly to him. Thus to attack the character of a ruler once rendered a man liable to be drawn and quartered. Every ruler of America had to submit himself to this sort of a thing as a part of the price he paid for his power.

In spite of herrings drawn across the trail the real issue was whether the Enchantress should rule or not. Cleveland's policy had thrown her henchmen into the Republican party, where they hid behind the name of Harrison, a grandson of the old hero of Tippecanoe. His success in 1888 was a triumph for the Captains of Industry, and McKinley set to work to draw up a tariff that made him famous and that surpassed all predecessors.

The people had been trained to regard the Tariff as a sacred charm which ensured prosperity. Now they began to feel that it was part of the web of the Enchantress, designed to hold the many subject to the few. The farmers never approved it, and there was an increasing group of merchants and professional men who found it an annoying impediment. A few were beginning to guess at the enormous profits it made possible, and joined the mugwumps in opposing it. The old current of Liberty and Justice was beginning to turn against the Tariff. The wave of public discontent was at last reaching ominous dimensions and the Democratic leaders were eager to turn the current into the channel of their party. The Democrats in their main plank in the Campaign of 1892 denounced "the Republican protection as a fraud, a robbery of the great majority of the American people for the benefit of the few." The wave of public feeling had at last risen to the height of the pinnacle where Cleveland had stood almost alone and he now had his reward for "standing for something." Senator Gorman, his former campaign manager, had turned against him on account of his position on the tariff. David B. Hill, the boss of New York and ally of Tammany, opposed him violently and both these men hoped for the nomination. The great orator Bourke Cockran poured forth denunciations of Cleveland and praises of Hill, but the current was running strongly now and Cleveland was borne along triumphant on the wave of popular enthusiasm. His opponents were snowed under at the first ballot and Cleveland was triumphantly nominated. He had no hope of winning without carrying New York, and that could not be done without the aid of the political current generated by Tammany Hall, which opposed him and refused to endorse him unless he yielded to the Political Spirit and gave the pledges they demanded. He faced Croker and Sheehan, the Tammany leaders, at a private meeting, and when they demanded pledges, he smote the table with his fist and declared solemnly: "I will make no secret pledges. I'll be damned if I will." He was out to fight that old current as well as the Tariff. When they found he meant business, and that he would withdraw and appeal to the public, they gave in and supported him without the pledge.

There are two kinds of democratic leaders,—those who sit with their ear to the ground listening for the voice of the voter, and those who stand by the truth as they see it and wait for the people to come to them. They do not seek for bait to lure the public favor nor do they follow the popular enthusiasm of the moment. They believe they are chosen to do what brain and conscience tell them is for the public welfare, and follow that course unshaken by the tides of popular feeling. They believe a leader is chosen to lead and not to follow. Cleveland was charged with the old current of Liberty and Justice. He radiated it and he believed that in time the people would once more be swept into its current. His election was a triumphant vindication of his character. No other man had been defeated for re-election and then come back in the next term and won an outstanding victory. For he gained an electoral vote of 277 against Harrison's 145, and with him went also a Democratic House and Senate, so that in 1892 for the first time in thirty-two years the Democratic party was in full control of the government.

In spite of this Cleveland found himself in turbulent seas, and storms and cross winds sprang up on every side. In spite of the strength of the current that swept him into power, the old Enchantress was too well intrenched to be easily overthrown. Even the tariff reform promised in the Democratic platform and demanded by the people, was by no means an easy measure to carry. An adequate bill passed the House, but when it came to the Senate it found the "Interests" well established. Although there was a Democratic majority, Gorman again turned traitor to his old chief and with Democratic aid emasculated the bill until it was little better than that of McKinley. Cleveland refused to sign it and it became law without his signature.

2. THE WESTERN HURRICANE

It was at this time when Cleveland, heading the old current that was working for reform, was beginning to break the web of the Enchantress, that the armies of the West started an independent attack that nearly wrecked the nation. They were set in motion by one of those terrific storms that break periodically upon the nation as the result of low-pressure centres of disaster and suffering.

Few will forget the hard times of 1893 and 1895. The expansion that had gone forward with such amazing rapidity had exceeded its normal limits, and there was a terrifying crash. Every boom burst. Failures multiplied. Money was almost impossible to obtain. Thousands were out of work and formed themselves into threatening groups and armies. Strikes followed in industries, mines and railroads. And the Pullman strike was so severe that Cleveland, in spite of the protests of Governor Altgeld of Illinois, took matters into his own hands and ordered out the Federal troops to quell it.

All the various storms whose beginnings we have described threatened to burst at once. The whole country seemed disorganized and on the verge of some great rebellion. During the administration of Harrison six new states had been admitted, and, with these new forces to aid, the western storm was rolling up into ominous proportions and taking definite form. A new party calling themselves the People's party, or Populists, had formed, and in 1892, to the astonishment and horror of the two old parties, they carried Colorado, Nevada, Oregon, Idaho, North Dakota, and Kansas. As in the time of Jackson the old Liberty spirit woke in the West and carried all before it, so again it reappeared in the same manner.

We have noted how this second attack on the money power began in the 1870s. Now it gathered all its forces, and, as before, mistaking its true enemy, struck at the foundations of its own prosperity—the Gold Standard. But there were new elements in the attack. The old spirit of Socialism from across the sea, which was not content to remedy the injustice of Capitalism, but sought to destroy the whole system, had gained a hold upon the West and was dominating the old American current.

This western tide had helped to carry Cleveland to victory, but as he saw it turn against what he considered to be the bulwarks of national prosperity and threaten to sweep them away, he took his stand against it, facing this time a storm of popular disapproval from his own followers, with the same fearless courage with which he had faced the enemy four years before.

The Populists had elaborated a formidable programme, which they thought would end the dominion of Capitalism. To destroy the money power, the detested Wall Street group, who in their view seized all the gold and made money so scarce, they advocated a silver standard on the 16-to-1 basis. To cut down the wealth of the Capitalist, they proposed an income tax which would pluck from him his unholy gains; and, to break his strangle hold on the public, they would turn all the public utilities over to government control. All the vast tracts of land held by corporations or alien capitalists were to be taken from them and turned over to the farmers. The inchoate rage of the poor man against his successful rivals was taking definite shape at last in an organized attack on the whole Capitalistic System. The barons and potentates had not realized the power that lay in the vote, and that their wealth and power could all be voted away from them. The Enchantress had gone too far in defying the public. A sullen growl of rage rose from thousands of homes where children were crying for lack of food as they read of plutocratic balls where tens of thousands were spent on flowers and decorations alone. It was evident that unless the Capitalists wanted to see their whole system go, something must be done to satisfy the demands of the crowd. They allowed the Sherman Anti-Trust Law to be pushed through. It sounded well, and it had many loopholes of escape for the Trusts.

The farmers were especially bitter against the railroads, who controlled the movement of their produce and by discriminating rates could ruin any man who did not obey them, and could wreak vengeance on any enemy. The roads had gained control of most of the legislatures and town governments, and in certain sections had set up an unbelievable tyranny. In their defence it must be said that all the state legislatures and town meetings had learned the game and lost no chance to hold them up for rights of way, and necessary privileges, so that the roads claimed that it was imperative to maintain lobbies and engage retainers to control them by bribery. Consequently they had built up a vast system of corrupt control against which the farmer was helpless. By banding together in granges the farmers finally managed to secure the passage of state laws regulating rates, and at last, amid great outcry from the rail-roads, the Interstate Commerce Act was passed, which was supposed to regulate all the injustice in ratemaking. Yet here also there were loopholes which were soon discovered.

An income-tax law was also passed, only to be declared unconstitutional by the Supreme Court. Those sops thrown to the hungry multitude by the politicians seemed only to whet their appetite. Cleveland's party had receded from him and left him standing alone. The Populists were swallowing up the Democrats. The whole nation was being swept into the battle against Capitalism, and the throne of the En-chantress was shaking.

3. The Web of the Enchantress Is Discovered

In the East the old Spirit of Liberty and Justice was alive again. All the grievances of fifty years had come to a head. The muckrakers were hard at work and people began to un-derstand how they had been gulled and exploited by the pol-iticians. City after city was waking up and turning out its bosses. New York had just had her eyes violently opened to what was going on. When Dr. Parkhurst first made the accusation that the police were in league with vice and were receiving large sums to protect illicit dives, the public was incensed at his venturing to attack that fine force which was so nobly protecting the city from crime, and he was told he had better get the country mud off his shoes before he tried to pick flaws in America's greatest city. When he pitched in and succeeded in proving that matters were a thousand times worse than even he had supposed, and the extent of that stupendous Tammany system of graft was revealed, then indeed people took a hand. Tammany was turned out in a thrilling campaign in 1894. Strong was made mayor and Theodore Roosevelt, as police commis-sioner, did as thorough a cleaning up as Colonel Waring did in the street-cleaning department.

Little by little it began to leak out that the graft of the saloons and houses of ill repute was but the small end of a system that had its grip on all city contracts and business undertakings, a system that embraced the bosses of both parties, one controlling the city and the other the state, who, though outwardly sworn enemies, were united in a secret partnership in which they jointly levied heavy contributions on every corporation that attempted to do big business. The web of the great Enchantress at last was revealed. We began to hear rumors of a regular meeting of these bosses with a prominent attorney who represented the corporations and who later occupied the highest position in the national councils, and we were told how, comfortably ensconced in their big leather chairs in the Equitable Building, they disposed of the affairs of the city, distributed the graft and franchises and special privileges and decided who should be favored and who should be hampered or crushed, while checks running up toward the millions were distributed to secure the privileges that were desired.

More clever than the Spirit of Reform, the old Political Spirit had provided safe outlets for the discontent of the masses. This vast system of graft was a means of keeping the proletariat of our great cities quiet and content under the Capitalistic system of whose product they would otherwise receive so small a share. Each man who voted the ticket was sure of a good job and of a share in the picnics and balls given by the ward boss. If he got into trouble, his cousin the Alderman could soon get him out; if he was dispossessed, his friend Paddy Divver, or Tom Foley, the ward boss, would see that his rent was paid. Or if his mother died and there was no money in the house, Tom, the poor man's friend, would see that she had as fine a funeral as any man in the ward. Some ward heeler always stood yonder on the corner, and any man in trouble knew how to find him, and could get the help he needed at short notice. It was a vast system for collecting toll from the superfluous wealth of big business and distributing it among the poor in terms of festivals and jubilations, of relief for distress, and, above all, it gave to each man, no matter how incapable and undeserving, the assurance that he would be looked after and that he was in touch with powers that he could call upon

in any emergency. The system, then, provided an outlet
through which the dissatisfaction and suffering of the submerged classes could find expression and relief, before it
reached the explosive point. Reform upset all this. Most of
the men, being somewhat inefficient or inclined to indulge in
alcoholic celebrations and neglect their work, soon lost
their jobs. There was no one on hand to pay their rent, or
give them advice. When they were in trouble there was no
cousin who was an alderman, but an unsympathetic man
from uptown who told them the sad truth that they deserved what they got. All the small hucksters, whose push-
carts or street signs had been overlooked by the policemen
in consideration of the trifling graft they received, were
now called strictly to account. There was no more wasting
of the city's money on picnics and drinks. In spite of the
fine efforts of the Reform District Attorney to get in touch
with the dissatisfied element it was not surprising that,
under reform government, New York, instead of being
peaceful and happy, should have swelled the great mass of
discontent in the country, the dissatisfaction of the farmers
who were distressed by a terrible drought, of the workers
and miners whose wages had been reduced, and the general
despair due to the breaking of real-estate booms, the collapse of watered stocks and the failure of innumerable
firms. The old current of Liberty and Justice swelled by discontent, and augmented by the Socialistic tide, had turned
to a raging torrent which sought not merely to break the
web of the Enchantress but to overturn the social order.
The war was changing to a revolution.

4. The Dynamo of the Western Current

We have noted that every great current of feeling has
centred about some man whose personality acted as a dynamo, which, once caught in the current, generated and radiated power. As Cleveland had gathered up the Reform
current, so, at the Democratic Convention in 1896, a man
appeared who put all their feeling into impassioned words,
and when he declared that capital should not "press down

upon the brow of the working man this crown of thorns and crucify mankind afresh upon a cross of gold," the assembly went wild, and the hitherto unknown Nebraskan became a leader under whose banner they twice assailed the entrenched forces of industry and finance. Seldom in modern times had any man so gathered the inchoate emotions of half a nation together and hurled them forth in a thunderbolt of flaming words. They struck the embattled walls of Capitalism with such an impact that all of Wall Street quivered at the shock.

The army attacking the great Enchantress was split in twain. Though still inspired by the Reform current Cleveland felt that this Western revolutionary current was as dangerous as the old corruption. He felt that the success of the Silverites would mean ruin to the country, and when the Democratic party began to swing in that direction, instead of adopting the silver plank and remaining their greatest popular leader, he wrecked all his chances of political success by denouncing them for their folly. He wrote to Dickinson: "I have never seen anything like this craze before, but my faith in the American people is so great that I cannot believe they will cast themselves over the precipice. But there is our old party with its glorious traditions and all its achievements in the way of safe and conservative policies and its exhibitions of indestructibility. Is it to founder on the rocks? Will not sanity return before we take the final plunge?"

Heroic as were his efforts he could not stem the tide. Here was another situation that made void the old party methods of handing out tempting bait to secure the support of the popular vote, and avoiding any stand on critical questions for fear of offending constituents. Just as in 1856 a great tide of violent emotion had carried away the party walls, and swept the old Whig party out of existence and aligned men on an entirely new basis with the drive of a great purpose behind them; so now this strange popular passion was sweeping across the lines of the old parties and creating a new political formation. The Western Republi-

cans under Senator Teller bolted from the party. The Populists and Prohibitionists intimated that they would bolt to
any party that would adopt the silver plank.

Such was the situation when the Democratic convention
met and Bryan made his famous speech. When Cleveland
tried to hold the Democrats to sound money, Bryan denounced him as a traitor and a "servant of the interests."
The abuse poured out upon him was beyond belief when one
considers his service to his country. His party repudiated
him and all he had done. A resolution endorsing his administration was voted down by a tremendous majority. He,
the strongest leader the Democrats had had since Jackson,
was literally put out of the party and left standing alone.
Not in vain, however, for it was undoubtedly Cleveland's
heroic stand for sound money that threw the votes of thousands of Democrats into the Republican column and defeated the measure he felt to be such a menace to the nation
and put him in a position where he could have been nominated in 1904 had he so chosen.

He was replaced by a leader of a different type. One of
those leaders had arisen that cause one to doubt Democracy,
one who was not merely a mouthpiece of the inchoate passion of the multitude, but an agitator who could stir them
to the depths. Bryan was sincere, honest, devoted to the
public welfare and deeply religious, and his words carried
the conviction that these qualities inspire. He understood
the common citizen and knew how to reach him as no other
American of the age. He made speeches, hundreds of them,
to tens and hundreds of thousands. No man ever spoke so
much or commanded such audiences. He was more of a
resonator than a dynamo. He reflected and concentrated
the current already flowing. He said what the people wanted
to hear, he proclaimed what they already believed, and they
applauded vociferously. His speeches, though eloquent, were
trite and commonplace and full of the sentiment that centres in the home and family. His religion was of the un-
shakable fundamentalist type that defies modern thought.
He had all the crudities of mind and manner that charac-

terize the "common" man and make him common, but with them, an extraordinary kindliness and quick perception of need or distress. Science, wealth, culture, society were all in that league whose centre and soul was Wall Street. They formed the great plutocratic current which he opposed as he would the devil and all his minions.

For thirty years from the time of his Cross of Gold Speech he dominated the party and the country at large with an influence few men have ever exercised. He was a tremendous fighter. No opposition could daunt or quell him. His rich sonorous voice cast a spell on men, regardless of what he said. His last great fight against his party for his beloved silver plank was a sight for the gods. Immovable on fundamentals, he would fish for votes with the crudest, most ill-advised methods. He had all the finest qualities of the common man as distinguished from those of the gentleman. Denounced by his enemies as a fraud and a wind bag, a demagogue and agitator—no name was bad enough for him. And yet he was no sooner defeated than he rose up again stronger than ever, and so great was his following that he could dictate his terms to the end of his life.

Some leaders, like Washington or Jackson, rule the people because they inspire the worship due to heroes, and some the people will follow blindly because they trust them. But Bryan ruled because he understood so perfectly what the people felt and expressed it. He was too much one of them to see the folly of their ideas, the emptiness of their hopes. He could not guide them into wise paths, he could only gather up all their feelings and ideas and give them eloquent expression. The great danger of democracy is that the people should choose not the wisest or the greatest as their leader, but the average man who understands them best, and this was what happened in Bryan's case.

There was something quite unprecedented about the campaign of 1896. The followers of Bryan were so sure they had found the one panacea for all the world's ills, and that with the free coinage of silver on the 16-to-1 basis, all the world's poverty and injustice and suffering would come to

an end, that they went into it with the spirit of crusaders. It
was pathetic to see their childlike faith in a remedy which,
though it might have brought temporary relief, seemed certain to bring ultimate ruin and doom upon them. Rather it
would have been pathetic, had it not been terrifying to witness their earnestness and determination to carry their cause
to victory.

On the other side feeling ran just as high. On the part of
the Barons of Industry and Lords of the Rail, there was
bitter resentment at the stupid and ungrateful underlings
who had turned to bite the hand that fed them, and mingled with the wrath a tinge of panic as the power of the
movement became increasingly manifest. Here were also
many thousands who felt that the overbearing Lords of
Capital deserved a lesson but who feared that the success
of the people would mean a greater disaster than they had
suffered before, and an increasing number of people who
believed that the system was all right, but that it needed
a lot of regulating to keep it in bounds and to protect the
public from its abuses. There were certain New York bankers who espoused the cause of free silver as a matter of
conscience, and with the spirit of the crusader and martyr
faced ostracism and repudiation at the hands of all their old
friends.

This was no old-time campaign in which politicians
pumped up emotion by "waving the bloody shirt" and making the eagle scream. This was a battle to the death, where
the passions of the nation were stirred to their depths, and
where the fate of the vast industrial system of the nation
was to be determined. Millionaires saw hands stretched out
to grasp their wealth, the politicians saw the threat to all
their power. McKinley, framer of the high tariff, was
chosen as their leader (though in earlier years he had favored the silver coinage) and after a desperate battle he
came out victorious, with 276 electoral votes against
Bryan's 176.

An unfortunate element in Bryan's leadership was that
his appeal was on sectional geographic lines, always a dan-

gerous situation. He carried the South and the West and got not a single state in the North, east of the Mississippi. Just what the defeated and disappointed people would have done when they found the old system more firmly entrenched than ever, we cannot state, for a new emotional storm was brewing which was soon to sweep over the land. We know, however, that the Anarchistic current from across the seas had swept into the midst of the welter of discontent and gathered it into a ruthless organization known as the I. W. W., which was beginning to spread widely through the West. They considered a capitalistic democracy a shade more diabolic than Czarism, for it deluded the workingman with the idea that he was free when he was in hopeless bondage. They held it was useless to try to unseat Capital by peaceful means, since the Capitalist had too firm a hold of the political machine. Violence and terrorism were the only means. The working man must seize the tools and machinery of his labor, and the farmer must seize the land. The tools should belong to the man who used them and the land to the man that cultivated it. The Capitalists who held these tools by craft and fraud, must be driven out and terrorized until they relinquished their claim. Deeds of violence followed words such as these, bridges were blown up, buildings fired, bombs exploded, and whole districts were terrorized. If the vote could not succeed, the French had proved there were other ways of putting down the mighty from their seats, and sending the rich empty away.

5. A Saving Cross Current

McKinley sat in a perilous seat, with enemies ringing him around, when suddenly their attention was distracted and a cross-tide of emotion swept across the nation, so powerful that for the moment grievances were forgotten. For some time the feelings of Americans had been stirred by the sufferings of Cuban patriots at the hands of certain Spanish administrators who had handled them with the utmost cruelty, slaughtered them without mercy and gathered their women and children into unsanitary concentration camps where they died like flies. The situation was rendered unendurable when Congress placed a tax on sugar which threatened the Cuban planters with ruin and threw thousands of men out of work, who joined the revolution. Our government protested against the cruelty of the Spanish administration, and Spain, though she intimated that her difficulties were due to American shipments of arms to the revolutionists, finally yielded and agreed to correct the abuses. Then suddenly the American warship *Maine* was blown up in Havana harbor with the loss of the greater part of her men. A wave of furious indignation spread over the nation. It was concentrated and pushed along by the yellow press which saw the chance to increase their circulation. Hearst had already published enough horror to stir a stone, and had made public a stolen letter of the Spanish Ambassador which was sufficiently insulting to secure his recall, and now it needed no red headlines to carry the war cry "Remember the Maine!" from shore to shore of the Continent. The American Ambassador cabled that Spain was ready to grant autonomy or even to cede Cuba to the United States, but all pacific intent was submerged by the popular hurricane. McKinley, whose political backbone Roosevelt had compared to a chocolate éclair, bent before the storm, suppressed the news from Spain and sent such a message to Congress that war was promptly declared.

The war certainly provided a cross wind that blew the clouds from the horizon. All the emotion the nation had to spare was let loose on Spain. The war was undoubtedly a blessing to McKinley and the Republican party. The turbulent and pugnacious element among the discontented had a chance to enlist and expend their pugnacity on the Spaniard, and the attention of the public was distracted from the evil deeds of the Captains of Industry by the victorious achievements of a new batch of heroes. Dewey, who deserved more credit for his resolution in passing the straits in the Philippines than for pounding to pieces the helpless wooden ships of the Spaniards at Cavite, made his triumphant progress up the North River with such a display of popular enthusiasm as the country had never seen before. Hero Hobson of the *Merrimac* made the tour of the country, now heroically attempting to protect himself from the embraces of adoring maidens. The Rough Riders of San Juan Hill received an ovation wherever they went. The whole country was in a turmoil of enthusiasm, and for the moment failed to note how terribly the army had suffered from grafting contractors, who supplied spoiled food and defective supplies, or to take account of the disgraceful mismanagement both in the army and in the medical corps, which caused the loss of far more men by disease than by bullets.

Bryan, however, was still hopeful. He could not believe that the angry wave of discontent that had been sweeping the country and clamoring for free silver, and the control of the industries and railroads by the people, and the taxing of predatory wealth, had flattened out. Moreover, he saw another issue on which he thought he might ride to victory. When war had been declared the Populist element in Congress had forced through a self-denying ordinance to the effect that the United States would keep no part of Cuba for herself. Nothing had been said about the Philippines, but Bryan thought that the old Liberty current that inspired America would never endure Imperialism and that this could be made a "paramount" issue. Congress was undecided what to do with this fruit which had fallen into its lap. When McKinley finally recommended the retention of the islands, there was so much opposition among Republicans and Populists that the measure could not be carried. It was then that Bryan entered the arena and, rounding up his followers, induced them to vote for the measure, which was thus triumphantly carried. As soon as it was accepted as Republican policy, he turned upon it, and attacked Imperialism and the subjugation of foreign lands as un-American, and started his campaign, with this issue in addition to his old platform of free silver. He did not realize how completely the old discontent and emotional turmoil had been ironed out by war enthusiasm. The Solid South stood by him, but the Western states had sufficient enthusiasm for the war and for expansion to throw them to the other side, and thus in 1900 Bryan received a much smaller electoral vote than in 1896.

6. The Anglo-Saxon Spirit Finds Its Dynamo

The threat had been sufficiently great to alarm the Republican leaders. The Political Current is a comparatively small stream and for its success depends on using the great currents of popular feeling for its support. Its leaders had lost no opportunity to capitalize the war enthusiasm which was their chief asset. Theodore Roosevelt, after straightening out the police system of New York, had run for Governor of the state and had succeeded in putting through a number of reforms by playing clever politics with Senator Platt, the state boss. As Assistant Secretary of the Navy he had attacked old-fogyism, and had kept the men at target practice, to the disgust of the old admirals, until he had made the Navy the most accurate shooting machine in the world. When the Spanish fleet came out of the harbor in Cuba where they had been bottled so long, every shot of the Americans took effect, and the splendid fleet of Spain was soon lying wrecked along the beach. Though the glory went to Schley and Sampson, who commanded, the people knew that credit was due to Roosevelt. In the meantime he had gathered a regiment of men from the Western plains, most of them old friends whom he had made when ranching out in Dakota, and these Rough Riders fought the only spectacular battle of the war at San Juan Hill.

These events put Roosevelt on a pedestal from which he could radiate through the nation such emotional force as he possessed. And he was a dynamo of no mean power who could generate such an unadulterated stream of the old Anglo-Saxon current as had not been felt in years. Popularity is a strange thing, compounded of achievement and character. Dewey had been put on an even higher pedestal, but in a few months all his emotional hold on the people evaporated. He was no dynamo. In every nation there are groups of many different sorts. Some leaders like McKinley succeed by listening carefully for the desires of the majority and obeying them. Others succeed when once placed in prominence by displaying their natural characteristics in full force, and trusting that there is a sufficient group in the nation to respond sympathetically. They are like magnets who, when lifted up, draw to them all men of a certain type. Bryan did this with the great half-educated small-town population of the Middle West. The appeal of Roosevelt was wider. An author and historian of no mean merit with the traditions of a gentleman, he could reach the cultivated class, but at the same time his life on the ranch had brought him in contact with the cowboys and hard men of the Western plains. He was a fighter of the old Anglo-Saxon school trained to hit hard and play fair. He had his code of honor, and no one could stand up to him and advocate anything dishonest or crooked or vile without feeling the breath of his condemnation. He aimed to keep around him a certain atmosphere which he called the "Oyster Bay atmosphere," and any one who transgressed by a word or sign was instantly excluded. It included men of the roughest type but it excluded any one who gave indication of meanness or crookedness, or lack of fine feeling. Such a man, raised to the public eye by his achievement, at once drew to himself the strong men of the nation, who held to the old Nordic ideals of hard fighting, strenuous endeavor, adventure and fair play. He attracted men of energy as Bryan drew the more pacific element.

To the Republican leaders his popularity was an asset, but his zeal for reform was a menace. They needed all the enthusiasm of the people he could arouse, but they wanted him where he could do no harm. They thought they had him neatly placed when they induced him to accept the nomination as Vice-President, contrary to the advice of his friends who fully understood their plans. Four times before, in the cases of Harrison, Taylor, Lincoln, and Garfield, sudden death had interfered to alter completely the course of the republic. For although one might suppose that an individual cannot seriously alter the purposes and direction of a democracy, yet these events prove that when the individual has his hand on the helm, he can carry the ship of state a long way from her course before he is replaced. The whole nation mourned sincerely for McKinley when the assassin's bullet struck him down, but none with such selfish fervor as the Republican leaders, who saw themselves turned over to the mercies of an erratic reformer who might wreck their organization any moment by some wild proposition. As a matter of fact he probably saved the Republican party from annihilation and the nation from revolution.

7. THE SLAVES OF THE ENCHANTRESS

Few, even to-day, realize how serious was the situation when the war enthusiasm died out. The old individualistic ethics still ruled in business and politics. No employer was responsible if his workmen were caught in the machinery and torn limb from limb. He had a free hand to keep them at starvation wages and take every advantage of their weakness and distress. He could defraud them by forcing them to take their pay in goods from the company store at twice their value. No moral sense checked him from crushing his rivals by any trick or fraud or from purchasing special privileges by bribery which gave him a strangle hold on the community. Everything was fair in business. It was "every man for himself and the devil take the hindmost."

The Revolutionary Spirit had beaten in vain against the throne of the great Enchantress. She still kept her seat and the web spun by the Spirit of Politics held the public at its mercy. We have shown how when men grew desperate and resisted, their strikes were crushed by injunctions and armed force. Every employer had a God-given right, protected by the Fourteenth Amendment, to deal with his employees as he chose, and any attempt to better their conditions by law was promptly thrown out by the courts as unconstitutional. The result was that the rich grew steadily richer and the poor poorer and more helpless.

I was living on the lower East Side of New York during

this period and was a witness to the frightful conditions and terrible sufferings of the poor. The worst tenements, in crowded courts without air, water or light, with hideous dark basements and narrow attics into which whole families of wretched children were crowded, were owned by the richest church in New York, which drew an enormous revenue from their property and felt no responsibility for its condition. Some of the worst dives in Chinatown were owned by men of prominence who never thought of inquiring whence came their income. Chatham Square was lined with lodging houses commonly known as "Bughouses" whose vast dormitories with double or triple decker beds consisting of strips of canvas on an iron frame, were filled with an army of wretched men out of work, who spent the day in trying to beg or steal the ten cents for their night's lodging. Hundreds of decent hard-working men were there, reduced to the last stage of misery. We would give them books to peddle or addresses to look up in the quest of a job and we would see them come in at night after tramping all day in the snow and sleet without food, and burst into tears from sheer exhaustion and despair. They would take any job that would keep them alive. One fine old woman from the island of Jersey was keeping her husband alive by finishing boys' trousers at twenty-five cents for a dozen pair. Another family, father and mother and two children, were trying to keep the wolf from the door by making Charlotte Russe boxes at the rate of $1.50 for 5,000. By working madly all hands at once, they could just clear enough for their rent and had to trust to luck for food.

Many of the men were longshoremen. Sometimes, between ships, they had no work and after pawning everything would go hungry till the ship came in. Then I have seen them work sixty hours at a stretch without sleep, and come home exhausted and weak to an empty, dirty tenement. Naturally they craved alcohol and drank till their money was all spent. I have seen little children come in in midwinter barefoot, clothed in one ragged slip, to tell me

they had been to school two days without food. It was no-
body's business, then. The schools were not equipped as
they are to-day. Where there are wide parks to-day, five-
story tenements were packed so closely that there was barely room to pass between. On each lot 100 feet by 25 feet
were two houses, four or five stories high, and on each floor
lived four families, many with six and eight children—and
even so they took boarders. The population was denser than
anywhere else in the world, and models were made of the
section to show the public what conditions existed. There
were no parks within reach, no movies, no amusements but
low dives, nothing save the saloons to give any relief to the
sordid misery. Each block was lined with saloons, and into
the back door of each passed long lines of women, each with
her pail, to get her mixed ale,—a terrible mixture of high
wines and various unsanitary ingredients. Night after night
I have been called in to stop fights in mixed ale parties, to
quiet women delirious from the stuff they drank, to keep
infuriated men from killing their children. There were base-
ment dives in Mulberry Bend where any wretch might rent
a "spot" on which to lie and as much beer as he wanted, for
a nickel. The beer was made from the rinsings of old casks
with enough lime to give it a "bead." Girls in department
stores were paid three and four dollars a week, and if they
complained of starvation were plainly told how they could
get along in comfort. There was an impenetrable wall between these things and Fifth Avenue. Save for a few ladies
who dabbled in Mission work, no one knew how the other
half lived, and they would have said it was none of their
business anyway.

While these things were going on the papers were full of
the extravagant absurdities of the very rich. Ward Mc-
Allister and his four hundred were on every tongue, and
the latest plutocrats were attempting every sort of display
to elbow their way into the charmed circle. Magnificent
palaces were built with interiors shipped bodily from French
châteaux. Paintings, rugs, statuary were bought by the
cartload, and the cost, in tens of thousands, arrogantly dis-

played. One woman had a special carriage and footman to take her pet dog up the avenue every day for an airing. Another bought her dog a diamond collar worth thousands. Balls were given where pearls and jewels were presented as favors. The Bradley Martin ball is still remembered as the acme of extravagance of that plutocratic age. It was at this time that I was calling on an old longshoreman. He had been captain and owner of a schooner from Maine, but his boat was wrecked and, working as hard as he could, he had been distanced by younger men. His wife was dying of consumption in a wretched tenement room and needed many little comforts. He had to go to work on the docks or see her die of starvation, yet he dared not leave her alone lest she might need his help and die in his absence. He was a fine old fellow, a typical old Maine sea captain. He pointed to a paper on the table with an account of some ball where $25,000 had been spent on flowers and the tears came into his eyes. "Wall," he said, "it don't seem hardly right for them to be spendin' all that on flowers, when just a few dollars would fix it so the old woman might pull through."

There were an increasing number who did not think it was "quite right." Among the working men the groan of misery and growl of wrath was becoming articulate as it found definite expression through various organizations. The Federation of Labor had a membership of 548,000 in 1900, and was to reach 2,000,000 by 1914. Intelligent workmen were looking restlessly for a cure for their troubles and reading Marx. In 1901 the Socialists and Debs came to the fore and by 1908 had actually secured a seat in Congress. Henry George propounded the Single Tax as his remedy and gained enough followers to run as candidate for mayor of New York. We have already spoken of the I. W. W. which became a menace in 1904 which none could overlook and which terrorized certain sections of the West. Terrible strikes in the mines and on the railroads resulted in bloodshed and the calling out of troops. But employers still maintained the old individualistic attitude and regarded with resentment any attempt to "dictate" in their business, or to arbitrate, and workmen grew more and more sullen and embittered as they contrasted the pittance they received and the sufferings of their families, with the extravagant luxuries of those who, as the workmen thought, by trickery, graft and cruelty had diverted the golden stream into their own pockets. Any one in constant touch with the working man and the poor in those terrible years just after the Spanish War, could feel the steadily mounting tide of wrath and discontent and hatred.

8. The New Current Breaks the Web

As we look over the history of the past one may think of the common people as some huge wild beast of the jungle, captured and trained to obedience, as is the elephant of India, by blows and starvation, but which if aggravated or suffering beyond a certain point turns upon its masters. Then it either tramples them in the dust, or it is conquered to live on in drudgery and slavery with a broken spirit. So when the emotion of the people reaches the boiling point it bursts forth, either to break the bonds of the social order that has confined it, or to be mastered anew and reduced to slavery. A third way out has been provided once or twice in the world's history. The wealthy and powerful class, seeing the sufferings of the poor and the approaching crisis, might surrender voluntarily their power and share their privileges with the poor. The nobility of Japan who held in their hands all the power and wealth, voluntarily surrendered it for the good of the state in 1868. Those who were watching conditions in America in those years around 1900, could only wonder whether it would end in chaos and bloodshed or if there would be some great change in the character of the ruling class and in the industrial system. It seems almost a miracle that just at that time the change came. All these various causes were operating to transform the American character. New emotions and attitudes were becoming dominant.

The old Anglo-Saxon current had been split in twain. One branch which stood for the old Individualism was an active part of the Plutocratic Current that upheld the great Enchantress. The other branch inspired those who had come to see that the only path to Liberty for the masses was in the restriction of this dominant individualism. Roosevelt, by nature a true exponent of the old Anglo-Saxon fighting current, saw that this Spirit of Independence which advanced as the champion of the Plutocracy to demand Liberty, was an imposition and a fraud, and that true liberty could only be attained by its overthrow. He became, therefore, a dynamo for this modified branch of the old current, which we might term the Spirit of Social Responsibility. In the tide of the old current every man had sought liberty and justice for himself. The new current was one which carried a sense of responsibility to see that others secured liberty and justice. If this could be done only by restrictions it meant that the current of Liberty must build restrictions instead of sweeping them away in the old fashion.

It was this new modified branch of the old heroic Spirit that, under the leadership of Roosevelt, at last broke the web of the Enchantress, and overthrew the throne whence she had ruled for thirty years.

Already there were storm conditions among the Western farmers and in the great group of industrial laborers, but now the well-to-do, intelligent portion of the Nation in the East as well as in the West were becoming aware of the game the politician and the Captain of Industry were playing over their heads. In 1888 Lord Bryce's book, "The American Commonwealth," laid bare many of the secrets of the politician and sounded a wholesome warning. A host of journalists sprang up who began to pry into the inner workings of every political machine and every trust, and all the unsavory mess was spread before the public, awakening a true sense of horror on every side. The common citizen had supposed that Standard Oil was the only offender; now he discovered that even those stocks from which he derived his income were tarred with the same brush. It was a soul-racking time and the consciences of all honest men began to stir. Thus the old Reformation current, always in the background of the American mind, awoke again, and joined with its old ally, the Spirit of Devotion to Liberty and Justice. Combined with the great Spirit of Humanity that was also waking to life, these three formed that great tide which we often term Public Spirit.

Robert Woods had started his settlement in Boston, and other settlements began to appear in New York and Chicago, where young Collegians studied the conditions under which the other half lives. Jacob Riis began his agitation for more air and better homes for the poor. It became a fad for young men of education to explore social conditions. The horrors of the packing business were so vividly portrayed that fastidious folk began to fear for their digestion and swore off meat for a time, fearing that some working men might have been chopped up in the sausage machine. And although they worried more over their health than over the working men, still the message percolated. Girls like Carola Woerishoeffer took jobs in the New York laundries, or associated themselves with the striking cloakmakers. They investigated the immigrants working under contract and often done to death by cruel and unscrupulous bosses. Under a deluge of muckraking city after city woke up and began to clean up.

The first effort was to bring the government back into the hands of the people and to break the web of the Enchantress. It was the political machine that controlled everything and the first step for the honest citizen was to free himself from the domination of the old Political Current. It is surprising how quietly this was done by a series of moves any one of which would have been impossible ten years earlier. In New York all the tramps and hoboes were handed the price of their vote, from one to five dollars, and herded to the booths where they were watched until they voted the right ticket. To obviate this the Australian secret ballot was proposed, and, after bitter opposition from the machine, was adopted in Massachusetts in 1888, and gradually pushed until within twenty years practically all the states had adopted it.

But the machine in secret caucus could still pick its candidates and the honest voter had no opportunity to remonstrate if the tools of Big Business were chosen. In 1897 La Follette proposed the Direct Primary, that the people might select the man of their choice. Ridicule and abuse followed, but in 1907 Hughes took up the cause, and by 1910 the Direct Primary was in use in nearly all the states.

Men were awake now and searching for means to break the hold of the old Political Spirit on the government and to enable the people to work their will. So many measures had been put over by the politicians that robbed the people of their rights, that men cast about for a means of defence, and in his platform of 1896 Bryan advocated the Initiative and Referendum, giving to the people the right to demand a referendum on any measure passed that was contrary to their interest, and also to initiate legislation when the politician refused to act. "Arrant Socialism" it was called then, but by 1902 six states had adopted it, and by 1912 it was the law in sixteen states. In many situations the courts had proved themselves to be under the orders of big business, but when the Recall of Judges was proposed there was a terrific outcry, for it seemed unwise to subject the Judiciary to the whims of the people. But even this measure was passed in eleven states by 1912. Ever since the bill of 1883 civil service measures had been gradually replacing the old Spoils System and now another abuse was taken up. The seat of the control of Big Business had been the Senate, and now it was proposed that the Senate should be elected directly by the people. In 1908 Taft took this up with the endorsement of Roosevelt, and in 1912 the Seventeenth Amendment was passed, making the popular election of Senators the law of the land. Thus at last the old web of the Enchantress was completely broken.

A question that had an even more vital effect on politics was that of woman's suffrage. The women had very strong feelings about many questions affecting the national life, especially those which concerned children and the home, but as they had no representation their feelings were bottled up in a separate compartment and ignored, so that there were vast emotional currents that had no effect on the national life save as the women were able to cozen their husbands and sweethearts. In Wyoming, where women were rare and treasured members of the community, the suffrage had been given them in 1868, but in the East the suggestion was received with ridicule and abuse. Politics was not woman's sphere. By her sweet influence in the home she should control the destinies of men, and not soil her hands with vile contacts involved in politics. The machine knew well that with women in the ring the whole atmosphere of politics must change, and they managed to get certain women to oppose it with virulence so that they might say chivalrously, "The women don't want it. If they did, why then—." Although the first crusaders, Susan B. Anthony and Anna Shaw and others, had much to suffer, the opposition was not as bitter as in England, for most men in the Western States were sufficiently chivalrous to be willing to give women anything they wanted. In 1895 Colorado, Utah and Idaho had granted suffrage, and in 1910 seven more states, so that when Wilson took it up in 1918 it was not difficult to pass the Nineteenth Amendment.

In a few years such amazing changes have seldom been quietly made in the history of a nation. The old lords and barons who had controlled the nation and all its industries through the political machine, found themselves robbed of their power and the people now held the control if they chose to use it. There was no need of bloodshed. Now they had only to vote away the wealth of the rich by placing any kind of tax they wished.

The web was broken, but there still remained the Great Enchantress, the Spirit of Gain and Greed.

9. THE ENCHANTRESS IS TRANSFORMED

As stated the great menace to American life had lain in the strangle hold which the Barons of Industry and Lords of the Rail had upon the government and through it upon the people. It was against their "get rich quick" methods that the great revolt had started. While many were men of fine character who did much for the public welfare, there were others who manifested an utter indifference to the public welfare, and to the sufferings of their employees, which even the old-time individualistic fighters began to find a bit off color. For example, Roosevelt in his oft-quoted letter to Lodge in 1906, notes the calm indifference of the plutocrats to the sufferings caused by their acquisitive methods, and makes it evident that he thought that present conditions demanded some alteration in the rules of the game. In time past only Kings and Emperors had had such power over the lives of their fellows, and history had proved that no man can be trusted to control the destinies of thousands without some check. Democracy while arming itself against political control by a King or tyrant had never thought of the possibility of an industrial control which would prove even more tyrannical and merciless.

These great combinations controlled by a few potentates with power to crush all rivals and grind their helpless work-men down to starvation, had been a new product of the age. The Sherman Anti-Trust Law had been enacted to curb them in 1890, but big business had found so many holes in it that it scarcely worried them. Roosevelt, however, saw it as a valuable tool. While Police Commissioner he had prowled around through the slums and, almost alone of all the men in politics, he understood the popular discontent and the imminent danger. He knew that either a new spirit must enter the trusts or their power must be broken. He did nothing until he was well established, and then he brought the Anti-Trust Law down in blow after blow upon the more unscrupulous trusts. There were twenty-five prose-cutions during his administration and forty-five more under Taft, who followed up his policy. He started with the big-gest and most powerful. The Standard Oil, Copper and Su-gar trusts and the U. S. Steel Corporation were all attacked and their questionable proceedings brought to the light of day.

It was fortunate for Roosevelt that at this time he could secure the support of the intelligent middle classes who also had a grievance and sway them by the tide of the new current of Public Spirit. The methods of big business in manipulating the New Haven road had reduced a gilt-edged stock almost to worthlessness to benefit a few financiers, and thousands of the more intelligent and cultured classes were robbed of the savings of years by this and other similar operations, so that they were as indignant as the laboring classes and backed Roosevelt in his attack on such methods.

The farmers had attempted to check the railroads in their unfair rates by the Interstate Commerce Law of 1887, but that too had proved a farce. In 1905 it was estimated that the railroads collected one hundred million dollars by unfair rates. In 1904 Roosevelt attacked them in his message and in 1906 the Hepburn Law was passed, making it possible to nullify unfair rates. In 1910 the Mann-Elkins Law was passed to prevent the roads from raising their rates. Thus it came about that with their rates fixed by a commission and their wages fixed by the Unions, the railroads were tied up so tight that even legitimate earnings were hard to secure. By the mere passage of a few bills, millions of dollars had been taken from the pockets of the plutocrats and put into the hands of the farmers and wage earners. In other revolutions, by slaughtering and plundering the aristocracy, the proletariat has transferred much wealth to themselves, but it is doubtful if such a vast transfer of weath from the rich to the poor as was accomplished quietly by the passing of these bills during the administrations of Roosevelt and Taft was ever achieved elsewhere. The reformers kept urging Roosevelt to crush the Trusts. He had a better idea,—to win them to a better spirit until they would work with him.

Another great abuse had been the manner in which the trusts and railroads had gained possession of the public lands and deprived the nation of its forests and available assets. Roosevelt discovered an old law authorizing the President to set aside forested land for the public use, and promptly began his great crusade for conservation and the preservation of the forests and water power. Before Congress checked him in 1907, 150,000,000 acres had been thus set apart, beyond the reach of big business.

If fifty years ago any one had suggested taking from the plutocrats two-thirds of their income and turning it over to be used for the public welfare, it would have been called arrant robbery, on a scale never attempted by any bandit. But even this amazing transfer of wealth was accomplished. In 1894 an Income-Tax law had been passed and declared unconstitutional. But so great was the outcry against the enormous incomes of the plutocrats that in 1907 Roosevelt began to advocate it again, and Taft in his campaign, with Roosevelt's endorsement, stole Bryan's Income-Tax plank, and in 1909 proposed the Sixteenth Amendment which finally made it the law of the land. This resulted in taking for the use of the public two-thirds of the income of those who were wealthiest. At the same time laws were passed protecting the working man from unduly long hours of labor, and making employers responsible for injuries received in their employ. This shifted all the vast expense associated with injuries and sickness from the workman to his employer. Such an astounding revolution probably never took place in the world before—transferring power and wealth and privilege from the few to the many, from the rich to the poor, from the employer to the worker. If one could calculate the billions thus transferred it would make the loot of the treasury of the Romanoffs look like a pittance. We can imagine what a stir it would have made in the world if the working man, in a burst of rage, had held up the plutocrat at the point of the pistol and compelled him to hand over two-thirds of his wealth. Here it had been accomplished by legal methods so quietly that few realized what had happened.

It was not accomplished without friction. On every side politician and plutocrat arose and cursed Roosevelt for a meddler and a socialist and a wild and crazy boy. He was wrecking the country and overthrowing the whole business system. To break up the emotional tide that was behind him they tried to start counter currents by the usual trick of appealing to the prejudices of the public. The most absurd and outrageous slanders were circulated. He was described as being so intoxicated that he had to be carried to bed, regardless of the fact that on the occasion mentioned, there were many who saw him and who could bear witness that he was perfectly sane and sober. Roosevelt was not the man to take attacks lying down. He waited until some responsible paper published the slander, and then sued for libel. The most eminent men from all over the country bore witness for him and his slanderers were snowed under by the abundance of testimony. He won the case, his detractor apologized. He was awarded damages but would take only a nominal six cents.

He was called a rash, unbalanced slanderer and vituperator, but, pugnacious as was his temperament, we are told by Thompson, who was with him constantly as reporter, that he so held it in check that he never said a word he did not mean to say, or uttered a statement he could not prove. He attacked violently, indeed, but after suing him for libel and finding he could prove his statements, his enemies grew cautious. He differed from other politicians who attack the rich when they have an audience of the poor, and vituperate England when among the Irish. Instead of floating with the emotional stream that surrounded him, he loved to stand up and fight his way against it. He attacked the Southern policy when he was in the South, and the British when he was in England, and Big Business when he faced its representatives. His enemies made the most of every opportunity. They spread it through the South that Booker Washington had been invited to a meal in the White House, and in every way by slander and caricature they tried to start counter waves of prejudice to break up the growing tide of enthusiasm and hero worship. The Republican leaders did not understand that by adopting these progressive measures he had saved the Republican party from wreckage and made it the people's party. He had prevented overt revolution by bringing about the greatest revolution the country had ever known by means of the ballot.

The result was most extraordinary. The new current of Public Spirit was now running strongly in the channel of the Republican party. The Socialistic tide animated the Populists, and the Politicians in the Democratic party decided to make it a channel for the current of dissatisfied feeling emanating from the forces of Big Business and inspired by the Spirit of Plutocracy that the Democrats had flouted so arrogantly and disastrously under the leadership of Bryan. If they could win back New York and the East by means of this wave of hostility against Roosevelt, they might then re-establish themselves once more in the seats of the mighty. Accordingly they chose Alton B. Parker, a sound-money man, and attempted to shelve Bryan and free silver. This was not so easy. The old Western current was still running strongly in the party and the old War Horse succeeded in preventing the insertion of a sound-money plank. Parker then countered by sending a message to the effect that he was a sound-money man and if they did not want sound money he requested them to withdraw his name. Bryan, though exhausted by his labors, rose from his bed, returned to the fray and made the most eloquent speech of his life; but in vain. Parker and sound money were chosen. It was an absurd situation. The Democratic party, after spreading its sails for eight years to catch the tornado of discontent from the West and from the dissatisfied workers, finding that Roosevelt had blanketed them, now shifted sail to catch the Eastern breeze awakened by the discontent of Big Business with progressive policy. But Parker had no emotional dynamic. The great tide of enthusiasm and hero worship swept Roosevelt to victory with a tremendous majority in 1904, and gave him four more years to carry on his progressive policies. At the end of that time he had the country and the machine completely in his hands and could dictate his successor.

As one reviews the astonishing changes of these years and considers the violent prejudices that were overcome, and the vast losses inflicted on the dominant element in society, it seems impossible that they could have occurred without some terrible cataclysm or fierce battle. The fact that they occurred step by step, so quietly that men hardly knew what was happening, was due to the gradual change in the spirit of America to which we have alluded, and which was being brought about by the union of these great currents of feeling that had been latent so long and that now united in an overpowering flood. Most astonishing of all, the Great Enchantress herself, the old Spirit of Commerce, was transformed from a cruel and hideous witch to a Fairy Godmother. For if the employers and heads of Big Business had not also been transformed in spirit the change could never have come so quietly. But many of these, stirred with sympathy for their employees, and disgusted with the old political methods, helped to bring about the change. Gradually there had been produced this general transformation from the old attitude of the Anglo-Saxon pioneer, that of independence and individual initiative and resentment of all interference by government, the "laissez-faire" attitude in short, to that of social responsibility, co-operation and public spirit. As admirably outlined by President Tucker of Dartmouth, it was a progress from liberty to unity. The spirit of independence had been essential to the earlier development of the nation, but it had worked itself out to a demand for liberty which meant slavery. In a closely articulated social and industrial system such as had now developed, the old-time independence was impossible.

The Spirit of Devotion to Liberty and Justice was still alive, but it was now fighting for Liberty and Justice for all men and not for oneself alone. Many causes had aided in this change of spirit. In the first place there was greater knowledge. The hidden web was dragged into the light of day. After a decade of diligent muckraking, the crookedness and graft and greed of every political machine and every business corporation had been brought forth into the public view. The solid honest citizenry saw it with disgust and abhorrence, and understood how they had been gulled.

Moreover, there was a deeper knowledge of conditions. Through the settlements, and through the study of sociology the youth of the country had come to understand how the other half lives, and the suffering and injustice of the lot of a large portion of their fellow beings. The church, which at first hand had supported the existing order, began to turn its attention from personal ethics and the evils of intoxication to social ethics. Men like Washington Gladden and Rauschenbusch and Graham Taylor followed in the footsteps of Maurice and Kingsley and began to preach a social gospel, and everywhere young people were studying the Social Teachings of Jesus. In spite of the exhortations from church wardens to keep to the spiritual gospel the new teaching would not down. It appeared in the press and in the novels of the day, such as "The Inside of the Cup."

The new generation who took over the leadership in industry were ashamed of the methods of their fathers. The policy of John D. Rockefeller, Jr., showed at once a marked change from that of his father, and he won the approbation of the country by the way in which he faced the strikers in Colorado and settled their difficulties. It was not merely that public opinion was against the old-time method. When the leaders of business once abandoned their old emotional attitude of resentment at interference with their business, intelligence began to operate and they grasped the idea that co-operation paid better than domination. Instead of seeking to crush their subordinates to blind submission and grind them beneath the heel, they discovered that the profits were greater with the intelligent co-operation of contented workers. And if they were given a share in the profits it was found that the profits increased yet more. Shorter hours and higher wages, instead of reducing the income, increased it. Thus profit-sharing came into being and the big corporations became anxious to have their stock taken up by the workers. Welfare organizations provided pleasant quarters and restaurants and amusements for workers. Some big organizations, like Filene's store, allowed their workers to organize and manage part of the business and discipline themselves. It became a disgrace to provide unsanitary quarters and to pay starvation wages, and firms where such conditions existed were blacklisted, and held up to obloquy. Men proved that honesty paid better than fraud in the long run.

10. THE REVOLUTION IN SPIRIT CREATES A NEW WORLD

Little by little the new ideas gained ground, even the old timers found that more pay and shorter hours brought bigger profits. The new sense of social responsibility brought many other changes. Tenement House Commissions altered the slums, and made new laws concerning housing, doing away with the old rookeries and death traps. In the blast of public condemnation the old corporations, like that of Trinity, for shame's sake tore down their disreputable Cherry Street tenements and built better. The overcrowded blocks, like Mulberry Bend, were destroyed and replaced by playgrounds, parks and public baths. Public-health commissions investigated conditions and appointed doctors and nurses to tend the children in the schools, to give treatment for disease and infection, for eyes and teeth, to eradicate tuberculosis, and to see that the pupils were properly fed. Girls were trained to cook, to keep house, and to make a pleasant home. And perhaps most important of all was the introduction of cheap and wholesome amusements in the moving pictures and public-recreation grounds, in place of the old saloons and dives.

A new world was created by this sense of social responsibility which swept over the country like a wave. Men had decent homes to which they could return, in place of the dirty, crowded rookeries; pleasant places in which to spend their spare time, libraries where they could read, and amusements within the reach of a slender purse. In the same slum district where the children were once in rags and the women lived in filth and squalor and the only amusement was a drunken carouse and mixed ale party, in 1929 the homes are neat and well-kept, and the women appear in

silk stockings and furs, and some even have motor cars. It
is unbelievable, this great American revolution, that took
place so quietly that no one realized what was happening.
Back of this change in the laws, which meant a shift in the
division of the profits of labor, by wages, profit-sharing
and taxation resulting in the transfer of billions of dollars
from the pockets of the few to the use of the many, was
then this real change in the character of the American
citizen. Though the progressive legislation was fought with
violence, the majority of the people were for a fairer deal,
and the new spirit of social responsibility in the end so took
possession of the men of wealth that they have devoted
enormous sums to public health, and research, to libraries
and public amusements. The list of gifts to the public by
such men reaches a total which fairly staggers the imagination. Of course there are still mean men in the world, and
industries where conditions are bad, but they are becoming
fewer and fewer. In fact the shoe seems to be on the other
foot. The Labor Unions are at times so tyrannical and unjust
that the employer suffers grievously. Such a reaction is
almost inevitable. When the working man finds that he has
the power, he often shows less restraint and public spirit
than even the old-time unscrupulous employer, and he has
created unreasonable strikes from which the public has suffered to such an extent that strong feeling against the
Unions was aroused. The Unions suffered from bad leadership, unscrupulous walking delegates who deceived and
forced the laborers. In the main, however, labor also has
felt the spirit of co-operation—and has realized that conflict is disastrous to both employer and employee. As the
working man is given a fuller knowledge of the business
and a greater share in its profits, he sees that his interests
are at one with those of his employer, and that the road to
prosperity is through co-operation and not through antagonism.

Such was the quiet revolution that freed America from
the despotism of the plutocrat and the boss and made it the
most prosperous nation in the world. Conditions in the

United States had never been as bad as in the old countries where there are static conditions of poverty and destitution that continue from generation to generation and where no individual hopes to rise from the class and condition to which he was born. There were sections of the great American cities where there was desperate poverty, but it was not the same people who were poor. Any one who lived in such "slums" soon noted that within five years nearly everyone had moved to better conditions. The Polish and Italian immigrants who lived in utter destitution, as their children grew up with an American education, were lifted out of their environment by the younger generation and moved from the lower East Side to Brooklyn and the Bronx, and their places were taken by other destitute immigrants. There has always been the opportunity for advancement, and now that the conditions of life are changed and everyone has so much more to live for, and so much more to interest and occupy him, and so much larger a share of the product of labor, it is hard to find enough dissatisfaction to form the groundwork of a revolutionary party. It is a gradual process by which the working men became capitalists through owning stock and an automobile, and all have enough stake in the existing order to turn them against anything that savors of Bolshevism or Revolution, save in sections where for the moment conditions are unfavorable, as, for example, among the textile workers of New England, or at times when some cause like a panic in the stock market produces general unemployment.

The interesting feature about this revolution is that it was not the result of an upheaval of the people of any concerted attempt to overturn the existing system, as in the case of all other revolutions. It was due to the intelligent leadership of the men in command, and chiefly of Roosevelt, who sensed the growing spirit of dissatisfaction and unrest, and headed it off by relieving the pressure before the boiler burst, and by guiding the public discontent into channels through which it could attain relief and satisfaction by legal methods and without a social upheaval. As we have suggested, if the men of wealth had opposed it to the end with all their might, there might have been a real revolution, but the astonishing feature was that so many of the most influential seemed to catch the new spirit and actually to be eager, like Mr. Carnegie, to rid themselves of their wealth in behalf of the public. If one could have watched events with an X-Ray eye, one could have seen a situation similar to that which preceded the French Revolution. On the surface an unexampled display of wealth and luxury, of gayety and splendor, while deep underneath in the section then unknown, where the other half lived, hunger and want and suffering, like volcanic fires, were raising the temperature to the explosive point. And the few who saw were tunnelling anxiously to provide a vent for public feeling before it was too late, slightly aided by the gathering discontent of the upper middle class. And just at the time when matters were most critical the younger generation of the very men who had built up these confining barriers that imprisoned the poor, stirred by this new feeling of sympathy and social responsibility, fell to and aided in demolishing the walls that for so long had confined the helpless masses. And they did this not because they feared a revolution, for few of them seemed to grasp the gravity of the situation, but because for the first time they had become aware of the terrible conditions under which these men lived, and because this new incoming tide of sympathy and social responsibility moved them to take action.

We have described that Great American Drama in which the old Anglo-Saxon spirit played the leading part. It appeared in different costumes, now clad by Jefferson in old Colonial vestments, now arrayed by Jackson in the deerskin and coonskin of the pioneer, and outfitted with a uniform by Lincoln, and dressed in modern clothes under Roosevelt, but everywhere we can trace the same old features—the devotion to liberty and justice, the sense of fair play, the good sportsmanship that have been handed down in a steadily flowing current from ages past. It has often slept, but has waked to take the leading part in every forward movement. Unsuccessful alone, it has always needed some ally, to hold its followers in union. We have watched the gradual change from that spirit which assisted the liberty of the individual, to one which fought for the liberty of the slave, and finally sought liberty and justice for all. The great battle has always been against the Spirit of Gain, which, when it dominates a nation, assumes the form of the Great Enchantress, casting spells upon the minds of men, and weaving a web which holds the masses under a rule as cruel and autocratic as that of any ancient tyranny.

We have shown how the old spirit faced the spirit of Revolution on the one hand, and the Enchantress on the other, and, summoning as ally the great Spirit of Humanity, won the victory which transformed American life. The old current, altered and modified, now turned its force into the great dominant tide of Public Spirit, which sought for justice and freedom, not through independence but through co-operation, and caused a change in the character of the individual so fundamental that the American of fifty years ago would utterly fail to recognize the description of the American of to-day in the pages of Siegfried and other modern writers.

CHAPTER IX

AMERICA AS A WORLD POWER

1. ISOLATIONIST AND IMPERIALIST

CORRELATIVE with the great struggles between the Spirit of Liberty and Justice and its enemies in the internal development of America, there was also in progress a conflict as to the relation which America should bear to the outside world. The old currents of feeling that swayed the American mind combined with or counteracted one another in a rather surprising fashion, and ended by producing two streams of feeling that were strongly antagonistic and that met in combat over every question of foreign policy.

We have spoken of the period when America was swept by storms from across the Atlantic and was liable to be torn asunder between the adherents of British aristocracy and French democracy, and we have shown how Washington strove to erect a barrier between this continent and the old world which would make America immune to the atmospheric conditions of Europe. He succeeded so well that for many years America was almost as much apart from European politics as was Japan. It was a wise measure that allowed the new nation to develop undisturbed by the old racial and political animosities and prejudices that plagued the old world. French and Germans, Austrians, Hungarians, Croats and Italians, Russians and Jews that lived once in perennial mutual suspicion and animosity, once settled in America, lived peaceably side by side with their old differences forgotten. There were, of course, some exceptions, notably in the case of the Orangemen and the Irish where there was a violent emotional eddy which resulted in perpetual riots, but in the main America was apart from the prejudices of the old world, and undisturbed by its cataclysms.

We come now to a period when America was again caught up into the stormy atmosphere of Europe. Once she had been so weak that storms from abroad swept over her. Now she was so strong that her own storms affected Europe, and no question could be decided without her aid. But during the period of isolation a definite emotional attitude toward foreign powers had developed, which found its expression in the Monroe Doctrine. It was in some measure the product of the old Liberty and Reformation currents of feeling, that made Americans suspicious of the autocratic political and religious system of Europe, and created a determination to keep their continent free from its influence. A second element supplied from the same source, was the feeling that America should never subject any other people to their domination, as was the habit of European nations, nor should she in any way become entangled in their affairs. This current of feeling ran so strongly in early America that it soon had produced its fetishes and phrases with high emotional charge, such as "entangling alliances," and the Monroe Doctrine became a sort of Palladium for which many would fight and die, though few understood exactly what it meant. For the sake of clearness we may call this whole attitude of suspicion toward foreign nations and resentment at their interference, with its associated emotional phrases, the Isolationist Current.

We have already described the rise of a current of feeling inimical to it, at the time of the annexation of Texas, which we termed the Imperialistic Current.

Instead of viewing America as a peaceful and pious housewife weaving diligently the tapestry of her own prosperity behind lofty harem walls, that secluded her from all possibility of flirtation with foreign princes, they saw her armed like Britomart with casque and spear, and striding forth to champion the oppressed and subdue wild and savage lands, that she might bring to them all her gifts of liberty and knowledge, and gather them into her kingdom of justice and truth. America has been greatly misunderstood from a failure to understand that the Imperialistic Current sprang from two entirely different emotional sources as we shall shortly endeavor to show.

In the meantime we must review briefly the period in which the Isolation Spirit was dominant and note the beginnings of the Spirit which created so great a change in the fortunes of the country. The Monroe Doctrine had been forged originally as defensive armor, to keep the old world autocracies from gaining any further foothold, and to prevent this continent from being swept into the whirlpool of European dissension because of disputes as to possessions in America. At first it was hardly taken seriously by European powers, but as no question of moment came up they allowed it to ride. Nothing could have been more inimical to this feeling of antagonism toward foreign interference than the attempt of Napoleon III to set up an autocracy in Mexico, but the United States could do nothing until the Civil War was ended. Then notice was served upon the ambitious French potentate that the United States Government regarded this effort to establish imperialism on the continent as a menace to the people of America and was prepared to back its opinion with solid shot. At that moment Napoleon had no wish for further complications and withdrew his French regiments and left the unfortunate Maximilian to be executed by his subjects.

If the first principle of the Isolationist was to warn off all foreign powers from any attempted conquest on these shores the second was that in return America would never seek any conquests beyond her own borders. We have already noted the violent protest that was made when Texas and California were taken from Mexico. Seward's attempt to annex San Domingo was quashed, and it was only with difficulty that he succeeded in putting through the purchase of Alaska from Russia. Invitations to interfere in European affairs were curtly declined in 1863 when America was asked to join in a protest against the Czar's treatment of the Poles, and in 1885 when Cleveland refused to participate in the Berlin Conference to regulate the injustice in the Congo Free State.

It was soon discovered that the Monroe Doctrine not only provided a defensive shell, but was also plentifully supplied with teeth and claws. It was strange that this implement, designed to keep America out of European wars, should have been first vigorously applied in a fashion that might easily have precipitated the United States into a foreign war. Venezuela appealed to Washington in a dispute with London over the boundary of British Guiana, and Richard Olney, then Secretary of State, sent a vigorous demand to London in July, 1895, that the question should be submitted to arbitration. This very demand made by the Isolationist Spirit proved to be the means of awaking its chief enemy the Imperialistic Spirit, and for the time we see emerging a new concept of America as a world power, a champion of the weak against the injustice of the old world, —a concept that was to grow and spread until the Imperialistic Current dominated American thought. This demand was expressed in terms that might well have stirred the old British lion to get up on his feet and growl, and at best the authorities in Downing Street must have felt that the young American state was feeling its oats in a fashion that deserved punishment. Olney said, "The United States is practically sovereign on this continent, and its fiat is law upon the subjects to which it confines its interposition. It is not because of the pure friendship or good will felt for it. It is not simply by reason of its high character as a civilized state, nor because wisdom and equity are the invariable characteristics of the dealings of the United States. It is because, in addition to all other grounds, its infinite resources combined with its isolated position, render it master of the situation and practically invulnerable against any or all other powers."

The authorities in London, doubtless remarking to one another that the American urchin was waxing somewhat fresh, replied calmly and coldly refusing to arbitrate. Then Cleveland suddenly voiced the New America. He said it would be "the duty of the United States to resist by every means in its power, as willful aggression upon its rights" the attempt of

Britain to appropriate lands which "we have determined of right belong to Venezuela." And he added that war was better than "a supine submission to wrong and injustice and the consequent loss of national self-respect and honor." Here was the old Spirit of Liberty and Justice opening the channel in which the Imperialistic tide was to flow.

Moreover, it was prodding up the lion in dangerous fashion and few who lived through that crisis will forget the wave of excitement that swept over the country. Wall Street was hit by a panic that roused the brokers to a frenzy against Cleveland as a crazy jingo jeopardizing the business of the nation. But from the rank and file there was a rather jubilant response, something perhaps of the spirit of the small boy who has knocked off the gentleman's silk hat with a well directed shot. But back of it all was this newly awakening sense of America as a world champion,—big enough and strong enough to stand up to any one and declare her principles. In one way or another Cleveland certainly sent a thrill through the whole nation, and from that day the Imperialistic Spirit, that seemed to have gently expired after the Mexican War, began to renew its grip upon the American mind. To the astonishment of everyone England at once acquiesced in Cleveland's demand. She was perhaps so sure of her case that she did not fear arbitration, and also she did not wish America lined up against her in any world combination. Her acquiescence was justified, for her claims were granted. Moreover, the principle of the Monroe Doctrine was maintained before the world.

A similar episode in 1903 confirmed the position of the United States as arbitrator of the New World. England, France and Germany threatened Venezuela with their warships in the attempt to collect their debts, and Roosevelt again told them to submit their claims to arbitration. England, in view of her previous experience, promptly agreed, as did France. The Kaiser, however, haughtily refused, and it was not until Roosevelt informed the German ambassador that he was sending Admiral Dewey with the fleet to Venezuela that the Kaiser decided to arbitrate his case.

This, however, was after the Spanish War, when the American navy had proved its power, and Europe knew that the United States was a force to reckon with. It was no such bolt out of the blue as Cleveland's defiance.

Before we consider the events that enlarged the American republic into an empire with possessions in the far corners of the earth, held by force of arms, contrary to her most fundamental ideas and feelings, we must consider what the emotional forces were that enabled the Imperialistic Current to rise to such a height that it overwhelmed the old current of Isolationist feeling.

2. THE ENCHANTRESS AND THE MISSIONARY SPIRIT COMBINE

There were two great motive forces that drove America into her Imperialistic attitude. One was the same old Spirit of Gain that as the Great Enchantress had established her iron rule over the nation. Just as, in America, the great leaders of industry and finance had pushed forward their plans in pursuit of the almighty dollar regardless of any one who stood in the way, so now they began to reach out for profits that might come to them from establishing American domination in other lands. This is a spirit which other nations understand and which to this day they believe to be the underlying motive in the foreign policy of the American people. But along with this motive there was another so diametrically opposed to it that many authors have refused to believe that it was sincere and have interpreted it either as hypocrisy or as a form of megalomania. I refer to what we may term the Missionary Spirit, by which I mean a deep sense of responsibility for the welfare of others and a real and often passionate desire to help them. It was, in part, a product of the Reformation Spirit, and we have described its astounding power and the somewhat disastrous effects which that current had on the minds of the Abolitionists. A recent French author notes this American characteristic with some irritation and interprets it as a desire to interfere in other people's business and to demonstrate one's own superiority by enforcing moral and religious standards on them,—in short as a sort of megalomania. There are persons of this type in America, and the old Reformation Spirit undoubtedly had at times this effect on human character, but it also produced a spirit of self-sacrificing humility as far as possible removed from it. A Frenchman should be able to understand it, for some of the noblest Frenchmen, such as Francis Xavier and Isaac Jogues, were possessed of it.

It would seem needless to say that when the primitive Christianity, which reawoke in the Reformation, truly possesses a people, this is one of its essential fruits, and in spite of all that was selfish and hard in the American, this is what did happen to quite a large percentage of the people. No one who has seen poor women stitching away to earn a few extra pennies for the "heathen," or young men giving up a promising career to plunge into the heart of Africa or China, can doubt it. This sense of responsibility for others, or sympathy with them, is of course variously directed according to the beliefs of the individual. To-day in case of a terrible plague abroad our doctors and nurses volunteer to go and help. Fifty years ago a large percentage of our population believed that the pagan world was on the verge of suffering infinitely greater and more certain than that of the plague, and there were constant pleas of the most earnest and passionate sort to send them help. We are not discussing here the theological or religious side of the question, but merely the effect of this constant agitation in stirring people who held the Christian point of view to a sense of responsibility for the outside world and of interest in it. Those who have never felt or seen this spirit will probably continue to regard it as hypocrisy or megalomania. It is not peculiar to Americans or Protestants, although they seem to manifest it in a form peculiarly aggravating to foreigners. I remember a French missionary among cannibal savages, who smiled when they asked why he stayed on, and who said to me, "Why try to understand? Call it a kind of madness if you will." But there are those who can understand that a man can have a really passionate devotion to his fellow men which will lead him to undergo great suffering and toil to bring them the help he thinks they need. Even if his ideas are wrong and the help he brings is not needed, that does not affect the reality of the spirit or the sincerity of the man. It should be unnecessary to say as much in a Christian country, but many recent authors show such misapprehension of the attitude of America that it is essential to call attention to its origin.

Now at the time when America was being shut in upon herself and kept apart from the outside world, save as big business was looking for a chance to get a grip on the wealth of some foreign tribe, this spirit was constantly being generated and was reaching out in the effort to help the so-called "heathen." While some New Englanders were sending rum to Africa and carrying slaves on their return, there were others who were sending missionaries and teachers and physicians. They were moved by a feeling akin to humanitarian sentiment but differing in that it accepted the whole wide world as its responsibility, while humanitarian sentiment acts usually on the case at hand. Although American sentiment was against any attempt to subjugate or include any foreign nation within our boundaries, there was a considerable number of our New England population who showed increasing enthusiasm for the subjugation of the ends of the earth to the Kingdom of Christ. It was really most amazing that so large a number of people of mediocre education, shut up to the narrow interests of the local village, should thus have reached out to the farthest confines of the earth and developed a sense of responsibility for them. It had its results on the national development.

A group of heroic men who had heard that Captain Cook had been killed and eaten by the savages of Hawaii, devoted their lives to missionary efforts in these islands, and all the churches of America were thrilled when practically the whole nation went over to Christianity. Thus at the same time that American business was beginning to break down the barriers of sentiment that kept America apart for

Americans, and was seeking to dominate foreign lands for purposes of gain, there was this other spirit at work, a constantly growing interest in foreign lands, kept alive through the reports of hundreds of missionaries, an interest which sought to gain nothing, but only to give of the best that America had, in education, health and religion, to the needs of the world. It is necessary to study the workings of both these spirits if we are to understand the surprising development of American feeling in the twentieth century.

All our foreign relations in these important years of expansion were determined largely by these two currents of feeling, the spirit of business enterprise which sought gain and conquest, and the Missionary Spirit which sought to help, and to relieve distress. The two currents have been mixed and commingled in the most surprising fashion, which is probably the reason why most foreigners regard America as hypocritical.

3. THE FIRST CAPTURE OF THE IMPERIALIST. THE HAWAIIAN ISLANDS

Hawaii is an example. As just stated, the missionaries went there with the desire to help and were prepared to sacrifice their lives. Business entered also and the government followed, securing the rights to Pearl Harbor in 1875. By 1890 there were many engaged in raising sugar and, among them, the children of the first missionaries were making large profits, and were swept away from the aims of their fathers into the tide of the Commercial Current. They saw that if Hawaii were annexed to the United States they would have no duties to pay and their profits would be increased. King Kamehameha had granted a constitution, and in the government thus organized these business interests had a powerful influence. In 1891 Queen Liliuokilani overthrew the government and made herself autocrat of the islands. The foreign interests organized a rebellion against her, turned out the Queen, and asked for annexation to America.

This was about to be granted by the Senate when Cleveland came in in March, 1893. He investigated and found that the revolution had been engineered by outsiders. He offered to reinstate the Queen if she would restore the constitutional government. She haughtily refused. Cleveland withdrew and the people of Hawaii organized an independent Republican government in July 1894, which was duly acknowledged by the United States. It then became evident that some great power was almost certain to gobble up the islands. The United States Navy was most anxious to secure the islands and feared their occupation by a hostile power. Business interests naturally desired annexation, but it is doubtful if they could have overcome the old American anti-imperialistic sentiment but for the alliance of the Missionary Spirit. The story of the Missions had led a large proportion of the people to feel that the Hawaiians were the adopted children of America and that she was responsible for their welfare and should share with them her privileges.

Annexation was brought up again in 1898 and successfully passed the Senate. The possession of the islands was undoubtedly a great advantage to a nation with imperialistic aspirations, and those who were planning to make America a dominant world power exulted in their acquisition. It was natural that the foreign powers should see only this, and regard the altruistic motives set forth to catch the current of the Missionary Spirit as pure hypocrisy. It is, however, probable that none of the expansion measures of this period could have been carried unless their sails had been set to catch the Missionary Spirit as well as that of good business.

The same spirit had a powerful influence in our relations with China during the same period, and it was this that made so marked a difference between the Imperialistic Spirit of America and that of other nations. The American people had to be convinced that their rule was necessary to the welfare of a country before the government was allowed to take it over. European nations had few such inhibitions. In 1895 Japan took Formosa, in 1897 the Germans seized Kiao Chau and dominated Shantung. In 1898 the Russians took Port Arthur, and the British Wei Hai Wei. Then in 1899 came the Boxer Rebellion and the slaughter of foreigners. The Allies marched into Pekin and prepared for reprisals. It was then that America came forward with her policy of the Open Door. This has been sneered at as a desperate effort of America to get in on an equal footing with the rest in the general robbery. In the minds of the public it was far from this, and Hay knew it when he said: "I do not think public opinion would justify this government in taking part in the game of spoliation now going on." Although there were interests eager to have a share in despoiling China, the solid sentiment of the country was moved by the other spirit that wished to help rather than rob, and when the government returned to China the indemnity exacted, stipulating that it should be used for the education of Chinese boys, the whole country approved.

4. IMPERIALISM AND "THE LITTLE BROWN BROTHER"

Much more serious and vital were the problems left by the Spanish War. Although the sugar interests in Cuba undoubtedly had something to do with the beginnings of that war, it was the other spirit that was the moving power, and any who lived through that period can remember how America responded to the terrible picture painted of the sufferings of the Cuban peons under the administration of Weyler. It was the sinking of the Maine that touched off the explosion, but the Isolationist sentiment was so strong that, when war was declared, it was distinctly provided that America should retain Cuba only long enough to see a good government established. Porto Rico and the Philippines were not in the range of public thought at that time. Undoubtedly the Commercial Current was running strongly and there were those in the government who planned to make America a world power and who were heartily glad that these islands were captured before the people had a chance to put in a proviso like that of Cuba.

It was what the Imperialist called "Manifest Destiny"

that put the Philippines under American control. This was the phrase used to catch the old Reformation Current and to win conscientious objectors. The Philippines were on the verge of a revolution against the injustice of the Spanish control. The great patriot Rizal had just been brutally shot and they welcomed the Americans as their defenders. They expected the government to be turned over to them as soon as the Spaniards were evicted, but this was not so simple as it would seem. In the chaos of a revolution when the only government that existed was overthrown, when there were no men trained in Republican government, and affairs were in the hands of adventurers, the Missionary Spirit would never permit America to withdraw and leave this people to their fate. There were, of course, men in the government and especially in the Navy determined to keep these islands as a stepping stone to world power, and there were business interests anxious to control the Philippine trade, but again it was the appeal to the other spirit,—our duty to the famed "little brown brother," our responsibility, having created a bad situation, to see it set right before abandoning it,—it was this appeal that moved the mass of the people. It was touch and go. The Isolation current was still strong and a vast number felt that it was un-American to interfere at all, and that the Filipinos should be left free to govern themselves in their own way.

In the meantime a clash arose between the American troops and Aguinaldo, which resulted in a guerilla war which lasted three years before the islands were finally subdued. Then the question appeared again and once more the sails were spread to catch both spirits. In spite of the sneers of foreign potentates there was a large mass of the American people who took very seriously their responsibility for the Filipino and who felt that they had no right to retire until everything possible had been done to provide for his education and health, and until a responsible government had been created which could be relied upon not to rob and plunder the poorer folk as had been done under the Spanish rule. It was largely because of this appeal made to the people of America that McKinley and Roosevelt were able to carry out their plan for the occupation of the islands.

The Philippines prospered under the able administration of Taft as Governor General. Schools were organized and hospitals built, and a government organized in which the people elected the lower house while the upper house was appointed. But it is not so easy to turn over the government to the Filipinos. The problem is complicated by the fact that there are many different tribes and races in the islands which distrust and hate one another, and if left to themselves, there is certain to be trouble. For example, the Moros in the Southern islands, after a long fight, finally decided to submit. The Americans told them that if they would surrender their arms they would be treated justly and protected, and they trusted the Americans and gave up their weapons. Then, to satisfy the demands of the Filipinos, the Americans withdrew and they were put under Philippine officials, age-long enemies, whom they hated and despised. When they resisted, having no arms, they were shot down by the constabulary, saying that they had been betrayed to their enemies by the Americans.

It was the appeal of facts such as these to the sense of responsibility of the American people that determined the decision to remain in the islands for the present, although imperialism was twice made an issue, and there was a strong sentiment against holding any people in subjection against their will.

5. "MANIFEST DESTINY"

Under the stimulus of the Commercial Current and the Missionary Spirit the Imperialistic Current began to gather head. It developed its emotionalized phrases, like all similar currents, such as "America as a World Power," and "Manifest Destiny," which had their appeal, and a conception grew up of Imperial America, crowned and throned like Ancient Rome, and dominating the Councils of the Nations by her inexhaustible youthful energy and her lofty ideals. Thus, after the Spanish War, America, that had been regarded by the Nations as a negligible quantity in world affairs, and by the British as a sort of hobble de hoy country cousin, leapt suddenly into the arena, fully armed, to be recognized by astonished Europe as among the first, if not the strongest, of the world powers.

While there were still many of the old-time Isolationists, the average man could not but be conscious of a thrill of pride as he saw America step forward into the front rank, triumphant and defiant, mistress of the Western Hemisphere, and unafraid to face any of the world's powers in defence of the principles she had sworn to maintain. Roosevelt had seized upon the imagination of the people. Everywhere men caught the vision of America grasping the world's sceptre and ruling mankind according to her principles of justice and fair play.

The American chest that began to swell when Cleveland started to twist the lion's tail, expanded another notch when Roosevelt notified the Kaiser that the American Navy was sailing for Caracas. The people knew then that America meant business and intended to maintain her ideas of justice in this hemisphere and was not afraid to defy the strongest war machine of the age.

In 1907 when the powers threatened to seize the customs of San Domingo, America again warned them off, took control of the situation and settled their claims.

Thus Uncle Sam, with the Isolationists hanging on to his coattails, and the Spirit of Commerce pulling him madly forward, was finally urged step by step into foreign lands by crises which aroused his sense of responsibility and brought the Missionary Spirit into action.

In accordance with the agreement, Cuba had been set free and given a government of her own, but in 1906 revolutionary disturbances took place and America again took over the government and held it until a stable administration was established. New troubles in San Domingo occasioned the establishment of a protectorate there in 1907. A rebellion in Haiti also resulted in an occupation by American troops until order was restored. Troubles in Honduras (1911),

Guatemala (1920), and Nicaragua (1921) were adjusted by United States troops sent in on request to preserve order.

Such action was a corollary of the Monroe Doctrine. The powers virtually said, "If you do not allow European forces to collect just debts or to protect their citizens in the revolutionary disturbances on your side of the Atlantic, then you must see to it yourself that justice is done and order is maintained." Many a time Englishmen have said these very words to me during the disorders in Mexico when America was hesitating to interfere and yet would not allow the British to intervene. There were many who sincerely felt that a definite responsibility to maintain law and order in the Western hemisphere had been placed upon the United States, and this tended to establish her upon the Imperial throne of the Western world.

It was by no means an easy position to maintain. The stronger South American powers were jealous of the United States and resented her interference, and to conciliate them and secure their co-operation, the Pan-American Union was formed. This satisfied the sense of responsibility, if not the Spirit of Gain, for the important point was that some one should be responsible for law and order in this hemisphere, and prevent the chaos of constant revolution, and if the South American powers were willing to share in that responsibility it was all the better.

6. The Enchantress Manipulates the Missionary Spirit

The great Enchantress was as clever in spinning her web and in manipulating the current in foreign affairs as at home. She assisted in arousing the Missionary Spirit and with every forward step she caught some new country in her web and subjected it to her subtle but inexorable rule.

It is hardly probable that Roosevelt in taking over control of these various chaotic governments was interested in furthering the prosperity of the Sugar Trust or any of those monopolies which he was so vigorously attacking. The fact remains that certain groups did make large profits

from the activities of the government, and it is probable
that they pulled wires to secure personal advantage in various ways. At any rate the result was such that the procedure of the government during this period acquired the
name of the "Dollar Diplomacy" and foreign critics as well
as the cynical group of American writers gave to the world
the impression that every move was made to secure profits
for American business and protect it from interference and
to exclude foreign competitors. That powerful business organizations that maintain a lobby at Washington are able
to influence the government to some extent should be self-
evident. We are considering, however, the great currents of
feeling in the American people, and to them the appeal of
the trusts was certainly very feeble. If the people endorsed
their plans it was because the trusts were clever enough to
appeal to the missionary or humanitarian spirit, this sense
of responsibility for the welfare of the weak, and also to
the growing ambition of the nation to exercise a controlling
influence in the world.

7. The Dynamo That Connected Atlantic and Pacific

One would suppose that by this time the Imperialistic
Current would have been strong enough to put through so
important a project as the Panama Canal, but the matter
hung on in the doldrums of endless discussion. It is rare that
one individual can radiate sufficient emotional force to carry
a democratic nation along a new course which is obstructed
by constant cross currents. Roosevelt did not believe that
the President was chosen to listen for the voice of the people and then to carry out their will. He accepted the theory
that the people chose the best man they could find to show
them the way, to tell them what to do, and then to carry out
with all his might any plan that he saw to be of benefit to
the nation. This is a totally different conception of the
Presidency from that of most men who preceded and followed him. This was the idea of the first Presidents, and
Andrew Jackson was a man of this type, but since his day,

with the exception of Cleveland, the Presidents had usually taken the other attitude. Roosevelt had acquired sufficient emotional dynamic to carry the people with him in most of the schemes he proposed. He had won the bitter enmity of Wall Street and Big Business by his attacks on the Trusts which had been characteristically venomous, vitriolic and vituperative, and for a time there was no name too violent or abusive to express their feelings about him. The people, however, had made a hero of him and cheered him to the echo.

There had long been talk of an Atlantic-Pacific Canal. The French company that initiated the Panama enterprise had failed, and in the endless discussion as to the relative merits of Panama and Nicaragua the whole affair was in the doldrums, and the average man believed that nothing would ever be done about it. Roosevelt saw its enormous importance to America, and that it made very little difference whether it was Nicaragua or Panama provided it was done. There are those who would have us believe that the real impetus came from the men who had bought up the shares of the French company and who influenced the President and Congress to choose the Panama route and to buy the privilege at an exorbitant price. This may be, though it is hardly likely that the President was a party to it.

The success of any popular leader depends on keeping a strong wave of popular enthusiasm behind him. Every plan that he carries out is sure to rouse the antagonism of some group, and is likely also to give some opportunity for graft to other unscrupulous persons. Roosevelt kept his following by putting through his plans to make America great with a strenuous energy that radiated throughout the country and everywhere awakened the Imperialistic Spirit. The current was strong enough to override much opposition in Congress and elsewhere, but he also knew where compromise was necessary in order to prevent too violent an opposing wave to roll up against him. Men had wasted decades in idle discussion. The Canal was a vital matter. He proposed to build it now. The end should justify the means.

It was of course necessary if America was to put millions into the Canal, that she should control it. When Colombia went back on the price agreed upon and began her attempts to hold up the American Government for more cash, so that it seemed that the work would be indefinitely delayed, a revolution was fomented in Panama, which declared its independence of Colombia. A price for the Canal strip was quickly arranged and the work begun. Directed by the genius of Goethals and supplemented by the marvellous health control of Gorgas, it afforded the world an instance of rapid and efficient construction under the greatest difficulties, that was unexampled and astounding.

A howl of rage arose from the disappointed grafters in Colombia, who accused America of fraud and injustice, and there was some echo in America from the enemies of Roosevelt and from certain political purists. But in the main the people were enthusiastic over the great achievement and applauded the vigor of Roosevelt in defeating the various attempts to hold up his great project. In spite of the dubious means, Roosevelt's prestige was increased rather than diminished, for the Canal was built and controlled by America and the benefit to the world and to America in particular was great enough to outweigh in the mind of the public any doubts as to the means.

Some difficulty arose with England over the tolls. By the Hay-Pauncefote treaty America had agreed to give equal privileges to all nations, but the American shippers claimed that the coastwise trade did not compete with international commerce, and that American ships trading between New York and San Francisco should be allowed a reduction in the tolls. This was passed by Congress under Taft's administration, and at once strongly protested by the British, so that considerable ill feeling was aroused, on both sides, the British claiming that America had deliberately broken a solemn treaty. Both this question and the payment to Colombia remained sore spots which aroused violent discussion all over the country until finally settled by Wilson.

8. America Becomes the Arbitrator of Nations

Still another matter which brought America forward as arbiter in world affairs and caused the breast of the citizen to swell yet more with the consciousness of power and pride was the Russo-Japanese War. American sympathy had been chiefly with the little men in their tiny island empire who had not been afraid to stand up against the aggressions of the greatest of the World Powers, and who had defeated the Russian navy and with incredible heroism had captured the impregnable fortress of Port Arthur. Feeling against Russia had at one time been very strong, owing largely to the crusade of George Kennan, who had vividly pictured the horrors of the Imperial prisons and the sufferings of the Siberian exiles who had been torn from their homes because they had spoken some word in favor of liberty or even of education. Some of this feeling still lingered, so that a majority of American citizens rejoiced to see the humiliation of the Russian giant. But the little men had now reached the limit of their endeavor. The war had become a stalemate in the Manchurian plains, and Japan was at the end of her financial resources. Her people were overtaxed and bankers, seeing no issue to the war, refused credit.

Roosevelt had abundant information that both sides would welcome any solution that would save their face, and therefore offered the services of America as arbitrator. The offer was accepted, the delegates met at Portsmouth, and America gained the prestige of settling a war between the great world powers. The Japanese Government had not confided to the people their critical financial situation, and they were at first infuriated with Roosevelt, because he obtained for them no indemnity from Russia, but their leaders were most grateful for the settlement which gave them a free hand in Korea and Manchuria, and the people soon came to a more friendly attitude toward America. As for the citizens of America, all these events put them in vital touch with the current of world affairs. As in Colonial days they had to think about the Old World because they were dependent, so now they had to turn their thoughts thither because the Old World was becoming dependent on America; not merely the missionary societies, but the whole nation was coming to feel a responsibility for the whole world.

CHAPTER X

THE CONFLICT OF THE PROGRESSIVE AND REACTIONARY SPIRITS

1. RIVAL PROGRESSIVE DYNAMOS

BEFORE we go on to the final crisis which established America as leader among the nations, we must turn once more to note a new conflict which arose in internal affairs.

The Revolution in Spirit had transformed the character of the Great Enchantress, for the leaders in Industry and Finance were now working for the public welfare, as well as for their own profit. The old Political Spirit of Graft and Greed was, however, more bitter than ever, and sought in every way to re-establish its domination. Public feeling seemed gradually to gather around two opposite poles. On the one hand were those who felt that more power should be given to the people, and more laws framed to restrict the power of wealth and privilege, and on the other, those who distrusted the people, who felt that too much had already been done to hamper the great corporations, and that the prosperity of the nation depended on restoring power and privilege to the dominant class. The latter pole drew to itself the old Political current and the Commercial current and the static aristocratic and plutocratic elements of society, while to the former gathered the Western current, the Eastern reform current, a portion of the Socialistic current and some elements of the old current of devotion to Liberty and Justice. From the fusion of these elements there rose two antagonistic currents of feeling which we may call the Progressive and Reactionary, and which increased so rapidly in voltage that they issued in some of the sharpest conflicts in American politics.

One might suppose that there were merely two different political theories, but they were much more than that. They

were two attitudes toward life, composed of strong prejudices and violent enthusiasms. The intellectual content was
small compared to the emotional. In short, they were what
we have termed emotional currents.

In their fundamental essence and extreme form these
two go back to the beginning of civilization. The one is the
same seen by the author of the Revelation as, clad "in
purple and scarlet and decked with gold and precious stones
and pearls, having a golden cup in her hand," she sat "upon a
scarlet beast having seven heads and ten horns," and "on her
forehead a name written: 'Mystery, Babylon the Great.' "
And in the other we might recognize that wild, ragged,
half-starved Spirit, Demos, that, turned to Demon, as Ten-
nyson says, and running amuck, has overturned thrones,
and slaughtered fair ladies in savage cruelty. But now both
are dressed in modern clothes, tamed and civilized, and only
in rare moments do we catch glimpses of the spirit that
lurks within. Nearly everyone in America was subject to
one or the other, for both currents ran crosswise through
both political parties and through all institutions. They
created great confusion, which was increased by the fact
that the progressive current centred about two figures that
radiated great emotional force, but who were radically and
fundamentally antagonistic.

Roosevelt and Bryan were now the outstanding figures
in politics. Each of them could radiate tremendous emotional power and both had their main stronghold in the
West. But Roosevelt had cut the ground from beneath
Bryan by his progressive legislation, and had become the
hero of the New America. In spite of the wrath of big
business he had the country in his pocket for the moment.
He had determined not to run for another term in spite of
the popular clamor, and he sought for a successor who
would carry out his policies. It was difficult, however, to
find one who would carry out progressive ideas and at the
same time win the support of that wing of the Republican
party that was strongly animated by the Reactionary Spirit
and to whom his ideas were anathema. He finally picked

Taft, overriding his wish to become a judge, and by the tremendous force of his personal influence and of the machine he controlled, he put Taft over at a convention that was wild to nominate Roosevelt, and which was only controlled with the greatest difficulty and dexterity.

The Democratic party was in difficulties in this year of 1908. Its success depended on catching some great wave of public dissatisfaction and riding into power. But the only such wave of importance was that of the reactionaries, and Roosevelt had cleverly scooped that in by getting the old guard to endorse Taft. Consequently the Democrats had to turn to personal dynamic. The only man who could hope to create a counter wave against Roosevelt was Bryan. And thus after two campaigns aimed at the White House and ending in the ditch, Bryan sprang Antæus-like from the mire of defeat, seeming to gather strength each time he was thrown to earth. On the first ballot of the Democratic convention, he got 888 votes out of 994. It was an amazing illustration of the tremendous dynamic of personal influence. Even when men's feelings seem definitely directed, a powerful personality passing over them, like a magnet over iron filing, may depolarize them—or repolarize them. Through his campaigns and lecture tours Bryan had made his personality felt by nearly half the people of the United States. His magnetism had started a vortex which sucked in many thousands. But this was not enough. Each campaign was supposed to have a "Paramount Issue" and it was hard to find one. To overthrow the Roosevelt regime some issue must be found that would gather up all the dissatisfaction that was floating about.

Bryan's chief hope was to catch the old-fashioned isolationist and anti-imperialist, who felt that Roosevelt had wickedly enslaved the Philippines. The party leaders managed to get him to avoid conflict with the Reactionary current, and to concentrate his efforts on stimulating the Isolationist current against the tyranny and imperial aspirations of Roosevelt. But Roosevelt, though hated by Wall Street, was the idol of the people at this moment, and it would have taken a bigger volcanic eruption than Bryan could engineer to throw him from his seat.

Bryan, the indomitable, went down to a third defeat so decisive that he was at last convinced that the people did not want him for a President. He won only 162 electoral votes against Taft's 321. The Democratic Political current carried the South for him, but Roosevelt captured from him his old stronghold of the West. Roosevelt had proved himself their champion against Pride and Privilege and they found that his creed of the strenuous life and his code of honor at all costs suited their digestion better than Bryan's pacifistic pabulum.

Taft had been accepted as Roosevelt's representative, but he soon proved to be a misfit for Roosevelt's shoes. His genius was static rather than dynamic. One would not suppose that so static a person could have roused such general irritation or have become so violently unpopular in so short a time. It is one of the mysteries of the public mind and the unexpected way in which it reacts. Before and after, as Viceroy of the Philippines and as Chief Justice, Taft has had the enthusiastic approbation of the people and has been admired and loved. But as President, few men have made themselves more unpopular. Apparently various innocent remarks were misunderstood and misinterpreted. He began by carrying out the Roosevelt policies and actually put through more prosecutions of the trusts and more reform legislation than Roosevelt himself.

It was hard to keep the balance. The conflict of Reactionary and Progressive over every step kept raising feeling on both sides to a higher pitch. The Public Utilities, Industries and Financial interests which were the backbone of the Nation's life and created its prosperity, naturally could see no good in the Progressive legislation which hampered them, and termed any one who favored it a Bolshevik or Anarchist, while the Progressives, irritated in turn, called Wall Street a nest of robbers and regarded the Captains of Industry as robber barons. Under Taft the scales seemed to tip gradually toward the conservative side.

A new tariff was put through which aroused the Progressive wing of the Republicans to fury by its "favoritism." A deadly blow was struck at Roosevelt's conservation policy through the discharge of Gifford Pinchot who had been its chief apostle. Various scandals, such as that which involved Ballinger, gave the public the idea that Big Business was once more getting its grip on politics and on the national resources, and that the old Enchantress was climbing back upon her throne.

2. A Personal Quarrel of National Importance

At the end of the four years the Progressive current had reached boiling heat. There was a large wing of the Republicans under La Follette heavily charged with anti-Wall Street sentiment, who demanded progressive legislation and were ready to break loose. In the meantime, by overthrowing the conservation policy, by his general reactionary attitude, and by certain unfortunate remarks, Taft had roused the indignation of Roosevelt. The latter had used the whole force of his political power to make Taft President and he now asserted that Taft had betrayed him to his enemies. A violent controversy arose between the two old friends which had the most disastrous effects on the Republican party, and the most surprising results on the future of the nation.

It seems hardly credible that an individual quarrel should alter the fate of a great nation and change the whole course of events. Although no poet has sung of it, this modern quarrel had a greater effect on the destiny of nations than the wrath of Achilles against Agamemnon before the walls of Troy. A controversy between two men who are exalted on the pedestals of position and popularity reverberates through the nation like a thunderstorm and brings the whirlwind with it, and in this case each man had a powerful current of feeling behind him. From various remarks that he made one must conclude that Taft, stirred by the attacks of Roosevelt and swung into the reactionary current by the influence of his friends, had actually come to feel that his old friend and patron was the most dangerous demagogue and revolutionary in the nation, and that he must on no account be allowed to get his hands on the reins again.

In the meantime Roosevelt had returned from his famous tour abroad where, in spite of the somewhat dictatorial manner in which he told King, Kaiser and Pope their duties, he had been received with almost royal honors. America was proud of him and when he returned popular clamor saluted him as the next President. At first he refused to allow his name to be used and then, convinced that La Follette had no chance, and that he alone could lead the Progressive element to success, he proclaimed that his hat was in the ring. The Big Business interests had already classified him as a public menace and feared him as a demon incarnate, and naturally did not wish that he should again control the nation. It was impressed upon Taft that it was his duty to keep Roosevelt out.

The way in which Root and the Republican old guard managed to throw the Republican convention to Taft showed that the old Political Current had not lost any of its power to make the wheels go around. It was termed a supreme example of steam-roller methods, and aroused the admiration of the business interests and the violent wrath of the progressive elements who claimed to have a majority at the convention. Roosevelt has called it the greatest robbery of the age and his animosity toward Taft and Root was increased a hundredfold, and he succeeded in radiating it in dynamic waves all over the country so that Taft became yet more unpopular. It seems foolish to attempt to over-ride so large a section of the party, for the sense of injustice always adds a violent charge to an opposition current and makes it more dangerous. The Reactionary Current, however, had been so accelerated by fear and prejudice that it rushed madly to its goal, blind to consequences, although the leaders knew that the election depended on holding the party together. They generated more feeling than the cohesive forces of the party could contain and it burst asunder. The Progressives held their own convention where they organized the Bull Moose party and Roosevelt was enthusiastically nominated. His popularity was so great and his spectacular personality so appealed to the mass of the people that it seemed as if he might win.

A characteristically dramatic event added emotional dynamic to the cause. As Roosevelt was about to address a great political meeting, an attempt was made to assassinate him and he was shot through the chest. He went through with the speech nevertheless, stanching the flow of blood with his pocket handkerchief. Such pluck stirred the public as never before and must have won him many votes. Taft knew that he could not win, but he and the great interests were determined to keep the reactionaries out even if it meant a Democratic victory. Roosevelt, who had used all his personal dynamic to put Taft in, was now using every ounce to keep him out.

The Democrats had learned something in the past few campaigns. The old Southern current of feeling, charged with hatred of the Republican party, was still running so strongly that the Democrats were sure of the South, but in other districts the great issue was now between the reactionary and progressive sentiment. The Democrats had proved that with a radical candidate like Bryan, they could not carry the pivotal states in the East, and that with a reactionary like Parker, they could not catch the breeze from the West. Their mistake had been to come out too decidedly for one side or the other. Now the Republicans had fallen into their error and divided into two wings, one Progressive and one Reactionary and the Democratic tactics must be to set their sail for both winds, as Taft had done in the last campaign. The successful candidate at this period seemed to be the man who could present himself as the enthusiastic supporter of both Reaction and Progressivism without committing himself to either. He could not sit on the fence; he must sit on both sides of it at once.

3. The Inarticulate Masses Become Vocal

The Democratic Convention held this year, 1912, was one of the most remarkable in history. The battle between the Conservative and Progressive forces here reached its most violent point, and the prejudice and animosity of both sides was here concentrated and expressed through the lips of their spokesmen so that the two opposing thunderclouds were here discharged in sparks. Big Business in league with Tammany gathered the most violent part of the Political and Commercial currents to the support of Harmon of Ohio, while the main tide of popular feeling was for Champ Clark of Missouri. He was said to be under the patronage of William Randolph Hearst.

Every one seems to have strong feelings about Hearst, but few know of the remarkable discovery that gave him his power. He discovered a large section of America that was inarticulate and deaf to the clarion trumpet of the press, and gave it ears and a voice. A large part of the great cities was submerged and unreached by the press save by certain local sheets, elsewhere unknown. At the time of the reform movement in New York that put Mayor Strong in power, I was living on the lower East Side. That section did little reading of newspapers. The only sheet that was generally taken was the *Evening News,* which was practically unknown on Fifth Avenue. The general popular dissatisfaction that accumulated during the reform administration was also unknown, for it had no organ through which to express itself. In the following campaign every paper in New York was strongly for the reform candidate except the *News,* and as no one uptown ever saw that, every one expected a sweeping victory for the forces of Reform, and was thunderstruck when Van Wyck went into power with a great majority. Hearst had evidently studied the situation and determined to reach this great inarticulate element, unexploited by the press. He bought up the *News* and the *Journal,* and set about creating a sheet that would awaken the interest of the uneducated laborer who never opened a book and shunned the daily press. He printed enormous headlines partly in red, put in pictures and diagrams of every event, that displayed it plainly to the ignorant eye, and sent out an army of reporters to hunt out "Life Interest" stories—which meant any little personal gossip with a thrill to it—love interest and crime preferred —and he reduced the price of his paper to one cent where others cost from three to five cents.

The result was that he reached this vast element that hitherto had taken no paper, or at most only such a small sheet as the *News,* and gradually educated them into news readers. He secured as his editor a real genius in Brisbane and the influence of his editorials was soon seen, and often for good, on the manners of the people. The ignorant laborers had little if any manners when Brisbane began and the change was noticeable. After an editorial, for example, on the value of courtesy, which implied that the true American would always give his seat to a lady, it was interesting to note how the tired working men in the elevated would jump up and awkwardly offer their seats to women who were standing.

Hearst influenced the people, but he got his hold by studying their feelings and giving them expression. All their bitterness and resentment against the rich and privileged classes he expressed in burning and vivid words. The same process was repeated throughout the country, until in every large city there was a Hearst paper, reaching the element that hitherto had been isolated, uninterested in news or public affairs, uninformed and inarticulate. These all woke up and began to take interest. They found their resentment and bitterness, which had smouldered dully hitherto, given vivid expression, and a whole vast element of the American people became suddenly vocal, and a force to reckon with. It was an astonishing performance, but as it released a great tide of feeling against the established order, it naturally aroused the wrath of the conservative element. At the same time there was something to be said for it. In the first place it trained a vast number of citizens to inform themselves of public and even of foreign affairs, and I have been told by men on other papers that their circulation was increased because of those who first learned to read the Hearst press, and then, being dissatisfied, went on to a higher grade of journalism. Also it is dangerous for a country to have a large element of the population inarticulate, and it is safer when their desires and feelings are openly expressed and understood.

On the other side it must be said that much of the class feeling, though smouldering deeply, had hardly reached the consciousness of the masses, and might never have found expression but for the Hearst press which became its brain and mouthpiece. It was not at all the ordinary Progressive Spirit, which had constructive aims, but a tide of bitterness and resentment on the part of the submerged class toward those who had what they wanted, and was destructive in tendency. It therefore added a new violent element to the Progressive current. Though it must often have opposed Hearst's property interests, his press became a tremendous machine through which he could exert his power and gain his personal ends. He first attempted to run as Mayor of New York, and so great was the influence of his papers that he almost carried the day against a press united against him.

Now he was making an attempt to control National politics, and he had adopted Champ Clark as his candidate in the battle of the masses against the classes, as Clark was supposed to stand for the farmer and wage earner against the privileged classes. Most of the delegates from the progressive West were instructed to vote for him—among them Bryan and the Nebraskans. Of all those who were swayed by the great Progressive current and opposed the industrial and financial interests, Bryan was the most ardent and the most prejudiced. To him they were all thieves and robbers. He suspected Clark of insincerity and thought that if Clark were hard pressed he would make a deal with the New York reactionaries and Tammany, which Bryan regarded as a "Covenant with hell."

4. The Progressive Spirit Fights for Control

It is a strange fact that when two such violent currents of feeling meet in conflict, they tend to throw out of the welter a leader of quite a new type, and it was now that both Republicans and Democrats were divided in the fierce clash of Progressive and Reactionary that such a leader became the dominant figure in America if not in the world. There were three different currents of feeling that must be brought into unity if the Democrats were to win the election, the old Southern current, the Progressive current which flowed chiefly from the West, and the Reactionary current drawn largely from the cultured element in the East, and the Democratic politicians sought a man who would appeal to all three, but who would really be dominated by the Political Current.

Wilson had been unexpectedly taken from the Presidency of Princeton and made Governor of New Jersey. The politicians undoubtedly thought that a man thus inexperienced in politics would be easily guided and would have to depend on them for support. He astonished them, however, by gathering up the reins with surprising dexterity, and by gaining such control of the legislature that before they knew it he had put through a series of progressive laws that were quite out of line with their intentions. He proved himself such a clever manager that they supported him in spite of themselves and before they realized what he was doing he had put through all that he wished done. He came thus into the public eye as a possible candidate for the Presidency. Princeton men all over the country, who did not belong to the New York clique that hated him, organized Wilson clubs and soon every one of influence was talking about him. Through his family relations he appealed to the South, his progressive legislation interested the West, and his reputation as President of a great University and author of a history of the United States, attracted men of culture in the East. But Bryan distrusted him and suspected him, as well as Clark, of affiliations with Wall Street and was therefore doubtful on which side to throw his influence.

As soon as the convention opened the battle between Progressive and Reactionary began in a fight over the chairmanship. When Parker was nominated, Bryan declared that this meant throwing the convention into the hands of the reactionaries. He appealed to both Clark and Wilson. Clark's letter was somewhat ambiguous, but Wilson came out so strongly against the reactionary control that Bryan was apparently convinced that he was the true candidate for the party. Bryan plunged into the battle from the first moment and never ceased to fight with all the strength that was in him until the end. Hated by a great number, despised by others, with no longer any political position, he was nevertheless the dominant influence of the day. With all his strength he was out against the forces of reaction. The Reactionary current was not strong enough to dominate openly and hoped to succeed by crafty manipulation, but Bryan drove them into the open by offering a resolution stating that the Democratic party declared themselves "opposed to the nomination of any candidate for President who is the representative of, or under obligation to, J. Pierpont Morgan, Thos. F. Ryan, August Belmont or any other member of the privileged hunting class" and farther "that we demand the withdrawal of any delegate representing the above-named interests." Ryan and Belmont were seated there when this unexpected volcano suddenly burst loose. Pandemonium reigned. Bryan was hooted at, abused, insulted, almost assaulted. Calm in the midst of fury, he kept calling for a roll call until he got it, and as no one wanted to go on record as in favor of the interests, he carried his resolution, even New York delegates voting for it while they gnashed their teeth. It was a clever move, but few would have dared to make it or have been able to stand out and put it through.

After that the nomination of Harmon was impossible, and New York soon withdrew its votes from him, throwing them to Clark; which gave him 556 votes, more than a majority but not the requisite two-thirds. Wilson gave up all hope and his manager was ready to turn over the Wilson votes. Then an extraordinary thing happened. The people had evidently been charged up with enthusiasm for Wilson, for from all over the country telegrams came pouring in upon the delegates urging them to vote for Wilson. Never before had such a mass of telegrams descended upon an assembly, fairly burying the delegates with the weight of the public demand. Many of the delegates favored Wilson and were only bound by their instructions to Clark. They began to break loose.

On the fourteenth ballot Bryan rose and precipitated another earthquake. The fact that the New York delegates had transferred their votes to Clark instead of recommending Clark proved to his mind that the latter had an understanding with Reaction and Tammany and intended to deliver the Progressives into their hands. Stating then that he believed Clark to be in league with the forces of evil, he withdrew his vote from Clark and transferred it to Wilson. Again there was pandemonium, but from that moment the landslide began and went on until on the forty-first ballot Wilson had 602 and Clark only 329. On the forty-sixth Wilson had 990 and the vote was made unanimous. It was an example of what one man can do by sheer force of will and inexpugnable determination when he feels behind him a great mass of popular feeling. Heedless of abuse and threats, of reproaches and accusations and actual physical force, Bryan had stood up, hurling his denunciations of Privilege and Capital, refusing to be downed, until the candidate he trusted and believed to be an honest representative of the people had been chosen. Whatever any one may think of Bryan as the Defender of Free Silver and of a world made in six days, let this stand to his credit that America did not enter the World War with William Randolph Hearst in control of the government. Hearst had been trying to get control of this great wave of animosity to Big Business to use it for his ends, but Bryan had checkmated him. The picture of America in war time controlled by Hearst is enough to make one gasp and but for Bryan the plan would have succeeded.

Wilson proved astonishingly successful as a speaker and he and Bryan combined to make a great impression on the American people. The division in the Republican ranks was fatal to them, and Wilson won the most crushing victory ever gained in American politics, gaining 435 electoral votes to his opponents' 96. Taft carried only Vermont and Utah, and Roosevelt's following in the West and in Pennsylvania was not sufficient to stem the tide.

5. THE RULE OF THE PROGRESSIVE SPIRIT

Wilson entered upon the Presidency less embarrassed by pledges than any candidate for many years. After Bryan's service it was but fair to appoint him Secretary of State. His ideas were quite different from those of Wilson, however. While Wilson thought that if a man applied for a position it was sufficient reason for refusing him, Bryan had been long enough in politics to be dominated by the old Political Current and felt that he should reward all faithful Democrats who had been so long without perquisites. There was naturally a tremendous rush for that portion of the pork barrel which he administered and he seemed to enjoy handing out the prizes.

Wilson was as great a surprise in National affairs as in State legislation. Although he seemed to stand alone, and the public complained that the men whom he appointed were not of first grade, and although the politicians were all suspicious of him and ready to oppose any progressive move, he nevertheless acquired a control over his party and over Congress which very few Presidents have had.

A series of radical measures which had been in the air for a long time and which the politicians of both parties had been dangling as bait for the progressive wing, but which they had no idea of passing, on account of the offence they would give to the reactionaries, he put through, one after another, with astonishing success. Greatest and most vital of all was the Federal Reserve Bill, which stabilized the banks of the country and prevented the possibility of any such disasters as had resulted from earlier panics. It also took the money power out of the hands of a small Wall Street clique.

The income tax which had been declared unconstitutional was legalized by an amendment to the Constitution and a curb was thus put upon the enormous fortunes that had been rolling up.

A Child Labor law was passed and also a law which irritated capitalists more than any other—that of the eight-hour day. A law was passed controlling the issuing of injunctions which had at times been used with notable unfairness against the unions.

The parcel-post was established against the violent opposition of the express companies, and, finally, the tariff was revised and its notable absurdities corrected.

Wilson had started with a fair amount of popularity, and we mention these familiar measures because they were the starting point of the terrific wave of antagonism, part real and part artificial, that rolled up against him.

These new laws were enough to rouse Reactionary feeling to the point of insanity, for they seriously upset the programme of Big Business and limited the income of the Privileged Class. They felt that Wilson was sending the country to the dogs and truckling to the working man, and robbing the employer of his just profits. They sincerely felt that he would wreck the great industries and destroy the prosperity of the nation, and that any measures were justified if he could be discredited. The success of a leader in a democracy depends, of course, upon his ability to voice the desires and feelings of as many powerful sections of the country as possible and to offend as few as possible—in short, upon the amount of emotional drive he can get behind him.

In his Income Tax Law, Wilson had satisfied the clamor of the submerged section that Hearst had made vocal, when bitter class feeling had been aroused by descriptions of the extravagance of the wealthy in comparison with their own want and hunger. It was the climax of the movement begun under Roosevelt, for, though in another party, Wilson had slipped into Roosevelt's place as leader of the great Progressive current. In his tariff reduction he satisfied the demands of the farmers of the West and also of a large section of the South, although, since manufacture had begun to creep into Carolina and Alabama, their sentiment toward the tariff was changing.

In his eight-hour law he satisfied the demands of the labor unions, which had become very powerful and wished for more leisure for their members. From the point of view of safety there is much to be said for the eight-hour law among railroad men, and engineers can hardly be blamed for accidents when they are compelled to work twelve or fourteen hours at a stretch. Mr. Ford has stated that while it was of primary importance to interest a man in his work, there were, nevertheless, large numbers who preferred to regard their work as mere drudgery through the performance of which they acquired sufficient money to enjoy themselves in their leisure hours. This group is sufficiently large to create an ever-growing demand for leisure time, in which working men could go to the parks and the cinema and find relief from the drudgery of daily toil. At any rate, there were vast numbers to whom the eight-hour law brought great satisfaction. The Child Labor Law was in response to the demands of the reformers, rather than the result of any popular demand; for the poor usually wanted to force their children to work in order to get more money.

6. The Reactionary Spirit Attacks

No laws, however, could have been better designed to arouse the antagonism and prejudice of the privileged classes—the employers of labor, and the leaders of the great industries. Instead of finding in Wilson a sympathetic gentleman of culture, as his reactionary supporters expected, they found him entirely impervious to their demands. Though other administrations had at least lent an interested ear to their point of view, Wilson proved utterly unapproachable and unsympathetic and they determined to rid themselves of him at the first opportunity. Though in his management of legislatures he had shown great tact, his uncompromising attitude toward the conservatives would seem to show a lack of that quality, and won him enemies at every turn.

Quite a large wing of Roosevelt Progressives had come to his support, but his next move served to alienate some of these. Colombia kept insisting that she had been defrauded by the United States, and Wilson appealed to Congress to reverse the policy of Roosevelt and pay Colombia twenty million dollars. The friends of Roosevelt raised a great outcry and said it was a weak submission to blackmail. There were many, however, who felt that the friendship of Colombia was worth the sacrifice and that America would profit by smoothing out her relations with the South American states, and the measure was finally carried under Harding in 1922.

Wilson made a similar reversal of Republican policy in the Panama tolls. The British were still protesting that America had broken her word by giving special privilege to her own coastwise trade and Wilson managed to get Congress to reverse its decision and charge the coastwise trade with the same tolls that the British paid. Both these measures roused violent feeling throughout the nation.

If he had taken Roosevelt's place at the forefront of the Progressive movement, he certainly did not replace him as the Imperialistic leader. The old Liberty Current ran strongly in him and this threw him to the side of the Isolationists.

In the Philippines he took steps toward turning over the government to the natives and gave them many of the important posts which hitherto had been held by Americans. This satisfied the anti-imperialistic wing that had been protesting all along against the occupation of the Philippines, but it naturally stirred Imperialistic feeling to violent protest, and Republicans claimed that it had disastrous results which it would take many years to remedy. The disastrous effect may have been due in part to an unfortunate appointment, and, with the right man as Governor General, Wilson's policy might not have had such unfortunate results.

All this time reactionary feeling, at boiling point, was waiting for some loophole in his armor through which he could be attacked in a vital point, but in most of his measures he had carried with him a strong current of feeling. In his Mexican policy, however, he laid himself open to his enemies, for even his friends found it hard to defend him. As this was the crux of the emotional situation we must stop to review these well-known events. Huerta had executed Madera and seized the government and Wilson refused to recognize the government he established. This left Mexico in a state of chaos, to the disgust of all foreign nations who had interests there, and put the Commercial Current throughout the world in a ferment. He called his policy "watchful waiting," but it seemed to those who watched a most hopeless blundering. He created an impression throughout the country of confusion and bewilderment. Embargoes on arms were placed and removed. He refused to interfere in Mexico and then sent the Navy to Vera Cruz and became involved in a battle which necessitated calling in South America to arbitrate. He was in two minds about recognizing Carranza, and tolerated Villa's depredations until suddenly he sent Pershing with an army into the midst of Mexico to pursue Villa at enormous expense and loss, and with no result save to rouse all Mexico against him. The Mexicans were utterly bewildered by all these contradictory manœuvres. Americans who had interests in Mexico were infuriated, foreign powers were exasperated, and all South America was alarmed and distrustful. There may, of course, have been logical reasons for each change of policy. I am speaking of the impression on the general public who knew nothing of the inside.

The Reactionary current had at last found its loophole. He had roused Imperialistic feeling by refusing to interfere, and had stirred up the Isolationists by attacking Vera Cruz and Villa. He offended his Progressive friends by refusing not only to take the advice of those who had studied the situation and could have given him accurate information, but even to see them and talk with them; and the emissaries that he did send, such as John Lind, were thought to be the least capable of understanding the situation or of giving him correct advice. It is claimed that he was afraid of being craftily influenced by the Reactionary powers, but the result was that he opened to their propaganda a wonderful opportunity to appeal to the prejudices of his friends.

They were not content to attack his real mistakes. While one appreciates the suffering of certain of the industries under his measures, one can only regret that his enemies should have launched an attack upon his private life and character which subsequent investigation has proved to be so entirely unfounded. When prejudice and antagonism reach a certain point men are ready to believe anything of their opponent. When accused of intoxication, Roosevelt fought back and forced a retraction. Wilson made no such attempt. The harm was done at any rate. Prejudice was awakened and that once roused is almost impossible to quell.

One unfortunate characteristic of the American people is the unbalanced violence of their opinion, or rather emotion, concerning their public men, due in large measure to the skill of the political propagandists in awakening the prejudices of the people. Few of the people of culture who reacted so strongly against Wilson because of the stories told about him, recognized their political origin and that the politicians, in sheer desperation at Wilson's attitude, were using every sort of ammunition on which they could lay their hands. It is an interesting commentary on the intensity of the feeling against him. The result of all this violent propaganda in America is a public opinion so unbalanced as to be ridiculous. A man is either a hero or a villain, a demon or an archangel, instead of an ordinary man who is doing his best and making many mistakes. I was sitting in the club one day during this period, when the man next me began an attack on Wilson, ending up by saying that he regarded him as a veritable Judas Iscariot; whereupon another man opened up with the remark that he considered Wilson a second Saint Paul! This was a sample of what one heard everywhere. The whole country was so swept by violent prejudice with reference to Wilson that any balanced judgment of his achievements and failures seemed impossible.

Then on top of it all, war burst forth in Europe.

CHAPTER XI

THE GREAT TRANSATLANTIC STORM

1. HYSTERIC ATMOSPHERE

ONCE more, as in the days of the French Revolution, there was danger that America would be swept by a hurricane from across the sea, in a storm more terrible than any which the world had known.

With American citizenry composed so largely of those who had recently come from Europe, the first fear of those in authority was that the country would be torn asunder by the currents of national and racial feeling that were rising to such torrential levels, and Wilson's first act was a proclamation urging all loyal Americans to put up the barriers and remain completely isolated and neutral in act and thought. Even Roosevelt joined in this at first, though he soon changed his position.

But no barrier could shut out currents of such high voltage. There were connections through which the current was bound to flow. The Eastern cities, through close affiliation with England, were strongly pro-ally. The middle Northwest, from Saint Louis through Wisconsin and Illinois, where the Germans had settled, was involved in the German war current. The West and Southwest were dominated by the Isolationist current. They were indifferent as to who won the war, and they had a very strong feeling against being drawn into it in any way. There were large numbers who had come to America to escape military service, and to avoid any chance of those wars in fear of which Europe so constantly lived, and such men did not propose to be dragged into the mêlée.

It did not take the flames long to lick up the barrier of neutrality and a furious emotional conflagration was soon raging all through the Eastern states. Both sides fanned the flames by vigorous propaganda. It did not make so much difference what was said. Beneath the veneer of Americanism were the old racial loyalties and antipathies that sought any justification at hand.

In Saint Louis, Chicago and Milwaukee, one heard how the enemies of Germany had ringed her around with their secret alliances waiting the chance to crush her, and how the old Fatherland in her desperate extremity was putting up a fight to save their noble Kultur and keep her place in the sun. In the Eastern cities the great Irish population, always bitter against England, were telling how the British, jealous of the German navy, were trying to crush another free people as they had crushed the Irish, and how they had plotted with France and Russia to take Germany by surprise. The Hearst press played up this side, and ministered chiefly to the pro-German element.

But it was when Germany started to march through Belgium and von Bethmann-Holweg cast the "Scrap of Paper" to the winds, that the allies had their chance at propaganda. Roosevelt broke loose at this cynical violation of a solemn treaty, although apparently it was what Germany had always planned to do, and what all the experts had expected. The strongest card of the propagandists was a sworn list of atrocities committed by the Germans, attested and circulated by Lord Bryce, whose name carried great weight in America. No one could read that booklet without being violently stirred.

The situation grew more complicated and feelings more violent, as the British, in attempting to enforce their blockade, seized on ships carrying American merchandise, and roused to wrath the powerful Commercial Spirit. On the other hand the German submarines started sinking without warning ships conveying Americans and many lives were lost; the old American Spirit of Liberty and Justice was stirred again to anger. Wilson was caught in the clash of the two currents, Desire of Gain insisting that he should compel the British to cease from seizing merchandise, and the National American tide demanding vociferously that if Germany killed any more Americans, America should at once enter the war. In all this raging vortex of emotion between pro-ally and pro-German and violent anti-war sentiment, with the old currents of Commerce and Liberty, of Isolationist and Imperialist boiling up between, it was hard to keep the ship of state on an even keel. Wilson wrote his series of admirably phrased protests that compelled recognition, but was attacked by both sides as a futile and pusillanimous note-writer. It might be supposed that the sinking of the *Lusitania,* with the loss of a thousand lives, like the sinking of the *Maine* would have swept the whole nation into the war current, but Isolationist feeling was too strong in the West, and they were willing to accept the German defence that the *Lusitania* got only what she deserved as she was carrying shells to destroy German lives, and that the Germans had been very magnanimous in warning the passengers.

The East was now in an emotional state bordering on hysteria. German plots and German spies were seen everywhere, and the most absurd accusations were made on every hand. It was at this critical time that the Presidential election of 1916 approached. With all the opposition of the Reactionary current and the new War current against him the hold of Wilson on his party had never been so strong. At the convention, ex-Governor Glynn paid him a tribute in his opening speech so eloquent that it made even Bryan weep. Wilson was nominated by acclamation at the first ballot, and his name was received with a burst of cheers that lasted steadily for more than an hour.

The Republicans succeeded in gathering Roosevelt back into the fold, so there was no fear that they would lose the progressive element, so long as they did not put up too reactionary a candidate. Roosevelt, whose progressive thunder had been stolen by Wilson, was now absorbed in a new issue—that of Americanism and Preparedness. He called it saving the soul of America. It was really an attempt to arouse our old hero, the Anglo-Saxon fighting Spirit. He was urging that it was America's mission to stand for justice in the earth, to punish such outrages as the violation of Belgian neutrality—and, in general, to stop her wealth grubbing and her absorption in her comfort and prosperity and listen to the call of honor and duty. Above all, since war was inevitable in the end, she must prepare herself to meet it as a first-class power. He wanted a candidate like General Wood who would come out strongly for war and preparedness. The reactionaries favored any preparedness that would stimulate industry but they would not accept Wood. Finally they compromised on Hughes. The advantage of Hughes was that no one knew exactly what he would do and consequently he did not find so many actively opposed to him. He had been a reform Governor of New York and had cleaned things up well, so that the progressive element supported him. He had greatly obstructed the old Political Current and the old guard feared him, but thought him sufficiently related to the Reactionary powers in New York to be amenable. The one aim of the conservatives was to get Wilson out and they knew it could not be done without decoying the Progressive Current.

2. THE ISOLATIONIST AND PACIFIST CURRENT

The Democrats relied on the fact that they had become the main channel of the Progressive Current, which must support them on the strength of their achievements, and they put before the public their amazing record of progressive legislation which they claimed surpassed the accomplishment of any other President. They promised yet further reforms, and Wilson even forced in a plank advocating the latest progressive measure—Woman Suffrage. For many years there had been a fight over this question which, though not as fierce and bloodthirsty as the battle in England, had yet involved the persecution and ridicule of the Suffrage leaders. Much of the violent opposition came from the women. Apart from the politicians, the average American man seemed to feel that the women should have it if they really wanted it. The time of battle was over now, and state after state had adopted Woman Suffrage. The Southern conservative current in Wilson had kept him aloof from it, but Progressive feeling triumphed in him and he pushed strongly for a national amendment.

The imminent question, however, was whether the Anglo-Saxon current stimulated by Roosevelt was strong enough to overcome the Isolationist and Anti-War feeling in the West, and the German and Irish racial currents which were all pushing against it, and carry America into the war. The Democrats were out to catch all the Anti-War feeling and inserted a strong neutrality plank in their platform. Some enthusiast in a campaign speech had said of Wilson, "He kept us out of war." The phrase was taken up and spread all over the country. On the other side the militant East, now roused to a passionate enthusiasm for war, found its spokesman in Roosevelt who attacked Wilson with his usual energy for not declaring war as soon as the Belgian territory was violated, stating that Wilson had chosen the "path of dishonor" and shown a "mean timidity" and that he had dropped the "Big Stick" and taken up the "Dish Rag."

Hughes started out in similar line, but as he progressed Westward and felt the temper of the people, he dropped all allusion to the war, and contented himself with denouncing the Democrats and promising a high tariff to protect the American working man. He evidently found such strong Anti-War sentiment that he dared not speak positively.

In addition to the old Isolationist current which had swept up so many foreigners who came to America to escape European domination, there was a new Current of Pacifism which had been gradually built up by the propaganda of the Peace Society, and which had carried with it many young enthusiasts for World Unity, and had as well the support of the old Quaker current of non-resistance, with powerful religious feeling behind it, and also the Tolstoian current, which was strong among Social workers. Though strongest in the East, this Pacifist Current reached mothers all over the country with its emotionalized phrases such as "I did not raise my boy to be a soldier."

Facing this combined current of Anti-War sentiment Hughes found it inadvisable to follow Roosevelt's lead. Nor could he advocate Progressive measures as most of his support came from Reactionaries. This gave Wilson the opportunity to make a clear issue, to designate the Republican party as the reactionary organ and to demand the whole Progressive vote for the Democrats. His campaign statements said, "The issue is whether the government shall be run for the special interests or for the people." He was content with this appeal and made few speeches.

The result proved that Wilson understood the temper of the people far better than those who had been urging him to declare war. The mass of the people in the West did not want war, and had no interest in it. "He kept us out of war" was the phrase that captured this Anti-War Current, and his legislation turned the Progressive Current in his direction and away from the Republican party, so that nearly 3,000,000 voted for him who before had voted for Roosevelt. His popular vote in 1916 was 9,000,000 instead of 6,000,000 in 1912. When the first returns came in with a strong majority for Hughes in the Eastern key states, the election was granted to him by the Democratic papers. Then the Western reports began to come in and it was found that the old Republican strongholds— Nebraska, Kansas, Idaho, Washington and Wyoming— had all gone over to Wilson, and finally after long doubt California and Minnesota swung to the Democratic column, and Wilson was elected. He had understood the people of the West, and they sustained him.

In spite of all the Reactionary forces could do to appeal to prejudices and to broadcast his Mexican failures and his unfortunate phrases such as "Too proud to fight," the Progressive Current and Anti-War sentiment carried him triumphantly to victory. Once more it was the West against the East. The Progressive spirit of the West was no longer wildly revolutionary as in Bryan's day, but constructively directed, and it triumphed once more as in the day of Jackson. For a time Roosevelt had dominated it, but Anti-War sentiment had switched it away from him. Wilson, although "he kept us out of war," knew that he could not continue to do so with unrestricted submarine warfare. He was not an Imperialist. The old Liberty current in him had a new and larger aim—to free not individuals but nations, and if he went into the war he hoped that it could be so directed as to result in ending wars and in giving smaller nations their freedom and a chance for autonomous development. He learned, however, of the secret treaties of the Allies by which they were to divide up all the territories of their enemies in a fashion that he felt was unjust and sure to cause future wars. Mr. House states that he made propositions to aid the Allies on condition that they would abandon these treaties, and they refused. This gave him a poor opinion of their statecraft and led him later to make the assertion that their aims were practically the same as those of Germany. As neither the American people nor the people of the Allies knew anything of the secret treaties, and had been taught that they were nobly sacrificing themselves for humanity, this statement raised a storm of indignation in England and France, as well as in America.

If he was to enter the war that strong current of Anti-War feeling in the West must be overcome or he would only meet disaster. Nothing that happened altered the Western sentiment—they took little interest in submarine depredations, and even the *Lusitania* left them cold. There were, however, latent currents of feeling that could be roused, among them fear of Japan and distrust of Mexico. The note of Zimmerman had come into his hands, in which that statesman urged Mexico to rise against America and suggested the co-operation of Japan in an attack upon the United States. To blow up the Anti-War barrier in the West, no more perfect explosive could be invented. The West had had experience of Mexican depredations, and to her Japan was a bugaboo that was always peering over the horizon, no matter how unlikely a Japanese war might seem to the people of the East.

This note was launched in the press, and while the East paid but little attention to it, it produced a most amazing effect in the West. I was there at the time and have talked with men strongly pro-German, who defended the sinking of the *Lusitania,* but who, when they read this note, declared that if Germany could thus attempt to turn loose enemies to destroy a neutral country where she had many friends, they were through with her forever. And they were. After that the West was ready for war.

3. Emotional Mobilization

As we look back to that period it seems unbelievable that a great Nation should have been so utterly transformed in a few weeks. All the conflicting currents of feeling, all the individual desires and ambitions, seemed to be swept into one all-engulfing torrent of war feeling. Every possible means was used to rouse and maintain that Spirit. Speakers were sent all over the country, speaking in every tongue and dialect to arouse the people. Children in the public schools persuaded their parents, Russians, Poles, Italians, who couldn't speak a word of English, to invest in Liberty bonds. Every other thought and desire was subordinated to winning the war. In the Composite Current of War-feeling the greatest amperage was in the old National Current of Loyalty that had been growing steadily since Webster's time and always redoubles in strength in war time. But the highest voltage was in the old Liberty current, which had given the main drive to all American wars, save the Mexican. Roosevelt had called on the people to avenge the Rape of Belgium and the Sinking of the *Lusitania,* and Wilson had summoned them to free the world from autocratic control, so the old Champion of Liberty once more occupied the centre of the stage in this last and greatest of wars. Usually, in a war, the Spirit of Gain takes advantage of the opportunity to graft and profiteer and defraud, but there was surprisingly little of that, for, instead of seeking their own gain, the leaders of industries that had fought against Wilson, now offered their services to the government at great personal loss. The people also were stirred to make sacrifices, to go without sugar or butter, to work at planting food-stuffs, or preparing lint or knitting socks. The Republican leaders hoped to get Wilson to organize a bipartisan government, but he kept everything in his own hands, although he appointed Republicans to head most of the great war commissions.

The mobilization of Germany was remarkable, but what America accomplished was miraculous. In a few months to turn a peaceful industrial nation of 100,000,000, with almost no army at all, into a great war machine with every available bit of energy in industry and agriculture concentrated on equipping and sending across the sea a huge army, with arms and supplies for millions of men; to build in France great city camps, with water supply and electric lights, with telegraph and telephone and railroads—was an achievement never equalled in the world before, and believed by the Germans, at least, to be utterly impossible. It could not have been done if the emotional power of the nation had not been so promptly and effectively mobilized.

The violence of the feeling was astounding when one considered how indifferent the nation had been but a few weeks before. Now any one suspected of pro-German sentiment was really in danger. The government became a great dictatorship which directed and controlled not only all activities but all thought and feeling. Any one who resisted the draft or uttered pacificistic sentiments was liable to prompt arrest and imprisonment. But the action of the government was not as violent as the feelings of the people. A real war hysteria swept over the land resulting in the most violent and unbalanced opinions and acts. But this was all a part of the necessary concentration of energy. A nation once roused in the passion of war and determined to win is no longer a group of normal human beings governed by intelligence, but a terrible wild beast, irrational, ferocious, merciless, bloodthirsty. There is no room for any opinion or feeling but one; and anything that conflicts—all the various peace societies for instance—are instantly crushed. The dominant spirit incarnates itself in a group or nation and suppresses intelligence and reason and all conflicting emotions, even the ordinary desires and appetites. Men went without luxuries and even without comforts, often when it was not necessary, and toiled at raising potatoes on their front lawns, and bought Liberty bonds when the sacrifice hurt. Thus under Wilson's leadership the nation was reduced to emotional unity, partly by force and partly by tact. The division between Republican and Democrat was forgotten. All were at one in the effort to win the war.

This tremendous current of feeling carried Wilson with it to a height seldom attained by man. When he went abroad at the close of the war, no American, and probably no human being, ever held such a position of influence among the nations of the earth. Although the current had already turned against him in America, the enthusiasm that greeted him as one saw it in France, passed all bounds. The common people looked to him as leader of the world, the smaller nations regarded him as a sort of Messiah. No one could have believed that in a few short months he would be abandoned by his people, discredited, hated, slandered, hounded by his enemies, even to the very last when he lay helpless and broken. It is an amazing instance of the fickleness of public opinion.

4. THE TURN OF THE TIDE

When for a long period normal feelings and old emotional currents have been overwhelmed and suppressed by such a powerful tide, there is an inevitable reaction. All that has so long been dammed up breaks loose. That is to be expected, but the force with which the returning wave of the Isolationist current struck the American people was an amazement to the whole world. It was aided by the Political Current, which had also been suppressed during the war. It was Wilson, who, unfortunately for himself, set this latter current in motion, when one would suppose he would have bent every energy to keep it in abeyance. The Republicans had supported him heartily in his war policy, but he doubtless feared they would turn against him and hamper him, and he made a very powerful and earnest appeal to the nation to elect a Democratic Congress. Nothing could have

irritated the American people more than this. It seemed like
an effort to make party capital out of the success of the war.
Most of the people had ceased to think about parties and had
worked only as Americans and here was a sudden attempt
to put the Republicans who had been helping him out of the
government. They were further annoyed that he took no
prominent Republican with him to the Peace Conference.

The Republican Political Current once more sprang into
action, resumed its league with the Reactionary Spirit and
set itself to break up the tide of popularity that had carried
Wilson to such heights. They were greatly aided by his determination to attend the Peace Conference. The surest way
for a man to lose his friends is to attempt to decide their
quarrels. Feeling is unreasoning, and in any just compromise all sides feel that they have been wronged and ignored.
If you review his procedure in the Peace Conference you
will see that it was an inevitable process of stirring up enemies for himself and hostility to America. The European
statesmen were bound by their agreements to stick as closely as possible to the old secret treaties, and week after week
passed with Wilson fighting for his new ideas of justice
and self-determination and the Fourteen Points, while they
stuck to their guns.

The Peace Conference involved a settlement of the claims
of all the various nations who had participated in the war,
some of which had already been agreed upon. The matter
was complicated by this new principle of self-determination
which involved the formation of half a dozen new states.
America demanded no territory and no privileges as her
share of the loot, but Wilson was determined to secure the
formation of a League of Nations which he felt was the
only hope for future peace in the world. He was hampered
by his former pronouncement of the Fourteen Points which
led men to hold him responsible for seeing that justice was
done to all, and that there should be no seizure of land contrary to the will of the inhabitants. In the whirlpool of conflicting interests such perfect justice was impossible, and
many thought that Wilson would have done better to with-

draw when he once sensed the situation. Whether bound by a sense of responsibility or conceit, or by devotion to the League, he stayed on. The other representatives each struggled to gain the advantages their people demanded as Wilson fought for the League. In that conflict of feeling, the French with whom I spoke regarded America as being just as selfish in seeking her League as England was in demanding the German ships and colonies, and felt that they were being cheated by both. Every decision Wilson made offended some group. The Italians left in high dudgeon, and feeling against Wilson and America ran so strong that American soldiers on leave could no longer cross the Italian line at Ventimiglia without a free fight. When Wilson returned he came no longer with the prestige of the enthusiasm of the nations of the world, but followed by a wave of snarling discontent.

5. DISILLUSION AND THE EMOTIONAL BACKWASH

After a great war ending in victory the conquering hero is accustomed to return to receive the enthusiastic plaudits of the people, who usually compel him to receive the highest office at their command. But there was a peculiar backwash to this war. After their passion of self-denial, the people reacted to selfish greed, and discontented grumbling. The men returned disillusioned and bitter. They had thought they were fighting to create a new world free from war, and "safe for democracy," whatever that might mean, and they found it was still the same old world, with the Allies squabbling over the booty and dividing it up without reference to the will of the people. They reacted against all their leaders and came back cursing their officers from Pershing down to the "shave tails." It was largely talk, for most of them were strongly loyal to any officer who had really led them. But I talked with many of them in France after the armistice, and was surprised to find how general was this attitude of disillusion and discontent. It seemed that the independent American had submitted to army discipline because he saw it was essential, but had resented it all along, and particularly such details as having to salute officers. A man stationed at Bourges told me that there was a real rebellion there among the men in the general-records department. They knocked down the commanding major and all took the train to Paris. I was told by a witness that at Nevers the men formed a ring and danced around the general in charge, shouting opprobrious epithets. It was really a critical situation.

To stem this tide of feeling, the authorities tried sending the men on leave. By strenuous effort the Y. M. C. A. managed to prepare amusement centres in the most beautiful spots in France which altogether would accommodate some 70,000 men at a time. No effort was spared to give the men a thoroughly good time in the best hotels and casinos in France. While I was at Nice, more than 160,000 men were sent to the four stations on the Riviera, and as many were sent to Aix les Bains and vicinity. But that was only barely enough to hold the discontent in check. The mass of the army carried back this mood of disillusion and dissatisfaction to America. The noble sentiments that had carried them into the war were "bunk," and they were resentful against all the authorities that had forced them to bear a part in such terrible suffering and in such foolish destruction of life and all its beauty and joy. This tended to rehabilitate the old Pacifist Current which had been suppressed during the war. Those who gave expression to pacifistic sentiment or who resisted the draft had been fined and jailed, and now was their opportunity to express their resentment against Wilson as dictator. Many others had suffered from unjust suspicions of their loyalty, and they too turned against Wilson.

There were, moreover, various national groups who resented Wilson's action at the Conference. The Italians were infuriated over the Fiume matter, and nearly all the Central European states had some grievance which was reflected in their relatives in America. A large group of Americans railed against Wilson for trusting the Japanese sufficiently to turn over Shantung to them.

6. The Isolationist Current Returns to Power

But greatest of all the currents of feeling which the politicians could use to overthrow Wilson was the Isolationist Current. Few realized how strong it had been or how violent would be its return wave. Most Americans, including many Republican leaders, such as Root, Hughes and Taft, had sympathized with Wilson's plan to end war by establishing a League of Nations, but this wave of reaction swept them aside, carrying with it a general distrust of Europe and a determination not to be dragged into any more European wars. Senator Lodge, who headed the Republican Political Current, was the first to detect that this tide of feeling, properly engineered, would supply the force to overthrow Wilson, and lost no chance to proclaim that by entering the League America bound herself to send over armies to straighten out every European dispute. The feeling spread that European statesmen were trying to use America as a catspaw, to back up their secret schemes for robbing one another, and that if once the United States were involved in the League, they became responsible for the Peace of Europe—a hopeless task since the Powers were determined to go on squabbling over territory as they always had done.

As the opposition developed, Wilson centred all his energy upon the League. To him it was the hope for the world, and he gave it an intense and passionate devotion which radiated from him to his followers, and set in motion a current of feeling which centred in the League and became a prominent influence in politics. To gain for the League the support of the Anti-War feeling he tied the League to the Peace Treaty ending the war, so that the Senate could not accept the one without the other. This only irritated the Senate the more. If making peace involved accepting the League, they preferred to let the war go on, on paper at least, and they threw the whole parcel into the discard, League, Peace Treaty, and all, and kept America technically at war for a year or so longer.

But the Isolation Current could do more than this to discredit Wilson. To induce France to disarm and withdraw from the German borders, Wilson and Lloyd George had guaranteed that if she were unwarrantably attacked, England and America would stand by. The Spirit of Isolation was strong enough to enable the Senate to repudiate this guaranty, leaving the French to declare that America had broken her word, and leaving Wilson discredited. When he left America, he had felt sure the people were behind him and ready to support his great plan. But this great receding wave, combined by the Politicians from all these antagonistic currents of feeling—the Isolationist, the Pacifist, the Commercial and the general disillusion—had left him high and dry and alone, repudiated by his people at the very climax of his great endeavor. The dissatisfaction of the French and British had its backwash in America. "It was Wilson who had got us into this mess" was the general comment. Moreover, there was the Prohibition Amendment, which had been carried against Wilson's better judgment, but for which he was held responsible, and which was resented in the Eastern cities.

Every one is familiar with Wilson's stupendous effort to carry the League on his return—his whirlwind campaign out to the West, the wild enthusiasm that greeted him, until he was struck down by adverse fate, and carried home helpless and broken.

Even then his enemies feared that he might rise again to power and assailed not only his policies but his personal character. Many feel that they exceeded the limit by bringing against him so many accusations that have since been disproved, when he was helpless and out of the game, but they apparently feared him as an evil magician who might come to life again any minute and were determined to leave no stone unturned to finish his career. The absurd extremes of American opinion were never better illustrated, for in contrast with those who called him a traitor and a fraud, and even more violent names, there was manifest a devotion toward him and a reverence for him such as few men have aroused, and not only among the Americans. I was astonished to have a young Oxford student tell me that he regarded Wilson as a saint and a hero. He was planning a pilgrimage to Wilson's home as to a shrine. So these two violent streams swirled around the bedside of the stricken man who still had power to send out dynamic waves to the farthest shores. His party looked to him for guidance and begged him to name his successor, but he would say but one thing: they must stand by the League. One Democratic leader after another who like Cox had been cold toward that League, after an interview with him, was galvanized into enthusiasm.

7. THE GREAT BATTLE ENDS IN PEACE

Cox, the final choice of the Democrats, put up a good fight, but, as the politicians foresaw, the great wave of reaction swept the Democratic party into the ditch. It seemed that in the general atmosphere of disillusion the people were determined to take it out of some one, for all they had been made to feel and endure. It was the task of Senator Lodge and Big Business to assist this gathering wave of hostile emotion to concentrate on Wilson and his party. Their watchword was "Return to Normalcy," which suited the reaction from the high emotions of war time and the idealism of Wilson. It may also have indicated to some minds a return to the good old days when a privileged group controlled the politics and resources of the country. Wilson called the Republican platform "the apotheosis of reaction." At any rate it succeeded. It was, however, the Isolationist current that triumphed and put Harding in power and not the Reactionary Spirit, as was speedily shown when the politicians attempted to steal away the victories of the Progressive movement. For a time the Political Current ran its secret course unimpeded, but at Harding's death its hidden web was again broken and its sinister grip on the public wealth was loosed.

Under Coolidge the long battle between Reactionary and Progressive seemed to end in a truce, under the guidance of one who saw the good in both. In his speech to the Massachusetts Senate he said: "Do the day's work. If it be to protect the weak, whoever opposes, do it. If it be to help a powerful corporation better to serve the people, whatever be the opposition, do it. Expect to be called a stand patter, but don't be a stand patter. Expect to be called a demagogue, but don't be a demagogue. Don't hesitate to be as revolutionary as science. Don't hesitate to be as reactionary as the multiplication table. Don't expect to build up the weak by pulling down the strong." His administration was to some extent an expression of these ideas.

Coolidge believed in progressive legislation where he thought it was needed, but he also believed that Big Business was achieving wonders in bringing prosperity to the country and that it should be helped rather than hindered. He went so far as to advocate the reduction of the income tax especially in the upper brackets, and he even dared to say that it benefited the country for rich men to have large sums at their disposal. This leads one to assume that he believed there had been a real change since the '80s and '90s when the working men in their destitution had been roused to desperation by the display of wealth of the magnates of that day, and that he thought the product of labor was now so divided that the working man lived in comfort such as he had never known in the history of the world; while on the other hand the men of wealth had become so public spirited that the excess of their profits would be used for the public welfare under direction of their brains even more effectively than if it were collected by government taxation. Needless to say, on this point there was violent difference of opinion, and there were many progressives who thought he was pandering to the interests of the rich, and accused him of being a stand patter, eager to bring back the old days of the McKinley régime. Harding had proclaimed unceasingly that the aim of his administration was to bring happiness to every home. Coolidge said little about it, but apparently believed that the prosperity of the country and of the working people supplied the material background for happiness, and that so long as they had enough for their comfort and happiness it was right for the rich man to have such reward as he could secure for directing this prosperity. The day when the Trust was looked upon as an unholy thing was past; men were disposed to look upon the great combinations in industry as adding to the prosperity of the nation, by the economy and efficiency they provided. In addition to the old combinations of firms in one industry, there now sprang up a new type of combination, a group of industries functioning together for their mutual advantage, such as that organized by Henry Ford, and the resulting prosperity was amazing.

8. The Fairy Godmother

To understand what the Great Enchantress, the Spirit of Commerce, has done for America, it is well to get the opinion of an outsider. As a foreigner and an expert Mr. Siegfried is well equipped to estimate her achievement. In his "America Comes of Age" he shows how after the war prices and wages both rose. If 100 represents prices before the war, by 1920 wholesale prices had crept up to 150 and were stabilized at that point, while retail prices went up to 170. After a time they fell off but wages which had been keeping pace kept on climbing. By 1925 prices had mounted again until wholesale rates reached 159 and retail 173. But wages, still climbing steadily, had reached 238 according to trade-union rates. Thus, though prices were higher, the greater increase in wages made the purchasing power of the working man equal to from 140 to 180 as compared with 100 before the war. In 1925 unskilled labor received from $3 to $5 a day, skilled labor $5 to $10, and special trades such as bricklayers $15 to $17. This meant that workmen were receiving ten times the wages which their fellows in Europe received. In addition they were housed in a fashion that would seem the extreme of luxury to those abroad. Practically all their houses were equipped with what Siegfried calls "confort moderne"—with baths, furnaces and electric lights, the perquisites of the wealthy abroad, and most working men owned at least a Ford. In 1925 there were 20,000,000 cars in the United States (one for every 5.6 persons) while all Europe had only 2,600,000. In California there was a car to every 3 persons.

Mr. Siegfried goes on to show that savings had shown as notable an increase. In 1914, 11,000,000 depositors had funds in Savings Banks to the amount of $8,300,000. In 1924, 38,000,000 depositors owned deposits worth $20,-400,000. In 1925 there were 83,000,000 life-insurance policies amounting to $60,000,000,000, two-thirds of them belonging to working men.

Not only did the working man have money in the bank, he also owned stock in the company in which he worked. In 1923 16 per cent of the stock of U. S. Steel Company was owned by employees, 33 per cent of the Goodyear Company's stock, 75 per cent of the International Harvester, 95 per cent of the Firestone Company, practically all of the stock of Procter & Gamble was owned by employees. Thus Mr. Siegfried shows us that the working man of America has been transformed into a capitalist, owning a share of the industry in which he works, with money in the bank and a car at his disposal.

Certainly the working man of America has exceeded the utmost dreams of any champion of the oppressed in any other age or nation. Nor would any economist of fifty years ago have thought it possible that the mass of the people of any nation should be able to live on a scale where articles of luxury which only the rich then possessed should be regarded as the necessities of their daily life. It is almost impossible for the people of other nations to understand the situation.

When I was in Russia in 1923 representing one of the famine relief organizations, I was held up on the train by three representatives of the Cheka or Secret Police, who flourished their revolvers and demanded credentials. I showed papers which gave some statement of the work of the famine relief and one of them said: "That is a fine work. It is the proletariat of America who do this for Russia, is it not?" I tried to explain that in America things were different, that there working men were constantly becoming capitalists and capitalists were in constant danger of becoming working men. This merely awakened his suspicions. He looked at me almost with horror and said: "You are not a capitalist, are you?" My funds were so low that I could say honestly and fervently, "Heaven forbid!" Whereupon he put up his pistol. It showed me plainly that it was impossible for men brought up under the foreign system to grasp in any way the situation of the working man in America. To them the Capitalist was the archenemy, a different type of being from the workman, and regarded with the horror we should feel of a mother who devoured her children.

With all the prosperity it must be admitted that there were still sections where there was great poverty and injustice and where men were still ground down to minimum wages. But on the whole we see the Great Enchantress, the old Spirit of Commerce and Gain, that for so long held the Spirit of Justice in her snares and kept the people in a slavery little better than that of an Oriental Despotism, now transformed to a Fairy Godmother who showers upon them gifts of which their grandfathers hardly dreamed. And thus the age-long battle of the Spirit of Liberty with the Great Enchantress ended in his union with a Fairy Princess, and we can only hope that they will live happily ever after, and that no loss of wealth or misbehavior on her part will lead to a divorce.

CHAPTER XII

RACIAL GROUPS AND ANTAGONISTIC CURRENTS

1. THE FOREIGN INVASION

WE have sought to sketch in outline that stupendous Drama in which vast spirits that rose out of the mists of the Past have contended for the mastery of a new continent.

We have traced the great dominant currents of feeling handed on from father to son, with their attendant prejudices and watchwords, and have noted how they lay stagnant for a time and then broke free again in a torrent of power to turn the wheels of destiny. In giving our main attention to emotion we do not wish to slight the value of thought. Ideas are the switchboard which throw the current of feeling into action and determine its course, and are therefore of supreme importance. We have chosen in these pages to follow the currents of feeling, rather than the development of the ideas that controlled them, which has been described by other authors.

In addition to these permanent currents of feeling we have had to describe some of the great emotional storms that rose from low or high pressure centres, and swept the country like a tornado.

It is our purpose now to consider emotional phenomena of a somewhat different type, and among them certain currents of feeling that we might term induction currents, since they are induced or aroused by the proximity of groups of different character. Chief among these are the racial groups. Nothing seems destined to cause more trouble in the world to-day than the prejudices and antagonisms caused by these racial contacts, and it seems as if America had become the meeting place of all the races of the world, so that the racial problem is of vital importance in her development. We have seen that America began with a fairly homogeneous group, dominated in the main by the same feelings, since they were driven from England by the same antagonisms and prejudices. But later conditions in Europe resulted in driving across the seas other groups who were dissatisfied or incompatible with the governments then in power. At first America had drawn chiefly from England, but oppressive conditions in Ireland had sent over large numbers of that race who had filled the ranks of unskilled labor. The Revolution of 1848 brought over many Germans of the better type, and many Scandinavians had come to occupy the rich farm lands of the Northwest. And now Russian oppression drove out quite a large proportion of the Finnish race, and pogroms in Poland and Bessarabia sent forth a constantly growing stream of wretched and destitute Jews. The poverty of Italy sought an outlet, and thousands of Sicilians and Neapolitans came to seek their fortunes and replaced the Irish as unskilled laborers, while the latter now found a place as craftsmen and policemen, to say nothing of politicians. Polack and Slavonian followed the Italian, the emigration being constantly stimulated by the industries that wanted cheap labor, and by the steamships, who derived their chief income from the steerage. These masses of foreigners were not intelligently distributed but collected in undigested lumps in various spots in the national anatomy.

I lived many years in a section of New York where on one side dwelt a solid mass of Polish and Russian Jews. Every sign was in the Hebrew script. On Friday evening nearly every window showed the seven-branched candlestick alight. On Saturday the streets were full of long-bearded men in their striped caftans and on the Feast of Tabernacles a booth of green shrubs was built in every tenement yard. The streets were crowded with push carts selling everything from old clothes to green lemonade, sour pickles, and broken eggs at five cents a cupful. It might have been a section of Warsaw, for even Jerusalem has not so many Jews.

On the other side was a city of Italians where every shop

had Italian signs and where the women hung out their gay garments on lines that crisscrossed the narrow courts and alleys, and vituperated each other in vigorous Italian exactly as in Naples. In a smaller section dwelt the Greeks and one read on the shop windows in old Greek letters the modern sign Καφφεῖον or Ξενοδοχεῖον, and on festivals the blue and white flag with its cross was displayed.

Across the Bowery one entered an oriental city over whose narrow streets swung Chinese signs in red and gold, over shops where were displayed queer dried animals hanging by their tails, or strange curios and beautiful china, where the streets were full of pajamaed figures that scuffed silently past, where the air was heavy with the scent of opium and where one could hear the vibrant squeak of the Chinese fiddle and the heavy beat of the drum.

In one street were only tall blond Scandinavian longshoremen. Other blocks were held by a tenacious group of Irish who had not yet given way before the foreign invasion. Here and there an old house with columned porch and mahogany doors and dormer windows bore witness to the fact that this section had once been solid with old-time Americans. Now in their place there were several foreign cities, each with its newspapers and churches or synagogues, keeping up the customs of the old world, so that one could hardly realize that it was America. And the same was true in every large city of the East.

Moreover certain sections in the country were possessed by certain nations, as the Portuguese on Cape Cod, and the Finns in certain towns around Boston, the Poles in the Connecticut valley. Wisconsin was a new Germany and Minnesota and Dakota a new Sweden. In New York and Boston over 70 per cent of the population were either foreigners or the children of foreign parents. Immigration increased by leaps and bounds until in the decade 1900–1910 fifteen million immigrants entered the country. Even though all these did not remain there was a net immigration of at least five and one-half million. And of these some 70 per cent belonged to the Jewish and Mediterranean races, who kept to their own customs and seemed to have few if any points of contact with the old-time American.

It is naturally a vital question what will happen to a country governed by public opinion, when such masses of people with totally foreign ideas and attitudes toward life are brought into their midst. The Polish Jews came from scenes where they had seen women and children butchered in the name of Christ, with the result that if the name of Christ appeared on the billboard in front of a church in their section, it was bombarded with all the rotten fruit and refuse in the neighborhood. The old Jews spat when they passed a Christian, and one day all the Jewish mothers raided the public schools in a panic and dragged out their children because they thought the children were being branded there with the Sign of the Cross. One might deal with a few such, but where there are more than a million in New York alone the situation makes one gasp.

We have shown that in early America, although there were diverse emotional currents, there was a certain amount of mutual understanding and the possibility of adjustment. But between such groups as we have described, what hope is there of any common purpose or common ideal? Certainly there seems no possibility of any understanding or co-operation in the old ideals and purposes for which the nation has stood, with men of such different race, religion, education and customs.

The country was in danger of becoming an agglomeration of groups with violent antipathies and no mutual understanding, a series of centres of violent emotion isolated by prejudices and suspicion. And the worst of it was that the politicians at once began to try to control the groups, to play upon their ignorance and their fears in order to secure their votes after they had been railroaded into citizenship. The problem was bad enough with the differences of the first colonies—now it began to look as if America were driving on to a situation utterly hopeless which must end in ruin.

We have stated that the contact of diverse groups tends to induce powerful emotional currents, in the group itself and in those that surround it. For every tribe or nation builds up around itself powerful emotional barriers. It has its customs and code of morals which receive their sanction from the religion of the group and this holds over them a curse if they neglect its tenets or forsake the way of their fathers. It trains them to feel a horror of the conflicting customs and beliefs of other groups. This makes it almost impossible for them to live in harmony with any different group. They feel that if they should be dominated by the other group or if their children should be influenced to lose their faith in the old religion and customs they would be ruined morally and lost in the world to come, and to a certain extent this is true. Nothing is more harmful than to take away the faith of the young in the old beliefs and standards of their race and to give them nothing to replace it.

During that early period I talked with many young Polish Jews who would say: "Of course, here in America we don't believe in that old Jewish stuff any more. We know it's all a fake and the only God there is is the almighty dollar." They had lost the fine old Jewish tradition with its high standards and real beauty, and they were becoming contemptuous of their parents and their past,—vulgar, irresponsible, dishonest, seeking only their own gain. Fortunately the leading Jews of New York saw the danger and took the situation in hand, giving the young people something to replace their old beliefs.

2. FOREIGNERS AND NATIONAL FEELING

When a country is filled with groups with different standards and religions which are continually charging one another with antagonistic emotion, something is certain to happen. There may be continual conflict or misunderstanding, or they may gradually neutralize each other. As the barrier of prejudice is removed and each begins to listen to the ideas of the other there comes a time when the emotional sanctions give way. They cannot believe in all religions and therefore they lose faith in any. If other standards are as good as their own, why trouble about any standard? It was this that wrecked Rome, when she accepted all the religions and standards of the Orient and so lost faith in her own high code of morals and standard of life.

This process seemed to be beginning in America. A younger generation of the children of foreigners was growing up with no convictions, no code, no standards, no strong sense of right and wrong, or of responsibility, swept hither and yon by the emotion of the moment. One dramatist depicted them as swayed involuntarily by Jazz, so that whatever they were doing, be it a funeral or a strike, or work in the fields, when the Jazz struck up they all started dancing in time. There was something tragically true about this absurd skit. The absence of any purpose, or anchor, or roots to life, so that the impulse of the moment is the one dominant element, tends to create an incoherent impossible national life.

In contrast with this there are certain groups, like the early Puritans, each of which feels that the only admissible solution is that it should dominate all the others and subjugate them to its standards and religion. Such groups try to keep their children from the public schools, and to train as many children as possible in their own schools. The public schools are doing their best to eliminate from the education of the young those racial and religious prejudices which cause controversy and antagonism, and to select those points in the old American tradition and standards upon which all can agree as a norm of education in which all children should be trained. If the virus were extracted from religion, each child could then be brought up in the religion of his fathers, controversial material being removed, and the sanction of the religion could be applied to the national code. Somewhat difficult this, to achieve, but there is progress in this direction. There is always the desperate fear of each group that its children will be influenced in the schools by some other group, and their morals thus ruined and their salvation put in jeopardy. In such a situation our hope is that all these racial antipathies may be dissolved in that great current of National feeling, whose origin and progress we have described.

Although definitely Christian instruction has been cut out from the public schools of New York, they have succeeded in selecting and training the children in those elements of the American tradition and standards which go to make up that great tide of National feeling in a fashion that is both amazing and inspiring. I have never heard the great sayings of Washington, Lincoln and Webster more eloquently quoted, or devotion to the highest ideals of America more beautifully or charmingly expressed than in the words of some dark-eyed Italian girl or young Jewish lad in the general assembly of one of the down-town schools of whose two thousand pupils probably not one had parents born in America. And I have never seen any one salute the flag with such reverence or sing "My country, 'tis of thee, sweet land of liberty, of thee I sing. Land where my fathers died, land of the Pilgrims' pride," with such real feeling as these youngsters, none of whose forefathers had ever seen the American shore. Our best public schools, then, are power houses for generating the American National Current. They are a vast manufactory for the production of American citizens. It remains to be seen how many millions of such children can be poured into this mill without clogging the wheels.

We have spoken of the effect of these groups on one another, but they also began to have an emotional effect on the mass of American citizens. The people of America began at last to change from their complaisant attitude of welcome to the oppressed of all nations and to realize that there was danger that the incoming flood would put out the old home fires, and that unless they bestirred themselves there would be no America left but only a continent dotted by settlements of every tribe and language and religion, each a city walled in by prejudice and suspicion and antagonism more impermeable than any walls of stone. America could afford to welcome individuals, but the moment a group reaches a certain size it becomes, as we have shown, an emotional dynamo that affects the community by its prejudices and threatens its standards; and immediately the community is up in arms to protect itself. Individuals of another race are nearly always cordially received, but when a large group appears, an emotional protective barrier of prejudice and hostility arises.

We find, then, that at present these racial centres exist all over the country in which powerful feelings are being induced by their proximity to other groups. These feelings may be negative, as antagonism or prejudice, or positive, as racial pride and ambition. They may be religious, political or social in character. They may centre in the desire to dominate other groups or in the wish to be let alone. They differ so greatly in these characteristics that it will be necessary to consider separately the leading groups.

3. THE NEGRO AND SOCIAL OSTRACISM

The negroes until recently were a passive group which generated within itself very little group emotion, positive or negative. They were notable for the emotional effect which they produced on the groups around them. But while they were the vortex around which swirled the bitter feelings which divided the white population into two sections, it was as slaves rather than as negroes that they produced this effect. Then the negro was the passive cause of strong feeling between two white groups. Now the situation is changed, and the main current of feeling is between the white and the black race. It has taken the negro some time to emerge from the feeling of inferiority that hedges in the slave. Education and wealth transform his emotional attitude toward the white man and he demands increasing privilege and recognition, and resents the restrictions which he once accepted passively. Discontented in the South where the whites now have the upper hand and exclude him from politics, and compel him to ride in separate compartments, and refuse to eat with him, or meet him socially, he has migrated in large numbers to the North which once appeared as his champion. It is easier to idealize and defend the negro at a distance than when he is sitting on one's chest, and when the North faced the problem and tens of thousands of negroes came pouring into Northern cities, the feeling toward him took on a surprising similarity to that of the South. In spite of his bank account, he was not welcomed at the Plaza or the Blackstone, nor were seats reserved for him at Sherry's.

Where two races come strongly into competition, feeling is almost sure to arise, and the maintenance of racial prestige becomes a vital question. In New York there are now some 250,000 negroes. The section of Harlem between 120th Street and 140th Street was once a prosperous part of the city with fine dwellings and handsome churches. Little by little the negroes filtered in, the whites giving way before them until now one hardly sees a white face in passing through that section. It is the largest negro city in the world—larger than any native city in Africa. Some of its inhabitants are men of wealth and culture, with fine libraries of first editions, rare paintings and bibelots. It is not surprising that this advance of the colored man meets with some expression of resentment. Only recently I was told by a young student that while he and his companions were walking through that Harlem section, they saw a colored man reclining in a handsome limousine driven by a white chauffeur, and were so indignant that they hurled after him whatever missiles came to hand, a futile and unfortunate expression of an emotion which seems to be fairly widespread.

At first the negro was submissive and accepted passively the position assigned him by the white man. Those who wished to help him attempted in institutions like Hampton and Tuskegee to give him such a thorough education in the trades and in agriculture that he would become essential to the community and would command the respect of the white man because of the valuable service he rendered and the wealth he acquired, and the South was willing to acquiesce in education of this type. There arose a group among the negroes, however, under the leadership of men like Du Bois who put up a violent plea for the social equality of the negro and their cause was taken up by the descendants of the old Abolitionists. Social equality, in the sense that a group of negroes is recognized to have the same privileges as a group of white men, it may be possible for them ultimately to attain.

But the negroes, like certain other racial groups, did not want their own social life; they wanted to be admitted to that of others. Now America is a white man's country and it is natural that the dominant groups should be white. In Abyssinia the Emperor and court are black, and white men must take a back seat, and doubtless they are not admitted to eat with princes of the blood. But they manage to bear up under this lack of social recognition and probably have formed a club of their own. America would be fortunate if the various racial groups would be content each to form its own social life. The negro probably would be content with this were it not for this continued agitation by a comparatively small set, who make it a principle to protest their equality at every point.

In a certain northern college where the negro comes as an individual, he has always been received on a basis of equality. Recently, however, a group of Southerners entered the college along with a negro. When they found him seated with them at the eating club they protested violently and said if he came again they would leave the hall in a body. The President assured the negro that he had a perfect right to sit at the table and was himself present at the next meal to insure that the negro was properly treated. After the negro had thus proved his right to be present, he was asked how he thought a gentleman would act if he found himself in a group where his company was not desired. The negro answered that he would gladly eat elsewhere, but that his father, who sent him to college, was one of the most earnest in the Du Bois movement and would withdraw him from college if he did not continue to assert his social equality. It is this element that creates real danger in the situation and continually injects more emotion into the question.

There are certain injustices which the South will undoubtedly correct as they lose their fear of being subjected to the negro. One of our foreign critics asserts that in South Carolina, where the population is 51 per cent negro, only 11 per cent of the education fund is devoted to colored children. So long as they are excluded from the vote, they have no opportunity to correct any injustice, and it is hoped that the South will find some way of giving them a fair representation without subjecting themselves to the danger of a return to the carpet-bagger rule. Now that the violent feeling resulting from the war is dying, the South is better able to handle the question without prejudice.

It is interesting to note that although the old negro kingdoms in Africa generated the strongest kind of antipathy to other groups, the negro group in America does not generate that negative type of emotion which would cause them to regard with prejudice or antipathy the groups around them. But they do seem to create in the groups that surround them a reaction of that sort. Some seem to feel a physical repulsion toward those of the black race which leads them to avoid all contacts. Many Southerners, however, have a deep affection for their old "mammies," and are accustomed to their caresses and keep the negro at a distance merely to preserve racial prestige. The emotional reaction caused by the negro is quite unique. It is not due to religious prejudice for he holds the same religion as the white men. It is not due to economic jealousy, like the feeling against the Japanese and certain other foreigners. While there may be a certain physical repulsion between the races, it is by no means general. The root of the difficulty is probably what other races term the "arrogance" of the white man, that instinctive feeling of superiority which every dominant group seems to generate and which induces a current of bitter resentment in adjacent races.

4. The Oriental and Economic Jealousy

If the South was first to defend itself against foreign racial groups, the West was not far behind. During the gold rush in 1849–50 and the building of the transcontinental roads, Chinese coolies came to California to work and were welcomed. But when they became a large group, sentiment changed. After 1870 they were denied naturalization and in 1882 a law was passed excluding all Chinese coolies. The difficulty here was neither social nor political, as with the negro. It was economic—though other reasons were assigned, such as the difference in religion and customs. The Chinese had such a different scale of living and were able to work so much more cheaply that they cut under American labor. They also prospered amazingly and there was jealousy of their progress. It was said that they could not be assimilated as Americans and also that they endangered American youth by bringing in foreign vices. At any rate the matter was taken in hand in time and the immigration was stopped before it had caused disaster. We should be hard put to it to decide what to do if America had a solid lump of ten million Chinese in her midst, as might easily have happened.

Next came the Japanese, who were imported to replace the Chinese labor, and who arrived in large numbers from Hawaii in 1898 after the annexation. They were so hardworking, capable and efficient that by 1904 it began to look as if they might capture the whole of California, and an effort was made to apply the Chinese exclusion law to them also. Although they had been liked as individuals, yet when they became a powerful group the most violent feeling was aroused against them—the defence mechanism of one group against another that threatens it.

The situation was most difficult. California insisted on their exclusion with real passion, but the national government wished to keep on good terms with Japan and knew that they were so proud and sensitive that to exclude them on the basis that they were yellow like the Chinese would be taken as an insult and as an assertion that they were an inferior race. This would inevitably lead to bad feeling if not to ultimate war. Washington sought to pacify California, but in vain. Here it was the case not of a mere local group, but of a group attached to a powerful nation, so that the emotions aroused reverberated in international affairs. Finally with great skill and dexterity, in 1907, the Gentlemen's Agreement was negotiated, by which it was explained to the Japanese Government that it was really the superiority of the Japanese as workmen and cultivators and not their inferiority that made the difficulty and their government agreed not to permit any who would be economically dangerous to migrate to the United States. That also was done only just in time. The Japanese already have fully half the arable land in some of the best counties of California like the San Joaquin, and they practically control many of the crops, such as asparagus, celery, onions and tomatoes. The public schools are filled with their children and the old settlers protest violently against having their own children crowded in with them.

Here again it was primarily the economic question. It was true that the American could not compete with the dexterity, frugality and endurance of the Japanese, and in a few years California would have been a new Japan. No people is quite altruistic enough to turn over their country to another race. It might have been done if the Japanese could divest himself of his distinctive characteristics and become merged in the mass of Americans, adopting their standards and ideas, so that in a generation no one could distinguish them from Americans—as proved possible in the case of the Nordic immigration. But the Japanese and Chinese remained unassimilable and California saved the nation from another and worse problem than that of the negro. The Chinese and Japanese who are in America constitute unassimilated lumps but they no longer arouse the violent emotional reaction which they once caused.

5. THE JEW AND RELIGIOUS PREJUDICE

When we come to the Jews we find racial feeling which is quite as strong, though different in character. Both religious and racial characteristics tend to generate in the Jew strong negative emotion or prejudice against other groups, and he also awakens similar feelings in them. The feeling is perhaps most violent between the Irish and the Jews, where religious prejudice enters in. I have seen Jewish hucksters tormented and robbed by young Irish hoodlums and I knew one youth who tripped an old Jew who was carrying a barrel so that his burden fell on his head and killed him. I started one day to stop a street fight where one man had the other down and was pounding his head on the edge of the curb, when an old Irishman pulled me aside and whispered, "They're both sheenies, let them kill one another." This feeling between Irish and Jew seems to be improving of late and it may be that the celebrated play, "Abie's Irish Rose," has had something to do with it.

There seems to be no political feeling against the Jew, for he has never sought to control politics for the benefit of his own race. On the part of the Anglo-Saxon the feeling against the Jew seems to be due in part to resentment at his success in business and at the rapidity with which he acquires wealth. Mingled with it is a certain personal antipathy which results from those slight differences in social and ethical standards which are often more irritating than great disagreement. One considers the other a fool, and the other thinks the one is no gentleman. It is singular how a great wall of prejudice can be built by slight divergences of character due to racial development. The suave indirection of the Jew and the truculent frankness of the Anglo-Saxon are mutual irritants. Here again social feeling comes in. The American grants the Jew equal economic, political and religious privileges but is prejudiced against any social intermingling. The Jews claim that there is prejudice against them in business, but the business positions from which Jews are excluded are usually those involving social relationship. It is among the newly arrived immigrants and orthodox Jews that one finds the violent religious prejudice against Christians—a result of the pogroms of the old country. I have seen the old rabbis spit when they met a Christian, and young Jewish boys throw missiles at every church they passed. As they become Americanized, the Jews cease to feel antipathy toward Gentile Americans and desire to be received socially in the same coterie. Hotel keepers in well-known resorts have told me that they cannot admit Jews, because when once a Jew enters, he brings all his friends. The Americans then leave, and when the Jews find the Americans no longer come, they also depart. Undoubtedly this is a prejudiced view, but it is held by many. Certain clubs exclude Jews, and there is a feeling among business men and bankers that even the best Jews have such different standards that they prefer not to deal with them. This also is probably prejudice in large part, for no men have been more devoted to the public welfare, or have manifested finer standards than such Jews as Jacob Schiff, Oscar and Nathan Strauss, Edward Filene, Morganthau, and many others whose names are honored by all Americans. The Jew suffers because of the great numbers of their race who have acquired wealth too rapidly and who try to push their way with rude and blatant assurance into company where they are not desired. This is a characteristic of uncultured *nouveaux riches* all over the world, but the Jews seem to include a greater number of that type because of their greater success in business.

In New York there are approximately a million Jews, more than in any other city of the world, and the question is therefore a very vital one. Racial prejudice is the result of their encroachment upon American life. With the best will in the world they do not seem to be absorbed into the American citizenry. Certain characteristics and attitudes seem to keep them a distinct race in the midst of this new environment as they have always been in the old world. Consequently there are eddies of antagonism against them in all the great cities. Lately they have been spreading into the country and have taken up farms in rural New England. Here also a certain emotional reaction against them is noticeable. In the South, where there are very few, the feeling is merely a part of that emotional reaction common to all primitive peoples against those of a different race and religion. The prejudice is unfortunate as a divisive element in the national life, but as it has little political or economic application, its effect is measured chiefly in terms of the injured feelings of social aspirants.

The Jew is seeking to merge himself in the life of America and is changing his name from Rosatsky and Goldberg, to Murphy and Gould, and it may be that he will succeed in eliminating his more protuberant racial characteristics sufficiently to be swallowed up in the American commonalty and thus bring the old prejudice to an end. As he forsakes the old orthodox Jewish religion for the Reformed faith, and the synagogue for the temple, the element of religious prejudice is lessened, and Jewish Rabbis such as Rabbi Wise are often invited to speak in Christian churches. In the case of the Jew, then, we may say that the feeling generated is primarily religious, and secondarily social, resulting in the first place in a barrier of prejudice and later in resentment at that barrier.

6. THE IRISH AND POLITICAL ANTAGONISM

When we turn to the Irish, we find here racial feeling of quite a different type. There is here no social prejudice, as with the negro and Jew, for Irish gentlemen of culture are received socially as readily as men of any other group. The Irish have great charm, are amusing companions, loyal friends, and bitter enemies and they love a fight better than their food. The chief feeling against them is political, and is due in the Eastern states, as indicated above, to a suspicion that the Roman Church is seeking to control the politics of America through the Irish. Whether this is true or not, the feeling is very strong and develops into resentment of the most violent type. It has happened that the Irish have interested themselves in politics more than any other race, and have risen rapidly to positions of influence, so that the politics of New York and Boston and of most of the Eastern states are controlled by bosses who are Irish Roman Catholics. They are naturally more clannish than most other races, and when in control they usually seek to oust the old-time Americans and replace them with men of their own group.

It has been repeatedly and publicly stated that this was done by the direction of the Church, and the press reported that when Mayor Mitchell of New York refused to discharge Protestants whom he knew to be good men, and defied the authority of the Church, he was promptly disciplined and put out of politics. Whether true or not, this is what is believed by the majority of educated American citizens.

The Irish party is well organized and if any attempt is made to defeat them, the accusation is at once made that those who protest and oppose the election of Irish Romanists are governed by religious prejudice, which should have no place in America. The better group of Protestants are so anxious to appear free from religious prejudice that they usually abandon all opposition and vote for the Irishman, while the resentment of the more ignorant Protestant group increases in bitterness. The question is complicated because in the South and in portions of the middle West, and of the far West, there *does* exist a violent prejudice against Roman Catholics purely on account of their religion. This creates confusion of mind. The prejudice which exists against a man purely because he holds a certain religious belief is a totally different matter from the resentment aroused against a group which is trying to control politics for the advantage of its own members. In their case the feeling is political, and not a prejudice against Roman Catholics, for, as we have already suggested, it would be equally strong against Lutherans or Methodists or Baptists if it was suspected that they were trying to gain all the political offices for themselves and to oust those of other religious affiliations.

The average American is willing that the next man should hold any religion he chooses and is usually willing to vote for him if he is the best man, with no thought of his religious belief. But if he thinks that man is the candidate of a religious group that is trying to get control of the government, his attitude changes, particularly if he knows that one article of the religion is implicit obedience to an authority who belongs to another nation. It may be, of course, that this general opinion is mistaken, but to the ordinary observer it appears that when in control the Irish make no effort to choose the best man for the office or to work in harmony with men of other religions. On the contrary, it is generally believed that under their control every Protestant, no matter how good, is eliminated as soon as possible and replaced by a Catholic no matter how poorly adapted to the office.

Moreover, whenever there is a feeling that such a group is working for dominance there is bound to arise an organization to resist them. America saw first the Know Nothings and then the A. P. A., who were especially strong at the period we describe. In Boston I was given a pamphlet showing how foreigners had gained control of the city government and giving a list of the hundreds of Irish Roman Catholics in the employ of the city. Strangely enough most of their names, like Donovan and Doherty, began with D. and the pamphlet was entitled "The Whole D— Family." The violence of this opposition in turn has created a reaction and there is a large group who are antagonized by their exaggerated attacks on the Catholics. In the case of the Irish, then, the feeling is not personal or social. Neither is it religious in the ordinary sense. It is an antipathy due to the general idea that this group is being used as an instrument by a powerful alien organization to establish its control in America.

7. South Europeans and Hyphenated Americans

There is a certain amount of feeling against the Italians and Polacks and Central European folk, chiefly because of the low standard of living of many of those who emigrate to America. Since they have joined the unions and are no longer cutting down wages, the feeling is less bitter, and is usually a mere dislike and contempt felt toward those who live in squalor. Other immigrants who have advanced to conditions of cleanliness and self-respect refuse to associate with them. This is really more a class feeling than one due to race. A study of the situation in New York shows that any racial group that has advanced to better conditions has this prejudice against any adjacent racial group which is in more squalid circumstances, and that although in their minds the prejudice is racial, it is really due to the conditions in which they live. The schools and playgrounds are working against racial prejudices by organizing Fiestas in which the children present the dances and poetry and music of the country from which they came, and each group thus learns to appreciate the art of the others.

With regard to the other European races, most Americans of the period 1900–1910 had a comfortable feeling that these foreigners were rapidly becoming assimilated and being transformed into good American citizens. Really there was being created in rather alarming quantities that strange being, the Hyphenated American, who is first German, Irish, Italian or Jewish, and only American so far as this country affords him an admirable field to acquire wealth.

This type of man takes no interest in the ideals or standards of America, but remains in the old world, talking the old language, reading it in his paper, hearing it in church and lecture, keeping to his old customs and really living still in the old country, though his hands work here. The war brought a sudden revelation of this new creature. The most violent cross currents of emotion at once appeared. It looked as if the whole country might be divided into a series of hostile camps and racial groups that would drag the national government hither and yon, pro-German, or pro-ally.

There was tragedy in the midst of all these vortices of emotion. I knew a young French-American girl who was married to a German-American and the feeling between them became so bitter and intense that a separation was necessary and their home was broken up. Finally the young German-American felt so keenly the collapse of the Kaiser that he went out of his head. The government ironed out a good many of the hyphens with a heavy hand, and the experience of the war, into which men entered as Swedes or Poles or Irish, turned them all into buddies, 100 per cent Americans. The French Homes Society were very cordial in entertaining American soldiers in France and they would frequently comment on the strange accent of the Americans, when talking to some Swede or Finn or Armenian. But in the war they were all fighting with all the grit they had for the old Stars and Stripes—Southerner and Yankee and Colored, Jew and Pole and Scandinavian, yes, and many a German-American, all fused together in a common comradeship. Heroism that would have commanded a sonnet in other wars was commonplace here, and a man at the dressing station, his face white and drawn and the cold perspiration on his forehead, would stand back and say: "Take my buddy first, doc; he's worse hit than me," when one was perhaps an Irishman and his buddy a Jew. With all its horrors and all that it revealed of the mean and despicable in human nature, the war was a great machine for the removal of hyphens and the creation of Americans.

At present it is rare that any violent feeling occurs in the case of any of the European races. If in each section where a certain racial group predominates there was violent racial antagonism toward the other sections, each group would soon demand independence and a government of its own, with state language and customs, and America would become like Central Europe. The French in Louisiana, the Germans in Wisconsin, the Swedes in Minnesota, the Italians in New York, the Poles in Connecticut, the Dutch in Pennsylvania, the French Canadians in Massachusetts, seem to live peaceably with their neighbors, forgetting the country of their origin, unless they are shoved at each other's throats by some European cataclysm like the Great War. The various racial groups in America are then fairly well localized and static, but they differ vastly in the amount and character of the emotion they radiate, from the violent prejudice that centres in the negro to the placid content of the Pennsylvania Dutch.

We may picture these various racial centres dotted over the country, surrounded by walls of prejudice of varying height and thickness, some positive in character and built up of their feeling toward their neighbors, others negative and created by the feeling of their neighbors toward them, and some both positive and negative and almost impassible. It suggests the Afridi villages at the top of the Khyber Pass, each surrounded by a high blank impenetrable wall, and surmounted by a tall watch tower from which the head of the house loves to fire pot shots at his neighbors. Fortunately every intermarriage bores a hole in these walls, and they are caving in under the pressure of American education.

8. THE AMERICAN INDIAN

The American Indian has always been a disturbing element in America. His differences are so radical that they have not only induced antagonistic feeling, but have issued in open hostilities. When two races so totally different in customs rub against each other for two hundred years and more, the induced currents of antipathy are constantly increased by friction. The cat and dog, though they have lived together for centuries, seem to come no nearer to mutual understanding. There are doubtless fundamental differences in their points of view. Though supposedly a reasoning creature, man seems hardly able to reach a better adjustment. The Indian had his own standards of honor and usually lived up to them, often showing the noblest qualities. These standards the white men did not understand, nor did the Indian understand the white man's methods, so that even with Indians that were friendly there were repeated clashes, resulting in raids and warfare, while the white man inconsiderately poured firewater upon the flame.

In warfare the Indian showed little regard for those international conventions and courtesies which a gentleman expects his adversary to observe. He scalped his prisoners or tortured them to death with the most hideous torments. This was in accord with his code of vengeance and of allowing his enemy to prove his fortitude. The settlers, not being trained in ethnology, regarded him as a demon, inhuman, and as incapable of mutual fellowship as a rattlesnake.

There were others, however, even in the earliest days, who aroused no little antagonism by standing up for the Indians. He had his friends, like John Eliot at Newton, and John Sergeant at Stockbridge, or David Brainerd, who devoted their lives to help him and who have their successors to-day in the Indian League. On the other side have been the settlers who suffered from his depredations, and who resented any gesture of friendliness. To the Indian, land can no more be bought and sold than sky or ocean, and when the white man thought he was purchasing territory, the Indians failed to grasp the idea that for a few gifts he was renouncing his fields and hunting grounds in perpetuity. Consequently they were as annoyed with the settlers upon their former territory as is an Englishman with a poacher, and constant strife resulted. The white men were stronger, however, and by force of arms the various Indian tribes were gradually herded into reservations.

There is a brutality about the advance of civilization which rivals that of the savage. Before that triumphant progress the savage has no rights. As soon as he was settled in one spot, the neighboring whites would begin to covet his land and commence an agitation at Washington to remove him. It is a tragic story of bitter injustice, of which no American is proud. The Cherokees and Creeks were gradually driven from Georgia far out to Oklahoma, and at last even this section, the old Indian Territory, was taken from them. By similar dealings other tribes were driven from fertile and pleasant lands to desolate and desert areas. Treaty after treaty was broken. When the Indians retaliated by raiding, the army was called out and they were hemmed in and slaughtered. It was unfortunate that their dealings were frequently with unscrupulous frontiersmen, who purposely stirred up trouble by supplying them with intoxicants and by irritating them in hope that they would rebel and be driven out by the soldiers. Most of the bitterest wars, such as that of the Apaches and Geronimo, were the result of exasperation on the part of the Indians at being driven from the reservations promised them, to desert places where they could find no suitable camps. There have been sad cases of treachery, as in the Black Hawk War, where the Indians were induced to come in under pledge of safety and then shot down without mercy. On the other side are cases of terrible atrocities and treachery on the part of the Indians, which roused the neighboring settlers to madness. It was the tragic story of a semi-barbarous race gradually crushed and overwhelmed by the advance of a civilization they did not understand and did not want.

Fortunately a league was formed of the friends of the Indian for his defence and protection, and of late years everything possible has been done to safeguard his interests. The bitter feeling against the Indians has died out. They are now the "wards of the nation," and each tribe has its reservation where they are, in the main, well cared for and prosperous. Many of the tribes have intermarried to such an extent that there are few distinguishing marks left, and in Oklahoma the Osages and Cherokees, through the ownership of oil lands, have become extremely wealthy.

Certain of the tribes, like the Navajos, Hopis and Pueblos of Arizona and New Mexico, have retained their old customs and traditions and in their wide reservations are practically untouched by the civilization of the white man. The Navajos send a few of their children to government schools, but most of the tribe live in their scattered Hogons and pasture their sheep on the wide plateaux of Arizona among the weird cliffs of the Monument Country and the vivid colors of the Painted Desert. It is supposed that Senator Fall as Secretary of the Interior profited somewhat at the expense of the Indians of New Mexico, but in the main they have been well protected by their friends, who have watched every bill introduced to rob them of their lands and privileges. Every year enterprising tourist bureaus take thousands of travellers to visit their more interesting settlements, such as Taos, Walpi and Acoma, and there is an increasing interest in Indian art as shown in their pottery, rugs and silverware. As they become civilized and settle down to work, they are gradually becoming American citizens, while those who keep to their own customs awaken no antagonism but are an object of increasing interest to the general public. In fact, there is an increasing protest against the attempts of the Indian schools to break up their old customs and dances and to Americanize them. The old bitter feeling is practically obsolete, and there is a general desire to preserve and protect them as an ethnological curiosity if nothing more.

CHAPTER XIII

EMOTIONAL POWER HOUSES AND RELIGIOUS CURRENTS

1. The Roman Static Current

If you are liable to shock from emotional currents you will doubtless be alarmed to find yourself in a country where innumerable power houses are generating currents of dangerously high voltage, the exposed wires from which you may encounter in any town and village. The situation is bad enough with those ancient power lines of racial current that cross here and there and emit sparks, without added complications. But every church is a power house where an emotional current of a special type is being generated, with emotionalized phrases and peculiar attitudes of its own. It is not long since these currents were so highly charged with prejudices and mutual antagonisms that an explosion resulted whenever they came in contact. Some of these currents, though dangerous at times, are of great value, and supply the power that runs the wheels of the social mechanism.

We have spoken of the Roman Catholic Church as the great dynamo whose power lines ran through the whole of Europe, carrying the current that maintained the social order. Although it originally created reverence for autocratic rulers, it has so adjusted itself that in America it is probably the most valuable stabilizing agency in the country. It generates a strong feeling of reverence for the law, of respect for women, of horror for immorality, for divorce, and for all revolutionary movements that threaten the sanctity of the home and the stability of society. By the promise of blessedness and the fear of its curse it keeps quiet and contented large sections of the population that in times of distress would easily be swept into the current of anarchy or communism. It carries in its current a great mass of dogmas and ceremonial commands and prohibitions which are as highly emotionalized as any ancient tabu. The system is designed to give an emotional content to nearly every act of the daily life, by associating it with prayer or with some religious observance. By creating a conviction of the infallibility of the supreme religious authority, it is able to place a tabu on any new thought that would tend to inhibit the flow of the emotional current. Based on the experience of ages, its psychology is almost unerring. By its assertion that in religious matters its statement of the truth is inerrant it comes into conflict with Science. As the corner stone of its edifice without which it would collapse is the conviction that the Roman Pontiff is the sole supreme religious authority, it comes into inevitable antagonism with other churches and religions and is prevented from apparent co-operation. But in spite of the prejudice and antagonism which it carries, the current which it generates aids greatly the endeavor of the other churches toward better conditions and a more stable home life. The fundamental difficulty is that an institution based on autocracy is an anachronism in a modern democracy. If, as Hilaire Belloc suggests, a conflict should occur between the authority of the Pope and the laws framed by the people, a very serious situation would be created.

2. Protestant Dynamic Currents

We have noted that America was settled by groups who crossed the Sea because they had rebelled against the old autocracies, under the influence of the Reformation Current of feeling and the old Anglo-Saxon Spirit of Liberty. This Reformation Current had its power houses in the Protestant churches, that were continually cultivating the sense of individual responsibility to God, and enforcing that deep reverence for law and morality which had its basis in the threat of the fires of Hell. It developed that sense of responsibility for converting the world and relieving its suffering which was the basis of the Missionary Spirit. It also charged the individual with a terrible sense of sin and fear of punishment, followed by a wave of rapture or of peaceful content. This extraordinary psychical change resulting from a full charge of the Reformation Current was known as conversion. There was always an effort on the part of those in authority to change these churches into power houses to generate reverence for the government in power, on the model of the Roman Church, but as soon as this was accomplished the old current would break loose and create a new set of dynamos.

The Protestant churches of America were, then, the power houses whence flowed three of these great currents of feeling which we have described, the Reformation Current, the Missionary Current, and, at times, the Current of Devotion to Liberty and Justice. As their organization was democratic there was nothing in it essentially opposed to the Spirit of Freedom, as there was in the churches of the old world.

To that extent they assisted in the main drive toward progress. But mingled with the positive current which each church discharged, were negative elements of antagonism and prejudice that had disastrous effects on the community.

The negative currents generated by adjacent groups of different race are powerful enough, but it is when they are combined with a religious current that they become most dangerous, as we have noted in the case of the Jews and the Irish. There is no virus more vigorous than the Odium Theologicum and when injected into a feverish racial situation it produces a dangerously high temperature. The dangerous element in the religious current is a claim to an exclusive monopoly of the means to salvation. Genial religions like the Buddhist, which admit the possibility of virtue and salvation in others, can live in peace, but those which claim this monopoly of salvation and assert that all others are lying instruments of the devil, designed to lure men with false hopes and land them in the flames of Hell—these religions naturally create emotional cyclones and violent antagonisms between their various adherents.

For if a man believes that his church and belief provide the only way to be saved, and that without them he is subject to eternal punishment, he must regard with horror all other religions and consider every attempt on their part to win converts among his friends as a hideous danger, and their teachings as a poisonous contagion to be shunned like smallpox.

In New York I learned that two little girls stopped attending meetings in a certain church because they were told by representatives of another religious body that every time they entered that church their souls became black. Of course statements of that kind cause a violent emotional reaction. No emotional cyclones are created because a religion claims to possess the way to salvation, but when it asserts that all other religions lead men into danger of eternal punishment, it creates toward them a most violent type of prejudice, a sort of horror, which is one of the most divisive and destructive emotions that can enter a community. It is difficult to know how to deal with it, for such beliefs are conscientiously held and so deeply rooted in the emotional nature as to be almost ineradicable. There was a time when almost every branch of the Church generated a current of this repellent type, carrying a heavy load of prejudice against all other religious bodies. The reason was that each claimed to possess some special article of belief or form of baptism, or ceremonial, which was essential to salvation.

Of late years most of the Protestant churches have been willing to admit that those outside of their communion could be saved, though one Bishop is reported to have said that no gentleman would take advantage of the opportunity. It has therefore been possible for the churches to work together for better conditions both in America and in the field of Foreign Missions, which has been amicably divided between the different denominations. Moreover, in America in small towns that once were making a vain effort to support four or five antagonistic churches, there is now a tendency for the Protestant churches, since they all produce a current of the same feeling, to join in a Union church, and worship together forgetting their former feuds. Fifty years ago in many small towns there were bitter feelings and many violent quarrels between Presbyterian, Baptist and Methodist. Episcopalians would enter a town where there were already four churches and do their utmost to win converts from the other sects, thus creating much animosity. There was a period when differences were emphasized and, instead of uniting, each church was split by divergences of opinion as to the essentials of salvation. The schism of the Congregational body, which was once the state church of Massachusetts, into Unitarian and Orthodox, produced a situation which divided the people of New England into two hostile camps. Nearly every church was divided, the Society and Church property usually going to the Unitarians, while the deacons and older church members stuck to the Orthodox faith and usually went forth to build another church. The Orthodox regarded the Unitarians as blasphemers for denying the divinity of Christ, and the Unitarians regarded the Orthodox as bigots for holding to the old doctrines of the Blood Atonement and the Inerrancy of the Scriptures. Fifty years ago the whole nation was involved in the vortices of these sectarian prejudices, and in many towns people of different sects would hardly speak and regarded each other with a sort of horror.

3. RECHARGING THE POWER HOUSE

Whenever the old current began to slacken in the churches, some dynamic individual, highly charged with the old spirit, would appear and proceed to recharge them. As these men were often free from the sectarian elements that divided the churches the effect was to unify.

From the time of Wesley to Billy Sunday, the country has been stirred by the preaching of some great revivalist nearly every decade and the tide of religious emotion thus started had a most amazing effect, not only on the personal life of individuals by inducing them to give up habits of self-indulgence, but also on the churches, by breaking up the various currents of antagonism and the walls of prejudice between them and also those between different races and classes, and by sweeping them all along on a common tide of fervid feeling. These revivalistic whirlwinds roused not only the old Reformation Spirit, but the Missionary Spirit as well,—that feeling of interest in the eternal welfare of others which finally came to include their temporal welfare, and which we recognize as humanitarian feeling.

The humanitarian feeling found its chief supporters at first in those branches of the church, such as the Unitarian and Universalist, which had lost faith in the imminence of eternal punishment. The current of altruistic feeling generated by the church thus took a new direction and sought to save men from suffering in this world. Both these sects were outside the sphere of revivalism and were regarded with a certain horror by the rest, who commonly distinguished between them by saying that the Universalists believed that God was too good to damn them, while the Unitarians held that they were too good to be damned. Be that as it may, it was largely this disbelief in Hell that turned their activities to philanthropic rather than missionary and revivalistic lines. They regarded with aversion the methods of the revivalist with his threats of doom for all who did not accept his creed, but the mass of the people responded to the appeals of such as Whitefield, Davenant, Jonathan Edwards, President Finney and Dwight Moody who held their meetings in city after city. In addition to his personal dynamic, Moody built up a powerful machine for generating emotion through the use of music, and the Moody and Sankey songs became familiar in nearly every Protestant American home, and proved to possess an amazing power to stir the feelings of a vast throng when they were roused to sing in chorus by the appeal of a magnetic leader.

There was a gradual shift from the emotional stimulus derived from the threats of hell fire to the appeal of Divine love set forth in music, but the threat was always in the background as a contrast to the Divine mercy, and without it revivalism would have found its main nerve severed. The effects of these emotional whirlwinds were unbelievable.

Hardened sinners broke down and wept. Others went into trances and convulsions. Among the negroes, and in more ignorant sections of the country, the camp meeting became a familiar means of arousing religious feeling to an orgiastic pitch, and such sects as the Holy Rollers have attempted to make it permanent at all their meetings.

Lately the revival has become a great business proposition involving the outlay of hundreds of thousands of dollars, in constructing vast power houses, where power is developed by the latest scientific methods. This meant the building of a tabernacle and the guaranteed support of all the churches, which are organized into an army pledged to attack every unsaved man and induce him to accept the creed of the revivalist. The revivalist must be an orator of unusual magnetic power, able to rouse a vast audience to laughter or tears, with a fund of wit, humor, and pathos. The ground is prepared for him by a carefully studied campaign, and his audience is aroused by the mass singing of emotional hymns. Certain revivalists start interest and excitement by denouncing all clergymen and church members who do not accept a certain creed and consigning them to perdition in picturesque language which wins the approbation of the non-church-goers. This scientifically constructed power house for generating emotion, with its calculated psychological mechanism, is in great contrast to the simple passionate sincerity of Wesley and his meetings in the open fields with all the churches against him. To-day the campaign usually ends in "love gifts" amounting to many thousands from those whose emotional nature the revivalist has aroused. To them it is undoubtedly as well worth while as it is to the revivalist. Dwight Moody was a man of great sincerity, earnestness and charm, who had pre-eminently the power to break down emotional barriers of hatred, prejudice and antagonism. His work still goes on through the educational institutions he has founded at Northfield, Mass.

4. The Consolidated Lines

This Revivalistic current finally resulted in a split which ran through all the churches. It swept the various sects into one great tide of the old fundamental Reformation Current with its fear of Hell fires, its exalted faith in the Blood Atonement and in the Inerrancy of the Scriptures, while those whose knowledge of modern science prevented their acceptance of these beliefs were left standing untouched. The scholarly Unitarians and High Church Episcopalians regarded these emotional ebullitions with some contempt, while the Revivalistic or Evangelistic wing of the church remained impervious to scientific discoveries and the teachings of Darwin, Huxley and Spencer, who were regarded as blasphemous atheists who denied the word of God. Little by little, however, science made its way, erecting a barrier of disbelief which the old current could not pass in the minds of many in all the Orthodox churches. Thus the barriers between the sects were broken down on the one side by the Revivalistic current and on the other by the advance of Science, leaving one great emotional barrier, splitting in twain nearly every sect and often individual churches—the barrier between those still dominated by the old current with all its emotionalized dogmas, and those in whom this current had been blocked by the conclusions of modern science. The same emotional attitude which once existed between Orthodox and Unitarian now existed between the two wings of each church.

The teachings of Darwin and Spencer were at first bitterly combated by all the churches. But in every church there were thinkers who accepted the findings of modern science and adjusted their theology to the advance of thought. The first great battle was in the 1880s at Andover on the question of the possibility of salvation for those who had never heard of Christ. The Andover controversy divided the Congregational Church into two wings and aroused the bitterest feeling. It issued in a lawsuit to dispossess the Andover professors as teachers of heresy, and this carried the excitement throughout the country.

It was followed in 1892 by the controversy at Union Seminary in New York on the question of the Inerrancy of the Scriptures, and the trial of Professor Briggs, conducted with that virulence of vituperation which often results from the conviction that the eternal verities are in danger, divided the Presbyterians into two parties,—Princeton Seminary still contending that Eve was created from Adam's rib, and that the whale swallowed Jonah, and seeking to prevent the ordination of any student of Union who had doubts concerning these cardinal facts. A similar movement was in progress in the Episcopal Church, where Cambridge Seminary, of which William Lawrence was then dean, represented the progressive element, while the General Seminary in New York and William Manning, rector of Trinity, upheld the Conservative doctrine.

Certain Baptist and Methodist churches joined in the progressive movement, but the great mass of the churches, especially those in the country and small towns, remained with the Conservative party for several decades. In the Roman Catholic church Archbishop Ireland led the progressive movement for a time, but by the centripetal force resident in an infallible central authority, the Roman church was able to restore her thinkers to an acquiesence externally indistinguishable from unity. Elsewhere, however, the progressive movement went forward, with the result that in place of the innumerable sectarian eddies, the emotional conflict is now resolved into the clash between Fundamentalist and Modernist, which by 1920 had divided Protestant America into two camps. The controversy between the sects is lost to view in this greater conflict between two opposing attitudes of mind. One clings to the literal interpretation of the Bible with all its miracles, and regards science as the handmaid of the devil, and the other seeks to adjust religious doctrine to the latest scientific thought. The Fundamentalist regards the Modernist with a very real horror. He is destroying the old faith and leading the youth of the nation to eternal destruction. The Modernist considers the Fundamentalist to be a bigot who makes religion contemptible or impossible to the intelligent youth of the nation. Each side is thoroughly conscientious, so that the emotional tension is high, and feeling at times reaches violent expression.

Fundamentalist revivalists such as Billy Sunday do not hesitate to denounce modernistic clergymen as emissaries of Satan, and gain a large part of their attendance through the excitement aroused by their vituperation. As already noted some such programme of denunciation is a valuable accessory in rousing men emotionally to the point where they will renounce habits of intoxication and self-indulgence. A similar programme of vituperation characterized Dowie and the Zionist movement, which induced thousands to renounce various forms of self-indulgence. Some consider that freedom from alcoholism is dearly bought when it involves a new influx of religious prejudice, but in the main even the Modernists are glad to further any campaign which will free men from such ignoble bondage, and are willing to sit on the platform while the revivalist denounces their errors.

At the present day, then, religion in America, instead of dividing men by walls of prejudice into innumerable sectarian groups, each of which has the only road of salvation and looks upon the rest with an antagonism little short of horror, is now dividing the people of the nation into two parties. The Modernist Baptist has more sympathy with the Modernist Presbyterian than with the Fundamentalist in his own church, and this seems to be generally true, save in the case of some old-time sects that still cling to their old doctrines. The Baptists for instance include a number of violently prejudiced sub-sects, some of which have no communion with the rest because of some special rite or belief which they regard as essential to salvation while others neglect it. But little by little science is doing away with the belief that any one religion has a monopoly of the way of salvation, and as this belief was the root of all violent religious emotion and prejudice, religion has ceased to be a divisive force of any moment, and the mass of the people

regard with indifference the divergences in belief of the
various sects and change their affiliations as convenience
suggests.

Certain sections, such as the Southern Mountaineers and
portions of the middle West, are predominantly fundamentalist, while the majority of the churches in New York
and Boston are modernistic, and occasionally in their national assemblies there is a violent clash, and a trial for
heresy is instituted which arouses general excitement. In
the main, however, the various sections go on their way
without any great emotional disturbance. In New York the
Baptists have been disturbed by the controversy between
the adherents of John Roach Straton and those of Dr. Fos-
dick, and the Presbyterians are divided between the old
Scotch churches and the advanced thinkers of Union Seminary, and the Episcopalians between Bishop Manning and
such modernists as the rectors of St. George's and St. Bar-
tholomew's, to say nothing of St. Mark's on the Bowerie,
but the public pays little attention to their disputes, and religion seems to have lost most of its dynamic as a divisive
force.

5. The Dominant Currents

Thus the powerful negative and destructive element in
the current generated by the churches has been reduced, and
they are of vast benefit as power houses for generating the
current of humanitarian feeling and for putting the drive
of conscientious feeling behind every movement for social
reform. For a time a large section of the church seemed to
be caught in the web of the great Enchantress, and every
effort of the Spirit of Liberty and Justice to find expression
was promptly quashed by trustees and wardens who feared
that the church would interfere with their autocratic control. But since the transformation of the Enchantress, the
church has been prominent in every forward movement, and
serves as a generating station of the old Spirit of Liberty
and Justice, save in special cases when the membership is
entirely reactionary.

There is an increasing feeling in favor of church unity. Men will always differ as to the method in which they prefer to worship, but even if different types of churches are preserved to suit the requirements of different individuals, there is no reason why all should not unite in generating the great currents of feeling that make for progress and in co-operating to improve conditions and combat evil, so long as they renounce the effort to claim a monopoly of salvation. Even among those who still claim such a monopoly, prejudice is growing less violent. Thirty years ago a Protestant clergyman could not pass through certain sections of lower New York without having Irish hoodlums salute him at every corner with insults as a "Black Protestant," and without seeing ancient Jews spit on the pavement as he passed, while to-day any such sign would be rare indeed. In those days each foreign church sought to maintain a barrier of religious prejudice around their constituents, and I have seen a German Lutheran minister threaten to leave the room if a Presbyterian clergyman was invited to participate in the service.

The Episcopalians have been most rigid in refusing to admit other clergymen to any part in their services, since they claimed that their apostolic succession alone possessed the unction essential to the performance of religious rites, but lately some of them have shown a willingness to recognize the spiritual qualifications of clergymen of other denominations. Such prejudice as there is seems to centre in a comparatively small group of the clergy. In the main, then, we may say that the emotion aroused by religion is ceasing to be really harmful as a cause of prejudice and antagonism between various groups and sections of the country. There are certain religious bodies where the separating emotional barrier is political, as in the case of the Presbyterians North and South, divided by feeling during the Civil War. In others the barrier is racial feeling, as in the Methodist church, where there is one division which includes colored people under white bishops, and another which asserts the equality of the black man and is controlled by negro bishops. There is much feeling here but it is racial rather than religious. The only significant religious feeling is that between Fundamentalist and Modernist, and that is doomed to disappear as scientific education advances, which must come about in spite of the efforts of certain legislatures to prevent it. The feeling between Catholic and Protestant is probably less than at any other period, and, as we have noted, where it exists on the part of Protestants, it is largely due to political rather than religious causes.

The churches of America are, then, the only organized power houses to generate the great currents of humanitarian feeling and of devotion to Liberty and Justice which are the main drive in all forward movements. Moreover, they add to these currents the tremendous force of the impulsion of conscience, and the sense that the Divine will is behind their endeavor.

6. FOREIGN CURRENTS

There was one power house which generated a current of such dangerous power that it seemed for a time a threat to the nation, and which aroused the most violent counter-currents. For many years the Mormons in Utah, Idaho and Arizona were surrounded by an emotional ring of prejudice, based not only upon their religion but upon their authorization of plural marriages. The story of their conquest of the desert under the leadership of Brigham Young is an heroic one. Many delicate women crossed the icebound Rockies in winter, their bare feet torn by stones and ice, as they pushed the carts containing their earthly possessions. Little by little they made desolate Utah a garden spot, and founded a community of hard-working, self-denying folk, who were ready to sacrifice all for their peculiar religion. Many strange stories are told of their mysterious rites which subjugate the women entirely to their husbands, and of their persecution of other religions, and very violent feeling existed against them all over the country. Since the admission of Utah as a state and their abandonment of plural marriages, this feeling has largely died down. They deny at present their old belief that women have no souls and depend upon their husbands for salvation, and as one meets them and watches them at work, they seem to be an earnest, Puritanical, hard-working folk, notable for their cleanliness and well-cultivated farms and ranches. Their missions will be found all through the South Sea Islands, and they even send forth ardent missionaries to convert the people of New England.

I had a long talk with two of them who had been trying to bring spiritual uplift to the hard-headed farmers of Connecticut. They said they believed in Christ and the Gospels, and I inquired if they could tell me the real difference between their doctrine and that of the Congregationalists whom they sought to convert. They responded that the difference was very simple, and when I begged for further enlightenment, they said, "Why, the difference is that ours is true." Further inquiry elicited that apart from this, the main difference was in their belief in the continued revelation of God through their elders at Salt Lake, who still receive the Divine commands, while other churches hold that the day of Divine revelation is past. They also believe in the pre-existence of the human soul, and that unborn souls await birth in great distress and anxiety.

In the main the prejudice of the Mormons against outsiders and of the general public against the Mormons has greatly diminished, and they live peaceably with their gentile neighbors both in Utah and in Idaho. Their influence in the latter state is sufficiently strong to make the anniversary of Brigham Young's arrival in Salt Lake the chief state holiday under the name of Pioneer Day. The current now flowing from the great Mormon Temple is one of reverence for the laws of God as promulgated through their elders, with a horror like that of the Puritans toward self-indulgence, and with great enthusiasm for faithful and honest work. It formerly charged the Mormon women with a feeling of inferiority and a dread lest by remaining unmarried they should lose the chance of salvation. It was the conviction that plural marriage was commanded by God that antagonized the dominant currents of feeling in the nation, and now that this is no longer expressed, the feeling against them has died down.

All along the upper valley of the Rio Grande may be seen certain windowless edifices known as Muradas. These are the secret meeting places of the Penitentes, a religious organization to which allusion was made in the introduction, which seems an incredible anachronism in Twentieth Century America. They are a survival of Spanish days, a branch of the Roman Catholic Church condemned by the priests, which nevertheless has persisted, and which has a powerful emotional effect on politics and social life. In Holy Week the traveller may see a procession headed by wailing women in black and melancholy flutists, followed by men stripped to the waist lashing each other with scourges tipped with iron or cactus till the path is red with blood. Following them again are from one to three men bearing crosses on pads of cactus, so heavy that they often fall beneath the weight, to be lashed by the men behind until they struggle to their feet and stagger on to the chosen spot where they are crucified and kept for three hours upon the cross. On the shoulder of these men there is a peculiar scar which is the badge of the initiate. I have been told that their influence was so powerful as to control the decisions of the courts, and that in order to gain their political support, even Protestant Americans have joined the order. The organization is so secret that it creates little emotional stir in the country at large, but in the neighborhood it has a powerful effect, the dominant emotion that it arouses being fear rather than prejudice. There are other peculiar religious communities in other sections of the country, for America is noted for the variety of its sects. The influence of most of these is purely local, and has little effect on the country at large.

For a time the Spiritualists had a powerful influence in America, and held great meetings attended by thousands, where the spirits of the dead were invoked. Of late the Society of Pyschical Research has done such a work of investigation that many of their mediums have been discredited. Many of the best are now working with the Society on scientific rather than religious lines. While there is violent prejudice against Spiritualism as a religion, the general attitude of intelligent men seems to be one of unprejudiced interest in the scientific investigations now being carried forward on psychic lines, through such mediums as have proved themselves to be honest.

The Theosophists have won some converts in California and have beautiful headquarters at Point Loma.

The Vedantists also have houses in several of the great cities and there are innumerable strange and foreign sects, none of which have aroused any very strong following among the general public.

The religious emotional situation is then a complex affair. It began with a vast number of power houses, connected up into rival systems, so that each had its station in every village, from which antagonism and prejudice was radiated. These numerous systems, though still keeping their names, are now consolidated into three main power lines, the Roman Catholic, Jewish and Protestant. The last is again divided into two networks which radiate mutual antagonism and suspicion, but are so arranged that one dominates the South and West and the other the North and East. But this Protestant network is so connected that the great dominant currents of humanitarian feeling which it generates, can sweep away at times these conflicting feelings and carry the whole Protestant Communion forward in some common endeavor for the progress of the world. The Jews are also divided into the orthodox, with innumerable synagogues as their power houses, where the old Jewish current is still generated as in past ages, and the Reformed, whose temples serve as power houses which produce not only a current of loyalty to the finest Jewish tradition, but also a powerful stream of humanitarian feeling which often unites with that from the Protestant Churches.

CHAPTER XIV

FRICTIONAL CURRENTS AND STORMS

1. CLASS FEELING

IF two small boys want the same piece of pie and are normally constituted, some emotion of an antagonistic character is sure to be generated. The same is true of groups of men who are struggling for the same prize. We may call feeling of this sort a frictional current, and it occurs whenever the interests of two groups conflict. A good deal has been said of class feeling, and this frictional feeling is supposed to exist between the different social classes. In the old world, where there was an impenetrable wall between the classes, it did not exist, because an emotional attitude of reverence and awe was cultivated in the lower classes, varying from the self-abasing worship with which the Pariah regards the Brahmin, to the respectful subservience of the Englishman to the gentleman or lord. Hereditary titles create an emotional barrier of surprising intensity and impenetrability. But where the lower classes suffer greatly through unjust treatment this attitude often changes to bitter hatred and revengeful animosity, as in the French Revolution.

In a democracy any class which attempts to secure special privileges for itself is at once exposed to frictional feeling. In America society is not stratified as in the old world. There is, of course, no such hereditary caste as the nobility —a subject of undoubted regret to certain social leaders who continually import samples from abroad—nor does the gentleman belong to a group distinguished from the tradesman by a special inheritance and training. In spite of such efforts as those of Ward McAlister to create a social barrier, no superior caste has yet been created. The gentleman in America is merely one who has availed himself of the opportunities for culture and refinement which the country affords, and although the majority of this class are probably among those who have been brought up in homes where the tradition of culture has been maintained for generations, like the so-called Brahmins of Boston, there are undoubtedly some of humble parentage who might claim the name in virtue of their own efforts. The class distinction which is most exploited in America is that between the employer and the employee, or between capital and labor, but as many of the greatest capitalists started as laborers, this distinction is by no means one that is hard and fast. Forty or fifty years ago, when the laborer and factory employee and miner received barely a living wage, it was extremely difficult for one of them to advance to a position of wealth and power. To-day it is possible, for any man of ability, by hard work to reach a position of influence and prominence.

What is termed class conflict in America has usually been a part of the battle with the great Enchantress, in which working men fought against a group, often composed largely of their former companions, who had gained the upper hand as employers, to secure a larger share of the product of labor. This is a perennial cause of friction between employer and employee, and it seems probable that there will be conflict over the division of profits between the laborer and the stockholder, until the laborer himself becomes a stockholder.

Another phenomenon which is termed class feeling is really the conflict of the Communistic Current with the American Commercial Current that no longer deserves the name of the Enchantress.

2. COMPETITIVE CURRENTS

In America men of the old stock who are working for a man of wealth consider themselves as good as their employer, if not better, and have little consciousness of a class barrier. If there is feeling against an employer, it is usually an individual matter due to injustice or arrogance. But whenever a certain group has gained special privileges and erected a barrier against others, feeling is sure to arise. In the period 1880–1890, when the Barons of Industry and of Transportation had gained such a stranglehold on the country, and enormous fortunes were rolling up, while the mass of the people were in great poverty, a great feeling of bitterness sprang up against the men of wealth and against Wall Street, as we have already stated. This was hardly class feeling in the sense that class is understood in Europe. It is the feeling of the man who is down against the man who is sitting on his chest, a feeling of bitterness among those who had not gained the prize toward those who had. When the working man is on his feet with enough money to buy silk stockings for his wife and a ticket to the movies and gasoline for his automobile, there seems to be comparatively little of this feeling.

There are those who fatten on animosities. The Hearst press consistently sought to exploit what feeling there was, as did certain walking delegates and Soviet emissaries. These all seek to develop frictional feeling between the man who has gained wealth and the man who has failed to do so. Since the days of Job the man of wealth has been subject to envy and satanic accusations, but in America where the working man of yesterday is the millionaire of to-day, this can hardly be called class feeling. Such feeling as exists is chiefly found, not among Americans, but among immigrants from Europe, who carry with them currents of bitterness generated in the old world. Russia is the main power plant for the Communistic Current, which carries violent class feeling as between the working man and the Capitalist, toward whom they have been brought to feel the same horror that an orthodox parson feels toward an atheist. As already noted, in the 1880's there was a large number of Communists, Socialists and members of the I. W. W. in America, who were animated by this bitter feeling against all Capitalists and the whole Capitalistic system, but most of their guns have been spiked, and they seem to have less and less influence in national affairs. The danger here is that in times of general distress they may carry the unemployed into the tide of the Communistic current, which is really a class current and seeks to put the whole of society under the domination of the industrial worker; which some declare to be a tyranny no less great than that of the Capitalist.

The Trade Unions form a group that stirred up very bitter frictional feeling when they were struggling with their employers for a larger share of the product of labor. In general it may be said that such groups as arouse emotional storms are occupational rather than social classes. The various Unions seem constantly involved in squabbles of their own which react to the misfortune of the innocent employer. In the main, however, they are leagued together, not to overthrow Capitalism, which most of them feel would be as disastrous to themselves as to the Capitalist, but to secure higher wages and shorter hours, or more money for less work, an aim which seems to have a vigorous appeal to the ordinary mortal, and which avoids those questions of economic theory which are so violently charged with prejudice that they split men by furious antagonisms. As stated, the intelligent working men have no class feud, but are engaged in a contest with their employers as to the division of the product of labor, and now that they are given stock in the company and a share in its management, the majority of them are capitalists themselves to such an extent that they can have no class quarrel with capitalism. Unscrupulous walking delegates, however, have succeeded in stirring up many emotional storms among men who would otherwise have been quite contented.

Those who work under conditions of difficulty or danger form a favorable channel for frictional currents. The coal mines have always been centres for strikes and violent outbreaks of bitter feeling between employer and employed, and it seems more difficult to reach an adjustment by which the miners will secure conditions of life and labor that satisfy them than it is in other trades. The mining sections still remain areas of emotional high pressure, ready to burst into revolt at any moment, in spite of all that has been done to improve conditions. In a mine which I visited recently there was a minimum wage of $8 a day, and an eight-hour day, which meant only six hours' work, as the men took an hour to get to their work, and an hour to return. There is certainly a vast change from the conditions under which wretched women and boys crawled half-naked with their heavy loads through the narrow passages of the English and French mines a few decades ago. But it will always be difficult to make underground work thoroughly attractive and to keep such workmen content.

Other centres of emotional disturbance are found in those industries, such as the cloakmakers, much of whose work is done in the so-called sweat-shops among the tenements, where women were employed at a trifling wage, often under starvation conditions. Here both employer and employee were usually foreigners, often unacquainted with the English language and with American customs. Frequent strikes were engineered by friends who are better informed, or by allied unions to enable them to better their conditions, and the tenement sections were thus kept in an emotional ferment.

We have already alluded to the emotional storm due to the friction between agriculture and transportation. The interests of the farmers seemed gradually to be brought into conflict with those of the rest of the country. Dependent originally on the railroads for the distribution of their produce, they suffered so greatly from discrimination in rates that actual warfare broke out in some sections, as in the San Joaquin Valley in California, between the ranchers and the Southern Pacific. They had too much of the old Yankee independence at first to band together in unions, and were at the mercy of railroad and middleman and of the grain-elevator companies and packers. Though the whole country depended on them for its food supply, they seemed helpless and grew all the time more embittered and hostile to the financial and industrial system that had them in its toils.

We have described the great Populistic movement which

swept the country under Bryan's leadership, set in motion by this wave of dissatisfaction and indignation which originated with the farmers of the Northwest. By combining and gaining control of politics and of the grain elevators, they greatly bettered their condition, but this section remains an area of emotional high pressure, dreaded by politicians and liable to burst into action whenever crops fail or conditions prove unfavorable.

There is quite a different emotional quality in the relation of occupational groups such as these, and that between class groups, one of which regards the other as almost demigods, while they in return are regarded as hardly human. In America it is merely a contest between two groups when their interests clash and there is suspicion of unjust treatment. As each industry meets unfavorable conditions and its workmen suffer, it becomes a centre where an emotional wave is generated which may find its expression in an attack on the employers, or in an effort to overthrow the political party in power, or in some form of communistic or socialistic endeavor.

When men receive enough of the product of their labor to live in comfort there is little frictional feeling. When they suffer want they begin to look for the man who is getting the larger share of the product. It is among men who are suffering that the most violent emotional storms are generated, and a natural corollary is that when there is a large number of unemployed, the barometer at once falls, and the weather becomes ominous. Large bodies of men who are suffering and idle and dissatisfied are the material from which the great emotional storms are brewed that rock governments and tear apart the social order with cyclonic effect. So long as men are at work and receiving a fair reward for their labor with opportunity of advancement, there is little likelihood of any violent class feeling or of an emotional storm in the realm of employment. But when a man is unable to find sufficient work to keep his wife and children from starving, he is goaded into an emotional attitude which may burst forth into action that endangers the commonwealth. It is then that men become the prey of the communistic and revolutionary currents that are always kept in motion by power plants across the sea and that are waiting the chance to sweep men into an attack upon the social order.

There is, of course, frictional feeling developed between any competing industries and organizations, but few of these are large enough to deserve notice here.

The emotional situation of any section depends largely on whether it is industrial or agricultural in character and to that extent there is some localization in these class or occupational disturbances. At present most of the frictional feeling is developed between the Unions and the employers, the farmers and the industrial sections, between non-Union and Union workers and in a vague and general fashion between the rich and poor, or as some would phrase it between the privileged classes and the proletariat. In a country where a railway switchman can belong to the President's cabinet it would seem that the privileged classes are those that possess ability and energy.

3. The Emotional Effect of White Collars

There is a certain feeling between the ignorant and the educated or between the manual laborer and the white-collar man, which has a peculiar effect. Many working men, though they do not aspire to enter the latter class themselves, are determined that their children shall enter its sacred portals, and this has a singular effect on the country. As civilized society is organized, the work of the world is done by large numbers of men who work under direction and supervision. For efficiency it is necessary that they should obey orders, and perform routine work which requires a minimum of intelligence. In normal circumstances the mass of the working class prefer to have a job which, when once learned, is easily performed, and requires no new mental effort. They acquire the most amazing proficiency at their task and are thus enabled to earn a living with the minimum of exertion. The work itself they do not pretend to enjoy, but it enables them to earn money which provides them with sufficient amusement to make life interesting. They become human machines for the production of wages. Their interest in life is outside their work rather than in it—this, of course, is opposite to the attitude of the artist, who finds his chief interest in his work, which is ruined if it becomes mechanical. As the number of jobs that provide any opportunity for the exercise of artistic ability is extremely limited, this is a fortunate provision.

Now, however, such working men are all ambitious for their children, and are sending them to high school, and in many instances to college. The result is that the colleges and higher educational institutions of the country are crowded with young people, many of whom have not the cultural background or mental ability to avail themselves of the education provided. Bees allow only a limited number to develop the qualities that fit them to be queens, but it seems that in America to-day everyone is seeking to qualify for kingship. Such an astonishing movement toward higher education was never known in the world before. There are literally hundreds of thousands of young people in the colleges of America to-day, all of whom expect that they will be thus entitled to enter a higher sphere of social life and a realm of activity in which they will direct others, or at least enjoy a white-collar job, instead of laboring with their hands as their parents had done. Most of them are receiving just enough education to make them discontented to work in a subordinate position, while they have not the ability to hold successfully the position of a director or organizer.

The result is that the country is flooded with young people who are looking for positions of prominence and responsibility, and who swell the ranks of bond salesmen and clerks and create a new class of doctors and lawyers of mediocre ability, while it is increasingly difficult to get efficient labor. When society as organized calls for one man in a thousand to be trained for a position of control, the country is in danger of educating one man in ten for such positions. The chief effect of a college education seems to be to produce an attitude of independence, irresponsibility and resentment to authority, admirable for kings, but unfortunate for a servant. The demand for kings is limited, and there seems to be great overproduction.

In the pioneer life everyone must be a man of initiative and independence. The complicated social order of to-day is dislocated when every man wishes to act on his own initiative and carry out his own ideas. Although machinery is doing away with the necessity for manual labor, America still needs a much larger number of folk who have not been educated to the point where they are unwilling to work under direction and to do as they are told, and this continual outpouring from the colleges of greater numbers of educated men than are needed to supply the positions that our social organization provides, is a menace to the future. It creates a discontented class who are prone to turn against the government and the social order, and who are ready to adopt any wild revolutionary scheme. Like certain Russians, they have just education enough to criticize and destroy, and not enough to construct or co-operate in any great progressive movement. The whole world to-day is suffering from this disease—a semi-educated group who consider they have a right to positions of prominence, and who, being unable to attain them, remain idle and devote their leisure to schemes for overthrowing the government or the social order, though they are incapable of any constructive plan by which to replace it.

In some future age it may be possible for the work of the world to be done by highly educated individuals who sit in easy chairs and push buttons, but at present society demands vast numbers who will work with their hands and work hard, and to educate our youth in such fashion that they scorn work of this type and remain an idle prey for communistic agitation, is a questionable benevolence. Those who have lived in British India state that the agitation which is in progress at present is due largely to young men who have acquired a smattering of Western education and are demanding superior government jobs of which they are morally and intellectually incapable and who in their disappointment and discontent are devoting their energies to driving out the British.

It is the presence of large groups of idle, dissatisfied, semi-educated folk all over the world who consider that they deserve more freedom than they can use wisely and a higher position that can be afforded them, that creates an unstable atmospheric condition in which the professional agitator and propagandist can arouse an emotional storm that endangers the public safety. Education should lift a man to a point where he can overlook the walls of prejudice that divide his neighbors, but a little of it seems only to reveal new grounds for bitterness.

The emotional map of America differs then radically from that of the nations of the old world. In India there is a horizontal emotional stratification that runs through every town and village separating each layer of the population from the next by impermeable barriers of feeling, built up of reverence and fear on the one side, and of contempt and disgust on the other. This stratification is less noticeable in Europe, but it still exists in some measure. In America the division is more often perpendicular and divides industry from agriculture, or separates the various industries by rivalry. Save where unreasonable demands are created by unwise doses of education, the frictional feeling that exists between horizontal classes or groups is usually due to injustice which creates suffering, and can be eliminated by adjustments which give a fairer division of wealth and opportunity. There is always danger that the Political Current may create a privileged class, which will again enthrone the great Enchantress and enable her to subject the masses to slavery. This is a danger to which democracies are always subject, but at present America seems unusually safe in this particular.

4. ELECTRIC STORMS AND PROHIBITION

The crash of thunder is one of the most terrifying phenomena of nature and is caused, we are told, by an electric discharge which splits the atmosphere asunder in such fashion that the divided sections rush together in a terrific clash which causes the roar of the thunder. There seem to be certain questions, which, when projected into the midst of the American people, cause a similar division and a similar clash of opposing feelings. To stir the mass of the people so vitally these must be questions that affect their fundamental appetites.

Apparently there is nothing that can arouse such violent feeling in a man as any question involving his food and drink, and Prohibition has stirred America to a greater pitch of feeling than any other question of the day. The present excitement had its origin in an agitation begun many decades ago, and carried forward chiefly by women through the organization of the Women's Christian Temperance Union. They met with ridicule when they tried to organize presidential campaigns, but they finally succeeded in carrying one state, Maine, for prohibition. It was not until the Anti-Saloon League came on the field that the movement began to arouse respect if not alarm. The saloon was an unquestioned abuse, in spite of its value as a "poor man's club," and the better elements united against it. By very clever political manœuvring the League advanced from one success to another until they held such a balance of power that the politicians were thoroughly terrified. State after state was carried and finally the Eighteenth Amendment was put through in 1918, as a sort of war measure, and the whole nation became legally dry. At first the people supported the law and it was claimed that great benefit resulted, in reduction of crime, increase of efficiency and wealth, etc. Then a reaction set in, and in many places the law became a dead letter.

No one questions the right of a government to exclude or limit the sale of articles harmful to the public welfare, such as narcotics and various other drugs, which, however beneficial they may be when rightly used, are a curse when the public is left free to use them according to its will. The question then is merely as to whether alcoholic beverages are sufficiently harmful to the public welfare to deserve being excluded or not. Those who enjoy them, and have never seen the harm they produce, or who consider that the enjoyment they get from them more than compensates for their evil effects, say they are not, and these have evaded the law in such fashion that widespread corruption has been the result.

This, then, involves a second question—as to whether a law that cannot be adequately enforced should be repealed or retained. On these two questions the whole nation is divided with an intensity of feeling and a violence of prejudice on both sides such that any intelligent discussion of the question has become impossible. Possibly it is just as well, for the question is so complicated that it is almost impossible to arrive at an intelligent conclusion. If the law could really be enforced for five years and the "experiment" carried through, it would then be possible to estimate exactly its benefit or harm to the national life. Since it apparently cannot, it is an undoubted danger to any community to have on its statutes a law opposed by a large and determined minority who have made up their minds to disobey it. A democracy is based upon the agreement to abide by the decision of the majority, but when a large minority refuses to do so, it means either a civil war to enforce obedience, or appalling corruption of the government. A question of this sort is certainly not worth a civil war, although Lincoln considered that the question behind it— that of obedience to the majority—was worth a fight to the finish. On the other hand the corruption resulting from disobedience is a serious calamity. The majority are as determined as the minority and in every test have refused to repeal the law. It seems absurd that a great nation of a hundred millions should be so violently exercised over the question of what they shall drink—and it is well for us to stop to enquire what are the emotional forces behind the question. Judging from the cartoons one would suppose that a group of self-righteous reformers with long faces and long-tailed black coats and tall hats, had forced their tyrannical Blue Laws upon the helpless public. It is not likely, however, that a great nation can be forced to change its policy in any such fashion as this, and we cannot hope to understand the subject unless we find the real emotional drive which swayed the will of the people.

In the first place there was behind it terrible suffering —such as drives men to extremity, and many of the so-called reformers who were ridiculed, like Carrie Nation, were men and women who had suffered intolerably. Everyone knows this, but unless he actually sees it, it is such an old story that it fails to make an impression. I saw a very little of it on the lower East Side in New York. Whenever the working men were paid off, it meant a prolonged spree, which often did not end until they had pawned everything in the house; and worse than that, it meant terrible treatment for their wives and children. I have been called in repeatedly to stop some man from beating his little girl to death, or killing his wife in a burst of drunken fury. Once I arrived just in time to stop a man, an ex-Hussar in the British army, from splitting his wife's head open with an ax, and sometimes I arrived too late and found the wife with a bullet in her head or covered with wounds.

The effect on the children was appalling. I remember rescuing one man from a mixed ale fight, and bringing him away with his head split open and a little golden-haired boy clinging to his hand and weeping. Where the woman drank it was even worse. I knew one woman who had killed her little girl by dragging her downstairs by her hair in a fit of drunken fury. I entered one tenement where the man was working and the woman had gone off on a drunken spree, leaving the children shut in. When I arrived they had just kindled a fire in the middle of the wooden floor. What would have happened to those flimsy crowded rookeries if I had not put out the fire, is beyond imagination.

It is futile to detail stories of this sort which are known to all, and yet forgotten. When seen they produce an impression. A friend who stayed with me a while, and who was accustomed to cocktails and wine on the table, said to me, "The problem here is simply the drinking. If that could be stopped all would go well enough with these people. You ought to stop all you are doing and try to put through some legislation that would prevent it." It did not seem to me the wisest way at the time, and I mention it merely to show how the average intelligent person who witnessed the suffering in the neighborhood was affected, and I am sure that if everyone had seen it, there would have been but little opposition to prohibition. People of this sort suffer dumbly, but when the opportunity comes, it is natural that they should express themselves.

Such conditions as these existed in many of the great cities and also in country towns. In addition there were peculiar conditions in certain sections which created strong feeling for prohibition. In the South the movement started among the white people as the result of fear of the negro, and of what he might do and had done, when intoxicated, and it had behind it a very powerful emotional drive. In the West the respectable folk were exasperated by seeing their towns shot up by intoxicated cowboys and miners, whose only idea when they were paid off was to celebrate in a fashion detrimental to the public weal. In addition in the East, the men at the head of the big industries, though they drank themselves, realized that they were losing thousands of dollars because many men who were paid off on Saturday were recovering from a spree on Monday, and unable to go to work until Tuesday, and the men at the head of the railroads realized the danger to the public from engineers and brakemen who drank. The movement therefore gained the support of most employers of labor, who believed in prohibition for everyone but themselves.

The movement thus had behind it the drive of suffering and exasperation and fear, and also the desire of gain and the economic pressure of good business. Moreover, after it had once been enforced, and it really was enforced the first two years—the women began to profit by it. Instead of going to the saloons, the family income went into trips to Coney Island, and to the movies, into furs and silk stockings and even a motor car, and having once enjoyed these things they were in no mood to return to the old ways. On the other side, however, were the irreconcilables who always wanted a drink, the society folk who wanted wine and cocktails at their dinners and clubs, the great mass of foreigners who were used to drinking without excess, and the young collegiate group, who resented any restriction on their liberties and who drank, in the usual defiant spirit of youth, just because there was a law against it.

In general the emotional attitude toward Prohibition was sectional—the South and West strongly for it, the East with its foreigners and great industrial cities as strongly against. In cities like New York and Boston, where sentiment was strongly adverse, it was almost impossible to enforce it. A sumptuary law of that kind must have at least a majority of the people behind it to be enforced. Otherwise it does more harm than good. For that reason wise statesmen have always recommended local option so that the sentiment of the community would be behind the law.

At present this question of enforcement is the most serious element in the problem. There has been created so large a class of men who profit by breaking the law that they are a serious menace to society. Their profits have been so enormous that they can afford to bribe the police and the city governments by huge sums, and a group has grown up in the large cities who feel that they can rob and murder and defy all the laws with impunity. Thus has come into being the racketeer, who has been able to levy a tax or blackmail on all legitimate industries—even on laundries and undertakers, under the threat of breaking up their business or of personal violence. It seems beyond belief that the people of any great city should submit to such domination, and it shows a lamentable lack of the old Anglo-Saxon Spirit. All this group of bootleggers and racketeers are active promoters of Prohibition as it supplies them with the wealth which makes their activities possible.

At present the law is so generally broken that those who looked to it for relief from intolerable suffering are finding it inadequate, and the evils connected with it are so great that feeling seems to be swinging against it. Unfortunately the question has become so highly emotionalized that logic and intelligence have little to do with it and the majority are swayed by blind prejudice and unwilling to listen to opposing arguments. Politicians shun the question like the pest.

In the Democratic Convention of 1920, Bryan, who was an ardent Prohibitionist, tried to force a dry plank into the Democratic platform and was opposed by Bourke Cockran who pleaded as vigorously for a wet plank. It was a great battle between two skilled orators, and the result was that the dry plank was voted down by 935 against 155, and the wet plank was defeated by a vote of 726 to 356. The which evidently showed that the politicians wished to leave the question severely alone. Their attitude was that the matter had been decided and it was no longer a national issue. It was an amusing instance of the way in which politicians avoid a question on which the public feel strongly. The Democrats of the South and West were strong for Prohibition, while those of New York and Boston were its chief opponents, so that any definite stand would have split the party in two. The Republican party has avoided the issue, but most politicians try to create the impression that they favor both sides.

It would be well for the country if the people would decide the question in one way or the other and then stand by their decision and enforce the laws they make. It was an old trick in New York state to pass laws which were not intended to be enforced but which enabled the police and government officials to levy blackmail, and Prohibition seems to have degenerated into something of that sort.

The racketeers and grafters have gained such incredible power through the enormous sums that they have acquired through Prohibition, which run up into the billions, that they now control the great cities of America. They can buy up police officials and even the judges and prosecuting attorneys, and so many supposedly respectable people are in league with them that it seems impossible to shake their hold. Their murders, committed with machine guns, bombs and automatics, actually run into the thousands, and very seldom is any one of them convicted. They can buy up the votes of the poor, and see that corrupt officials are everywhere elected. It is an appalling situation, and the worst is that even if Prohibition were now repealed, it would only turn loose on society organized groups of gangsters, used to gaining easy money, and determined to gain the wealth to which they are accustomed by murder and robbery if not by the present milder system of graft.

On previous occasions the old Anglo-Saxon Spirit has waked up and cleaned up such situations, when the government failed, by Vigilance committees and the determined action of the citizens, and there is reason to hope that this Spirit is not dead yet and that it will come to the rescue at last.

5. SUNSHINE AND CLOUD

Most of the currents of feeling which we have described are complex and are generated by specific circumstances and ideas. There are two great alternative currents, however, which are as all-pervasive as the sunshine and the rain and somewhat similar in their action on the public. There are individuals who radiate either one current or the other at all times, but there are also periods when each current seems to sweep over the country and carry everyone into its tide. These are the two currents familiarly known as optimism and pessimism. There are waves of pessimism that radiate from some catastrophe, and we have described the storms that have originated in some low-pressure centre of suffering and loss, and have swept over the country, creating the great panics that have such a vital effect on national progress. But in addition to these there seem to be pe-

riods of fair weather when everyone is cheerful and sure
of success and prosperity; and of cloudy weather, when a
shadow is over the land, and men fear to take any forward
step because of vague anticipated dangers.

Some persons are temperamentally optimistic, and are
great promoters and successful salesmen of bonds and life
insurance, while others are so fundamentally pessimistic
that they always anticipate the worst, and find a curse in
every blessing. But the vast majority are subject to these
changes of weather that sweep across the continent. There
is always undoubtedly some material cause that sets the
wave in motion, but the effect far transcends the cause, and
we see optimistic feeling mounting up like a tidal wave into
a great boom in which everything acquires a fictitious value
many times its worth, and again we see the wave retire and
leave wrecked firms and suicides strewn along the beach in
its wake. The barometer that registers these surprising
changes of weather is the stock market.

We have just seen a sample of what these waves can accomplish and of the astonishing way in which they reach
all classes and all sorts and conditions of men. Fifty years
ago the number of those who "played the market" was insignificant but it has been a notable mark of the transformation of the proletarian into the capitalist that of late folk
of all classes and occupations have invested their savings
in stocks and bonds, and have even acquired the habit of
buying on margin. In 1927 and 1928 an ever-increasing
wave of optimism brought tens of thousands into the market. Cooks, butlers, chauffeurs, farmers, small tradesmen
and even day laborers, saved up enough to purchase a few
shares, with the result that prices rose to incredible heights
bringing enormous profits on paper. This naturally increased the number and enthusiasm of the investors, so that
something akin to a craze swept the country. Nearly all the
industries, railroads and public utilities were making large
profits and paying extra dividends which naturally increased the enthusiasm. Then suddenly, without any apparent reason, the boom broke. A failure in London and a

political attack on the Edison Company of Boston apparently started the ball rolling, and the sudden calling in of a vast volume of broker's loans added to its speed. There was no failure in any of the industries, their prosperity remained the same, and there was no threat of war, but a sudden emotional wave of distrust swept the country. In this wave of fear everyone began to sell. The market fell so rapidly that those on margins were caught and had to sell at a sacrifice, some losing enormous amounts.

In view of the general prosperity a reaction was expected, but nothing could stop the emotional tide once it started. Prices fell lower and lower, and fortunes were wiped out. In the general distress men stopped buying commodities, and in place of the lavish expenditure on luxuries of all kinds which characterized the preceding months, all business came to a standstill. There had undoubtedly been great over-production and instead of increasing the purchasing power of the public to take it up, that power was cut in half. Consequently orders for merchandise were cancelled, production was limited, men were discharged and the whole country was soon suffering from unemployment and limited resources.

As nearly as one can discover, this strange reversal in business conditions and in the fortunes of many thousands was due to an emotional wave, with no great disaster behind it. Stocks had undoubtedly been forced up too far and paper profits had been pyramided and there was great over-production, but if optimism had remained and the public had continued to purchase as freely, it is quite probable that the leading industrial and public-utility stocks would soon have justified their prices. It was an extraordinary instance of the direful effects that can be produced by a wave of panic. Such panics were not infrequent in connection with the banks, and were not without reason when it was possible to exhaust the resources of the bank by a sudden run, so that the depositor was liable to lose his capital in the resulting failure. Recent legislation and the spirit of co-operation among the banks has rendered this almost impossible to-day. The failures among the banks and business houses were few and those that were in danger were rescued by their fellows.

Economists are now searching for a cause in the great falling off of American foreign trade, due to the high-tariff barriers on the one hand, and on the other to limitation of the purchasing power of Europe, resulting from unemployment and from the hard conditions in Germany, and also from the fall in silver which reduces the purchasing power of the Orient. In present conditions it is dangerous to be a creditor nation and to have such vast reserves of gold as are at present in America. The remedy seems to be to loan as much of it as possible to the nations where hard conditions prevail and to give some extra leeway in the payment of reparations and of the international debts.

Whatever was the cause, it was unknown to the mass of the people, who were swept by an unreasoning emotional whirlwind. At somewhat irregular intervals these waves of optimism and pessimism sweep over the whole nation, carrying to rich and poor, and those of all religions and all races and occupations, the same feeling of confidence or of distrust and depression. Such waves as that which centres in Prohibition differ in that, although they also sweep the whole country, they divide men into two opposing sections, each charged with antagonism and suspicion toward the other, so that every state, town and village becomes positively and negatively electrified, while optimism and pessimism come in alternative waves, each of which in turn dominates the whole community, so that the country is first positively and then negatively electrified.

6. LOCAL CURRENTS

If we examine any community we find that the emotional currents which have the greatest effect on the neighborhood are purely local, and tend to cancel out, so that they are not felt by the country at large. The social rivalry between Mrs. Smith and Mrs. Jones that generates such bitter local feeling, the competition between Brown's grocery and White's, the resentment of the Methodist circle toward the superior airs of the Episcopalian coterie, the bitter feeling engendered when Mr. Patrick Murphy replaces Mr. T. Fellowes Vandeveer on the school board—all these violent emotional whirlpools have little effect on the outside world, save as the emotion engendered is linked up with some general movement, as might happen if the opponents of Mr. Murphy should start a branch of the Ku Klux, or if Mrs. Smith and Mrs. Jones should take opposite sides on the Prohibition question. The local emotional currents are then turned in to swell the tide of national feeling.

It is this, indeed, which is happening continually, and the intensity of national emotional tides is due largely to these local currents which reenforce them with bitter personal feeling. The women of the community are probably much more interested in the supremacy of Mrs. Smith and her group than in the Prohibition question. We see, then, the country dotted over with these little power plants that generate in each village emotion of high voltage. It is quite possible to connect these up with some of the great emotional systems and to use them thus as re-enforcement plants which add greatly to the voltage of the National Currents.

7. TRANSFORMERS AND COMMERCIAL LINES

In the old days each village had its little emotional power plants which were separate and disconnected, but wires have now been laid which connect them up into systems so that emotion can be carried from one end of the country to another. The various clubs and organizations, which have sprung up all over the country, act often as communication lines and also as transformers by which violent personal or local feeling is transferred to national questions. A personal grievance against Mrs. Smith may throw the Jones family into the opposition camp, where their emotion is expended in working against the political and social aims of the club to which Mrs. Smith belongs. This seems at first absurd, but it would be a revelation to many to discover how much of the political, social and religious feeling that has national consequences, results from such transformation of local and personal grievances.

Many organizations that have a local object have expanded to a national significance. The Rotary Club in each town is an association of the energetic business men designed to promote the prosperity of the town and to draw trade and attract investors in real estate, as well as to create good fellowship. It has become a national institution. It radiates optimism and enthusiasm like an up-to-date heating plant, and through it the successful operations of the merchants of Oshkosh find an echo in Tallahassee and Tucson. It is a vast radiating machine.

Books have been written concerning the psychic aptitude of Americans for joining organizations, and they have been characterized as the world's greatest "joiners." This characteristic breaks up the isolation of individualism and assists in the development of group emotion. In the summer one can hardly travel without being surrounded by men in gorgeous turbans, ribbons and regalia on their way to some convention. The oldest organizations are the Masonic orders, which have as their basis the cultivation of high standards and fine feelings, to such an extent indeed that to some men they stand in place of religion. There are the Odd Fellows, the Shriners, the Elks, the Moose, and others, many of which are benefit societies which provide for members who are ill or crippled, and even support homes where those in need can be cared for. Some of them, like the Moose, include women as well as men, and they all create links through which different sections of the country are vitally connected.

All such organizations are like systems of telephone wires through which emotions and ideas can be quickly spread throughout the country. In general their effect seems to be unifying and not divisive like the old religious sects which developed so much rivalry and prejudice. Though each man is convinced of the superiority of his own group, he is not impelled by conscience to destroy the others. They also have their value in affording an outlet to the ambitions of men, as they have an aristocracy of their own, in which it is possible for a man to progress through some thirty-three different degrees of attainment, and acquire thereby titles and regalia, compared with which those of the King of England seem modest and unpretentious. A man who is Grand Master of the Thirty-third Degree can afford to look down upon the President of the Somerset Club. Working men can hardly be dissatisfied with their lot when they have such opportunities of acquiring recognition and title in an hierarchy so ancient and so stately.

There has been high emotional tension between the secret societies and the Roman Catholic Church, which has always opposed them and has forbidden its members to join their organizations. They were regarded as heretical and subversive of the existing order. Whatever may have been their anarchistic tendencies in the old world, they are not dangerous in America, and the feeling between them and the church is here much less marked.

Other channels of intercommunication have been created by the conventions which of late have been organized in nearly every branch of employment. The various branches of the church have always held their conventions at stated intervals. These have not always proved generating stations for the higher Christian emotions, but have more often provided a field in which the violent feeling between high and low church and broad and narrow, and between progressive and conservative, found vigorous expression, issuing sometimes in a heresy trial, sometimes in a revision of the prayer book, or the marriage service. As such they have been of value as affording a means of settling the questions concerning which feeling had become so violent as to threaten division. The political parties have held conventions to choose their candidates which, as we have shown, have been the arena in which some of the most violent emotional storms of the nation have culminated in a desperate battle.

There has been less emotion in the conventions organized by the various professions. We find that the physicians, and engineers, and architects, all meet in the summer months to discuss their problems and to confer honor on those of their profession who have rendered distinguished service. The convention movement has steadily grown. Dentists, druggists, grocers, hardware men—every type of employment, now has its convention, where men and their wives gather from all over the country, and in addition to discussing their difficulties and problems, have a joyous junket with their families. All this has a unifying effect and lays additional channels of emotional intercommunication.

So much has been said of the cinema or the "movies" as an emotional stimulus to the people that one hesitates to approach so trite a subject. No more powerful method of implanting prejudice, or awakening latent emotion in children or young people could well be devised than to show scenes which have all the vividness of reality, in which the strongest emotions are displayed with every adjunct that art and genius can supply to make them moving and vital. The cinema affords the most wonderful opportunity the world has ever seen for preparing in the minds of our youth emotional trains of the finest and most valuable kind, and some of the great cinema dramas have made use of their opportunity to the full. Unfortunately too many of the companies are in the hands of those who seek only to appeal to the cruder and baser emotions of the masses, and, instead of attempting to arouse that which is best, pander only to that which is worst. They can appeal to men with scenes of adventure and murder, but the surest appeal to both men and women is found in scenes that stimulate sex feeling. In the ordinary man this feeling needs control rather than stimulus, but the chief effort of the cheap movie seems to be to arouse to the utmost that emotion in its lowest forms of lust.

CHAPTER XV

THE VARIABLE AND ETERNAL FEMININE

1. Sex Attraction

WE know that two charges of positive electricity repel one another and we have also noted that when two men or two groups have the same prize in view, an antagonistic reaction usually occurs. For an example of the fact that charges of a different sort attract one another, we must turn to a most primitive division of the human race into two sections which carry emotional charges similar to positive and negative electricity, in that each radiates a subtle attraction for the other. I refer, of course, to the fact that man was created male and female. We are abundantly informed by modern realists that this attraction is merely the procreative instinct, and that all the sentiment that has gathered around it is mere "bunk." There are others who insist that men and women are the same in all fundamental qualities, and who seek to minimize the differences by copying the behavior and costume of the opposite sex.

Those who find in the emotional current between the sexes nothing but primitive procreative instinct have but little understanding of the characteristics of these currents of feeling. The basis or originating cause of the current is often vastly different from the current produced, which gathers up ideas and feelings which originally had no part in it, and sex feeling has collected many elements which did not belong to it ten thousand years ago. In the first place there are in it two elements which to me seem quite distinct, the primitive procreative instinct which is general, and a current of personal attraction which is individual and variable. While some may be impervious to such things, most of us are conscious that persons of strong personality radiate a magnetic current, from the eye or from the touch,

354

which may have a powerful attractive or repellent effect, and most of us feel that the current radiated by an attractive woman is quite different in quality from that which we feel in men. This is certainly not the procreative instinct, but it might be considered a stimulus to it. Modern literature has made us familiar with this attraction which Kipling once termed "It," and which seems to be the most important asset of every current hero and heroine.

Different tribes and nations react very differently to this instinct, and if one is to understand a nation one must consider this side of its emotional life, as well as that which has to do with politics. Just as we have traced the development of currents of political feeling as they have taken up new ideas and emotionalized them, so we must follow the changes produced in this current as civilization has progressed.

The primitive instinct is so powerful that it is dangerous to society save when directed in definite channels where it is confined by a wall of powerful tabus. Monogamy and the family, which are the basis of our social order, form such a channel.

It has been the experience of the ages that society has been most happy and prosperous when sexual desire has been limited to monogamy. But in dealing with the masses it does little good to tell them what is wise and best. They must be kept to the path of wisdom by walls of fear and shame. Thus every stable society has erected emotional barriers, and a feeling of guilt or disgrace is associated with every transgression of the bounds set by custom.

While thus providing a definite channel for the sexual instinct, many feelings have been associated with the original instinct, and a current of feeling has been created which includes many emotionalized ideas as to what is decent and right. Ceremonials connecting marriage with religion have added the feeling of reverence, and solemn oaths have brought in conscience and the sense of honor. The general current of feeling as to sex, then, includes many inhibiting emotions. There is no primitive instinct that has been hemmed in by such powerful inhibitory forces as the pro-creative instinct, for none have been thought to have such a devastating effect on the social order, or on the higher development of character, as that instinct when uncontrolled. Certain groups, as the monastic orders, have attempted to suppress it entirely and have developed a very real horror of it and a sense of sin in connection with sexual indulgence even in thought, which was appalling in its effects.

In dealing with the subject, then, we must bear in mind that in this current we have a third element in addition to the two primary ones. There is the instinct, which is natural and general, the current of sexual attraction which is natural but individual, and the current of feeling in relation to sex which is general and artificial, in the sense that it is the product of the experience of ages, and that it has taken up a host of feelings and emotionalized ideas which differ in every nation. In early America the current included a horror of any sexual indulgence beyond the bounds of matrimony and strong feeling against divorce save on scriptural grounds. It also included a sense of shame in connection with anything that had to do with sex or birth, so that it was felt to be indecent to say that a woman was with child; and to speak of a woman's lower extremities as "legs" was a serious social indiscretion. Many endured a torturing sense of guilt merely because they were conscious of the pull of the primitive instinct.

But aside from these inhibitory elements the current included many that were of great value and beauty, and it seems unfortunate that in ridding ourselves of those elements which were foolish and harmful we should lose others which add greatly to the charm of life.

It is a characteristic of this age, of which we shall speak later, to seek to break down all the old tabus and the feeling of right and wrong which held men in check, and to throw over with them all the feelings that have grown up in the course of history, as having no basis in reality, so that only the crude instinct is left.

From earliest time, men have thrown over the relation

between the sexes a veil of mystery which has had a charm of its own, and around all the course of love-making has developed a certain tradition which has had a peculiar beauty. It has been idealized in art and literature—the most beautiful poems and works of art have centred in it. Men of the most delicate feeling and the loftiest ideals have surrounded it with a mystic glory. Love-making itself has been an art with its own special forms of classic beauty. It is thus that the great emotional currents are created that endure through the ages. Civilization is a process of putting fine feeling and beautiful ideas into the crude bare facts of life, of clothing the hideous skeleton of reality with the flesh and blood of warm feeling and inspiring thought.

The process of eating has developed from the tearing apart of raw flesh with the fingers, in a cannibal orgy, to a noble ritual in which men sit about a table which is clothed with damask, ornamented with silver and glowing with lights, where every movement is prescribed in accord with graceful forms, and the whole is the expression of hospitality and friendship, and affords the finest opportunity for the exchange of thought and feeling. The great current of feeling concerning social custom and behavior at table includes scores of tabus and many pleasurable emotions and differs entirely from the primitive appetite from which it sprang. It is a work of art in terms of emotion. One would hardly gain by saying "All that is real here is the desire to fill our stomachs. Let us destroy the rest and be sincere and eat as the simple savage eats." And yet it seems to be something similar to this that is being accomplished by all the crude display of sex feeling in the cinema, the drama and literature of the day. Such public portrayal of its grosser side seems to tear from it all the mystery and beauty that have gathered about it through past ages, and to reduce it in the eyes and practice of modern youth to a combination of crude lust and rough comradeship. All that our forefathers screened as being so intimate as to have a real sacredness is dragged to the light and audiences are fed on long passionate kisses that endure to the point of disgust, and intimate boudoir and bedroom scenes that in their crudeness destroy all charm and beauty, and reduce us to the level of the primitive animal instinct.

It must be admitted that there has been far too much screening in the past, and that by concealing the vital facts of life from young people great harm has been done them. We are suffering at present from a reaction toward sincerity, a quality whose value cannot be overemphasized. It is, however, quite possible to be sincere and yet to retain beauty, to teach facts reverently in a manner that surrounds them with charm rather than disgust.

We have just discovered that the feelings of guilt and shame and horror that served to check harmful instincts in the masses are not necessarily authoritative and of Divine origin, and the tendency is to throw over all feeling as an unreliable guide, and to rely simply on the intelligence. The removal of the barrier seems to leave men free to indulge their primitive instincts. They have not yet discovered that feeling has an absolute value in itself, aside from its use as a tabu.

Certain feelings and currents of feeling have beauty and bring happiness and joy, and are therefore worth cultivating and maintaining, however they may have originated. If they are beautiful now and add charm and happiness to life, they are worth while. Having used our intelligence to discover that the authority that kept us virtuous by terror is only a bogie dressed up to frighten us, we are disposed to think that all feeling is a fraud. We have yet to discover that it is feeling which gives to life its value, and that intelligence is given us to discover which of the currents that have flowed down through the ages can fill life the fullest of beauty and charm and power, and to find means of cultivating that current and of keeping ourselves in its full tide.

Certainly of all the currents of feeling that have grown up through the ages none is capable of bringing more satisfaction and charm than the current of sex feeling at its finest, and there can be no better occupation for the intelligence than to filter out from it those elements that degrade

and coarsen it or that render it destructive and dangerous
and to keep it at its purest and best. The artist of the future
will be one who takes the crude feelings of humanity and
builds them up into emotional currents full of beautiful
ideas and delicate shades that will bring delight to all who
receive them.

There is danger in suppressing a powerful instinct by
tabus which is almost as great as letting it go free, and the
Anglo-Saxon race have been scorned as hypocrites because
of their efforts to keep sex feeling out of sight. The French
consider it better to give it free expression, although they
shield young girls from it with particular care. To give it
greater freedom might prove no more harmful than the exposure of the human form, if it were possible to prevent deliberate attempts to arouse the baser passions. The tabus
put upon it in early America produced an abnormal suppression of sex feeling as a deadly sin, and of all discussion
of it, save where there was a deliberate attempt to rouse it
by stories told in secret. And the result of so much suppression was a desire on the part of the young to know what
was hidden from them and to discuss in secret that which
was forbidden in the open. This created an opportunity for
unscrupulous men to create an underground current of feeling which took the vilest forms and had a most destructive
effect on character.

2. Destructive Currents

The peculiar character of every nation and tribe and
group is due in large measure to the emotional currents
that flow through it and we have endeavored to show how
large a part in the formation of America was played by the
old Anglo-Saxon current. Each group instinctively protects
its dominant currents, and regards with horror any influences which tend to interfere with them or which subject
the minds of the young to feelings hostile to them. There
has been in the Anglo-Saxon current, however, a feeling of
antagonism to all attempts to dominate men by these traditional currents, and at present there is a conflict between

the group feeling and this feeling for independence. There are certain currents of feeling that even the most ardent champions of independence regard as poisonous and such are excluded from the mails and from literature. There are others which are dangerous to the life of the group and which destroy by a subtle poison all that is finest in their character and tradition. It is increasingly difficult to detect and exclude such currents.

In the 1880s the country was overrun with vile literature and pictures which were secretly circulated, designed to pander to these suppressed desires and to stimulate the grosser passions of the young. Anthony Comstock started a crusade against such publications. He carried the matter to excess and attacked even the finest works of art as being a stimulus to violent sexual feeling. He stirred up a hornet's nest, not only among the publishers of corrupt literature and those who desired it, but also among artists, who started a campaign against him, and aroused the most violent feeling, so that he met with persecution of all kinds, from ridicule to personal violence. For a time the whole country was stirred and took sides pro and con. He kept steadily on, however, and finally succeeded in suppressing the worst features in the publications of that day.

Since then there has been a continual conflict as to what literature, pictures and drama should be suppressed and what should be retained. There are many who are still swayed by the tabus of the old current, and there are more whose æsthetic sense rebels against seeing a thing of beauty dragged in the mud. Apart from all question of tabus the desire of every intelligent person should be to see that the current preserves those elements that give the maximum happiness and charm to life. It is an extremely difficult question, for that which seems suggestive and corrupt to one man, seems quite harmless to another. There are certain things which public sentiment will not tolerate, but it is very difficult to state just where the line should be drawn, and there has been the bitterest controversy and the most violent feeling over some of the decisions of the censors. The main point of discussion lies between those who consider that artistic expression and beauty of phraseology excuses any amount of moral obliquity, and that anything which is truly art should be permitted, on the one hand; and, on the other, those who feel that beauty of expression only makes such literature or pictures doubly harmful, by giving to acts and words which are harmful and destructive a fascination they would not otherwise possess. In general, public opinion seems to incline more and more to the former point of view, and for the sake of its beauty much literature, art and drama is now permitted, which would have been rigidly excluded twenty years ago.

A most noticeable change has been in connection with the exposure of the human form. A few decades ago this was considered indecent and immoral. The prevalence of athletics has made the nude such a familiar sight that it has lost its suggestive significance and has less emotional effect than the display of an ankle thirty years ago. It is that which is contrary to custom which is suggestive. To a Mohammedan it is the unveiling of a woman's face that is indecent and stimulating to the baser passions. Her unclothed body has little emotional significance in comparison. It is unquestionably a great advantage to this generation to be accustomed to seeing the nude form, and to find no indecency save where it is intended, as in the cheap vaudeville. In literature and the drama the same holds true. Some is as innocent as a nude child, but there is more which, though beautiful, is deliberately designed to arouse the grosser feelings. This can hardly fail to be harmful in laying emotional trains that are liable to issue in disaster or in degradation.

As stated, the general tendency in America is toward a much freer expression of sex emotion in accord with the French idea, save that in France the old charm and mystery of the sex drama is maintained by screening unmarried girls from familiar contact with men. In America in school and college they meet with a freedom which, at best, results in a sort of boyish cameraderie, largely free from sex feeling, and, at worst, has its issue in sexual experimentation and freedom of contact which leaves little to the imagination.

It has been discovered that in order to transform a crude appetite into a more permanent emotional current which can gather up those elements of delicacy and beauty which give it charm, the appetite must be partially inhibited, and the emotional artists of the future will undoubtedly discover the scientific laws by which this can be most satisfactorily accomplished. In the meantime we know that one great value of sex feeling to humanity is that it has not always found immediate gratification, and has therefore found expression in other channels, through art and music and literature, through which the lover has expressed his feeling for his unattainable inamorata. It is through such sublimation of the grosser emotions that some of the finest works of mankind have been produced. Moreover, it is generally true that the immediate satisfaction of a desire kills all the higher emotions and more delicate shades of enjoyment that come as a result of partial inhibition. Just as the immediate gorging of the stomach would prevent the epicure's enjoyment of an exquisite meal, and render impossible the pleasures of a friendly dinner with all its appeal to the æsthetic side, and the social and spiritual elements that are involved in the sharing of food with congenial companions, so it may prove that the youth of this age, by their gross contacts and crude expression of the sexual relation, may find that they have become insensitive to the higher, more delicate shades of emotion and that they have lost much of the charm of the old relation. Moreover, as girls approximate the behavior and manners of boys, the mutual attraction and charm of the sexes for one another seem to decrease as the difference in potential is less.

The cinema and the drama and modern literature all combine to further the new attitude toward sex relations by the continual portrayal of crude passion and self-indulgence, and thus are constantly laying emotional trains in the minds of the young, which naturally are fired at the first contact with the opposite sex. The girls by the readiness and crudity of their response, may easily do away with that sublimation and refinement of emotion that resulted from the delay of desire and thus destroy much of the charm of the old relationship. From their point of view sincerity is of more importance than all these things, and they feel they are greatly the gainers by the change. They are no longer checked by custom and public opinion, but only by their own sense of decency or fastidiousness, and their conduct is a true expression of their character.

We see, then, in progress a process of undermining the old emotional barriers which have segregated the sexes in past centuries, and have preserved the current of sex feeling with its beauty and charm, by holding in check the violent passions of mankind. Just what will happen when these walls of modesty and shame come crashing to earth is hard to foretell. The ancient tabus are all walls erected by the experience of mankind to hold in check forces of which they were afraid. Whether it is yet safe to destroy them remains to be seen. It may be that there is sufficient appreciation of the happiness produced by family life, and by the traditional system of sex relations in its finest form, to preserve it without the enforcing walls of the old tabu.

3. Woman and the Liberty Current

We have been discussing the currents of attraction created by the difference in potential between the masculine and feminine. But there is a field in which the two sexes come into conflict and where currents have been created not of attraction but of antagonism.

In many countries the condition of woman was little better than slavery and it is natural that the old current of Devotion to Liberty after securing the freedom of the nation, of the negro and of the working man, should turn its efforts to the emancipation of woman.

Forty years ago in certain states woman was little better than a chattel. A husband owned all the property of his wife, and controlled her children, as well as being lord of her body and life. She was completely subject to his will and, having no money or property of her own, was dependent upon his whims and unable to leave him no matter how cruel was his treatment. Her morals were carefully supervised. She could not enter a hotel or restaurant alone, or smoke in public. Some states had more liberal laws, but in none save Wyoming did women have the vote. The first agitation for Woman's Rights was met in the East by the most violent prejudice and antagonism. The politicians wished to keep women out of politics and to preserve the mystery of their subtle methods. Husbands resented the revolt of their wives. Sentimentalists said that woman would lose all her delicacy and charm by meeting with men in the rude arena of politics. Her place was in the home. She could not hope to understand matters of national import. Many women were as violent in their opposition as the men, and feeling reached a point where the leaders of the women, such as Elizabeth Stanton, Susan B. Anthony and Anna Shaw, were attacked and insulted, their processions were stoned and broken up and obloquy was put upon them as bold unsexed creatures who had lost all modesty and sense of decency.

Such was the attitude in the South and East. The West, however, felt quite differently about it, and the men of that section were disposed to give the ladies whatever they wanted. One western state after another was won to the cause. There was no struggle at all in California. Woman's suffrage was proposed and granted as a matter of course. The movement spread rapidly, for where one state accepted it, it gained a preponderant vote, which the other states were eager to equal. Finally during the war, by an amendment to the Constitution, suffrage was granted to the women of the nation as noted above.

Great changes have naturally resulted in the laws governing women and their relation to husband and children. But laws have less influence on a nation than custom. The war did more than the vote to emancipate women. Everywhere women took over the occupations of men. A beginning had been made before the war, but there was strong prejudice against the few woman lawyers, doctors, and clergymen that existed and such women as held public office or entered upon men's work were looked upon askance. During the war, however, it was a patriotic duty to take up a man's work, and the women did so with public approval. It threw them into a new relationship with men, involving both competition and comradeship.

Since the war women have been unwilling to renounce the opportunities thus opened or to retire from the field of man's activity to the kitchen stove and the nursery. There are women at present in nearly every profession and every branch of business. Women have ben elected to state legislatures and have been governors of several states, and of late have even been elected to the National Congress. As a result the old attitude toward woman as a delicate, angelic creature set apart on a pedestal to whom every courtesy should be offered and every privilege granted—this old medieval attitude has largely disappeared, and woman takes her share of knocks in elbowing her way through the competing crowd. It is said that she cannot have both her rights and her privileges, and the woman of to-day seems to prefer her rights, as, strange to say, her privileges were combined, as already noted, with the greatest injustice in the attitude of the laws. She had been content to rule by charm without the right. Now she has the right, the charm may fail to work. She would rule the world not by rocking the cradle but by rocking the government.

Once it was a disgrace for any married woman to work, but to-day there are many who contribute their share to household expenses, and some whose husbands do the housework while they work outside. A woman's activities are necessarily limited by child-bearing, and there is a movement to recognize her service to the state in this respect by pensioning her during the period of childbirth. It seems not unreasonable that this form of production, which is certainly as valuable as any, should receive as much financial reward as the production of shoes and hats. Various mechanical devices have greatly lessened the work of household drudgery and make it possible for women to find outside employment without neglecting their homes. Those who have such employment are perhaps happier than those who have not, for there is an increasing number of women of the middle and wealthy classes who have not enough to do in the home to keep them busy in their husband's absence, and who become discontented gad-abouts. They play bridge or throw their energies into the activities of some woman's club. Although many of them have thus done valuable public service, they do not seem to find, as a rule, the satisfaction that the old-time housewife found in her work. A large element of the population that has not enough to do to keep them busy is always a danger, and a field in which destructive emotion generates.

Woman has been emancipated but does not yet seem sure of what she wishes to do with her liberty. Some make use of it to imitate men as closely as possible in costume and habits, and to lower their standards of morality to correspond with those of man. Whether woman will attempt to reverse the game of sex and become the proposer and pursuer, remains to be seen. Whatever they may be, her desires and feelings have become a serious matter with which the politician must reckon, and which affect vitally the development of the country. There is a certain group who maintain an attitude of rivalry and antagonism between the sexes, and a certain amount of bitter feeling against the tyranny of man still survives among them. But whether hostile or friendly to man, woman is now a dominant factor in American life, and the success of any party depends upon pleasing her.

It is interesting to note the efforts of various organizations to exploit emotions pertaining to woman and the home, as for example, the "Mother" feeling. Mother's Day has become an institution and every effort is made to arouse appropriate emotion throughout the country. The men have made a feeble competitive effort in introducing Fathers' and Sons' Day. Thus both sexes have taken advantage of the favorite American artifice of setting apart a day to develop enthusiasm for a certain cause or feeling of a certain type. Speeches are made, processions formed, bands play, emblems are displayed and everything possible is done to stir the feelings of the public. It is not only every dog that has its day in America.

4. THE EMANCIPATED FAMILY

The emancipation of woman has had a great effect upon the home and family life. The "tyranny of man" with all its cruelty had the advantage that it preserved the integrity of the home and the solidarity of the family. There were no divisions—the wife was compelled to obey her lord and master and to stay by him and her children no matter how she was treated. This was extremely hard for her, but a vast advantage for the children, for when the wife was of the proper obedient type, they were brought up under unified authority, and were sure of a home in which their life found its roots, and that secure background which is so essential to normal development. Now that a wife, at the first grievance, can run off and obtain a divorce and another husband, that stable element in the life of the nation is in danger of dissolution.

It can hardly be questioned that in the development of character nothing is so essential as a stable background of some kind, where children acquire certain definite principles and standards, and learn that there is a place in the world where they belong, a heritage to which they must be true, and a group of which they are an essential part, whose standards they must maintain. It is such a home environment that provides the emotional preparation essential to a strong nation. It is hard to imagine what standards can be acquired by children to-day whose parents have been divorced and remarried, so that they have no home conditions. Instead of possessing a house and garden of their own, too many families live in flats, and move from one to another with every change of season and employment. Even the wealthy, who might afford such home places as have remained for centuries in the hands of the aristocracy of England with their associations and traditions, in America move from Bar Harbor to Palm Beach via Newport and Lenox, with a brief season in New York, so that they acquire no family traditions or roots in the soil.

Another cause which deprives children of a stable background is the prevalence of mixed marriages. Formerly there was a very strong prejudice against the intermarriage of people of different race and religion, but to-day it is a common occurrence. The result is that there is either strife in the family as to the standards by which the children should be brought up, or else an indifference which results in their having no definite standard and tradition.

All these changes in the home create a condition of emotional instability throughout the nation. The young are swayed by the emotion of the moment, with no deep-rooted traditions and standards. That heritage of fine tradition that makes certain acts impossible, and other essential, does not exist. All is change and variation. Impulse rules. With an emotional atmosphere of this sort the situation of the nation is entirely different from that of fifty years ago. With the increased instability and the extraordinary facilities for intercommunication, through the radio and through the network of organizations, propaganda is made possible which might sweep the nation to almost any extreme of emotion or action. Such stability as exists is created chiefly through other agencies than the home. The schools, the Boy Scouts, the various clubs of which mention has been made, the various churches, all have their standards and traditions to which they hold their members with more or less rigidity, and it is through these that the stability of the nation is chiefly maintained. This, however, is hardly adequate as a stabilizer. How swiftly and forcibly the nation can be swayed was shown during the war, when all the means of propaganda were brought into full play, and there is danger that a similar emotional tide might be set in motion by less scrupulous hands and result in great disaster.

CHAPTER XVI

THE NEW FREEDOM AND THE NEW BONDAGE

1. Emancipation of Thought

THE Great American Drama has proved to be a series of knightly quests on the part of our hero the Old Anglo-Saxon Spirit of Devotion to Liberty and Justice. His mission has been to liberate the captive and the distressed. First he sought religious liberty, and rescued that distressed maiden, the Dissenting Church, by carrying her off from her persecutors to safety across the Seas. Then, in pursuit of political liberty, he donned his armor and fought to free the youthful maiden Columbia from the control of masters in the old world. The actual physical slavery of the negro roused him again to fight a desperate battle to strike off these material chains. That finished, he found the masses in financial fetters, starving and helpless, and started a long and weary struggle to break the enchanted web, and win financial liberty. With all these quests on hand he had left woman bound in medieval chains and at her cry turned at last to set her free. And all the time another battle was going on which had its effect upon the others and without which his victories would have been impossible—the fight to emancipate Intelligence, which had been shackled more closely even than woman. Filled with the excitement of the combat he has not always stopped to inquire if he might not be liberating some dangerous monster that might better be left in chains, or to consider if there was any one who could govern the unchained powers, or what would happen when the last throne was overturned and the last altar broken down, and no authority remained to prevent these liberated forces from tearing the world to pieces in their struggle for supremacy.

In the Middle Ages Intelligence was regarded as a dangerous and unscrupulous character, who, if left free, was likely to set fire to the house without the slightest regard to consequences. It was therefore kept carefully shackled and compelled to work as a slave. It was chiefly employed in constructing the magnificent power house of the Church which generated the feelings that served as a guide to men in the place of Intelligence. The current of faith, hope and love thus produced, kept men working contentedly without hope of earthly reward, and stimulated them even to lay down their lives in self-sacrificing service, while at the same time it shut them into the paths of virtue by tabu fences highly charged with fear and awe. The dynamo that ran all this vast system was built on the fundamental idea of a Divine Creator and King, who delegated his authority to Pope and Prince, and who would punish with unending torment all who rejected his authority and disobeyed the commands plainly written in his Sacred Word—all in fact who did not follow exactly the plan of Salvation explained by his ministers, a God who rewarded with eternal bliss those who gave Him their loyal service. Whenever Intelligence started picking at the mechanism of this dynamo or attacked any of the ideas on which it rested, prompt action was taken to throw the rash meddler into a dungeon.

We have explained how the Reformation short-circuited the current and cut out Pope and King and much ceremonial. The old dynamo remained in action, however, and still charged the fences that hemmed in the path of virtue and provided the main drive for faithful work unrewarded in this life, and for heroic endeavor and self-sacrificing service. Men still laid down their lives for duty's sake and in gratitude for the Divine Grace that had saved them from their sins. But in America as in some other countries the Spirit of Liberty struck off the chains that had confined Intelligence and, arrayed in the authoritative robes of Science and Scholarship, it soon started to poke into the mechanism of the great dynamo and to undermine the foundations on which the whole emotional system rested, thus causing the utmost horror and confusion among the good people of that day. Scholarship asserted that the Bible instead of being God's words and commands, dictated by the Divine Spirit, was a collection of ancient traditions, whose science and history were inaccurate and whose morals were questionable, and science undertook to demonstrate that the Power that created the Universe must be One quite different from the God who walked with Adam in the cool of the day. It also threw doubt on the miracles which had been regarded as positive proof of the Divine Mission of Bible characters.

We have described the effect which this had in dividing Protestant religion into two sections, one of which remained impervious to the new thought, while the other sought to adjust religion to it. An authority based on the gentle appeal of the character and life of Christ to the human consciousness is a very different type of authority from the absolute dictatorship of the terrifying Judge of all the Earth with the devils of the Pit behind Him, and the shift is certain to cause great changes in the emotional system of the modernists.

One result of this last achievement of the Spirit of Liberty in setting free the intelligence is that, for a large section of mankind, the old system of tabu has gone by the board. Among such men obedience to the laws, both civil and moral, can no longer be enforced by fear of eternal punishment or dread of the anger of God. Nor will they toil on contentedly without adequate pay in the hope of a heavenly reward. The standard of character laid down in the Bible for them has no greater authority than those of other religions, nor do they discover any reason why they should lay down their lives in the service of others. Faith, hope and love are no longer God-given and eternal to them, but delusions created by ancient instincts. They have knocked the foundation of ideas from under the whole emotional system and it no longer has any meaning. To those whose thoughts are entirely emancipated, no authority has any authority, and all real worth is taken from love and life. In the resulting chaos the only thing of supreme importance is their own desires. The old system trained men to feel that they were worthless worms under the wrath of God, and they were grateful for small blessings. For the emancipated there is nothing to check their egocentricity. They return to the childish sense that they and their wishes are the most important consideration in the universe. As the universe seems indifferent to them they are unhappy and discontented.

Although the effect on the general public is not so great as upon this emancipated group, it is still noticeable enough. In the first place the final campaign of the Spirit of Liberty seems to have changed the emotional atmosphere that creates the attitudes which form the basis of the national character. In the days of Washington the atmosphere was saturated with reverence. Everyone from childhood breathed in a dynamic mixture of reverence and fear, and it was this which lay at the basis of the social order in America, as elsewhere in the world. Every child was conscious of awe before the law, the judge, the governor. He was trained to reverence tinctured with fear for his parents and for their commands, for his school-teacher and the birch rod, or, if a girl, for the husband who was to rule over her. For back of them all and giving to them their authority as His representatives, was the overshadowing presence of the terrible God of justice, who had prepared the flames of eternal fire that were always waiting to engulf the disobedient.

In addition, there was a reverence for custom and convention and tradition, which no respectable woman, and few men of position, would dream of defying. It was this feeling of reverence that kept men obedient to law, that preserved the integrity of the family, and was the basis of good conduct and good works. It was the fear of the Lord that created virtue and benevolence. To-day that great basic emotion seems to have evaporated and disappeared. In the opinion of the masses, God has either moved farther away or changed his character. Reverence for law is certainly a negligible quantity in these days of prohibition. Children do not recognize the Divine authority of their parents, nor wives that of their husbands. In fact, they resent even the suggestion of authority. The rule of fear and of the rod in the schools is over. The fear of eternal punishment and the overwhelming awe before God as judge of all the earth, seems to have given way to other emotions, save in certain primitive fundamentalist sections. And yet the social order goes on much as before, although the power that turned the wheels has been disconnected. Men do not do good deeds to escape Hell fire or learn their lessons for fear of the rod. We shall find that there are other emotions which supply the driving power. There is a new dynamic in the atmosphere.

2. THE NEW DYNAMIC

Some think that to-day we have advanced beyond the childish stage when men must be governed by tabus and by reverence for authority, and that they should be ruled by intelligence. Whereas formerly obedience was compelled by fear and awe, now a man must be shown a reason why he should obey any man or any law. Unfortunately primitive instincts can seldom be checked by intelligence. They go on their way regardless of consequences. There are, however, certain feelings that can be used to replace the emotional system that has been destroyed. Fortunately the Anglo-Saxon current included a feeling of respect for law and real devotion to justice. Moreover there was in the current a strong feeling of good sportsmanship and a sense of honor that held men to an agreement or to a majority decision even when it proved to their disadvantage. This feeling still persists in the old American element, and it is cultivated in all the better schools and organizations for youth. Instead of being spied upon and punished when caught in transgression, boys are put on their honor. It is this feeling, instead of reverence, that keeps men obedient to law and faithful to agreements, and maintains the political and industrial structure.

When it comes to the emancipated family, where the husband and father once ruled by divine right, considerations of prudence and wisdom do not seem to be sufficient to preserve its solidarity. It is evident that if each individual insists on having his own way and on spending the family resources for his pleasure, there must be conflict and suffering. At present there is an effort to rely entirely upon love, and to make no attempt to hold the family together when that ceases to exist. This is the reason for the companionate marriage, which seems to be an attempt to make sure that enduring love exists before making the final agreement. When it does exist, each is willing to make the sacrifice necessary to successful co-operation. Where it does not, there is no emotional compulsion sufficient to hold the wedded pair together. The same is true of the children; if they are not trained to love their parents and brothers and sisters, there is no force that will hold them to the obedience and self-sacrifice that is essential to happy family life.

When it comes to the moral law the situation for the emancipated is more difficult. It is not merely that there is rebellion against all authority, but a feeling that no real authority exists, and that one type of conduct has no more worth than another. This is due to the breakdown of the old emotional system and to the fact that there has been no shift to a new basis. Having always done right because it was a Divine command and because it ensured heavenly bliss, when these reasons are removed there seems to be no reason for doing right. But right conduct has a deeper basis than this. Instead of being right because it was commanded it was commanded because it is right. In other words there are certain lines of conduct that have been proved to bring the maximum of power and happiness, and which have a beauty as great as that of any work of art. It will probably take some time to shift to this new basis and to train youth to see the value and beauty of right conduct, and to follow it because they love it and not because it is authoritatively commanded.

There are certain types of character or standards that have been built up through the ages, which have inherent beauty and worth. No one can read the Bushido, and see the picture of the ideal Saumrai, without appreciating that here is something very noble and very fine, and worth imitating as far as possible. In the same way the Christian gentleman presents a type or standard which must appeal to many. A totally different standard, but one of equal beauty, is presented by such men as Saint Francis. There are fine types of business men, of soldiers, of clergymen, of doctors and of explorers. If an artist finds interest in painting a beautiful portrait, there is a still more thrilling interest in realizing such a standard in one's own flesh and blood and brain. It makes little difference what standard one chooses, provided he is faithful to it, and eliminates incongruous elements. A good monk will have quite a different code from a good business man, but if he is faithful to his standard he will win honor and happiness and will be of value in the world. This, of course, requires discipline and a chief characteristic of this age is rebellion against discipline.

Youth says, "I see no reason why I should not always do as I wish, or why I should ever do anything I do not want to do." Discipline has always been enforced by authority and it will take some time before men will learn the advantage of enforcing it upon themselves. The boy sees its importance in training for the football squad, but he has not yet learned that it is necessary if he is to attain any goal in life. To attain a goal one must hold to his course against the blast of conflicting passions and desires. The man without discipline is a weakling, carried to and fro by every chance desire. The man without a standard is a formless, back-boneless creature, on whom no friend can rely, and for whom society has no use, for it never knows where to find him.

Moreover, happiness is impossible without discipline. Life is not so arranged that a man can always have what he wants, and the sooner he learns to adjust himself to it, the happier he will be. In the old days it was considered necessary to "break a child's will." This meant that he must be taught to get over the childish idea that he can get whatever he wants by insisting on it or by howling and making a sufficient disturbance. Many reach adult life with this childish point of view. The more wealth they have the longer it endures, and the more painful is the awakening when at last they face real life and death.

The emancipated youth cannot have his will broken for him. If he is going to get rid of the cancer of discontent, he must perform the operation on himself. Undoubtedly our youth will soon become expert at self-discipline and be as proud of their psychic muscle as they now are of their physical strength.

After a man has been kicked and pushed along through life by fear and conscience it takes some time to learn to run under his own power. He collapses into the arms of Chance and Fate. But there is a new emotional current in process of formation whose main characteristic is a deadly antagonism to these ancient worthies. Always Chance and Fate have sought to block the progress of man, to thwart and break his spirit. And men have called them the will of God and passively submitted. But this new Spirit, instead of yielding supinely to their leading, recognizes them as the great enemies of mankind, to overcome and thwart whom in the great battle of life is an endeavor that gives zest to every act. It is this Spirit which inspires men to turn in disgust from the cloying sweetness of satisfied desire, and fight their way along the path to the goal they have chosen, undeterred by the obstacles chance puts in the way, meeting the crushing blows of fate with a war cry instead of a whimper, finding in the battle with pain and suffering and injustice an exhilaration and joy that those who sink passively into the arms of Fate and Appetite can never understand. This Spirit was not unknown in the world of the past. It has inspired the great explorers and scientists and many an humble and unknown hero. We call it sometimes the Spirit of Adventure and sometimes by other names. It is this Spirit that must guide men now that the Spirit of Liberty has broken down the ancient barriers that kept them following blindly along the old road of virtue. The emancipated who fail to find this guide seem either to stray into the quicksands of the Slough of Despond, or to be captured by Giant Despair.

3. The Dangers of Liberty

We noted that in spite of heroic achievements, the Spirit of Liberty had serious defects of character, which caused disaster and confusion. Liberty in itself is of questionable value. One must discover what one is freed from, before one knows whether to be thankful or disconsolate. To be freed from all law and all religion is the aim of the anarchist, but most of us would find it a dubious blessing. These emotional torrents are prone to rush on further than reason would allow.

The old fetish of "Liberty" which formed the centre of so many emotional tornados in the past has swept forward on its way, its forces swelled by more recent allied fetishes such as "making the world safe for Democracy" and has created such an antipathy to authority of all kinds that modern youth even of the unemancipated type feels itself outraged if any limitation is put upon its will or activities. The emotional effect of this old fetish is really amazing. "This is a free country"—"No man has a right to control my life"—phrases such as these meet an immediate emotional response and create the conviction that each man has a right to do as he chooses and to resent any interference on the part of government or of his superiors. It is an emotional reaction independent of intelligence, for any intelligent person knows that to-day unity is far more important than liberty, that unchecked liberty means anarchy and chaos, and that it is only as men submit to direction and to authority that civilization and progress are possible.

After every revolution the "liberty" fetish has produced the same disastrous result—an emotional wave of defiance to all authority; and in England under Cromwell, in France under Robespierre and Napoleon, in Russia under Djerjinsky and the Cheka, it was found necessary to repress it by violent measures. Fortunately in America progress has been due to a gradual development and not to an emotional cataclysm and her citizens are accustomed to use their intelligence. Youth nearly always goes through a period of rebellion against authority when the boy is acquiring his independence of parental rule, and this reaction is somewhat exaggerated at present.

Aside from this group of growing boys and girls, the "liberty" fetish finds its chief field in the foreign element who have come to America to escape from authority and who feel that in a "free country" they should be able to do as they choose. It is all a misnomer with disastrous emotional effects. America is no more a free country than was Europe in the Middle Ages. There is just as much authority exercised and probably more. The difference is merely that the seat of authority is in the majority vote of the people and not in any one man, and that consequently the government is not conducted to exploit the people for the benefit of any group or individual, nor is it used to hold the mass of the people in slavery. They are free to express their will, but when it is expressed, obedience is exactly as essential as in an autocracy. It is not a free country, fortunately, or it would probably resemble France in 1793 or Russia in 1920.

The Great Spirit of Liberty has done its work under the direction of reason. Men found certain evils from which they wished freedom and they attained it. This unreasoning emotional charge on the abstract idea of liberty is a menace and the sooner it is withdrawn the better. It gives the anarchist a hold on the masses. If all the emotional store which these words have the power to discharge could be transferred to "co-operation," "public spirit" and "unity" it would undoubtedly be of vast benefit to the nation. We suffer from "hangovers." Liberty was the world's great need 200 years ago, and the charge of enthusiasm upon it has sufficed to overthrow all the autocracies of that day. And that charge still remains, although to-day it is in danger of operating not for constructive progress but for disintegration and destruction. It is a singular fact which we have already noted, that emotional charges gathered about some word or idea, which in the past have accomplished great and beneficial changes, persist after they have become useless and even harmful. Such are some of the watchwords of religion and politics, of vital value once but now merely a source of harmful prejudice, hatred and bitterness.

4. THE NEW BONDAGE

There is something strangely elusive in the pursuit of Liberty. Men throw off one bondage and proudly proclaim their freedom, unaware that some new tyrant now holds them in his thrall. It is amusing to see how emancipated youth has become subject to a new type of bondage which seems to be spreading through the nation—a slavery to group opinion. One often sees the most ardent disciples of the new freedom showing a slavish subserviency to the opinion of their own group. The college youth, though resentful of other authority, must wear a certain type of coat, and speak and act in strict conformity with the opinion of his set.

All over the country we see the old submission to recognized authority replaced by this slavery to group opinion, a domination to which the earlier disciple of Liberty would never have consented. He was reverent toward authority but he was also independent. In some ways this feeling of Independence seems to counteract the attitude of reverence, but it was the chief characteristic of the pioneer, who went forth to conquer the forest and the prairie, who wanted a free foot unhampered by government regulations, who wished to live his own life in his own way and carve out his destiny from the virgin soil of a new country, fighting the wild beast and the savage, unhampered by the conventions and customs of the cities he had left behind. It was such men as those in their coonskin caps and buckskin trousers who gathered to support Andrew Jackson. This same spirit of Independence in different form, dwelt also in the cities of the East. They were reverent toward God and their rulers, but they insisted upon freedom to choose what God and what ruler they should revere. They proposed to have no king or deity forced upon them.

To-day observant foreigners call attention to the fact

that the American does not prowl alone like the cougar, but follows his companions like the docile sheep. In short, they have discovered that America is completely dominated by the herd instinct—there is no independence, no individuality. Every man dresses like his neighbor, builds the same kind of house with furniture turned out by the thousands at Grand Rapids, all on the same model. Every town is just like the next, and all across the great Continent every town and house and man is standardized in clothes and habits and ideas. The foreigner considers that this is the fundamental nature of the American, but we, who have studied his development, know better. This criticism deserves notice since it is so generally made, and it is interesting to find out what has happened to America since the days of Independence. I can myself remember as a boy how the little New England town where I lived was full of quaintly original characters, who had an individuality as marked as the dry pungent New England idiom they spoke and the eccentric garments they wore. To-day the citizens of the town are all ironed out into a commonplace similarity. They would be ashamed to display any such idiosyncrasies as those of Bill Pratt the orator, or Abe Bunter, or old man Pettit, or D. K. Hunter with his sign, "A Yankee by trade and works at it."

Foreigners complain that all American products are standardized and produced by the thousand. There are none of those little individual artistic touches that make the work of the French craftsmen so charming. Our critics maintain that this is because the American wants to be exactly like his neighbor in everything he possesses, while the Frenchman is discontented unless his possessions have some individual mark that distinguishes them. Our critics go further and say that the American is completely dominated by the group to which he belongs. They intimate that this is due in some measure to the passion of the Anglo-Saxon for regulating the life of his neighbor. He feels it is his duty to see that his neighbor adopts the same code of morals and manners which he holds himself, and that he must regulate the conduct of his neighbor in every particular. With this goes a feeling of responsibility for the welfare of those about him, which to the Frenchman apparently seems an impertinent intrusion into the affairs of others. Thus the causes of this standardization of life in America are said to be found in this passion for regulating the lives of others on the one hand, and on the other in the herd instinct which leads the masses to submit to such regulation and to copy their leaders.

5. Social Responsibility

Now neither of these characteristics was noticeable in the early American, who, as we have repeatedly noted, resented all interference in his business or daily life, and whose lack of all sense of responsibility for the general public was well expressed in the oft-quoted remark of the financial leader of that day: "The public be damned." Nothing in American life is more striking than the astonishing growth of this feeling of social responsibility. We have noted the beginnings of the Missionary spirit which was based on religious conviction and involved a sense of responsibility for the souls of others, and which at first contented itself with an attempt to save them from the danger of future punishment. We have noted how, with the study of sociology and the interest in settlements, this feeling developed to a sense of responsibility for the conditions in the slums, to which even the churches had been so indifferent that they derived part of their revenues from tenements that were little more than death traps. Then, at the time of the Roosevelt regime, the feeling grew rapidly that business enterprise could not be left to go its way regardless of the public welfare and to assert its independence of all interference. There resulted the various laws regulating the trusts and railroads, which at first aroused as bitter resentment as they would occasion in France to-day, and they were condemned as unwarranted interference with private business.

Then little by little there grew up among the leaders of

industry and finance a sense of responsibility for their employees, so that welfare departments were introduced, and insurance, and profit-sharing, and a certain measure of self-government. It was this spirit which transformed the great Enchantress to a Fairy Godmother who, instead of deceiving and plundering the masses, has worked miracles in their behalf. As we review history it seems that those characteristics which to the Frenchman seem fundamental in the nature of the American, are a comparatively recent growth, and that the exigencies of national development have transformed a race which was once fully as individualistic and independent as the French.

It is this sense of social responsibility combined with humanitarian feeling which has taken the place of reverence as the emotion at the basis of the social order. The American obeys the law not because of any reverence for it as ordained of God, but because he feels his responsibility as a member of the community to see that its rules are obeyed. He does good deeds not to gain favor with God, or for fear of eternal punishment, but because he feels sympathy with those in distress and feels responsible for any suffering he can alleviate. He has travelled a long road from the individualistic attitude of the nations of the old world.

In Paris a young American lady of my acquaintance found a man lying unconscious on the sidewalk in front of her hotel. She asked one Frenchman after another to aid her in getting him to a place of safety, and they all hastily withdrew. Even the concierge of the hotel said it was none of his business, and she had reached a state of extreme anxiety and annoyance before she finally succeeded in ordering a taxi and getting him to a hospital. It was an admirable illustration of the individualism which shrinks from interfering in other people's affairs and which avoids all responsibility for others, as compared with the instinctive sense of social responsibility which so characterizes Americans that even a girl in a foreign city cannot see a man suffering and helpless without taking some action.

To-day this feeling has expanded into what the sociologists call social regulation—to the individualist the most annoying of all qualities—the sense of responsibility of the group which leads them to seek to prevent any member from transgressing their standards. This feeling is being developed throughout the country increasingly by the boy scouts, and in the schools, and in the many clubs, masonic orders, and fraternal organizations that have sprung up throughout the country. To our French critics it seems as annoying to be subjected to any such interference with his manners and morals as it would have been to the early American pioneer, and there are still many in America who share this feeling. Most Americans, however, are not conscious of being regulated, save when the regulation takes the form of a law. Their desire is to act in accord with the standard of the group to which they belong, and when they find themselves at variance with it, they are as uncomfortable as a man would be to find himself on Fifth Avenue without his trousers.

This sense of social responsibility expresses itself also in the emphasis on "Service" which characterizes modern American business. Every firm advertises its desire to "serve the public" and its success in so doing, so that the inexperienced foreigner might suppose it was purely a benevolent enterprise with no thought of personal gain. To certain foreign critics this appears as utter hypocrisy, or else an absurd fetish. It seems more probable that it is merely an adjustment to the spirit of the times. Men realize that the best service brings the best profits, but mingled with the desire for gain, in many cases at least, there is a real desire to serve, which is a part of this general attitude of social co-operation.

This growing feeling of social responsibility bears an increasing part in the development of the nation, and is becoming the fundamental emotion or attitude upon which the coherence of the social order depends. Where this feeling finds place graft and greed are checked, and it is counteracting the "get rich quick" spirit of the age.

As already stated, it is this feeling of social responsibility that brought about the legislation that so improved the condition of the working man, that caused the transformation in the slums and tenements and that changed the spirit of the business man in such fashion that he became anxious to serve the public on the one hand and on the other to provide his employees with such living conditions that they were contented and happy. Although it may also have tended somewhat toward standardization, we cannot regard it with the dislike evinced by our foreign critics.

The nations of the old world, based originally on autocracy, were stabilized by the emotions of fear and reverence which each man felt toward his superior. Those emotions were carried over into the new world regardless of the fact that they were antagonistic to the spirit of democracy. The spirit of independence and love of liberty, in those great battles which we have followed, has been gradually undermining these old-time emotions, but, fortunately, this new spirit has mysteriously arisen to take their place. The common herd, who are less influenced by these emotions, have been stabilized by fear of public opinion, which is equivalent to the herd instinct, an emotion useful for the moment, until all men come to feel the higher emotions, but nevertheless a clog on progress and free development. The old disciples of liberty resent strongly and despise the bondage of this emotion, not realizing its temporary necessity, and still keep up their attack on all the restrictions of organized society. They do not comprehend that until man loves his neighbor as himself he must be held in check by some lower emotion. This great shift in emotional characteristics is the most interesting feature in American life to-day—the change from control by fear to control by public spirit—and the fight of the individualist against the domination of this herd instinct.

6. STANDARDIZATION

Standardization in industry is a different matter from standardization of character. The former was caused chiefly by the desire for economy and efficiency, while standardization in the life and habits of the people was due chiefly to the herd instinct, rather than to the desire of the group to regulate the life of the individual, as our foreign critics suggest. In other words, the individual was more anxious to be like the group, than the group was to make him so. One can hardly give the same approval to this feeling that one gives to the feeling of social responsibility. As has been suggested it replaces the old reverence for authority, for in its essence it is fear of the opinion of the group, a dread of ridicule, or of appearing conspicuous by one's divergence from those about one. It is of value, for one can imagine the indecencies and vagaries of conduct and costume that might appear in a community unchecked by fear of public opinion. But it tends to destroy individuality, and to limit the development of art and of genius.

Fortunately it affects externals rather than the inner life. It is a man's dress and visible behavior that are subject to the criticism of those about him, and not his thoughts and standards of character. For example, boys in school and college in their dress and behavior must all copy one another exactly, so that it seems as if they had all been stamped in a mint with the same die. When it comes to their curriculum, however, there is much greater independence and more variety in the branches they study than in the old days. They pride themselves also on their independence in thought and in religion.

On the other side, however, we have the attempt of the group to infuse its members with the school or college spirit. They must adopt the standards and traditions of the institution, and support the football eleven, and cheer and sing in chorus, all of which tends to crush individuality and to merge the individual in a corporate whole. Lately there is developing a strong resistance to the college-spirit idea, although in externals of dress and habits the herd instinct seems as strong as ever.

The standardization that results from fear of public opinion seems on the whole more harmful than helpful. It weakens character and destroys much that is fine in the development of the individual. The standardization that results from an effort toward economy and efficiency is another matter, and it is due in large measure to this that American industry has achieved such remarkable success.

A recent French writer tells us that in his position as Secretary of Commerce, Mr. Hoover did much for industry in this way. He found that articles were being manufactured in a needless variety of patterns, which increased expense without offering any real advantage. He suggested a reduction of these patterns to a minimum which would meet the real needs of the case. According to the statistics compiled by Siegfried he found there were 78 different kinds of grape baskets, and reduced them to 11 patterns. There were 210 different kinds of bottles, which were reduced to 20. Patterns for automobile wheels were reduced from 175 to 4; styles of brick from 66 to 7, tires from 287 to 32. In all these cases the suggestions of government were gladly accepted by the manufacturer, who naturally saved large sums by the change.

In such matters it is hard to see any harmful result from standardization. When it comes to artistic products the same cannot be said. We are told that in the textiles America, with 800 looms, produces only 14 different designs, while at Lyons in France, with 200 looms, some 80 different designs are produced. Here the American method entails a distinct loss.

By specializing on mass production America is able to fill the markets of the world with a standard product, such that everyone knows precisely what he will get for his money. There is economy and efficiency but little variety. From the fruit of California which is sent out in standard sizes but with little if any variety in flavor, to the motor cars and sewing machines and agricultural machinery, all has its standard shape and quality and every man demands the same product that his neighbor possesses. When it comes to articles of luxury or the products of art, America is unable to compete with France, where the old individualistic tradition remains.

7. ÆSTHETIC EMOTION

It is so continually asserted authoritatively that while excelling in efficiency America is crude and raw and lacking in culture, that most of us believe it. There are those, however, who doubt and who maintain that there is no country where the mass of the people are as deeply interested in music and painting and sculpture, or where architecture is reaching a finer development. Certainly there is no country where there are more women's clubs anxiously seeking cultural development, or more opportunities for the common people to hear the finest music and see the greatest works of art. We have spoken of the cultural effect of the museums upon the children. Similar opportunities are afforded in music, and all over the country community arts associations are springing up where the people are trained in drama, music, painting and sculpture, and you find the plumber and the fish man acting Shaw's plays and the barber and the druggist playing in the orchestra.

The impression of lack of culture may be due in part to the type of American who is seen abroad. The character of a nation is judged from the few who emerge above the level of visibility. The mass of the people remain invisible and inaudible. In America there has been an astonishing emergence of those ordinarily invisible. Trades people, mechanics and workmen of all classes are making the grand tour—and young girls from the small towns whose ideas of the social amenities are derived from the movies, and one may well ask what impression America would have of European culture if the country were flooded by gigantic steamers laden with costermongers, butchers, brakemen, plumbers, grocers, etc., from England and France, as are the great Atlantic liners with similar folk from America. Considering their background they perhaps do as well as would a similar group from any other nation, were they suddenly to emerge into social prominence and international adventure. Elsewhere such folk have not the means to travel.

One of our French critics advises America, unless she

wishes to become increasingly detested by the nations of Europe, to prevent her citizens from all foreign travel for a season. It is characteristic of the uncultured classes in every nation to exhibit a somewhat blatant enthusiasm for everything that pertains to their homeland and a crushing contempt for every foreign custom or product that differs from that to which they are accustomed. This seems to be peculiarly true of that class of Americans who immigrated from abroad, who in the old country had been treated with contempt by the aristocracy, and who now, having acquired wealth as grocers or plumbers, delight to return to the land of their birth and show their superiority as American citizens to those who once despised them. It is then this uncultured class, who demonstrate a blatant Americanism, that is so much in evidence in Europe to-day. One can hardly expect foreigners to realize that fact and to disregard their utterances as the expression of a class which is usually inarticulate. This attitude on the part of newly made Americans is an interesting indication of the completeness of their amalgamation, since they are more American than the Americans themselves.

It is difficult for a foreigner to distinguish the aristocracy in America. In taking the Twentieth Century Limited unexpectedly one Friday night from Chicago to New York, I was only able to secure an upper berth. I found the train filled with a group of young people, many of whom seemed acquainted. One of them explained that they were buyers from the Chicago Department Stores who went to New York in season to spend the week-end there. He said there were fifteen from the store which he represented. They were provided with every luxury. Each had a whole section —two berths—to himself—to provide which the train had to run four sections. The nobility of Europe could hardly travel in greater luxury than the buyers and "drummers" of America, and it would probably take a Frenchman some time to discover that they are not representatives of aristocracy but of "good business."

CHAPTER XVII

THE BREWING OF TEMPESTS

1. EMOTIONAL PREPARATION

THE great storms that sweep across a continent do not occur without a certain preparation in atmospheric conditions. The areas of high and low pressure must be so disposed that a change in temperature suffices to spring them into action in a fashion not dissimilar to that in which a mine is laid and sprung. When we examine the development of human beings, we find a process continually in progress which is akin to the laying of a mine. Certain emotional reactions are being built up which may be discharged in the future with telling effect. We are just beginning to understand a little of this extraordinary process. We see grown people who react with almost uncontrollable horror at sight of a snake, or spider or caterpillar, and learn that this violent discharge of emotion is due to some childhood experience, now perhaps forgotten. Long ago the mine was laid and when the right stimulus arrives the explosion occurs.

We find that a similar reaction often takes place as the result of the influence of parents upon children. The most familiar form of explosion is that of fear, and a child of ignorant parents brought up to hear the constant expression of their fears concerning witches or warlocks or ghosts that haunt a certain cemetery will find that even in later years he cannot pass the place in question without an emotional reaction. The same principle holds true of other forms of emotion, such as antipathy or hatred or those various types of antagonism which we term prejudice. A child of Irish parentage, who continually hears Orange men referred to as the epitome of all that is cruel and treacherous and evil, can hardly escape an emotional reaction of antipathy when he meets a North of Ireland man, and I have seen a similar reaction toward Christians among the children of Russian Jews who had been through the pogroms of Bessarabia. Much depends on the sensitiveness of children. I call to mind one woman who traced back her violent prejudice against Armenians to a diatribe of her father's which she overheard as a child. Thus, through childish experiences, and through the emotional expression of opinion on the part of those to whom the child looks up in reverence, emotional mines are continually being set, which explode in later life—sometimes with disastrous effect.

In this fashion a horror of "Yankees" was implanted in the children of Southerners who survived the Civil War, which is still bearing fruit in American politics.

Religion is peculiarly potent as a mine setter, and the violent prejudices implanted in the minds of children in connection with their religious instruction are continually manifesting themselves in dangerous fashion. If a child is brought up by those who regard the members of another creed as under the influence of the evil one, in such fashion that contact with them or listening to their views or reading their books may bring a terrible curse upon him and cause him to lose his soul, he naturally feels a sort of horror in the presence of such persons that is difficult to overcome. These emotional reactions are entirely subconscious and independent of the intelligence. The train that has been laid is touched off and the inevitable result follows. The same facts hold true in reference to political opinions. Forty or fifty years ago, children were charged with a sort of horror or antipathy toward the Republican or Democratic party, as the case might be. As a result of the emotional atmosphere that surrounded them, the word "socialist" or "communist," or "standpatter" or "free trader," awakened a reaction of antipathy, although they may have been quite ignorant of the principles behind these names.

Education is an attempt to lift men above the power of these subconscious emotional discharges into a realm where their decisions will be made by intelligence and not under the influence of that blind rush of feeling that we term prejudice. Something has been accomplished in this way, but it is amazing to discover how far men are still governed by these discharges of emotion that had been stored up in childhood. We have mentioned the fact that the politician makes use of this situation to the utmost. He studies the atmospheric condition of his constituency—the emotions that are thus stored up, and knows how to use the stimulus that will set them free. As for example, the opponents of James G. Blaine made use of the "Rum, Romanism and Rebellion" speech. And the enemies of Roosevelt and Cleveland spread the accusation of drunkonness, knowing that they would set off an explosion of prejudice.

2. EMOTIONAL BATTERIES

We have spoken of certain organizations as batteries, meaning that they are permanent centres for emotional preparation, where men are so charged that they are certain to react in a certain way. It is through these batteries that the great currents we have described are kept flowing from age to age. Every home is such a battery. Every church or organization is a system of connected batteries, and everywhere we find clubs where definite sentiments are cultivated, such as hatred of militarism, enthusiasm for the Constitution, antipathy to capitalism, 100-per-cent Americanism, etc. One method of the agitator is to organize clubs in which a certain emotional reaction is built up in preparation for the critical moment when the proper stimulus can set it off. So Jefferson organized his Democratic clubs throughout the nation, and so to-day Communistic clubs are being organized in all our great cities. It does not accord with our ideas of freedom to interfere with such organizations; but to allow them to develop is as dangerous as to permit the construction of bomb factories. One has only to look at India to-day which is now ready to burst into a flame of insurrection, to see the danger of allowing the formation of these innumerable groups where hatred of the British was cultivated.

It must ultimately become a great question what emotions

a nation will allow to be definitely cultivated by organizations which are really designed as permanent emotional generators. Here we come up again against the individualists and disciples of liberty, who claim that there should be no interference. To-day the old-time devotee of political freedom who shouted, "Give me liberty or give me death," has joined hands with the modern individualist who resents any limitation upon the expansion of his personality or any restriction of his desires or appetites, and who resents all control in the home or school or government, and is continually attacking America as a travesty upon the "land of the free." This group is generating a type of feeling that is a serious danger to the national development. And what is called love of liberty to-day is no longer rebellion against unreasonable tyranny but resentment against all discipline no matter how valuable, and against all restrictions no matter how essential to the public welfare.

In these days of free intercommunication, it becomes possible for a small determined group by persistent propaganda to develop a powerful emotional charge of antagonism or prejudice against any individual or against the government. Unless they had learned to deal promptly and severely with such attempts it is probable that the government of Russia or Italy would not be long in existence. In America, up to date, the government has been sufficiently satisfactory to the people to render such action unnecessary. How long it will remain so is a question. Where the people have a legitimate grievance it is, of course, harmful to prevent its expression. We are now speaking of instances where no such grievance exists, where the people are contented and prosperous, until, by a definite process of propaganda, hatred and prejudice against the government are generated. The people of India are to-day more prosperous and happy than they have been for centuries. And yet a small group of agitators by persistent cultivation of hatred of the British has been able to bring the whole country to the verge of revolt. The more intelligent know that the British are working to turn over the government as soon as it can be done without disaster to the masses of the people, and that if British influence were removed now there would be endless riots between Mohammedan and Hindu, and continual feuds, wars and oppression on the part of their rulers, but it is not a question of intelligence. It is purely an emotional charge, developed by long cultivation, and now ready to blow up and create chaos and disaster.

3. The Stimulus to Dissatisfaction

There are certain emotional reactions in every normal man that can be counted upon. One is that if he thinks he is receiving less than he deserves he becomes bitter and discontented and antagonistic to those whom he considers responsible. Now it is a very easy matter to persuade the average man that he deserves more than he is getting, even when facts strongly indicate the contrary, and this is the path usually followed by the agitators who wish to develop a strong emotional charge which they can explode to their political advantage.

It is a peculiar characteristic of this age that every man tends to think more highly of himself than he ought to think, and to consider that society owes him a livelihood and the materials of happiness merely for condescending to exist. Instead of recognizing his enormous debt to society and his utter inability, if cast on a desert island or thrown on his own resources, to supply himself with any of the essentials of his daily life, all of which are created by the energy and intelligence of his fellow men, he is prone to find fault that he does not possess all the luxuries which in a lifetime of toil he could not dream of producing. He does not consider that every smallest convenience that we enjoy has cost years, even centuries, of toil and blood, as men have experimented and worked and starved to carry out their plans, or remember that every smallest article such as a pocket knife costs the labor of thousands, who have toiled in mines and smelters, and foundries and factories. When one considers the building of a house, and the labor involved, in securing lumber from the forest, in the iron work, and plumbing, glass, plaster and all the various appurtenances, a man should be in humble mood as he realizes that, for the trifling services he has rendered society, some hundreds of thousands of skilled workmen have been toiling for him. In the Middle Ages the doctrine of total depravity did much to keep down a man's idea of his deserts. It was dinned into him on every occasion that he was a wretched sinner, an object of loathing in the sight of God—that he deserved endless torture in the flames of hell as the reward of his innate wickedness, and that it was only by the mercy of God and the intercession of the church that he might hope to escape. Feeling, then, that he deserved the fires of hell, he felt happy and contented to be let off with a life of hard toil here on earth, in the hope of escaping his deserts.

Every man was then so charged with a feeling of unworthiness that, however small the rewards he received, he felt gratitude rather than discontent. In this age a charge of the opposite sort seems to have been laid in the minds of most of our youth. They seem to have been taught that society has done them a wrong in bringing them to birth and that it owes them reparation. We hear them announce that they did not ask to be born and that society, having produced them, owes them a life of happiness. Mormon doctrine teaches that it was only after centuries of pleading that they secured the privilege of being born, and it is not easy to prove which point of view is correct. At any rate, with the constant increase of population, society is more likely to find that its duty lies in eliminating superfluous youth rather than in providing them with happiness, and they may find that to preserve themselves from the lethal chamber it will be necessary to give more adequate proof of their value to society than they have yet supplied. In the meantime it is this element in society—which considers that its deserts are far greater than its achievements really warrant, or than it is possible for society to grant—that affords the great field in which agitators can store up those emotional charges of bitterness, hatred and prejudice, that become such a menace to civilization.

As we have noted, it is difficult to estimate the effect on the young of the continual expression of hatred or contempt or antagonism toward a certain individual or group or nation. It inevitably stores up an emotional charge which will probably explode without any regard to intelligence or logic. Possibly there is nowhere shown in the gospels a greater insight into fundamental causes than in the passage which consigns to the fires of hell the man who calls his brother a fool or a villain (for the word is stronger than "fool" in English) and who thus develops a charge of contempt or hatred which may be disastrously exploded at some future date without any adequate reason, and simply because the emotional connection has been made, just as a child, influenced by the attitude of others, reacts subconsciously against a cemetery in the dark.

The above discussion is merely an attempt to indicate the general emotional field in which the press, the pulpit, the cinema, the spoken and written word, are continually operating; sometimes to develop prejudice and store emotion, and prepare the storms of the future, and sometimes to touch off a mine of prejudice laid years ago. How far it is possible for any government to exercise control of such a field is doubtful. It is certainly worth while to keep it in view. Much can be done to counteract its dangers by generating wholesome enthusiasms; for it is just as possible to store helpful and constructive emotions as those that are destructive. The public schools and boy scouts deserve much credit for what they are doing to store the minds of children with fine enthusiasms for the great men of America and their ideals, and they may rest assured that such storage of right feeling is as sure to find issue in action as is the destructive emotion nurtured by certain elements of the press.

4. THE PREPARATION FOR PREJUDICE

Some of us can remember how as children we were trained in the schools to a feeling of antagonism toward the British as "tyrants" and "foes of liberty" which it took many years to overcome, and we know of certain sections in the country and certain elements of the press where a similar propaganda is in progress to-day. A book has recently appeared which attempts to prove that the chief aim of education in Russia to-day is to train its youth to a hatred of England as the chief exponent of capitalistic tyranny and thus prepare them for the conquest of India, where, on the Northwest frontier their representatives are already installed, wearing the emblems of the sickle and mallet, and inciting the tribesmen to insurrection. I have seen so much of this violent prejudice and utterly unreasoning horror of certain groups, subtly implanted in the minds of the semi-educated, that it seems to me the great danger of the age. No argument can affect it, for, as we have shown, it has nothing to do with the intelligence or reason, and is purely an emotional reaction. The individual has been so trained that the reaction must occur when the stimulus is applied, and any attempt to reason only awakens distrust and suspicion or a hostile reaction of some kind.

With all this in view it becomes a problem how to educate the masses of America so that they will be armed against prejudice of this sort, instead of becoming its victims,—an effect which the present system seems more likely to produce, through the discontent which it awakens. If a substitute could be found for the old doctrine of total depravity which would give the average man a more moderate estimate of his importance to society and of what he deserves at the hands of his fellows, we might find in it an adequate safeguard, but the tendency seems to be quite in the opposite direction, in the general effort to persuade us that we are supermen, of vast and undeveloped potentialities, unappreciated by the world. It is part of the childish spirit of which we have spoken and it must yield as men come to grips with reality and realize the need of self-discipline.

5. THE NEW AMERICA AND THE OLD

For the success and prosperity of any group there are two essentials: first, they must work together in a common spirit of mutual helpfulness; and, second, such elements as endanger their happiness and unity must be suppressed. So long as men's passions and selfish desires are stronger than their mutual love there must be laws to control them, and so long as there are groups who, through ignorance or evil intent, do harm to themselves or to others, they must be kept in bondage.

As men become more intelligent and as they are increasingly ruled by sympathy for others and by public spirit, it is possible to do away with the old bondage of fear and force in certain cases, and to rely on the guidance of reason and of neighborly feeling. Law and emotion are in a delicate balance. If man loved his neighbor as himself no law would be necessary, and we could be anarchists and prosper. The anarchist of to-day assumes that it is the law that makes man unbrotherly, but history proves that it is his unbrotherliness that makes the law. Communism is an attempt to force man by law to be brotherly, while our ordinary laws are content with preventing him from being violently unbrotherly. The anarchist would make man brotherly by doing away with law, the communist would make him brotherly by creating more laws. Neither method seems to succeed. The Spirit of Brotherhood cannot be created by law or by removing law. It requires a different sort of culture; the Christian church was designed as a dynamo to generate that current, but it has often been diverted to other ends. The Spirit is growing in the world but the methods of the anarchist and communist are more likely to set it back than to advance it. It is the progress of this Spirit that makes liberty increasingly possible.

We have shown how the Spirit of Liberty has freed group after group until the nation has acquired a freedom in religion and in politics, in their financial resources and in thought, such as the world has never known before. Men are bound not by fear but by the laws that their own intelligence creates. This would be well if all men were in the same stage of advancement, but unfortunately there seem to be representatives of every age from Adam down, who are still at large.

The world is a collection of missing links, or of links that should be missing by this time. It is they who make all the trouble, for they can only be controlled by force and fear. For the Spirit of Liberty to go further and set the desires and passions of these folk free from all control, would be as mad as to throw open the door of every cage in the Zoo. There are monsters none too safely chained that might easily break loose and wreck the lives of the innocent and helpless.

There is always danger that liberty will be transformed into a license that will produce chaos and degeneration.

The old Anglo-Saxon Spirit of Liberty, whose career we have followed, was protected by a strong feeling for justice which set definite limits to liberty and prevented it from encroaching on the rights of others. It included respect not only for law, but for the justice that lies behind law, so that when the law failed the representatives of this Spirit felt individually responsible to see that justice was carried out. A great danger to-day is that in the newer element in America there is a great demand for liberty without this safeguarding feeling for justice, which seems to be sadly lacking in them. This attitude is manifest in a sentimental sympathy with criminals, in attempts to do away with severe sentences, in unwillingness on the part of juries to convict; and it is reflected in the administration of justice throughout the country. There are so many ways in which a criminal can appeal his case that it is almost impossible to secure a quick conviction even in the most flagrant cases. Such a small percentage of murderers are now convicted that the law no longer acts as a deterrent, and criminals are ready to chance anything. When matters have reached such a pass that innocent girls are railroaded to jail by criminals in connivance with the police, a few days' imprisonment and a fine are hardly adequate as a deterrent, and it would seem necessary to return to some of the old-fashioned punishments such as the bastinado, that a cowardly man of that type would really dread. The result of such inadequate justice will probably be an increase of lynching or the organization of Vigilance Committees by the old-time citizens, who see their safety and property threatened by criminals who have little difficulty in escaping from the justice of the law. When the machinery of justice has broken down the old-time Anglo-Saxon has always taken the law into his own hands.

Without this safeguarding sense of justice, increasing liberty must always be a danger. In every nation or group there is usually a section that wishes to advance a little more rapidly than is safe and another section which would like to maintain conditions as they are or even to go back to former conditions. In America this division is accentuated by the large numbers of immigrants from other lands who have other ideas and feelings than those which animated the original settlers. This division is quite different from that between the Progressive and Reactionary.

The Progressive wing of which we have spoken in politics sought to pass laws that would favor progress, but the division of which I speak is more fundamental, and seems often to oppose the reform laws. In the main it is a cleavage between the Old America and the New, and is partly a result of the admittance of such large numbers of foreigners to American citizenship. The division probably originated in the resentment of the old-time American toward the recent citizen of foreign parentage.

We have shown how, even before the civil war, the feeling against the new foreign element found expression in the "Know Nothing" movement, and how later fear of the political control of foreigners created the American Protective Association, both of which were power houses for generating a strong anti-foreign current.

The A. P. A. was succeeded by a recrudescence of the Ku Klux Klan, which in its platform presented very noble aims such as preserving true Americanism, but which soon became an instrument of violent destructive prejudice. Trusting in their mysterious disguise, outrages were committed all over the country which were ostensibly punishments of evil-doers not reached by the law, though others claimed they were merely instances of private vengeance.

The Klan grew in power until it actually controlled the elections in several states, though it claimed to have no political function.

To the enlightened American this method of going about in a ghostly disguise under the direction of Kleagles and Grand Wizards to take vengeance in the dark on helpless foreigners seemed contemptible and un-American. Those who defended them said that, unless the Americans organize and take action, their land will soon be in the grip of some foreign group organized and equipped for the purpose. It was surprising to find how many solid honest men of influence in their various communities, particularly farmers, tradesmen and craftsmen, went into an organization that one would suppose utterly repugnant to Americans.

Its headquarters were chiefly in the South and West, though it also gained many adherents among the New England farmers. Among the mountain folk of Carolina and Tennessee the feeling against the foreigner and against Roman Catholics was perhaps at its strongest. Here was a group which was really medieval in its outlook. Feeling here was not only against foreigners but against all the modern thought that was attacking the old beliefs. The people were Baptists and Methodists brought up in the belief that the Bible was the inerrant word of God, and that the world was created in six days. The laws of the state of Tennessee actually forbade the teaching of evolution in the schools as sacrilege, and the trial of Scopes for teaching geology and anthropology according to modern science aroused the interest of the whole world.

We all remember how Bryan went to the aid of the state and assisted the prosecution. He felt as strongly as the people of Tennessee that to deny the creation story in Genesis meant to destroy all faith in God, and to wreck the morals of the nation, and he brought intense feeling and powerful oratory to their aid. He is reported to have said that the difference between Fundamentalism and Modernism was the difference between the Rock of Ages and ages of rock. With these people the question was supremely vital. Their salvation hung upon it and they felt that any one who sought to rob their children of faith in the old-time religion deserved their bitterest antagonism. A large element of the Baptist and Methodist groups throughout the country was in sympathy with them and felt just as strongly. There is no emotion stronger than those that centre about religion and in no case does prejudice run so high or become so unreasoning. It was from this group with its medieval feelings that much of the membership of the Klan was drawn. To submit their country to the domination of Roman Catholic or Jew was something they could only regard with horror and they were equally anxious to protect the country from the modernistic thought that threatened to overturn the old American ideals.

6. Anti-foreign Feeling in Politics

Under the leadership of the Klan this anti-foreign feeling acquired such strength that it spread through the nation and threatened to disrupt the political parties. It manifested its power in the Democratic Convention in June, 1924.

No such turbulent political gathering had ever been known in America. Feeling had already been aroused to a high point by MacAdoo's advocacy of Prohibition and the Unions, when a plank was proposed denouncing the Klan. Colby spoke for it and Bryan against it, and a veritable tornado broke loose. For a time it seemed as if all would end in a free fight, but at length the vote was taken and the plank defeated by 542 against 541. The Convention had become the battle ground of religious and anti-foreign prejudice. The delegates from the East were bitterly antagonistic to the Klan. The state bosses of Illinois, Indiana, Pennsylvania, Maryland, New Jersey, New York and Massachusetts were all Roman Catholics and resentful of the attacks of the Klan. Against them were the South and West where the fundamentalist Baptists and Methodists prevailed. The fight between these two forces went on for weeks, from June 24 to July 9 in fact, and finally MacAdoo had to withdraw.

The feeling reappeared in different form in the Campaign of 1928, when the Democratic party became the channel for the feeling of the New America against the Old. Their candidate represented the vast population of immigrants who had brought with them the varied customs and religions of the old world. They naturally were bitterly opposed to the Klan, but they also resented the dominance of the old Anglo-Saxon Protestant group that had stood for the education and culture of the Nordic type from the days of Washington down to Wilson and Coolidge. There were many who felt that in a great Democracy the head of the nation should be a representative of the common man and of this vast new element which had received some measure of training in American ideas and enough education to succeed at their jobs without the culture that marked the aristocrat. They thought that to have a woman of the people as first Lady of the Land to meet the Queens and Princesses of Europe would mean a great advance for Democracy. Their candidate understood the needs and desires of the man on the street. He had proved his honesty and intelligence as Governor of New York, his courage and force by his mastery of Tammany. He was a Roman Catholic and many felt that it was sheer prejudice that had hitherto prevented a Catholic from becoming President and that a protest should be made by electing him. Thus the Democratic party gathered in the New America and all those who were opposed to the old ideas and the old methods. Many felt that the Old America with its wealth and culture was in league with big business and involved in deals with the Republican party to secure special privileges and to dominate the country. Further, there were disciples of Roosevelt who maintained that the Old American group was now interested solely in prosperity and comfort and not in righteousness and justice, and that they should be thrown out of power and the common man should be given a chance. The state bosses of most of the Eastern states were still nearly all of them Irish Roman Catholics, as in 1924. Thus the Democratic party had become the channel through which the feeling of the New America against the dominance of the old Protestant Nordic America, could find expression. But this very fact involved the loss of that half of their constituency that had put up such a fight in 1924. The South was still strong in its opposition to the Roman Church and the foreigner. With many of the narrow-minded Baptists and Methodists the opposition was pure religious prejudice. With others it was due to a suspicion that the Irish Catholic group were trying to control politics to advance their own group and religion.

By thus turning the great current of feeling against the Old America into political channels the clash of the conflict was carried to the farthest corners of the nation by telegraph and radio. The astonishing power of the latter instrument to arouse interest and enthusiasm was abundantly demonstrated, and the whole country was soon thrilling to appeals on both sides. Every speaker of ability creates in his hearers a vortex of enthusiasm for the cause he represents, or a wave of antagonism against it, which often influences their decisions more than the most careful argumentation. When this vortex is extended beyond the walls of the hall to the farthest confines of the continent and the roar of applause spreads through walls of stone across deserts and forests and over mountain ranges to far-distant cities and solitary ranches on the prairie, it becomes indeed a vast and overwhelming force which sweeps along the public in a great tidal wave of feeling. Whether in the busy life of the city or on the lonely prairie, this voice of the President-to-be and the roar of the multitude coming thus out of mystery, causes the great questions of the day to impinge upon the quiet family circle, borne by a wave of emotion whose power it is hard to estimate. It swept to the polls a larger number than had ever before voted in any electoral contest in the world.

The vote seemed to secure, for a time at least, the supremacy of the old America. The force of the new current was not yet great enough to carry the nation, and for the first time since the Civil War, the solid South was disrupted.

The old bitter feeling against the Republican party that had endured for sixty-five years, at last gave way before other antipathies; loyalty to the Democratic party yielded before loyalty to the old America, and five at least of old original Southern states shifted to the Republican column. The alliance between the old Democracy of the South, representing the pure-blooded Americans and containing the old aristocracy, with the Democrats of Tammany Hall, the foreign industrial element and the Irish politician, was as incongruous as a wedding between Dolly Madison and Richard Croker, and was sure to end in divorce.

In the conflict of these two opposing currents both sides have created extremes of prejudice and bitter feeling, and we find the bigoted Irish politician opposed by the intolerant Klansman. But both sides have something to contribute toward the progress of America.

7. Old Authorities and New Thought

We have described the political issue, but that is only a small part of the conflict. The feeling is not merely political nor is it merely greed for power on the part of the new element. The cleavage is much deeper and involves a divergence of feeling that goes to the very roots of the national life, in art, literature, religion and in the home itself. It involves two attitudes toward life that are fundamentally opposed. It manifests itself as a reaction of resentment against the compulsion of the standards enforced by the old régime, combined with annoyance at the rigid moral control of the Anglo-Saxon, and it includes the antagonism of the individualist to measures enforced for the public welfare which interfere with liberty. Such measures are pictured as due to the activities of conceited reformers, who endeavor to thrust their arbitrary and unreasonable standards down the throat of the public.

This group finds some of its leaders among those emancipated in thought, and with them are certain temperamental folk, artistic and otherwise, and a number of young people nurtured on ultra-modernistic literature, and certain iconoclastic collegians who, having spent a few months between the Latin quarter and the Montmartre, consider the convictions of the mass of middle-class Americans who live on Main Street as provincial and intolerable, and ardently desire their overthrow and the substitution of the more individualistic ideas of the French. This combination of foreign elements and would-be foreigners, who are opposed to the old American ideas and standards may prove the centre for the great emotional storm of the future, which will determine whether America shall remain American or become a nation with the standards and characteristics of Southern Europe.

Any one truly familiar with European countries must realize that while some of them are much freer in respect to legislation that concerns the public welfare, they are nevertheless much more rigidly subject to governmental regulations, to arbitrary customs and to aristocratic control. When millions live together in organized social life some form of control is essential, and those who seek to overthrow the American type, which is based on the cultivation of a high standard of character and moral responsibility, probably fail to recognize what we have already sought to demonstrate—that the result would be either anarchy or the establishment of a dictatorship such as that of Italy or Russia, which involves a limitation of liberty far more rigid than anything yet experienced in America.

One can hardly hope, however, to control such emotional storms by reason, since they are usually mere outbursts of dissatisfaction which follow the channel prepared by plausible agitators. That there is a storm of this nature brewing any one can see with but half of his optical energy, and it will require the stern efforts of every intelligent man to avert it, or to turn it into channels where it may have some constructive value. There is undoubted value in every such outburst of the people. It usually indicates that something is wrong and that there is need of some adjustment. The danger is that unscrupulous agitators can usually succeed in turning such a tide of popular feeling into channels profitable to themselves but destructive to the public welfare.

8. PASSING PHASES AND PERMANENT VALUES

It cannot be claimed that the old regime was perfect. There was much in it that was narrow and intolerant. At present it is supremely important to the nation that leaders should be found with sufficient genius to make such concessions as will disarm the resentment of the newer element, while preserving all that was finest in the old, and who will be able to turn the new tide of individualism with its creative power away from iconoclastic attempts to destroy all authority, into channels where its energy will find play in constructive effort. Some leaven is needed to counteract the dominance of the herd instinct—some agency which will free the creative fire from the suppression of convention and custom. America is in danger of achieving unity by a uniformity which is disastrous bondage. It remains for future leaders to create a unity embracing the utmost possible diversity, accomplished, not by the compulsion of law or public opinion, but by voluntary co-operation in a spirit of devotion to the public welfare. And this can only be when all the various vortices of personal feeling and all the group antagonisms are merged in the dominant tide of public spirit.

Thus we may hope that prejudice may at last be so overcome that men can lay aside the restrictions that hamper, and all of the old authority that was narrowing and unwise, and cling the more firmly to those great ideals, loyalty to which has created the American Commonwealth and wrought the great miracle of modern times. For the story we have told is the story of the most amazing achievement in the world's history, the unification of men of every race and tribe and of the most diverse character into one self-governing nation so that their old feuds are forgotten and they are no longer Irish, Italian, Polish, French, German, Jew, Negro and Indian, but loyal Americans, proud of their nation and as ready as any native son to give their lives in its defence and for its glory. It is not strange that they should all have come to the land of plenty, but that they should have come to such a sense of unity as to hold together in a vital corporate union of 120,000,000 of people —here is the miracle—when we see these same people across the seas divided by jealousies, feuds and prejudice and living under the constant threat of war.

We can hardly doubt that this miracle is due in large measure to that group of men who came over with a certain standard, and certain ideals of liberty and justice, and with that type of character that we term self-regulating, so that they were more likely to be honest and just when unwatched and put upon their honor than when threatened with the punishment of a tyrant. Needless to say they were by no means perfect, and there were as many men who were unworthy and false among them as elsewhere, but they did have these ideals, which alone would have made democracy possible, and in some miraculous way succeeded in communicating them to the growing nation. Whatever dangers the future may bring these ideals must remain—the Sacred Palladium, which alone can secure prosperity and glory to the nation.

CONCLUSION

THE MAP OF HUMAN EMOTIONS

In the preceding pages we have viewed America in a variety of aspects. We have beheld an Olympian Drama in which ancient spirits rising out of the misty Past have met with other spirits summoned from the vasty deep, and have fought for the Soul of America.

At times the Drama has faded from our eyes and we have seen a great network of power lines ramifying through the country from power houses which generate currents of dangerously high voltage, some racial, some religious, some political, that emit sparks where the lines cross, and often threaten a conflagration.

Then again we have watched the weather conditions that prevailed over the continent and have traced the great storms that have swept across the nation. We have watched how, from some area of low pressure, a whirlwind has started that has carried destruction far and wide, and we have seen great storms conjured up by some cloud-compelling Rainmaker. The West has hurled its tornadoes upon the East, and the South has launched its hurricanes upon the North, carrying devastation in their wake.

As we look out to-day over the great continent with its towering mountain ranges and fertile valleys, its great cities with their teeming population and its barren deserts, its glowing sunshine and drifting clouds, we know that behind all this scenery that fills the stage are vast latent forces, unseen but ceaselessly working—forces that may break loose in storm and cyclone and tear the social fabric asunder, or that may be harnessed to drive forward the wheels of progress and to transform the world. It is this great hidden realm of force—the feelings of the people—that we have sought to describe. We have found that in the minds of men there are great currents of feeling that run on from age to age based on certain ideas, and generated sometimes by the churches, sometimes in the heart of the family, sometimes in the instruction of the schools. For all these are power houses, where strong currents are developed, and where old currents are re-enforced and raised to new power. Each child while yet sensitive and unformed, is charged by parents or teachers with these ancient currents of feeling and with emotionalized ideas, so that he goes forth into life with repellent feelings or prejudice toward certain men or acts or ideas, and enthusiasm or devotion toward others. We have seen how at first America was swayed by currents from across the seas and nearly torn asunder, until barriers of feeling were erected that shut them out. We have seen how those barriers were transcended by the Commercial Current or desire for gain, and by the Humanitarian or Missionary Spirit; and how in spite of the conflicting Isolationist current America was swept again into the vortex of International affairs.

Just now that Isolationist current seems to be dominant again, and it is doing its utmost to keep America out of European affairs, and to secure prosperity for America alone at the expense of the rest of the world by high tariff walls and by refusal to co-operate with the needs of Europe, while America accumulates vast reserves of gold by exacting payment of debts which threaten the foreign governments with ruin. The immediate results have been a falling off of more than a billion dollars in the foreign trade of America with resultant "hard times" and unemployment, and added to that a feeling of hostility toward America on the part of foreign nations who are in her debt, or who are injured by her tariff policy. We can only hope that the new Current of International feeling will eventually wipe out this old exclusive current which belonged to a past age and has no place in the united world of to-day, for instead of preserving America there is continual danger that it will precipitate war and disaster.

We have followed that great Current of Devotion to Liberty and Justice that originated with the old Anglo-Saxons as it has influenced the development of the nation and freed men from various types of bondage, until in its rebellion against all authority it has become a danger to the public welfare.

We have seen how the old current of Greed for Gain in alliance with the Political Spirit was opposed by the New Spirit of Social Responsibility and the New Public Spirit, and how the forces of Reaction fought against the Progressive Spirit.

As we look over the map to-day behind all the stage scenery we see these forces at work. If the map were colored to represent racial origins we should find it as checkered as that of Central Europe. In each such section we can detect the induction currents that are being generated by the proximity of conflicting racial ideas and purposes.

We can also hear the hum of the dynamos in the public schools—as they generate that great National Current of loyalty to American ideals which, in the children at least, must neutralize these hostile charges and sweep them forward in a common devotion.

All over the country in every city and little village we see the power houses of the great religious currents with their interlacing wires, charged with prejudice and animosity, but now tending to fuse into two great power lines, of modernist and fundamentalist feeling, which generate certain animosities but which can be combined to further the great forward movements.

And we can detect how in the struggle for wealth the friction of competing groups is constantly generating hostile feeling, between employer and employee, Union and non-Union, or between Agriculture or Industry and Transportation, until some intelligent adjustment lowers the charge by lessening the friction.

We need no electroscope to discover how the whole nation is positively and negatively electrified by the question of Prohibition so that every ear is deaf to intelligent argument, and the politicians are afraid to open their mouths;

and we can feel in our own bones the great waves of optimism and pessimism that sweep the land in alternation.

It takes a more subtle instrument to detect how the charge of sex feeling that draws man and woman together in mutual attraction is altering the ancient emotional current that in past ages has controlled sex relations. And we discover with surprise how powerful is the old herd instinct as it counteracts the rebellion of the Spirit of Liberty against authority.

Such is the Emotional panorama spread before our eyes as we survey the continent to-day. And now we detect everywhere a general movement in these conflicting currents as they seem to unite in two great Streams, one of which combines all the conservative feelings of the Old America, while the other gathers up all the insurgent impulses of the New America, and piles up in opposition to the centres of the old-time religion, and the established social order and the vast organization of the Capitalistic System, a tide of free thought and foreign ideas—all the incoherent aspirations, socialistic and individualistic, of the new element in American life that is seeking to break down the old tradition and to dominate American thought and politics.

To some extent it represents the struggle of the individualist against the gathering power of the old herd instinct, and the rebellion of youth against the restrictions of authority, and against those forces that hold the nation together and maintain its order. We have shown that in a democratic nation which is not controlled by fear and despotic authority, there must be other powerful emotions to consolidate the people and maintain the laws. Even here there is danger that in preserving unity progress may be prevented. Unity and progress, these two, are the essentials of greatness and prosperity. They can only be secured by the most delicate balance of centrifugal and centripetal forces.

We must have such forces as custom and convention, respect for law, fear of public opinion and the herd instinct, which hold men together, but there is always the danger that they will crush individuality and restrict progress. On the other hand defiance of them means anarchy and chaos. We may hope that the protest against them may be sufficient to permit progress and not so violent as to produce chaos.

The harmony of individualism and unity can only come when each individual has enough sympathy for his fellow to respect his rights and relieve his distress, and enough public spirit to prefer the progress of the community to his personal success. There is sufficient of the old spirit of greed to make one despair at times, and one can only hope that the various centripetal forces will maintain unity until the increasing tide of public spirit has time to sweep through the nation and penetrate both the slum and the sanctum of the bank president, the exclusive club and the excluded foreign quarter, until all the antagonisms and prejudices of race and religion, the rudimentary residuum of past conflicts, are carried away, and the nation, assured of unity in the devotion of its citizens, may go forward to a progress in which the peculiar abilities of each individual may find free play in the realization of his most beautiful dreams and loftiest visions.

INDEX

INDEX